Turkish Islam and the Secular State

Contemporary Issues in the Middle East

Turkish Islam and the Secular State

The Gülen Movement

Edited by
M. Hakan Yavuz and John L. Esposito

 Syracuse University Press

First Edition 2003
       05   06   07   08   6   5   4   3   2

The paper used in this publication meets the minimum requirements of
American National Standard for Information Sciences—Permanence of
Paper for Printed Library Materials, ANSI Z39.48–1984.∞™

Library of Congress Cataloging-in-Publication Data

Turkish Islam and the secular state : the Gülen Movement / edited by M. Hakan Yavuz
and John L. Esposito.
p. cm. — (Contemporary issues in the Middle East)
Includes bibliographical references (p.) and index.
ISBN 0-8156-3015-8 (alk. paper) — ISBN 0-8156-3040-9 (pbk. : alk. paper)
1. Islam and politics—Turkey. 2. Gülen, Fethullah—Views on Islam. 3. Turkey—Politics
and government—1980– I. Yavuz, M. Hakan. II. Esposito, John L. III. Series.
BP173.7.T875 2003
322'.1'09561—dc22   2003060641

Contents

Preface

THIS VOLUME aims not to provide a comprehensive historical study of the neo-Nur movement associated with the Turkish spiritual and social leader Fethullah Gülen, but rather to examine the intervening role of market forces in the interaction between the secular Turkish republic and Turkish Islamic sociopolitical movements through the study of Fethullah Gülen and his movement. The various chapters on the Gülen movement seek to assess its significance in the shaping of the contemporary Islamic sociopolitical scene in Turkey.

Within these parameters, we have chosen those articles in which the interaction between the secular state and the religious, cultural, and sociopolitical manifestations of Turkish Islam is assessed with regard to current seminal developments in the country—the most obvious being the rise of a Muslim-oriented Anatolian bourgeoisie and the sweeping electoral victory of the Muslim democratic Justice and Development Party in 2002. Each chapter focuses on different aspects of the interaction between Gülen's ideas and leadership, on the one hand, and this broader evolving sociopolitical context, on the other. Analysis of the growing accommodation between modern Turkish Islamic identities and idioms and the democratic, market-oriented Turkish state also sheds important insights on similar challenges facing a number of large Muslim countries.

We have placed the Gülen movement within the larger context of the Nur movement. Gülen and his following cannot be understood without considering the founder of the movement during the early republican period, Said Nursi. Many of Gülen's followers object to this linkage between Nursi and Gülen, but we feel that understanding the genesis of the movement and its significant permutations necessitates a consideration of the formative role of Sufi tradition in general and of Said Nursi in particular. In Gülen's neo-Nur movement, one can discern both the legacy of traditional Islamic sociopolitical activism and the modern challenges faced in the reproduction of Islamic identity in a large and developing secular state.

The Center for Muslim-Christian Understanding at Georgetown University helped make this project possible by hosting a conference on the Gülen movement. This volume is an outcome of the papers presented at that conference. We thank the Rumi Forum for Interfaith Dialogue for their financial support. We also owe a special debt of gratitude to Ali Aslan and Hüseyin Sentürk for their unstinting generosity, which greatly facilitated our work.

The Rockefeller Foundation and the Kroc Institute of the University of Notre Dame provided a year of support for Hakan Yavuz to work on this project, and this assistance is gratefully acknowledged. Yavuz also thanks the Summer Institute of the Alexander von Humboldt Foundation of Berlin, Germany.

Eric Hooglund played a crucial role in preparing the manuscript and provided valuable criticism; without his help, publication of the present volume would not have been possible. Mujeeb R. Khan also read a number of chapters and provided his customary keen editorial insight and comments. Finally, we also must thank Mary Selden Evans of Syracuse University Press for her excellent guidance and support throughout all the stages of publication.

M. Hakan Yavuz
John L. Esposito

Contributors

Bekim Agai is a researcher at the University of Bonn, Germany, and a former fellow of the Volkswagen Foundation in the Junior Research Group, focusing on educational networks in the national and transnational context. His doctoral dissertation is entitled "Between Network and Discourse: The Educational Network Around Fethullah Gülen; The Flexible Implementation of New Islamic Thought. Three Countries in Comparison." Agai earned his M.A. in Oriental studies at Rheinische-Friedrich-Wilhelm University in Bonn. He also studied at Cairo University. He has lectured on Said Nursi, Islam and politics in contemporary Turkey, and the political culture of Turkey. His current research interests include the impact of Said Nursi on Islamic discourse in Turkey and Islam in Europe.

Yasin Aktay is associate professor of sociology at Selçuk University in Konya, Turkey. He received his Ph.D. from Middle East Technical University in Ankara. In 1991, he founded the quarterly intellectual journal *Tezkire,* of which he is editor, and the publishing company Vadi Yayınları. He also is on the editorial board of the journal *Sivil Toplum* (Civil society). During 2001, he held a postdoctoral fellowship at the University of Utah. His publications include translations of several Arabic and English books and articles into Turkish. He is coeditor of *Postmodernism and Islam, Globalization, and Orientalism* (1996, in Turkish) and of *Sociology of Religion* (1998, in Turkish); he is coauthor of *Word Was at the Beginning: On Hermeneutics* (1996, in Turkish). His most recent book is *On the Possibility of a Turkish Religion* (1999, in Turkish).

John L. Esposito is professor of religion and international affairs at Georgetown University's Walsh School of Foreign Service. He is the founding director of the Center for Muslim-Christian Understanding and editor in chief of *The Oxford Encyclopedia of the Modern Islamic World* (1995), *The Oxford History of Islam* (1999), and *The Oxford Dictionary of Islam* (2003). He is the author of *Islam: The*

Straight Path (1991, expanded ed.); *Islam and Politics* (1998, 4th ed.); *The Islamic Threat: Myth or Reality?* (1995, rev. ed.); *Islam and Democracy* (1996, with John Voll); *Political Islam: Revolution, Radicalism, or Reform?* (1997); *Islam and Secularism in the Middle East* (2000, with Azzam Tamimi); *Makers of Contemporary Islam* (2001, with John Voll); *Iran at the Crossroads* (2001, with R. K. Ramazani); *Unholy War: Terror in the Name of Islam* (2002); and *What Everyone Needs to Know about Islam* (2002).

Hasan T. Kösebalaban is a doctoral candidate in the Department of Political Science at the University of Utah, where he is completing his dissertation, "Multifaceted National Identities and Foreign Policy: The Case of Turkey and Japan." He is a native of Turkey and received his B.A. in political science from the International Islamic University in Kuala Lumpur, Malaysia. He subsequently pursued graduate studies at the International University of Japan, where he obtained an M.A. degree in international relations. During 1997–98, he was a visiting researcher at the University of Tübingen in Germany. He has published several articles in English- and Turkish-language scholarly journals, including most recently "Turkey's EU Membership: A Clash of Security Cultures" in *Middle East Policy* (2002) and "Turkish Media and Sports Coverage: Marking the Boundaries of National Identity" in *Critique: Critical Middle Eastern Studies* (forthcoming). He also is the author of *Güneydoğu Asya'da Islam ve Siyaset* (Islam and politics in Southeast Asia, 1997).

Ahmet T. Kuru is a Ph.D. candidate in the Department of Political Science at the University of Washington. He is the author of essays on identity and politics in Central Asia and on Islamic movements, published in journals including *Central Asian Survey* and *Cahiers d'études sur la Mediterranée et le monde turco-iranien*. He is currently studying church-state relations in the United States, France, and Turkey.

Thomas Michel is a member of the Indonesian Province of the Jesuits. He presently serves as secretary for Interreligious Dialogue of the Society of Jesus and ecumenical secretary of the Federation of Asian Bishops' Conferences. He studied Arabic in Lebanon and Egypt and received a Ph.D. in Arabic and Islamic studies in 1977 from the University of Chicago. His doctoral thesis, completed under the instruction of the late Fazlur Rahman, focused on the thought of Ibn Taymiyya. Dr. Michel has taught for many years in Indonesia and the Philippines. In Turkey, he has taught in the theology faculties of universities in Ankara, Izmir, Konya, and Urfa.

Elisabeth Özdalga received a Ph.D. in sociology from Göteborg University in 1979 and presently is a faculty member in the Department of Sociology at Middle East Technical University in Ankara. Her main research interests are religion and society in the Near East, Central Asia, and Turkey. She is affiliated with the Swedish Research Institute in Istanbul; as its previous director, she organized four major international conferences on aspects of Islam. She edited the proceedings of these conferences in four books: *Civil Society, Democracy, and the Muslim World* (1997); *Alevi Identity* (1998); *The Naqshbandis in West and Central Asia* (1999); and *Sufism, Music, and Society in Turkey and the Middle East* (2001). Özdalga also is the author of *The Veiling Issue* (1998).

Zeki Sarıtoprak holds a Ph.D. in Islamic theology from the University of Marmara, Turkey. He also studied Arabic for several years at Al-Azhar University in Cairo. He is the founder and president of the Rumi Forum for Interfaith Dialogue in Washington, D.C. He currently is a professor of Islamic studies at John Carroll University in Cleveland, Ohio. He also has taught at Harran University in Turkey; Berry College in Rome, Georgia; and Catholic University and Georgetown University, Washington, D.C. His fields of specialization include *kalam,* Sufism, the Qur'an and hadith, Islamic sects, and contemporary Islamic movements. He is the author of several books and articles in Arabic, English, and Turkish.

Berna Turam is a doctoral student and lecturer at McGill University in Montreal, Quebec. The title of her thesis is "Shifting Linkages Between Islam and the Secular State: The Case of the Gülen-Community Movement." She received her M.A. in sociology from McGill in 1996 and her B.A. in political science and sociology in 1993 from Boğaziçi University in Istanbul. Her primary research interest is political sociology with a focus on civil society, state, nations and nationalism, and ethnic and identity politics. A secondary area of interest is gender, focusing on patriarchy and civility.

John O. Voll is a professor of Islamic history and associate director of the Center for Muslim-Christian Understanding at Georgetown University. He is a past president of the Middle East Studies Association. Among his books are *Islam: Continuity and Change in the Modern World* (1994, 2d ed.) and *Islam and Democracy* (1996, with John L. Esposito) and *Makers of Contemporary Islam* (2001).

M. Hakan Yavuz is an assistant professor of political science at the University of Utah. He obtained his B.A. degree from the University of Ankara and his

M.A. and Ph.D. degrees from the University of Wisconsin at Madison. He is the author of *Islamic Political Identity in Turkey* (2003).

Ihsan Yılmaz is a lecturer in law at the School of Oriental and African Studies (SOAS) at the University of London and vice director of the Center for Ethnic Minorities and Law at SOAS. From 1999 to 2001, he was a research associate at the Center for Islamic Studies, Oxford University. He holds a B.A. in political science and international relations from Bosphorus University in Istanbul and a Ph.D. in law from SOAS. His research interests include legal pluralism, legal postmodernity, the interaction of Muslim law and identity with British law, Muslim laws vis-à-vis the West, the sociology of *fiqh*, Muslim political participation in the West, and Turks in Britain. His articles have appeared in *British Journal of Middle Eastern Studies, Journal of Ethnic and Migration Studies, Journal for Islamic Studies, Journal of Muslim Minority Affairs,* and *Middle East Journal.* His most recent publications are "Muslim Surfers on the Inter-*madhhab*-net and Neo-*ijtihad*," in *The Madhhab,* edited by Ruud Peters and Peri Bearman (2001); and "Inter-*madhhab* Surfing, Neo-*ijtihad*, and Faith-Based Movement Leaders," in *The Islamic School of Law: Evolution, Devolution, and Progress,* edited by Frank Vogel, Peri Bearman, and Ruud Peters (forthcoming).

Introduction

Islam in Turkey: Retreat from the Secular Path?

M. HAKAN YAVUZ AND JOHN L. ESPOSITO

THE TURKISH STATE'S conception of Islam is informed by its understanding of secularism as the only path to modernity, progress, and state power. This "otherness" of religion in general and of Islam in particular constitutes the meaning and role of the secular in Turkey. As a result, the discourse of secularism, even more than the real acts of Muslims, shapes the policies of the Turkish state and the secularist elite (Gellner 1994b; Mert 1994). The elite's aggressive policies are an extension of this construction of Islam, as can be seen by the way the elite read and interpreted the actions of Turkey's Refah/Fazilet Party. The Kemalist position—the ideology of Mustafa Kemal Atatürk (1881–1938), the founder of modern Turkey—on secularism can be summarized in the following way: modernity and democracy require secularism. Islam, he believed, was neither secularizable nor privatizable. Thus, in order to bring modernity, Islam had to be either kept under strict state control or confined to personal conscious.

In order to understand the cultural struggle in Turkey, one needs to privilege the concept and practice of secularism. This examination is crucial for our understanding of interweaving relations between politics, modernity, and religion.[1] Because the Turkish elite's conception of Islam is very much informed by their understanding of secularism, we first explore the concept of secularism and its realization within the Turkish context. Then we discuss the background of this cultural struggle and its divisive effects on religion. In fact, it was only with the openings of new social and cultural spaces that the state relaxed its control of

---

1. For more on the role of Islam in Turkish society, see Mardin 1989 and Göle 1996b. Indeed, modernity is not about time, but about a new configuration of social relations in which the rise of impersonalism and the inclusion of the masses as citizens play an important role.

Islam, which, in turn, allowed religious groups to reinterpret Islam according to the needs of modern society.

The Nur movement provides a case study of an attempt to cultivate faith without becoming embroiled in a confrontation with modernity. Moreover, it demonstrates not only multiple patterns of modernity but also a constant fluctuation in the understanding and implementation of secularism. The chapters of this volume reveal the transformation, not the decline or extinction, of religion in modern Turkish society.[2] Thus, they provide not only a reexamination of the secularization paradigm but also an exploration of the possibilities of multiple modernities.

Secularism as an intellectual and political project in Turkey has a long history of differentiating, marginalizing, and excluding large sectors of Turkish society.[3] In the examination of Islamic social movements, one needs to take this exclusionary history of secularism into account. Secularism in Turkey is different from secularism in the United States because in Turkey it involves an attempt to control the "lifeworld" of and impose a way of life on the people (Habermas 1984, 287, 398). The history of Islamic movements demonstrates that Muslims do not act passively when their lifeworld is colonized by the forces of a centralizing bureaucratic state, the market economy, and expert opinion, but rather involve themselves in a process of negotiation and readjustment. Many Islamic groups understand secularism as part of a strategy to preserve the authoritarian elite's domination as it uses secularism to rationalize its exploitation and exclusion of ethnic and practicing Muslims from the decision-making processes. This forced modernization in Turkey has made Islam an important resource for challenging the secularist project. However, Islamic movements utilize Islam not only to resist this hegemonic system, but also to promote change by vernacularizing modernity with Islamic practices. Islamic movements embody two contra-

2. On the "decline" paradigm, see Tschannen 1991 and Wilson 1982. Those who are critical of the "decline" paradigm and propose a new secularization theory include Casanova 1994, Demerath 1995, Finke 1990, and Stark 1994.

3. In the decisions of the Turkish Constitutional Court, only the secular public sphere is assumed to offer peace by removing any form of difference rooted in ethnicity or religion. The state wants to make sure that the Turkish public sphere is homogenous and unified without any religious marking. In other words, religiously rooted arguments in the public sphere are treated as divisive and dangerous for the peace and stability of that sphere. Secularism has become an authoritarian state ideology intended to root out religious and ethnic difference in the name of enlightenment values. The assertion of universal equality and nonviolence has become the source of inequality and oppression. The symbolic violence and denial of any religious presence in the public domain have become public policy.

dictory aspirations: the development of a contemporary terminology to deal with contemporary social and political issues, and the preservation of authentic Muslim identity and ethics. These trends toward modernity and conservation punctuate internal debate within Islamic tradition.

Secularism as a Source of Normative Conflict

What is secularism? How has secularism translated into public policy? What is the connection between nation building, secularism, and modernization? How does our understanding of secularism inform our conception of religion in general and of Islam in particular? What are the consequences of state-imposed secularism in terms of widening the normative conflict in Turkey?

Secularism, defined as the removal of the domination of religious authority from diverse spheres of society or public life, is the key constitutive category of modernity.[4] European secularism emerged as a solution to the wars of religion in Europe. Thomas Hobbes, the father of modern philosophy, created independent ethics outside of Christianity by excluding religious concerns and values from the public sphere. Because of ongoing religious wars in Europe, secularism became a necessity for civil peace and stability, and states soon refused to pursue any religious goals. The separation of the state and religion became the bedrock of the European state system, and secularism became the constitutive feature of modernity. Utilizing this European experience, scholars and philosophers previously emphasized a great transformation from the traditional to the modern world; from religion to reason; from a hierarchical and status-based society to a rights-based and impersonal society, with the inclusion of the masses into politics as citizens (Taylor 1998). The founding fathers of sociology—Auguste Comte, Émile Durkheim, Max Weber, and Karl Marx—in different degrees examined and predicted a steady shift from a religion-centered worldview to a secular, science-based, and reason-centered worldview.

Whereas in the European experience philosophers and politicians tried to expand the power of the state and restrict religion to the private sphere, in the United States secularism shielded diverse religions from state manipulation. Thus, two modes of secularism evolved from two different contexts. The first

4. One needs to disaggregate the concept of secularism in terms of its social, political, and philosophical meanings. Politically it means the separation of religion and politics. Socially it means a this-worldly orientation and recognition of individual reason and science as the means to engineer society. Philosophically it means that religious views and beliefs are regarded as humanly constructed rather than as divinely ordained and mysterious. See Berger 1973.

model of secularism, or *laicism,* which evolved in France, is antireligious and seeks to eliminate or control religion. The second model of secularism, evolved from the Anglo-American experience, seeks to protect religions from state intervention and encourages faith-based social networking to consolidate civil society (Esposito 2001a, 9). In short, the first model sees the state as the agent of social change and the source of the "good" life, whereas the second treats the state with suspicion and sees civil society as a source of change and of the "good" life.

Turkish secularism is based on the radical Jacobin laicism that aimed to transform society through the power of the state and eliminate religion from the public sphere (Berkes 1998). This Jacobin faith "in the primacy of politics and in the ability of politics to reconstitute society" (Eisenstadt 1999, 73) guided Mustafa Kemal and his associates. (It is this Jacobin tradition that would set a model for political action for the Islamists, the nationalists, and the leftists.) The Kemalist project treats secularism as above and outside politics. In short, secularism draws the boundaries of public reasoning. Any attempt to use religious discourse in public debate, even in the Turkish Parliament, can be used to ban that party or exclude the group. In Europe, philosophers sought to overcome sectarian conflicts by replacing religious argument with reason and universal philosophy. Not God but rather the moral subject became the source of ethics. Moral philosophy and rational religion became the source of morality. William E. Connolly, in *Why I Am Not a Secularist,* argues that although Kantian rational religion sought to get rid of the Christian God, it nevertheless has four ecclesiological features:

> First, it places singular conceptions of reason and command morality above question. Second, it sets up (Kantian) philosophy as the highest potential authority in adjudicating questions in these two domains and in guiding the people toward eventual enlightenment. Third, it defines the greatest danger to public morality as sectarianism within Christianity. Fourth, in the process of defrocking ecclesiastical theology and crowning philosophy as judge in the last instance, it also delegitimates a place for several non-Kantian, nontheistic perspectives in public life. (1999, 32)

Thus, secularists seek to perpetuate the Kantian "effects" by preventing any form of religious intrusion into public life.

By presenting the secular as modern, progressive, and European, many scholars have characterized colonized countries and their traditional ways of life as "backward" and underdeveloped. In the construction of the secularist view, they have created an Oriental "other": Islam. Many argue that political and religious authority has become increasingly separate in the West since the Reformation and increasingly unified under Islam in the East. They tend to defend the myth of the unity of religion and politics in Islam; in this defense, they are led by Bernard Lewis, who argues that "Islam was . . . associated with the excessive use of power from the very beginning. . . . This association between religion and politic, between community and polity, can . . . be seen in . . . the religious texts in which Muslims base their beliefs" (1994, 135–36). Lewis concludes that religious authority and political authority in Islam are not separate but one. This unexamined idea unfortunately has dominated Turkish studies (Berkes 1984; Tunaya 1964, 1991).

A group of scholars have challenged this Orientalist assumption on two different grounds. First, they argue that politics and religion are elusive and contextual (Lapidus 1988; Voll 1982). The boundary between the religious and the political is not fixed or text centered, but rather fluctuating and porous. Second, they argue that Islamic social movements are not a conservative reaction to modernity but an attempt to create their own version of modernity (Asad 1993; Piscatori 1983, 1986). These movements seek to raise Muslim consciousness and expand the boundaries of the public sphere. Ira Lapidus challenges the assumed "separation" of religion and politics in the West and their "unification" in Islam by arguing that

> The European societies are presumed to be built upon a profound separation of state and religious institutions. This view ignores the variety and complexity of the European cases. It ignores the numerous examples of state control of religion, the phenomenon of established churches (such as the Anglican Church in England), and the concordats in Italy. It ignores the integral connection between religious and political nationalism in such countries as Ireland or Poland. (1996, 3)

In fact, there is no single pattern of interaction between religion and politics in Islam, but "rather several competing ones. Moreover, in each of the models there are ambiguities concerning the distribution of authority, functions and relations among institutions" (Lapidus 1996, 4). John Voll (1982), another leading authority on Islamic politics, emphasizes the complex and context-sensitive relations between religious and temporal authority in Muslim societies.

In many developing countries, secularism became a theology of progress and development. In this regard, it is important to study Turkey for a number of reasons. Normative fault lines of modernity are nowhere else as clear as in Turkey. The interaction between secularism and Islam plays an important role in normative and ethnic conflict, in cultural politics of remembering and representing the past, and in the formation of new social movements in Turkey. The forced secularization process, which has sought to "civilize" (that is, Westernize) Turkey, created a major normative struggle around the following questions: Who are we? How are we to live together? What are the moral boundaries of the community? For theoretical and empirical reasons, Turkey is an important country. The Turks not only developed one of the most comprehensive models of ethnoreligious coexistence qua the Millet system, but also were the first to experience the modernization project in the Muslim world. This shift from an ancien regime to a "modern" society and a nation-state is the source of many normative conflicts in different societies.

Three major outcomes of modernity in Turkey were nationalism, secularism, and, more recently, the pluralization of beliefs and values. Despite different challenges and conflicts, the premodern Ottoman polity had a reasonable framework for maintaining a unified normative charter that could command the allegiance of the great majority of Muslims, Christians, and Jews. With the introduction of modernity, the politics of nationalism and secularism raised the question of legitimacy and shattered the traditional framework of coexistence.

Neither nationalism nor secularism divorced from their European context helped to solve this problem in the former Ottoman regions of the Middle East, the Caucasus, and the Balkans. Secularism in Turkey did not bring peace and stability to fighting religious groups; instead, it worked toward modernizing the state and homogenizing society. The Kemalist principles of nationalism (i.e., the attempt to create a homogenous nation) and secularism (i.e., the attempt to form a modern society based on rationalism) destroyed the multiethnic character of Turkish society by getting rid of Greeks and other Christian communities and by denying the Kurds their cultural rights. The source of Turkish political morality became nationalism to serve the state. Nationalism did not replace religion, but it managed to nationalize religions, which, along with secularism, became the sources of ongoing tension. In the current post-nation-building period, pluralism, as a result of globalization, has become a key virtue—peaceful coexistence by recognizing diversity within "nation-states."

Although our work recognizes the vital role of democratic institutions to navigate competing norms and interests, we stress that normative charter is essential for deliberative democracy and the coexistence of diversity. Nondenominational or nonsectarian Durkheimian "collective conscience" (what may be termed *normative charter*) is sine qua non for the adjudication of sectarian ideas and interests. A religiously based normative charter is necessary to answer some of the most important questions: What is the purpose of our existence? How are we to live together with our differences? As long as late modernity raises the question of difference, we cannot assume a society without normative charter, but instead need to develop an inclusive normative charter. Thus, the Nur movement in Turkey is significant because it deals with the formation and dissemination of a nondenominational Islamic ethics of engagement with religious, cultural, and ideological difference.

The Origins of Turkish Secularism: Positivist Philosophy

In order to understand the current normative conflict in Turkey, we need to examine it in the context of the Ottoman legacy. The source of power in the Ottoman Empire was the complex web of relationships between a military and a bureaucratic system, on the one hand, and Islamic institutions, on the other. The system had a deep understanding of the autonomy and unity of institutions. The major source of tension was between state institutions and Islamic sects and Sufi orders. Sufi orders and networks served as the protective shields against the excesses of state power because they contained and nourished the civil code of interactions. European colonial penetration and the loss of territory in the nineteenth century forced the Ottoman bureaucracy to complete modernization by removing societal centers of resistance.

The modernization of the Ottoman system started with the goal of "consolidating and strengthening the state" (not society) to resist European penetration and ethnoreligious rebellions in the Balkans. The nineteenth-century Ottoman elite consolidated state power primarily by modernizing the army. This process transformed the army into an agent of ordering society in accordance with the needs of the state. The second instrument of consolidation of state power was the introduction of science and technology for economic development. For the Ottoman bureaucratic intellectuals, science became the progressive force to order and regulate society and to alter modes of thinking.

The affinity between the positivist worldviews and the interests of the bureaucratic elite who carried out these reforms needs to be examined. The "carriers" of positivism had very special characteristics. Their vested interests were attached to their ideological position. They exploited the reform campaign to consolidate their power vis-à-vis religious intellectuals by framing all opposition to their view as "religious fanaticism." The republic used this Young Turk (1908–18) legacy of division not only to delegitimize all forms of opposition by characterizing them as struggles between science and religion, progress and fanaticism, but also to criminalize those forms of opposition.

The Young Turks presented themselves as progressive because they had a "modern" scientific education and were guided by science and reason, not by religion. The major characteristics of the Young Turks, who were trained in secular schools, were: (*a*) unquestioned faith in positivism as a guide to polity and society; (*b*) determination to create a modern society to consolidate the power of the state; and (*c*) a passion for elite rule. Owing to these three characteristics—positivism, statism, and elitism—the Young Turks were neither liberal nor democratic. Although they stressed the significance of the parliamentary system and constitutionalism as a way of coping with ethnic challenges in the Balkans, their first and foremost goal was to protect and consolidate the power of the Ottoman state. Even the attempts to create "Ottoman citizenship" were aimed at expanding the social basis of the Ottoman state. Thus, for the Young Turks, the ancestors of the republican elite, identity was constituted by two contradictory trends: radicalism (which stresses science and a rationality-based society) and conservatism (which seeks to consolidate state and group power). They presented themselves as "revolutionary" in their intent to change the society, but they also used the state to consolidate their own power (Mardin 1983a). As a result of nineteenth-century reforms, the legacies of an authoritarian state structure and a new administrative military-civilian bureaucratic elite punctuated the establishment of the Republic of Turkey.

Mustafa Kemal, just like the Young Turks during the wars in the Balkans and World War I, never hesitated to utilize Islam to mobilize the population against the invading European armies and always treated Islam as the glue to integrate and blend all Anatolian Muslims into the Turkish nation.[5] In the formation of the Turkish nation, the republic assumed that Muslimness was a sine qua non for becoming a Turk. After achieving national independence, however, the republic implemented a rigid positivist project by denying any role for Islam in the formation of the new polity.

In the late 1920s, laicism became the constituting principle of the Kemalist project of building a nation-state. In the Fourth Congress of the People's Republican Party in 1935, Mustafa Kemal codified his ideas and goals as "Kemalism," which consisted of six eclectic principles to guide the party, the state, and the nation: nationalism, secularism, republicanism, statism, reformism, and

5. For more on the connection between nationalism and Islam in the Turkish context, see Yavuz 1993 and 1995c.

populism.[6] The Kemalist doctrine was informed by the dominant European authoritarian ideologies in the 1930s and perceived modernization as Westernization. In practice, Kemalism became the ideology and practice of eliminating class, ethnic, and religious sources of conflict by seeking to create a classless, national (unified as Turkish), and secular (cleansed of any religious sign or practice in the public sphere) homogenized society. Thus, fear of differences became the guiding principle of the Kemalist state. Moreover, owing to the impact of French positivism, the Kemalist project's sole legitimate agent of change has been the state itself. Change is "modern" and acceptable only if it is carried out by the state. Thus, in the process of making a Kemalist state, any form of bottom-up modernization of civil society became a source of worry and suspicion. Because Kemalism saw the nation and state as one and the same, Islam was excluded from the definition of these entities. Kemalist reforms tried to create a new society and a *Homo kemalicus,* a persona guided by voluntary positivism and forced amnesia (in other words, no deeper sense of identity). This Kemalist ideal was neither democratic nor liberal but authoritarian, elitist, and ideological. Although some scholars—such as Tarık Zafer Tunaya, Niyazi Berkes, Ergun Özbudun, and Feroz Ahmad—have justified this tutelage system as a transition to democracy and civil society, their ex post facto explanation ignores the societal factors and authoritarian aspects of Kemalism.[7]

Nothing shaped and guided the Young Turks and Mustafa Kemal as much as positivism (Mardin 1981; Timur 1971, 132). The republican elite adopted the Comtian idea of "progress within order." Positivism shaped the domains of politics, economics, and society. Expert opinion became the final reasoning in terms of setting public policy. Science and technology were regarded as the means to economic development. Faith in positivism became the guiding principle of the Turkish educational system. As the Mustafa Kemal saying went, "Science is the truest guide in life" (*"Hayatta en hakiki mürşit ilimdir"*). So Kemalist laicism is not about the separation of politics and religion, but rather about restructuring society in accordance with positivist philosophy. In practice, this restructuring means preventing religious influence in the spheres of education, economics, family, dress code, and politics.[8] This top-down nation-building

---

6. There are a number of good works on Kemalism; see, for example, Köker 1990, Öz 1992, Parla 1992, and Tuncay 1981.

7. On the official view of Kemalism, see Karal 1981.

8. Only with the democratization and the evolution of the market conditions did the Turks gradually overcome these divisions.

project not only widened the previous fault lines in the Ottoman society, but also added new ones: Turks versus Kurds, secularists versus Islamists, Alevis versus Sunnis. The next section examines the secular fault line in Turkey.

Turkish Secularism: Reconfiguring Laicism as Identity

In the context of Turkey, the adjective *secular* (*laik* in Turkish) became the identity of the ruling elite. This *laik* identity consists of being progressive (having faith in science), modern (i.e., European), and nationalist (Turkish). Laicism constituted the hegemonic ideology and informed state policies. In fact, it became the *identity* of the ruling elite, the *ideology* of the national-security state with a built-in code of violence to exclude anyone who does not fit the state's definition of a *"laik* Turk." Owing to these exclusionary practices in Turkey, laicism has very little moral power to guide political action. In the context of Turkey, unlike the United States, secular values and forms of identity are affirmed as in opposition to religion. For instance, in Turkey, morality, or moral conduct, is the preserve of the family, the neighborhood, and the community, whereas many Turks regard the political domain as the space of dirty tricks and duplicity. They consider this moral emptiness of the political domain as the source of corruption. Because they also equate secularism with the domain of politics and the state, it has not fully penetrated everyday interactions and regulations. Instead, contrary to Kemalist goals, religion remains the source of family, neighborhood, and community interactions. People are expected to be honest and rule bound within their families, neighborhoods, and community, but not in politics or in the state. This sharp division between moral community and the political sphere is the source of many problems in Turkey.

In the process of secularization, the most important division emerged between European and local lifestyles, or *"à la franga"* versus *"à la turca."* This division is most significant because it punctuates everyday life, including lifestyle, dress code, taste in music and art, ritual cleanliness, and the type of furniture one seeks to own. Thus, almost all Turkish homes are divided between a sitting room, where full privacy is practiced and preserved, and a European "salon," where guests are welcomed and served according to formal rules. Both rooms require separate furniture, codes of conduct, and clothing. So almost all Turks learn to live in a hybrid world of European and Muslim forms of conduct. In other words, Turkish modernity created the possibility of sharing European and Muslim identity at the same time.

For Islam, as the constitutive framework for and the source of ethics in Turkey, the idea of secularism, which does not include a similar ethical charter, remains an alien ideology, as does the identity of the ruling elite in Turkey.[9] In short, it is the ideology of the self-declared Westernized elite to maintain their privileged position through the state. Although the usual antonym of *secular* is *religious,* in recent years the antonym has been *opposition to hegemonic order.* Secularism in the Turkish context means excessive state penetration into everyday life and the exclusion of ethnic, religious, or regional difference. Contrary to its aims, the Kemalist project of nationalism and secularism actually helped to construct an oppositional and ideologized Islam. Thus, religious revival became the internal dialectic of Kemalist modernity.

The Evolution of the Islamic Social Movement, 1950–1980

Although the Turkish state always has tried to use Islam for its own goals, it never allowed the free expression of religion and religious practices. The Turkish republic established the Directorate of Religious Affairs to "administer and regulate" people's religious needs and affairs in the public sphere. By not allowing society to regulate its own religious affairs, the republic prevented the emergence of an alternative vision of Islam and banned all civil society-based religious networks. This skepticism, or fear of society, was the major feature of Kemalism's attempt to create a secular nation-state. With the socioeconomic transformation of the society, however, new political, economic, and cultural opportunity spaces emerged (Yavuz 2003). These new spaces for political parties, actions groups, associations, reading circles, newspapers, and market and fashion shows became sites of contestation and negotiation between Islam and modern lifeworlds. Because Islam is regarded as the major source of the constitution of the self, religion increasingly became more important in these new urban spaces. As a result of the Turkish experiment with modernity, a number of religious, ethnic, and ideological movements have punctuated the state's political history. Next to Kurdish ethnonationalism, the Islamic movement has been the most powerful claim-making movement (Yavuz 2001). In short, the structural transformation (urbanization, industrialization, and education) actually empowered the marginalized sector of Turkish society and facilitated its return to politics, economy, and education. The return of religious activism and religiously framed movements is not a fearsome "return of the repressed," but rather an attempt to *vernacularize modernity.*

9. Taylor aptly argues that "an authoritarian programme designed to diminish the hold of religion on the masses, as in Turkey under Atatürk, or China under Mao" does not bring peace and stability (1998, 37).

This contemporary religious activism is an outcome of four interrelated socioeconomic processes: the geographic mobility of the population to new urban centers; the expansion of mass education, which led to the questioning of the state ideology and to access to diverse reading sources; political participation and utilization of religious networks for political purposes; and a search for new values to cope with the modern challenges of identity and morality. Because Islam organizes everyday life, community action, and the constitution of the self, these new opportunity spaces for political action groups, markets, foundations, media networks, and cultural associations helped Muslims to live as "conscious Muslims." Islam, just like other religions, became a moral framework within which to discuss identity and justice in society.

In the 1960s, as a result of economic development and the new legal framework of the 1961 Constitution, which created a number of legal spaces as rights, a new set of agents of modernity emerged. Kemalism, which sees only the state-guided reforms as modern, did not know what to do with or how to respond to these new societal actors. The major issue was who should define what institution, dress code, or practice as "modern." The Democratic Party, which had come to power after the transition to a multiparty system in 1950, identified the newly emerging bourgeoisie as the agent of modernity. The major feature of the Democratic Party that differentiated it from the People's Republican Party of Mustafa Kemal was its recognition of societal forces as the agent of modernity and change. In the end, though, Kemalists, the self-declared guardians of the republic, became very suspicious of empowering society and ended the Democratic Party government with bloodshed by hanging the prime minister and two prominent ministers. Thus, the conflict between top-down and bottom-up modernization was the major source of breakdown in the 1960 coup.

Economic and social changes forced the Kemalist guard to give up its dream of creating a "classless society" and of redefining Kemalism as the national-security ideology of the state. Its main goal became the protection of the state and its purity against societal penetrations. Thus, in response to newly emerging social and political actors, Kemalism became a more conservative ideology to protect the state against assertive religious and ethnic identities. In the 1960s and 1970s, leftist intellectuals, grouped around the weekly magazine *YÖN*, redefined Kemalism as an anti-imperialist and "national liberation" movement (Özdemir 1993). They stressed the statism aspect of Kemalism and sought to consolidate state power against the bourgeoisie. The deep divisions and radical politicization of society in terms of left versus right, Alevi versus Sunni, and Turk versus Kurd dominated the 1970s. Extremist leftist movements and Kurdish nationalism started to undermine the security and stability of society. In the second half of the 1970s, Turkey became a battleground where more than four thousand people were killed.

The military intervened in 1980 to stop the fragmentation of the state. The multiparty system in Turkey created new political spaces for Islamic movements to work closely with political parties. In addition, the Cold War and the communist movement in Turkey forced the state to use Islamic movements as an antidote to the left. These two factors—the deepening of electoral democracy and "the repression of democratic leftist forces" (Lubeck 2001, 4)—created political opportunities for Islamic movements. Thus, the 1980 military coup disrupted existing power arrangements and created opportunities for new actors who desired to restructure power relations and the distribution of resources.

On 12 September 1980, when Turkish generals intervened to stop escalating left-right violence and to curtail a growing leftist movement, they utilized Islam not only as an antidote to communist movements, but also as a resource to mold a more obedient generation. Turkey's excluded groups were mobilized during the 1983 elections when the state identified the leftist forces as the threat to national security. These historically excluded groups benefited from this new political opening and activated their indigenous religious networks, such as the Nakşibendi and the Nurcus, to seize material and cultural rewards. Between 1983 and 1990, religious networks were mobilized to offer welfare services, communal solidarity, and mobility to those newly educated classes and businesses. Prime Minister Turgut Özal's expansion of the freedom of association, speech, and assembly removed the state monopoly over the broadcasting system and further facilitated the communication and dissemination of local and global idioms. As a result of these factors, Islamic movements constructed an activist "consciousness" to shape the sociopolitical landscape of Turkey.

The "modernizing" republic had full official control over education and telecommunication until the early 1990s. This control enabled the state to organize and monitor the public sphere to ensure that it was adhering to the official national (i.e., Turkish) and secular (i.e., European) identity. Moreover, the state used high tariffs to create a pro-statist and secular, but not necessarily national, bourgeoisie by implementing exclusivist policies against Armenian, Greek, and Jewish merchants who hitherto, with the aid of Western imperial powers, had dominated trade in the Ottoman state. Although the formation of a culturally diverse bourgeoisie had begun in the late 1960s, the economic policies implemented by Turgut Özal following the 1980 military coup helped to crystallize and expand a countercultural bourgeoisie class with Anatolian roots. In the 1980s and 1990s, Özal's free-market policies were supported by small-scale provincial businessmen and the petite bourgeoisie of the cities. This sector—

which includes peddlers, dealers, builders, restaurant owners, small and midsize industrialists, and food processors—received no public funding and thus opposed state intervention in the economy in favor of economic liberalization. Özal was a member of the İskenderpaşa Nakşibendi Sufi order, and he promoted in particular those businessmen of Anatolian origin who had close ties to such Islamic circles.

There are three interrelated reasons for the growing influence of Islamic discourses in the late 1980s (Kasaba 1998). First, Islamic discourse produced a new vision of identity composed of national and religious symbols. Second, it managed to disseminate its ideas by utilizing all forms of communication networks and media. Third, it developed intimate ties with the Anatolian bourgeoisie. Muslim entrepreneurs, who were not dependent on state subsidies and were concentrated in foreign exchange-earning export industries such as food processing and textiles, were particularly well placed to prosper in this period. This economic elite funded many prominent new publications, including the newspapers *Türkiye, Zaman,* and *Yeni Şafak,* as well as many national and regional television stations. Özal's neoliberal economic policies created and enlarged economic and political space in which people could establish new contractual ties. Therefore, neoliberalism, by creating gaps between the rich and poor and spaces between religious and secular groups, led to a more pluralist society marked by differences rather than by unity. The economic liberalization and growth of the Özal period created a dynamic Anatolian entrepreneurial class and numerous opportunity spaces such as independent newspapers and television channels, which could not be muzzled in their demands that the political sphere be broadened. This transformation became a source of fear for the hegemonic elite.[10]

Privatization of the Public Sphere: The Process of Desecularization

Because of Özal's neoliberal economic policies and political liberalization, along with the introduction of new media technologies, a complex religious "market"

10. The "soft coup" launched against the Refah Party in 1997 is just the latest in a cyclical series of such interventions by the Kemalist establishment to suppress civil society. The greatest threat to this autocracy composed of bureaucrats, generals, state-supported industrialists such as the Koç group, and their media outlets are not Muslim politicians or Kurdish activists, but the prospects of political liberalization that would curtail their sweeping powers. It is questionable, however, how long this counterattack against civil society and liberalization can be sustained because it faces a law of diminishing returns.

evolved in Turkey. In this expanding religious market, Nakşibendi orders, the Nur movement, and the politically active National Outlook Movement of Necmettin Erbakan, competed over the "true" meaning and proper "action" of Islam. One of the major impacts of liberalization was the simultaneous process of pluralization and expansion of Islam in public spaces. Like other markets, the religious one consists of diverse buyers and a set of firms seeking to serve potential customers. The opening of this market led to the transformation and pluralization of the religious sphere and, most important, to the expansion of religious idioms and networks to other spheres of life such as the economy, the media, and charity.

The Nur movement of Fethullah Gülen has benefited the most from this political and economic liberalization. One of the most influencial Muslim leaders of Turkey, Gülen has utilized the ideas of Said Nursi to establish an extensive education system. This neo-Nur faith-based movement focuses on identity and ethics to overcome the normative conflict in Turkey. A closer examination indicates that for the Nur movement, Islam constitutes a social capital that can be mobilized for diverse instrumental ends. The Nur movement uses the values and norms provided by Islam to channel conduct in a certain direction, promotes the circulation of information and knowledge, and shapes long-term interaction within a framework of trust and mutual obligation. By using new structural opportunities in the market and society, it has created its own vernacular modernity by directly addressing needs previously ignored by the Kemalist ideology and Turkey's state structure.

The case of Turkey indicates that secularism should not always be read as the telos of development and modernity. Secularism does not always evolve with modernity, development, rationality, and emancipation. Jose Casanova's pathbreaking comparative historical sociology of religious movements demonstrates that not all religious movements are fundamentalist, but rather that some are tied to democratization, social justice, and leftist agendas: "Throughout the decade [1980s] religion showed its Janus face, as the carrier not only of exclusive, particularist, and primordial identities but also of inclusive, universalist, and transcending ones. The religious revival signaled simultaneously the rise of fundamentalism and of its role in the resistance of the oppressed and the rise of the 'powerless'" (1994, 4).

The case of Turkey supports Casanova's conclusion that (*a*) not all religious expressions are conservative; (*b*) the domain of religion is not a permanent fixed site of particularism and exclusiveness; and (*c*) the deprivatization of religion is the dominant trend in some countries. Indeed, in modern societies, religion "finds refuge in the newly found private sphere" (Casanova 1994, 40). However, it is in this private sphere where religious activism is charged and extended to the public sphere.

Modernity did not create a sharp division between public and private, but rather a contingent and flexible boundary where private becomes public or vice versa. Increasing penetration of the state and market forces activated a religious charter to defend specific lifeworlds against colonization and to protect human dignity (Casanova 1994, 40). The public "focus of [religions] is no longer the state but, rather, civil society" (Casanova 1994, 63).

The study of the Gülen movement reveals not only the processes of "deprivatization" of Islam but also its increasing publicness in modern Turkish society. It indicates the social and political conditions under which faith can become a source of social capital to empower society. The chapters in this book adopt a bottom-up approach by focusing on different sites of interactions such as education, media, economics, and civic associations in recording such events.

The Fethullah Gülen Movement

In the past two decades, the extraordinary vitality of Islam has led to a reexamination of religion and its role in Turkish society. The embrace of modernity, in fact, has proven to stimulate rather than to diminish the attraction of Islam for millions of people. It is true that many of the early religious responses to the secularizing reforms were manifested primarily in small and antistatist movements and defenses of tradition. But new religious movements revitalized traditional religious institutions, which thereafter emerged in a second wave. These religious institutions not only have survived, but also have often provided the rationales and structures for struggles over control of modern institutions.

This volume focuses on the Gülen movement, its ideas and worldview, as well as its educational, economic, and media activities. It looks at how the Gülen community is shaped by the sociopolitical context of Turkey and by Said Nursi's ideas and how it constitutes multiple arenas of Turkish society and their interaction with and response to modernity. Among the critical questions examined are: What ideas inform the Gülen movement? What is the connection between Said Nursi and Gülen? To what sectors of society does the Gülen movement appeal, and why does it appeal to them? What is its position on cultural and political diversity in the society? How does the movement translate its ideas into practice? What is the dialectic between ideas and practice?

The volume covers the social context of the movement as well as the sources of Gülen's ideas and of the educational practices of his movement. In order to understand what is new about the Gülen movement, in chapter 1, "Islam in the Public Sphere: The Case of the Nur Movement," Hakan Yavuz explores the ideas of Said Nursi, the founder of the Nur movement, and the movement's transformation as a result of new social and political conditions in Turkey. When Gülen became known in the late 1960s, Turkey had a democratic civil society as a result of the liberal 1961 Constitution. Moreover, during this formative period, the major challenge for the state was communist insurgency, against which the state elite did not hesitate to use Islamic groups. When the Özal government privatized the economy, education, and telecommunication networks, well-organized Muslim groups were empowered to carve new spaces for themselves. Under these better conditions, Gülen was able to translate privately formed piety into public activism. As a follower of Nursi, he seeks peace based on justice on earth and the hereafter through intellectual and spiritual enlightenment. Following up on this discussion, in chapter 2, "The Gülen Movement: The Turkish Puritans," Yavuz discusses how Gülen utilizes educational networks to achieve intellectual and spiritual enlightenment and to put the values of Islam into practice.

In chapter 3, "The Gülen Movement's Islamic Ethic of Education," Bekim Agai looks at the translation of Gülen's ideas into practice. "Education as Islamism" is the core theme of Agai's argument. He discusses the relationship between education and Islam and the way in which Gülen seizes national and global opportunities to advance his cause of training a new elite, armed with both modern sciences and the Islamic ethics of serving humanity. Gülen, for Agai, has moved beyond leading a purely religious movement to become more social and educational by presenting himself as a "modern" educator and social innovator. Agai also examines how this educational mobilization, in turn, has shaped the worldview and practices of the Gülen movement. Those trained in the summer camps of the 1970s became the teachers of the new generation of teachers, missionaries who carried the ethical message of Islam all over the world. Agai argues that the movement was first transformed by its educational practices while it was seeking to transform the society. Since the 1990s, the movement has presented its educational mission as a cure for identity conflicts, a bridge between local and global groups, and a basis for interreligious dialogue.

In chapter 4, "Fethullah Gülen as Educator," Thomas Michele examines Gülen as an "educator" who seeks to "integrate [students] with their past and prepare them intelligently for the future" (Gülen 1996a, 59). This pedagogic vision is based on the assumption that, as Michel puts it, "the effective process of modernization must include the development of the whole person." In the realization of this vision, the educator plays a formative role; it is the educator "who has the ability to assist in the emergence of the students' personalities, who fosters thought and reflection, who builds character and enables the students to interiorize qualities of self-discipline, tolerance, and a sense of mission."

Elisabeth Özdalga, in "Following in the Footsteps of Fethullah Gülen: Three Woman Teachers Tell Their Stories," chapter 5, discusses the more individual aspect of Gülen's educational practices: the formation of the self, ethics, and inner space through religious practices. Islam helps to create the necessary ethics of honesty, solidarity, and respect. The three women teachers spotlighted in the chapter do not negate their "self" but rather form a unique self by utilizing common Islamic idioms of community, ethics, and identity. In short, Özdalga's study demonstrates that there is no self without the shared idiom of Islam. Because Gülen's schools do not teach courses on Islam or ethics, they introduce ethics through the exemplary conduct of their teachers. This approach is morality by conduct, not by a strict curriculum. Teachers are expected to foster thought and reflection and to help students to internalize qualities of self-discipline, self-sacrifice, and tolerance. This movement is based on an ethics of education—that is, engaging with difference and cultivating individual moral character. Its two pillars are presentation of Islam (*tebliğ*) and representation of Islam by labor (*temsil*). One is expected to communicate and present Islam through his or her good labor. In other words, this is not a preaching or doctrinaire Islam, but rather Islam in life, communicated through the teachers' good works.

Another of Gülen's significant contributions is his attempt to problematize the boundary between secular and religious time, or religious and secular activity. He calls Muslims to engage fully in the production of knowledge and action in accordance with Islamic ethics. In chapter 6, "Fethullah Gülen's Search for a Middle Way," Ahmet Kuru argues that there is no "biblical" or "merchant time" in the writings of Gülen, but rather holistic action in the name of God. Time in itself is less meaningful than action. Time and space become important in acting and engaging. This emphasis on time-space is pivotal in Gülen's interpretation of the Qur'an. The "middle way" reconciles the perceived dichotomies between (*a*) modern science and Islamic knowledge, (*b*) reason and revelation, (*c*) modern understanding of progress and Muslim tradition, and (*d*) the free will of modern humans and the Muslim understanding of destiny by accepting them as two faces of the same reality. Kuru argues that Gülen tries to reveal a dynamic interpretation of Islam that is compatible with and at the same time critical of modernity and Muslim tradition, rather than creating an eclectic or hybrid synthesis of modernity and Islam.

Yasin Aktay argues in "Diaspora and Stability: Constitutive Elements in a

Body of Knowledge," chapter 7, that Gülen reflects the larger trend in modern Turkish Islamic thought. He treats Gülen in terms of the diasporic conditions after the abolishment of the caliphate and the introduction of a new idiom of politics and society, and in terms of the deep sense of statism and nationalism among the Turkish ulema. He also examines how Gülen seeks to cope with this seismic shift from Islamically shaped political language to pure secularist forms of politics.

Islam, for Gülen, leads believers to perfection. Because Islam consists of morality and identity, Gülen's main goal is to cultivate and nourish these elements through education. Although Gülen realizes the need for ritual, he regards moral uprightness as lying at the heart of the religious impulse. In addition to its ethical aspect, Islam, according to Gülen, is about having a conscious identity. As Zeki Sarıtoprak argues in "Fethullah Gülen: A Sufi in His Own Way," chapter 8, Gülen calls this identity *"muhasaba-i nafs"*—the notion of questioning yourself before being questioned. The knowledge of self is the key to knowledge of God, so "he who knows himself knows God" is the guiding principle of Islam. Thus, raising religious consciousness means the formation of both one's identity and one's morality at the same time.

Gülen believes that humanity would become more peaceful if there is a close balance and interactive relationship between rational and spiritual enlightenment. He seeks an interactive relationship between reason and spirituality. He wants to "educate and train" hearts and minds by calling his readers and followers to develop an interactive framework to understand the connection between reason and revelation. He therefore argues that

> Neglect of the intellect . . . would result in a community of poor, docile mystics. Negligence of the heart or spirit, on the other hand, would result in crude rationalism devoid of any spiritual dimension. . . . It is only when the intellect, spirit and body are harmonized, and man is motivated towards activity in the illuminated way of the Divine message, that he can become a complete being and attain true humanity. (2000c, 105–6)

By employing a constructivist theoretical framework, Hasan Kösebalaban's "The Making of Enemy and Friend: Fethullah Gülen's National-Security Identity," chapter 9, analyzes Gülen's conception of foreign policy. As a leader of a faith-based social movement, Gülen does not divide the world into two clashing groups of Muslims and non-Muslims. Rather, his view of international politics is marked by three distinct perceptions of external others, with varying degrees of separation from the self. Utilizing Alexander Wendt's discussion of cultures of anarchy, Kösebalaban discusses Gülen's conception of the "other" in terms of Hobbesian (enemy), Lockian (rival), and Kantian (friend) perspectives. Gülen views Iran as the Hobbesian other of Turkish state identity and thus as the most important threat to Turkish security. He perceives the West, however, as a *rival* to compete with, rather than as an *enemy* to confront. He suggests that Turkey needs to integrate into Western economic and political systems in order to increase its economic prowess. In contrast, he internalizes the Turkic world and the Muslim communities in the Balkans in Kantian terms of friendship. The main line of his approach to foreign policy is that Turkey should follow multiple orientations in its foreign policy, maintaining close relations with the West, on the one hand, but also strong links with the Turkic world, on the other.

Berna Turam's study "National Loyalties and International Undertakings: The Case of the Gülen Community in Kazakhstan," chapter 10, examines the Gülen community as civil society, in the face of ongoing tensions and confrontation between Islam and secular regimes. Turam discusses the ethnic underpinning of Gülen's educational networks in Central Asia. Based on extensive ethnographic data, this study reveals a new Islamic conception of the "nation as the state" and shows how the Gülen community accommodates ethnicity. Specifically, it focuses on the ethnic politics that Gülen pursues in Kazakhstan through the movement's educational projects. Her findings paradoxically suggest that strong national loyalties endow Gülen with legitimacy and recognition as an international social actor.

In connection with this view, a slow but steady process of renewal is evolving in Muslim sociopolitical and jurisprudential discourses and practices, leading to a new Muslim politics and international relations and paving the way for a modern and harmonious society as a result of a bottom-up approach. The reality of different types of Muslim legal pluralisms poses both challenges and opportunities regarding new reinterpretations (neo-*ijtihad*) and renewal (*tajdid*) of Islam in decades to come. In this regard, the evolution around the ideas of the charismatic figure Gülen provides an example of a renewal with the potential to influence the Muslim world. Ihsan Yılmaz's chapter, *"Ijtihad* and *Tajdid* by Conduct: The Gülen Movement," demonstrates the extent to which Gülen successfully has mobilized many people to establish institutions that will put into practice his discourse in more than fifty countries and to realize his ideals of raising a "golden generation" and achieving general global peace. Preliminary observations and evidence indicate that Gülen is not only renewing Muslim discourses and practices, but also transforming the public sphere. In this regard, the movement based on Gülen's discourses is an example of a renewal that has the potential to influence the Muslim world. This transformation process is definitely a *tajdid* in the Turkish public sphere, if not in the whole world. The reality of internal Muslim legal pluralism requires that different *ijtihad*s, shaped by local conditions, take place in different parts of the Muslim world at the same time. Thus, other renewalist movements elsewhere are quite possible. With the increasing importance and weight of the Turkic world in global sociopolitics, Gülen's model for *tajdid* will be more influential. It already has been contributing to Turkey's potential leadership in the region, and his followers have been spreading the "renewed word," as it were, by their conduct throughout the world.

In chapter 12, "Fethullah Gülen: Transcending Modernity in the New Islamic Discourse," John Voll argues that Gülen presents a significant example of an emerging mode of faith articulation that is becoming important in the twenty-first century. By focusing on the interaction between the global and the local, he examines the role of transnational networks in the evolution of the Gülen movement.

Turkish Islam and
the Secular State

1

Islam in the Public Sphere

The Case of the Nur Movement

M. HAKAN YAVUZ

DESPITE THE EXCLUSIONARY and delegitimizing efforts of the Kemalist state in Turkey, a gradual yet profound social transformation has been taking place at the grassroots level as a result of the emergence of new, alternative social, cultural, and economic public spaces.* The economic and political liberalization policies of former president and prime minister Turgut Özal in the 1980s accelerated the formation and expansion of such spaces. Culturally and economically excluded groups, such as Muslims, have used them to create their own "parallel society." For instance, deregulation of broadcasting has empowered Islamic voices to express themselves on diverse radio stations and television channels and in magazines and newspapers. Moreover, the growing Anatolian bourgeoisie, commonly called Anatolian "tigers," has formed its own association, called Müstakil Sanayici ve İş Adamları Derneği (MÜSİAD, Association of Independent Industrialists and Businessmen).[1] These new alternative spaces have served to empower Islamic groups in Turkey.

*This article emerged out of my research while I was a Rockefeller Fellow at the Kroc Institute of the University of Notre Dame in 2001–2002. I thank the Kroc Institute and especially Scott Appleby, its director, for their continuous support. Some parts of this chapter were published previously in *Middle East Journal* 53, no. 4 (1999): 584–605. I would like to thank Michael Dunn, editor of that publication, for allowing me to use those parts here. I also thank Astma Afsaruddin, Nilüfer Göle, Fred R. Dallmayr, Charles Hirschkind, Dale F. Eickelman, and Ali Ünal for comments on earlier versions.

1. MÜSIAD was formed by businessmen excluded from Türk Sanayicileri ve İş Adamları Dernigi (TÜSIAD, Association of Turkish Industrialists and Businessmen), a powerful, pro-state business association. Some secular groups claim that the "M" of MÜSIAD stands for *Muslim* rather than *müstakil*. Indeed, many MÜSIAD members do not hesitate to present their organization as an association of Muslim businessmen.

As a result of economic liberalization, the introduction of private media, and the changing legal system, Islamic movements are under transformation. The evolution of the Nur movement illustrates this transformation and the expansion of Islamic practices and discourses in diverse spheres of social and economic life. By examining the Nur movement and its involvement in publication, finance, media, broadcasting, and education, I argue that one can see the formation of a new Muslim consciousness alongside a powerful network community. The case of the Nur movement challenges the argument that Islam and modernity are inherently conflictual and antagonistic. Rather, I show the way in which they can interact with and transform each other. New opportunity spaces in the media, education, and economy empower and transform Muslim actors and help the process of cross-fertilization of the universal and the particular, modernity and Islam, discipline and freedom. As a result of the formation of these more dynamic spaces, the Nur movement has become an identity- and ethic-oriented faith movement with major instruments of social control and empowerment. On the basis of the Nur movement's experience, one can argue that Islamic movements do not necessarily have to be revolutionary, but rather can be a reinterpretation of tradition in light of modern debates in the expanding public sphere (Habermas 1997a, 2001; Hirschkind 2001). In its utilization of new public spheres within a contested zone over identity, authority, and resources, the movement stresses both religious and secular education to create an inclusive language of public discussion. Said Nursi sought either to discipline diverse opinions and practices or to open up conceptual space in opposition to the hegemonic positivist discourse by empowering believers with new ideas. In the reading circles, known as *dershane*s, which serve as spaces for meeting, discussion, and literary socialization, the movement prepares the Nurcu, a follower of Nursi's teaching, for public discussion by cross-fertilizing religious and rational modes of thinking.[2] Thus, Islamic movements are not necessarily formed in reaction to modernity, but rather they represent participation in its vernacular production. Religion has provided both solidarity and ethics to facilitate the positive aspects of modernity. The Nur movement demonstrates this modernizing potential of religion (Kasaba 1998).

This chapter argues that Islam in Turkey operates as a source of social stability and as a motivational force rather than as a radical political project. I begin my argument—that religious ideas are not fixed in practice but are protean and open to change—by examining the sources and the context of the Nur movement, a

---

2. I thank Fred R. Dallmayr for assisting me in rethinking the spillover effect of religious practices and ideas into the public sphere.

religiosocial movement that takes its name from its founder, Said Nursi.[3] Nursi's case illustrates the ability of religious traditions to absorb global discourses of democracy, human rights, and the market economy. Second, in my examination of Fethullah Gülen's life and ideas, I focus on the four cycles of the neo-Nur movement and its new modus vivendi between Islam, on the one hand, and secularism, democracy, and cultural pluralism, on the other. This analysis further points to the movement's ability to cross-fertilize diverse discourses and to use new political, economic, and technological opportunities.

Although Gülen's movement derived its conceptual framework and ideas from Nursi's writings, Gülen leads a different form of movement, one that is more praxis oriented and seeks to transform society and institutions by expanding its circles of sympathizers and supporters. The Gülen movement has been transformed by its own outcome (its teachers, schools, and media outlets) and by the means it uses to achieve its goals. Gülen wants to engage with and participate in social and political institutions, whereas Nursi pursued a rigid civic resistance and refused to compromise with the system while also rejecting violence and confrontation. Like Nursi, however, Gülen uses ideas as his weapons, stressing the significance of persuasion in religious and public discussions. The use of persuasion rather than confrontation, combined with the expanding public sphere in the 1980s, consolidated the tradition of pluralist Islam in Turkey.[4] The practice of persuasion in the *dershane* networks function as a preamble to public discussion about common issues.

The Life of Said Nursi

Said Nursi (1873–1960) authored several volumes of Qur'anic exegesis known as *Risale-i Nur Külliyatı* (The epistles of light) and was the founder of the most powerful text-based faith movement active in Turkey. An ethnic Kurd, Nursi was born in the eastern Anatolian province of Bitlis.[5] He spent half of his life in

3. For the full Turkish collection of Said Nursi's work, see *Risale-i Nur Külliyatı,* vols. 1 and 2 (Istanbul: Nesil, 1996). These two volumes include virtually all of Nursi's writings. Nesil is one of the most intellectually active and independent Nur circles in Istanbul and operates several radio stations throughout the country. The Nesil circle includes prominent Nur intellectuals and is closer to Fethullah Gülen than any other Nur group in Turkey. See Mardin 1989.

4. A number of good studies examine the connection between pluralism and Islam. See Akpınar 1993; Ocak 2000a, 2000b; and Sachedina 2001, for example. Ocak, a leading Turkish historian, examines the historical origins of pluralist Turkish Islam in Anatolia.

5. Most Kurds in Turkey belong to the Shafi'i School of Sunni Islam, whereas the Turks belong to the Hanafi School. Some Hanafi Turkish Nurcus follow the Shafi'i rites during their daily

exile or in prison. During these exile years, Nursi wrote what is among the most sophisticated and appealing interpretations of the Qur'an, his goal being to raise religious consciousness. In his work, he developed new ways of understanding Islam and society that oppose the expanding influence of positivist epistemology in the Muslim world. His reading of Islam and the strategies he employed to reform society and polity began the most powerful Islamic movement in contemporary Turkey. Islam, for Nursi, means three things: a normative order and a moral order to differentiate right and wrong; a worldview that informs one's understanding of human reality and the world; and an inner force to constitute the self and to empower oneself against the odds of modern society. Nursi's main focus was the last layer of Islam: the individual level that would constitute and transform society.

The Nur movement (also known as Nurculuk) differs from other Islamic movements in terms of its understanding of Islam and its strategy for transforming society by raising individual consciousness. As a resistance movement to the ongoing statist modernization process in Turkey, it is forward looking and proactive. Nursi's work offers a conceptual framework for a people undergoing the transformation from a confessional community (gemeinschaft) to a secular national society (gesellschaft) and shows that circles of communities can coexist within Islam. These frames constitute a map of meaning and include updated concepts and strategies for dealing with modern challenges. They revive and redefine folk Islamic concepts and practices in order to establish new solidarity networks and strategies for coping with new conditions in everyday life.

Because Nursi lived during the turbulent collapse of the Ottoman Muslim state and the emergence of the new republic, he had to respond to the dominant debates of his time. Consequently, there were, as he has described, three "different" Nursis: the Old Said, the New Said, and the Third Said. These Saids correspond to the different orientations and strategies he employed at different times to raise Muslim consciousness. Even though Nursi had a traditional education, he was critical of traditional Islamic learning as insufficient and was attempting to introduce a new rationalistic method. His main goal in his commentaries was

---

prayers because of their loyalty to Said Nursi. Said Nursi was consciously Kurdish, yet he always rejected Kurdish nationalism and considered Turkey the common homeland of the Ottoman nation. Because of the prevailing political situation since the establishment of the Kurdish Workers Party, many Turkish Nurcus react strongly to any mention of Nursi's ethnic origin. Some Kurdish nationalists seek to nationalize Nursi's personality and writings as Kurdish; see, for example, Malmisanij 1991, a book that has been banned in Turkey. For Nursi's official biography, see "Tarihçe-i Hayat" in Nursi 1996b, 2109–242.

to prove that science and rationalism are compatible with religious beliefs. He wanted to contemporize Islam by Islamicizing contemporary institutions, practices, and discourses. He wanted to "protect" the people "from unbelief, and those in the *madrasa*s from fanaticism" (Nursi 1996b, 1956). In short, his writings have three interrelated goals: (1) to raise Muslims' religious consciousness (self-transformation is very important); (2) to refute the dominant intellectual discourses of materialism and positivism; and (3) to recover collective memory by revising the shared grammar of society, Islam. This faith movement empowers communal life by stressing the power of knowledge, freedom, and initiative to build stable Muslim selves and communities.

In an effort to bring the natural sciences together with Islamic sciences, Nursi visited Sultan Abdülhamid II in 1907 to seek his support for a university in Van. However, the sultan rejected his proposal to reconcile scientific reasoning with Islam. Nursi was very critical of Sultan Abdülhamid II's oppressive policies and the way Islam was reduced to a state ideology. He eventually joined the nationalist Young Turks and became actively involved in constitutional reforms.

Owing to internal and external events, the Young Turks came to power in 1908. After nine months, the government of the Committee of Union and Progress (CUP) failed to meet the people's expectations, and the increasing social and political discontent expressed itself in the 31 March Rebellion in Istanbul on 13 April 1909.[6] However, the CUP-controlled Operation Corps entered Istanbul on 24 April 1909, arrested the leadership of the rebellion, and restored the CUP government. Although Nursi did not play any role in the instigation of the rebellion—on the contrary, he actually convinced a group of soldiers not to join the rebellion but to return to their barracks—he was arrested because of his involvement with the Society for Muslim Unity, which was accused of inspiring the rebellion. At his trial, Nursi delivered a long speech defending the virtues of constitutionalism and freedom[7] and subsequently was acquitted. However, the 31 March Rebellion became a defining event for state-society relations in the late Ottoman Empire and the republican period. The CUP presented the rebellion, which was prompted by social and political discontent, as a "reactionary" (*irtica*) event against a progressive government. Since then, the central government has framed almost all anticentralization and anti-Westernization opposition as "reactionary." This discourse became the popular tool for excluding religious people from politics and for delegitimizing any form of religious entry into the public sphere. According to İsmail Kara, the most prominent scholar of late Is-

6. See Akşin 1994, Albayrak 1987, Baydar 1955, Danişmend 1961, and Rıfat 1996.

7. His speech before the Ottoman Martial Court in 1911 is in Nursi 1996b, 1917–36.

lamic thought in the Ottoman Empire and the early republic, the 31 March Rebellion has been construed as a framework to represent as reactionary any form of opposition against forced homogenization.[8]

After his acquittal, Nursi returned to his hometown and began teaching the Kurdish and Arab tribes about the ideals of constitutionalism and freedom. He collected his lectures and conversation notes and published *Münazarat,* in which he treats freedom as an integral part of faith (Nursi 1996b, 1937–59). Nursi identified poverty, ignorance, and internal enmity as the problems of the Muslim community. The individual requires freedom to realize the power of God, and through this realization that individual will in turn be freed from man-made oppression and persecution.[9] Nursi invoked Islamic terminology to vernacularize constitutionalism, liberty, and elections. He argued that democracy and Islam are not contradictory concepts and that democracy and freedom are necessary conditions for the existence of a just society.[10] He also called on the people of eastern Anatolia to transcend their narrow tribal and regional loyalties and thus stimulated a consciousness of Islamic nationhood.

In early 1911, Nursi visited Damascus and delivered a sermon on the causes of the social and political decline of the Muslim community, stressing enmity, despotism, egoism, and the death of truthfulness in sociopolitical life as the major sources of this decline.[11] In this speech, however, he also offered some general solutions to these problems.

During World War I, Nursi fought against the Russian-Armenian forces and wrote his famous *İşarat'ül İ'caz* in Arabic.[12] He was captured by the Russians and spent two years in a prisoner-of-war camp before escaping in 1918 and returning to Turkey via Europe. Back in Istanbul, he again became inner oriented and found himself in deep spiritual crisis. During this period, Ahmed Sirhindi's *Mektubat* helped him to overcome the crisis and to take the Qur'an as his guide and master.[13] Sufism was the most powerful layer in the formation of his ideas and personality.

After the war, Nursi published "The Six Steps" in Istanbul newspapers,

8. Author interview with İsmail Kara, 4 August 2001, Istanbul.

9. For one of the best analyses of Nursi's political philosophy, see Mürsel 1995.

10. For more on Nursi's ideas on democracy, see Nursi 1996a and 1996b.

11. His speeches were published in Arabic under the title *Hutbe-i Şamiye;* for Nursi's own translation of this work into Turkish, see Nursi 1996b, 1959–96.

12. This is his first and only traditional Qur'anic commentary; see Nursi 1996b, 1155–272.

13. Sheikh Ahmad Farrooqui (1564–624), also known as Imam Rabbani and Ahmet Sirhindi, lived at a time when Islam faced the greatest threat in India.

sharply attacking British plans to occupy Istanbul. He mobilized religious opinion against the British and in favor of the emerging national movement led by Mustafa Kemal (1881–1938). This support resulted in Nursi's being invited to Ankara, where in 1922 he delivered a series of lectures asking the new Grand National Assembly to obey Islamic precepts, institutionalize the rule of law, and respect popular democracy. However, he was disappointed in his exchanges with Kemal and other officials, and in April 1923 he took a train from Ankara to Van, a trip that he later referred to as a "transitional journey" from the Old Said to the New Said. This journey was a form of intellectual *hijra* (migration) to achieve self-transformation.

At this time, Nursi realized that the problems were at a microlevel and could not be solved by macrotransformations. For him, the minds of the reformist elite had been colonized by positivist philosophy. In order to free Muslim minds and to overcome the tension between desires and resources, the New Said sought to "bring God back" by raising Muslim consciousness. The Old Said, in contrast, was very much a political Islamist, an activist who believed in societal transformation through political involvement in state institutions. He now realized that the problem did not lie in the institutions, but rather in the necessity to develop an alternative way of understanding.

Nursi believed in the power of ideas and in a cognitive revolution. His goal thus became the construction of an Islamic consciousness and a new map of meaning to guide *everyday* life. His main struggle was not with modernity, but rather with the positivist epistemology that sought to uproot human beings from their sacred origins. The New Said, therefore, was characterized by his withdrawal from politics and public life. This "internal emigration" or withdrawal into contemplation (*tefekkür*) marked his thinking and writings. As a result of three years of contemplation in Van, he wrote his first essay, *Mesnevi-i Nuriye,* to set the conceptual framework of his lifelong work, the *Risale-i Nur.* During this period of withdrawal, Nursi lived an ascetic life in Van and spent his time writing books. Also during this period, Sheikh Said led a Kurdish-Islamic revolt against the homogenizing, nation-state-building reforms of Mustafa Kemal (Olson 1989; Yavuz 2001). Although Nursi refused to take part in this revolt, the state considered him a potential threat in the area and subsequently forced him into exile in Burdur.[14]

Because of his continued activity, however, he was soon moved to Barla, Is-

14. Some scholars, such as Heper 1997, 39, still sloppily confuse Nursi with Sheikh Said; for a more accurate and balanced view, see Mardin 1989, 95.

parta. During this eight-and-a-half-year period in exile, Nursi wrote almost half of his entire *Risale-i Nur* collection.[15] Because the state banned all reading and discussion of his works, copies of his commentaries were scribed by hand and distributed via a confidential network, known as the *nur postacıları*, the postmen of the epistle. This secretive solidarity network became the foundation of the "textual communities" known as *dershane*s, which in turn became one of the embryos of civil society in Turkey. His followers made more copies of his work and distributed them widely throughout Anatolia.[16] When a core group of followers began to emerge and thus became known, Nursi was arrested and tried by the Eskişehir Court on the charge of creating an illegal Sufi order and subsequently was imprisoned for eleven months. It was this court that dubbed his followers "Nurcus."[17] During the second stage of his life, Nursi carefully avoided politics and focused on raising Muslims' consciousness.[18] When Turkey moved to a multiparty political system, he leaned toward the Democratic Party. This period characterized the "Third Said." Nursi died in Urfa in 1960 at the age of eighty-seven. Even his body posed a "security threat," however. After his funeral, military coup leaders exhumed it and reburied it at an unknown location (Şahiner 1996).

Why were Nursi and his followers perceived as a threat to the Kemalist project? What made him the "enemy" of that project were his alternative ideas regarding science, identity, personhood, and the rule of law, all aimed to form a vernacular modernity that was more appealing for common Muslims than the imitative top-down Westernization of the Kemalist state. Nursi rejected instrumental use of Islam as a national liberation movement or as an ideology to empower the state. Religion, for him, was a source of normative charter for forming morality and identity. His conception of the state also differed from the Young Turk and Kemalist views in that they treated the state as the agent for determining what constitutes a good life and as an instrument of modernizing and guiding the society. In other words, the official modernization project sought to empower the state and used all means to engineer a new "official" public sphere

15. He wrote some of his best work in jail; for instance, he wrote *El-Hüccet'tüzzehra and İsm-i Azam* in Eskişehir jail in 1935.

16. Nursi wrote all his commentaries in Arabic script, so his followers insisted on copying the writing by hand to perpetuate Arabic alphabet education in Turkey.

17. *Nurcu* literally means "follower of Nursi." The Eskişehir Court gave the name "Nurcus" to those who were arrested for possessing Nursi's books.

18. During the republican period, Nursi wrote *Emirdağ, Kastamonu,* and *Barla Lahikaları.* These works were collected by his students and include his communications with his students and followers. To raise Muslim consciousness, he wrote the following commentaries, *Sözler, Mektubat, Lem'alar,* and *Şualar.*

based on binary oppositions: secular versus religious, *à la franga* versus *à la turca,* salon versus family room, science versus religion, and modern versus traditional. This approach, in turn, worsened relations between the state and society as the state tried to impose its exclusivist secularist ideology on the population.

Nursi's Ideas

Nursi's understanding of human nature sprang from his understanding of Islam—that is, from the Qur'an. Nursi believed that faith is the result of the innate nature of human beings *(fitrat),* which is "turned toward" God. Religious faith was the outcome of human desire to create a meaningful life and harmony in society. According to him, humans are in a state of constant tension between desire and reason because they have infinite appetites and desires but limited resources.

This tension can be managed only by developing a full connection with God. Nursi sharply criticized positivist epistemology and its desire to control nature and humans simultaneously. Because he felt that religion is innate to human nature, he saw the lack of religion as the source of many conflicts and wars. He expanded this concept of tension to the societal level, where the absence of God in the public sphere was the source of people's problems. His goal, therefore, was to bring God back to the public sphere, which required a response to the dominant positivist epistemology. Connecting to God, for Nursi, meant introducing new conceptual resource tools to shape and lead human conduct. His project offered a new "map of meaning" for Muslims to engage critically in the public sphere and to guide their conduct. He did not offer an Islamic constitution or an Islamic order, but rather a mode of thinking about reconnecting with God.

According to Nursi, Jewish, Christian, and Islamic revelations are the "Word" and their interpretations can vary according to time and space. The meaning of the Qur'an is thus changeable in this way. Moreover, the Qur'an is not the source of scientific discoveries, but all scientific discoveries reveal the depth of its message (Voll 1999). For instance, "As time grows older," Nursi wrote, "the Qur'an grows younger; its signs become apparent." In this case, Nursi, unlike other Islamists, treated scientific discoveries as an attempt to "further deepen understanding of the Qur'an" (1996a, 447). As human knowledge expands in nonreligious areas, so does our understanding of Qur'anic revelation, according to his way of thinking. By linking a better understanding of the Qur'an with scientific discoveries, Nursi sought to open a new and radical reading of the Qur'an.

Nursi was also fully aware of the impact of print technology and print culture on Muslim societies. His concept of the world becoming "a global city" dates back to his earliest writing in *Mesnevi-i Nuriye*.[19] He wrote several short essays on the social consequences of radio, which was an innovative means to raise religious consciousness among ordinary people. He celebrated the advent of the multigraph (*teksir makinesi*) as a "Nurcu," a follower of *Risale-i Nur*, with multiple hands, because *Risale-i Nur* was duplicated by handwriting (1996b, 1753). He called on his followers to employ the new communication technologies in the service of Islam. The current Nurcus' use of modern media such as radio, television, magazines, e-mail, and newspapers is a direct result of Nursi's earlier encouragement.

Nursi's Qur'anic commentaries are different from other traditional commentaries in terms of their language and methodology. Nursi utilized a rich mixture of Persian, Arabic, and Ottoman Turkish expressions to articulate his ideas and to create a common idiom among Muslims. He also used the narrative form to explain the existence of God and other concepts. This narrative form of religious discourse allowed diverse sectors of society to read and communicate his message. Nursi's work was based on three sources of knowledge: the Prophet, the Qur'an, and the universe, which he regularly referred to as "the Grand Book of the Universe" (Nursi 1996b, 1277–1407). He examined the Prophet Muhammad as a source of ethics and justice (Canan 1996). By continuously drawing parallels between the Qur'an and the universe, he argued that there is no contradiction between religion and science (Karabaşoğlu 1996). He used scientific laws to illustrate the existence of order in nature and then presented this order as a sign of God's existence. He employed scientific discoveries to "prove" the existence of their creator. Because these discoveries expand our knowledge about their creator, it follows that scientific activity is religious activity. They help one reach a full understanding of the Qur'an. Nursi thus developed the notion that scientific discoveries are manifestations of the *esma-ül hüsna* (attributes of God in the universe).

Nursi's ideas appealed to a large segment of Turkish society in part because of his development of a new conceptual bridge for the transition from tradition to modernity, from oral to print culture, and from a rural to an urban environment. He imagined a gradual transformation in three basic stages: (*a*) raising Muslim individual consciousness, (*b*) implementing faith in everyday life, and (*c*) restoring the shariah (Nursi 1996b, 1641). The first stage, the period of raising

19. This book was written between 1918 and 1922 and reflects the transition from the Old Said to the New Said, who is more Sufi oriented; see Nursi 1996b, 1277–78.

Muslim consciousness, which can be realized only within a free and just society, is treated as sine qua non for the realization of his goal: a shariah-based society—that is, "a society of the rule of law" (Yılmaz, chap. 11). He expected conscious individuals to mark their practices according to Islamic norms, transforming society from within. Nursi sought to equip Muslims with the necessary conceptual tools to participate in the public discussion and to live their lives in accordance with Islamic precepts. Although he had no open political project, these goals have the inevitable political consequence of a shariah-governed society. Nursi's notion of the shariah is different from that of contemporary Islamists. He did not treat the shariah as a sacred law, but rather as the opinion of jurists. According to his thinking, laws are to be made by an elected assembly of the people. By a "shariah-governed society," he meant a law-governed and just society.

Nursi's understanding of the state differed from that of the Young Turks and of the later Kemalists, for he treated the state as the servant of the people and argued for a neutral state without any ideology. The state should be molded according to the needs and desires of the people. He argued that citizens and communities are rivers and streams, whereas the state is a pool: a change in the quality and quantity of the "stream is going to have direct impact on the pool; if the problem is in the pool, it will not have an effect on the sources of the stream" (1996b, 1945). Because the state is a servant of the people, its employees do not need to be Muslims because their duty is to serve the people in accordance with the law. The state must be based on five principles: justice, freedom, respect for human dignity, the will of the people, and security.

Because raising Muslim consciousness can be realized only within the framework of a free and just environment, both freedom and justice constitute two integrated concepts of Nursi's writings. Justice is the critical concept, and he always presents two images of justice: absolute justice (*adalet-i mahza*) and relative justice (*adalet-i izafi*) (Nursi 1996b, 1844–50). Absolute justice stresses individual rights regardless of how insignificant or impractical they may seem and rejects any form of compromise in favor of public interests. Relative justice is based on the protection of the state or public interests against individual rights. Nursi argues that a stable society requires the implementation of absolute justice to protect freedom. According to his vision, "the right of an orphan cannot be suppressed for the good of the entire society; similarly, an individual cannot be scarified for the security of a nation. There is no question of weak and strong as far as justice is concerned. The rights of the weak cannot be overlooked in favor of the strong" (1996a, 55–56).

After justice, the second most important concept for Nursi is freedom for self-realization. He declares: "I can live without bread, but I cannot live without freedom" (1996b, 1682). He argues that all social and political organizations must be based on the protection and advancement of freedom. For Nursi, freedom means freedom of speech and thought. He identifies poverty and oppression as the enemies of freedom. Oppression, *zulüm,* for Nursi, is the source of economic and intellectual backwardness and of constant conflict and enmity. His solution to these ills is freedom within the rule of law (*hürriyet-i şeriyye)* to institute rights and freedom of information and thought in order to overcome ignorance and enmity.

After the Old Said "died," Nursi always remained reluctant to become involved in politics. He considered the realm of politics to be a place where diverse identities, interests, and organized groups conflict. He believed religion should not be used as an instrument to advance particular interests because it is the grammar of *all* society. If religion were identified with one party or faction, it would become impossible to represent the "true" Islam. He was opposed, therefore, to the idea of an Islamic party. Indeed, he considered such a party specifically un-Islamic. However, he supported the presence of Islamic ideas in the public sphere in order to consolidate the communitarian notion of polity. In his writings, he emphasizes that change is gradual, spreading from the individual to the community and from the community to the political sphere. He considered politics to be the art of persuasion to build a public consensus by utilizing communal values.

The new Nur communities in Turkey are at the forefront of developing an interfaith dialogue with other religious groups. Nursi advanced an inclusive argument and avoided defining any religious tradition as "oppositional" to Islam. For him, there were three enemies: ignorance, poverty, and dissension (internal enmity), and he called on Muslims to cooperate with other religious groups against these problems. After making a careful distinction between faith (*iman)* and religion (Islam), he concentrated on the construction of faith in the age of skepticism (Nursi 1996a, 477). The Nur movement, therefore, is not a political Islamic movement, but rather a faith movement that seeks to raise religious consciousness and to work with other faith communities. Faith precedes Islam and any form of ethnolinguistic solidarity. This interfaith solidarity has been reflected at the political level—for example, in the Nur movement's support of Turkey's integration into the NATO alliance against the antireligious communist system. Because Turkey had no colonial experience, Nursi never developed an anti-Western position, and he divided Europe into two categories. The Europe that he supported "follows the sciences that serve justice and right and the industries beneficial for the life of society through the inspiration it has received from true Christianity." He was critical of the second "corrupt Europe, which, apart from beneficial science and the virtues of civilization, holds in its hand meaningless, harmful philosophy and noxious, dissolute civilization" (1996a, 643).

Textual Communities: Dershanes as a New Religious Public Sphere

From the beginning, the Nur movement has emphasized the transition from an oral culture to a print culture (Yavuz 1996b). The *Risale-i Nur* became the basis for the formation of a number of reading circles, known as *dershane*s. These reading circles evolved into a number of textual communities in which membership is defined by reading and internalizing the philosophy of the text *Risale-i Nur*. The Nur movement seeks to move Islam from an oral-based tradition to a print-based medium and to raise religious consciousness through education and reason. The reading circles gradually spread throughout Anatolia and updated Islamic vocabulary in terms of the global discourses of science, democracy, and human rights. These reading circles have institutionalized themselves with the purchase of homes or apartment floors where members of the circles can assemble to read Nursi's writings and where university students can live temporarily. Today there are more than five thousand reading circles in Turkey. The number of Nur adherents varies between two and six million. As of 2001, there are fifty-three *dershane*s in the Central Asian republics, fifty-seven in Germany, seven in Holland, four in Austria, two in Belgium, and one in Sarajevo.[20]

Nursi's writings helped the formation of new mechanisms of sociability (*dershane*s, foundations, magazines, and philanthropic associations) and of intellectual exchange, as well as a raised consciousness about public opinion. The Nur movement has utilized its informal network of reading circles as a stepping-stone in the construction of a new counterpublic. By a "counterpublic," I mean a public informed by religion, ethnicity, gender, and class, as well as by a different normativity and a sense of the "good life" (Hirschkind 2000). Moreover, the counterpublic under certain conditions absorbs the "official" public because the goal of the counterpublic is to change both the normative foundations of the official public and the strategies of framing social issues.[21] For instance, Turkish

20. The first book on Said Nursi in the Bosnian language is Godzo 1998. Author's interview with Murat Şengün, 22 Aug. 2001, Hamburg, Germany.

21. Nilüfer Göle, a prominent Turkish sociologist, was instrumental in stressing the connection between privately formed practices and their utilization in the public sphere. She was the first scholar to unpack the "official Turkish public sphere" and stress the positive role of religion in the

nationalism created an "official" national public in which any religious or ethnic discussion was marginalized and forced to create its own illegal counterpublic. Only with the liberalization and economic diversification of Turkey have religious and ethnic publics been gradually integrated into the public sphere.

*Dershane*s are spaces for socialization and community-oriented virtues, enacted through conversational readings, discussions, and prayers. In the 1980s, informal *dershane* networks, along with media networks, created several social outcomes. First, they showed how the diverse policies of the state, the new privatized market conditions, and new communication opportunities can create counterpublics in which the "new" Muslim actor may be constituted. Second, they facilitated not only the formation of a global ethics of engagement with internal and external others, but also the construction of a new religious consciousness. Third, they challenged the boundaries of public versus private, national versus transnational, and secular versus religious. The *dershane* circles have demonstrated the role of normative foundations of mixed public and private spaces and the utilization of privately formed "social trust" to shape new public goods. Islamic ideals of responsibility and good work can inform Muslim activism in Turkey now. *Dershane*s, as new religious public spheres, have played an important role in the circulation and cross-fertilization of ideas and civil skills of activism. They are places where public opinion either is formed or is critiqued through the utilization of religious ideas. Indeed, these spaces are not a Habermasian public sphere, but in terms of their consequences they are vital for the formation of a larger public sphere (Habermas 2001). Their role in the constitution of the public requires a new understanding of the public. Privately built trust and a new cognitive map for understanding the meaning of the good life have social consequences in terms of constituting a framework of public discussions. Coming together in *dershane*s to read Nursi's writings is a public act because of its consequences. In these *dershane*s, Islam becomes a source of solidarity and a chart of social responsibility in the constitution of Muslim self and community. It has become clear through them that being Muslim is never an exclusive identity, but rather a moral foundation of tribal, ethnic, regional, and other forms of identities.

The Nur movement uses the opportunities created by the activation of the free-market economy and the liberalization of the legal system in Turkey to cre-

---

thickening of civil society. My understanding of the "counterpublic" and the "official" public is very much informed by the Turkish experience and also by Göle's research circles in Germany, which examine the role of Islam in the public sphere. Author's interview with Göle, 13–14 May 2000, Essen, Germany.

ate new counterpublic spheres and to transform the "official" public sphere. Nurcu actors use the media to speak back to the state. Furthermore, the locally built social trust in *dershane* networks is translated into activities in education, media, the economy, and politics.

Fragmentation of the Nur Movement

After Nursi's death in 1960, the Nur movement pluralized along ethnic, class, educational, generational, and regional lines (Yavuz 2003). Yet the sense of collective identity and shared moral orientation formed a sector of Nur movements that continues to work together on many issues. One of the reasons for the continuation of this collective Nur identity is the Nurcus' commitment to Nursi's text and to the perpetuation of the same moral orientation. The Nur identity is derived from Nursi's writings and cannot be reduced to any organization or leader. Moreover, in the 1960s, the center-right, defined by social conservatism and Turkish nationalism, absorbed the Nur movement into its own anticommunist front. The Turkish state supported this new nationalist-religious coalition against an assertive communist ideology and an increasingly Arab-centric radical Islamism. It even supported a degree of Islamization of Turkish nationalism in order to contain radical ethnic (Turkish) nationalism. Many prominent Nurcus welcomed this new nationalist-Islamic alliance as a way of expanding their opportunities to disseminate Nursi's message without fear of state persecution.

Fission is the lifeblood of the Nur movement and the secret of its success. Different groups within the movement support and develop cordial ties with each other; they also compete over interpretation and service to promote the movement's message. There is a powerful motivating force within the movement, a "do-it-yourself" force, which helps to form many different and dynamic Nur groups. In other words, Nursi's writings do not allow room for clerical control or the hegemony of a single mode of interpretation, but invite every reader to become his or her own religious authority. Each group seeks to share Nursi's mental world to understand the message of his writings. In the *dershane*s, people are asked to see Nursi as their *dost* (friend) with whom they converse on intimate terms, and the narrative form of communication is more common among them than generalized theological formulae. They like to tell stories about Nursi and about themselves. Salvation, for a Nurcu, is to understand the power of God and to become a friend of the Prophet Muhammed. The metaphorical writings and readings help Nurcus to validate their own religious and social identities. Another contradiction within the Nur movement is found in the "paradoxical process [wherein] a more autonomous self [is] achieved through surrender or recommitment to the claims of a moral order" (Cucchiari 1988, 418), much like Pentecostal conversion.

The first major split in the movement resulted from the struggle between publishers and scribes to control the meaning of Nursi's text. The scribes, known as Yazıcılar, led the secession from the Nur movement with their insistence on providing the *The Epistles of Light* in handwritten form. They argued that handwriting (*a*) makes the text more humane and facilitates its internalization; (*b*) develops a bond to the text; (*c*) makes the Nurcu a part of the text; and (*d*) helps to maintain the Arabic script. In contrast, publishers stressed the significance of mass production and rapid distribution. This group of Nurcus, later known as Yeni Asya, established its first newspaper in 1960. After several of these earlier newspapers failed or were banned by military authorities, *Yeni Asya* was established in 1971. The goals of this newspaper were to protect democracy by taking a position against all antidemocratic movements; to present alternative views against communism and atheism; to support closer ties with the Western countries; and to develop close ties with other Abrahamic religions and institutions to create a common front against communism and atheism. The Yeni Asya community defines itself in terms of

> accepting the *The Epistles* as the only modern interpretation of the Qur'an. We believe that *The Epistles* is the sole and effective means maintaining faith and living a pious life. Besides, we accept the *The Epistles* as a basic reference in religious, social, political, economic, and cultural areas. [Our community] seeks to disseminate the message of Nursi through communication networks and believes in the information society and seeks to empower Muslims with knowledge.[22]

The second source of fragmentation in the Nur community was the political positioning of the movement. Mehmet Kırkıncı and Fethullah Gülen supported the 1980 military coup and adopted a very statist position. They reimagined the Nur movement as a "Turkish Islam" and nationalized it. When a religious movement seeks legitimacy from a secular state that either excludes religion from the state structure or seeks to control it through inclusion, the only method of gaining legitimacy and support is through nationalism. In other words, religious groups must seek to maintain their relevance and legitimacy before the state by stressing their contribution to nationalism and national culture.

Yeni Asya experienced the most dramatic separation in 1990 when a group

22. Şener Boztaş, vice director of the Yeni Asya Foundation, provided this statement to the author on 13 Mar. 2001.

of younger and very influential Yeni Nesil (New Generation) adopted a pro-Özal and more modern attitude. This latter group now dominates the interpretation of *The Epistles* by organizing high-quality conferences and seminars. As a result of their commitment and hard work, *The Epistles of Light* has become a source for academic study and examination. They have adopted a more critical reading of Nursi's writings and regularly invite foreign scholars to present their view of *The Epistles*.

The third major source of division in the movement is marked by the overall ethnic tension in Turkey. A group of Kurdish Nurcus formed their own group, the Med-Zehra. This Kurdish group established its own publishing house (Tenvir Neşriyat) and in April 1989 began to disseminate its views through its Kurdish nationalist *Dava* magazine. This group is led by Muhammed Sıddık (Dursun) Seyhanzade; it supports Kurdish political rights and opposes the Turkish state, and it has close ties with some radical Islamic groups. Sıddık accuses other Nur communities of supporting bigoted (i.e., anti-Kurdish) policies.[23] The Kurdish Nurcus tend to treat Nursi as a Kurdish nationalist, whereas the Turks stress his pan-Islamism. Many Kurdish nationalists interpret Nursi's exile and persecution as a prime example of the persecution of the Kurdish identity. However, the court cases against him show that his persecution was the result of his struggle to renew Islam against the social engineering of Kemalist reforms, rather than because of his Kurdish ethnicity. Owing to Sıddık's rigidity and desire to control the movement, Med-Zehra experienced a major division in 1990. A group of younger Nurcus, under the leadership of İzzeddin Yıldırım, formed Zehra Eğitim ve Kültür Vakfı and began to focus on education rather than on Kurdish nationalism. Their major goal has been the republication of *The Epistles* in the Kurdish language.

Eight major Nur communities are divided currently in accordance with their political positions and relative utilization of modernity. The scribes Kurdoğlu Cemaati, Mehmet Kırkıncı, and Mustafa Sungur represent a conservative outlook in their interpretation of Nursi's writings and a defensive attitude toward modernity. The modernist and progressive groups include Yeni Nesil, the Gülen community, and Yeni Asya. The ethnic and radical sector is represented by Med-Zehra.

I suggest that owing to state political oppression, a new form of Islamic activism evolved out of the Ottoman-Turkish intellectual tradition. Said Nursi formulated a new way of religious renewal through collective reading circles, the *der-*

23. Sıddık interviewed in *artıHaber* (20–26 Dec. 1997), 17.

*shane*s, to raise religious consciousness. The primary impact of these reading circles on social and political life is that religious participation has spilled over to other social spheres by offering people ties, networks, and opportunities to build civic associations. A closer examination of the reading circles indicates the various pathways that religious networks use to mobilize, recruit, and train members to become active participants in society. Nursi formed a dynamic connection between religious ideas and social action. He sought to give a rational account of why he believed in God and how people can renew their faith constantly through questioning. He stressed the role of the cognitive experience over the affective experience in Islam. One can identify Nursi's writings as the foundational text for Fethullah Gülen because Gülen always has used Nursi's method of raising Islamic consciousness and the reading circles to create transnational religious networks.

Indeed, the Kemalist secularization project begun in the 1930s in Turkey created new public spheres free of religion. Yet the same process, in turn, redefined the meaning and role of religion as an oppositional identity—an alternative source of defining the self and a different way of becoming a moral person. The boundary between the secular and the religious is thus now contested and fluctuating and is shaped ultimately by the parameters that state authorities have allowed. Although the Nur movement is situated in a secular and strictly demarcated Turkish polity, its ideas and practices are infecting and transforming the Turkish project of top-down modernization.

2

The Gülen Movement

The Turkish Puritans

M. HAKAN YAVUZ

THE MOST POWERFUL of the Nur circles is Fethullah Gülen's education-oriented neo-Nur community. He benefited from Said Nursi's model of the *dershane*s (reading circles), but he transformed them into "lighthouses" (*ışık evler*) and stressed the ethics of education and work for transforming Muslims and their environment. He sees the economic and moral poverty in the Muslim world as a result of spiritual and intellectual decline and has utilized a number of strategies, especially private and public education, for the renewal of the Muslim tradition. The strategies and means of the Gülen movement have changed constantly over a forty-year period.

Gülen's community uses Nursi's flexible ideas to promote a nationalist, global, and free-market orientation. Gülen's faith-inspired education movement is different from Nursi's exclusively faith movement. Gülen is an inspirational leader of a transnational education movement, whereas Nursi was the formative giant of intellectual discourse. Although Nursi was focused on *personal* transformation, Gülen has focused on *personal* and *social* transformation by utilizing new liberal economic and political conditions. As a combined ulema-intellectual persona, Gülen not only preaches inner mobilization of new social and cultural actors, but also introduces a new liberative map of action. His goals are to sharpen Muslim self-consciousness, to deepen the meaning of the shared idioms and practices of society, to empower excluded social groups through education and networks, and to bring just and peaceful solutions to the social and psychological problems of society. Gülen, as a social innovator, focuses on the public sphere more than on the private sphere and seeks to turn Islam and Islamic networks into social capital. The Gülen movement does not constitute a series of reactionary convulsions of the marginalized sector of the Turkish population, but is rather a bourgeoning middle-class movement that seeks to utilize new economic and social spaces in accordance with Gülen's ideological framework.

Life and Ideas: Dadaş Islam and Turko-Ottoman Nationalism

Fethullah Gülen (b. 1938), as a prominent Nurcu leader, commonly is called "Hocaefendi" ("Master," or higher religious authority).[1] According to his memoirs, his boyhood in Erzurum kept his heart pure as his mind matured and allowed him to stand ethically erect in the public life.[2] Born in a community of farmers, young Gülen chose not to farm but to become a religious scholar. Islamic moral principles that informed his early preferences also served as guide marks for behavior at crucial turning points later in his life. In his moral training, his family—especially his mother—and his Sufi teacher played formative roles. He learned Sufism from Sheikh Muhammed Lütfi, called Alvarlı Efe, who was the most influential personality in his early education.[3] His unofficial Sufi education strongly affected his ongoing spirituality. Unlike nearly all his male friends, he never smoked or indulged his pleasure-oriented passions.

Gülen's writings and worldview create a marriage between religion and science, between tradition and modernity (Gülen 1996a, 43–48). Although he was born in Erzurum, a conservative town, he worked most of his life in İzmir, the most modern Turkish city. In 1966, he was appointed to the Kestanepazarı Qur'anic School in İzmir to teach courses on Islamic sciences. While serving as a teacher, he regularly traveled to different coffeehouses, mosques, community centers, and other public spaces to preach about Islamic ethics and the natural sciences, commonly utilizing Nursi's ideas. For Gülen, serving God means raising "perfect youth" who combine spirituality with intellectual training, reason with revelation, and mind with heart.[4] Combining his personal abilities with the social resources available in İzmir, he formed a powerful transnational religio-cultural movement that today includes thousands of loose networks of like-minded people. However, he has not limited himself to Nursi's writings, but has included the work of socially conservative and politically nationalist intellectuals

---

1. This section is derived from Yavuz 1999b.

2. For more on Gülen's life, see L. Erdoğan 1997 and Hermann 1996.

3. Author's interview with Gülen, Üsküdar, Istanbul, 25 Apr. 1997.

4. This goal eventually would dominate Gülen-guided activities aimed at raising a "golden generation"; see Gülen n.d.a.

such as Necip Fazıl Kısakürek, Nurettin Topçu, and Sezai Karakoç.[5] As a man of action more than ideas, he is concerned about the application of ideas and moral norms in public and private spheres (Ünal 2002). He does not want to confine Islam to the private domain but rather stresses the role of public religion in the formation of morality, identity, and a just community.

Gülen's Conception of Turkish Islam and Nationalism

The Gülen-inspired network community thus differentiates itself from other Islamic groups by stressing Turkish nationalism, the free market, and modern education.[6] Gülen is the engine behind the construction of a "new" national Islam of Turkey marked by the logic of a market economy and the Ottoman legacy.[7] In order to carry out his mission of shaping the future of Turkey, Gülen has met with many high-level politicians, including presidents.

Gülen's followers generally are more predisposed to tolerance, electoral politics, moderation, and a market economy than are other Islamic groups in Turkey, for two contradictory reasons. First, Gülen always has stressed the communal religious consciousness as the sine qua non for the realization of a just society; and, second, he insists that the state is absolutely necessary for the survival of Turkish Muslim society. According to members of the Gülen community, religion is primarily a personal or communal matter as opposed to a political or state matter. Their understanding of Islam is very much conditioned by the experiences of the Ottoman state and the Republic of Turkey. The movement does not seek to negate or challenge the processes of modernization. Rather, it seeks to demonstrate the way in which a properly conceived Muslim project can affirm and further the most crucial ends of modernity, such as the formation of conscious actors who are armed with both religious and secular knowledge. Gülen seeks ways to contribute to the vernacularization of modernity by redefining modernity not as Westernization, but rather as a set of new economic, technological, and legal opportunities for authentic societal transformation. Modernity, for Gülen, offers new resources for a renewed Islamic consciousness and a Muslim presence in the new public sphere (Özdalga 2000). Gülen's ideas

5. For Gülen's intellectual evaluation, see L. Erdoğan 1997 and Can 1996.

6. For a more critical treatment of Gülen's community, see Yavuz 1997a.

7. For more on the debate on the Islam in Turkey, see Can 1996, 33, Vergin 1998, and Kara 1997.

and actions introduce the possibility of being both modern and Muslim at the same time (Yavuz 2000a, 7, 14).

The state-centric understanding of Islam among Gülen's followers is the outcome of the culture of insecurity in Anatolia that evolved from the legacy of the disintegrated Ottoman Empire. Nursi and his first generation of followers witnessed the elimination of Muslim hegemony in the Balkans and the Caucasus and the partition of Anatolia by the Sevres Peace Treaty of 1920. Subsequently, the Nurcus, in particular those from eastern Anatolia—such as Gülen and Mehmet Kırkıncı, a prominent Nur leader and personal friend of Gülen— viewed the state during the Cold War as the first condition for the survival of their religion against the expansionist Soviet neighbor (Kırkıncı 1993, 1994). The Turkish state came to regard the Nur movement as a barrier against the left- ist, communist movement in Turkey. Indeed, many prominent Nurcus, such as Gülen, became involved in the foundation of the Türkiye Kominizmle Mü- cadele Dernekleri (Turkish Association for Struggle against Communism), and the Nur movement has been the major pro-NATO and pro-American Muslim group in Turkey.

Gülen's personality is very much influenced by the regional culture of east- ern Anatolia. Communally based Islamic identity in Erzurum existed not in a rei- fied sacred doctrinal form, but rather in the rhythms of everyday life in which Gülen was socialized. Islamic identity is like a vernacular language, allowing inti- mate communication between members of a community. This form of Islamic identity evolves from historical experience and emerges as persons become aware of their own context in a community with a distinct set of historically based practices. Gülen was aware of the power of Islam in the everyday life of people in Turkey, and his main concern early on was to bring this excluded iden- tity to the public sphere and to give legitimacy to it. He became aware of Nursi's writings in 1958, which facilitated his shift from a particular localized Islamic identity and community to a more cosmopolitan and discursive understanding of Islam. Nursi's writings empowered him to engage with diverse epistemologi- cal systems.

Erzurum is a major eastern Anatolian city with a long and rich history as a Turkish frontier zone against both the Iranians and the Russians. The people of Erzurum also are known by the subregional identity of *dadaş*. Regional commu- nitarian Islam, marked by *dadaş* identity, therefore is punctuated by the culture of frontier conditions, which stresses community over individual and security over other concerns.[8] Owing to this geographic frontier position and the presence of

---

8. See further Yavuz 1996a and 1997a.

immigrants from the Caucasus, the cultural identity of the region always has been highly politicized, with Islam and Turkism as its codeterminants (Gülen 1997f). Mustafa Kemal (1881–1938) organized the first national congress in Erzurum, and the city was a center of national liberation.[9] This regional culture and the religion teacher Muhammad Lütfi molded Gülen's early personality and his understanding of Islam as nationalistic and statist.

Gülen seeks to restore the nation by remembering its past rather than forgetting it, and he calls on people to "rediscover the self" that has been "embodied within Islam and the Ottoman past."[10] The past from which Gülen wants to derive the contemporary self is not the historical past, but rather the past of choice in the present. This cultural revival of Islamic circles in Turkey seeks to criticize the current Kemalist project and its future orientation by constructing the past of the Turko-Muslim community. In other words, by reimagining the cultural content of the Turkish nation, Islamic groups can reconstruct the political nation as Muslim, Ottoman, and Turkish. The politics of nationalism in Turkey has been embedded gradually into the politics of culture. There is an attempt to free the definition of the nation from the statist elite. One of the major effects of the politics of culture is the reconceptualization of the nation and its cultural connection with Central Asia and the Balkans. Therefore, the neo-Nur movement, in constructing the present by "remembering" a past of its own choosing, operates in simultaneously modern and nonmodern times (A. Ünal 2002, 89–94).

By constructing the cultural past of the Turkish Muslim community, Gülen constructs his own version of nation by giving up imitative forms of modernization. Although some Kemalists read this goal as an attempt to form an Islamic state, I would argue that their reading of Gülen's project is superficial. Gülen and his close circles do not hesitate to critique the policies of Westernization as a derivative imitation that led to the total collapse of the Ottoman state. His movement, in contrast, is constructing its own modernity with its own available means.[11] It aroused justifiable fears of social conservatism and unjustifiable (though understandable) fears that this project of "remembering" the past would lead to religious republicanism.[12] There is not much evidence to support the latter fears. Yet a large segment of the population has celebrated and sup-

9. On 23 July 1919, the Congress in Erzurum decided to mobilize all forces for the liberation of the homeland.

10. Author's interview with Gülen, Üsküdar, Istanbul, 25 Apr. 1997.

11. On the connections between modernity, emancipation, and the new political consciousness, see Göle 1996b.

12. For one of the best critiques of Gülen's movement, see Insel 1997; see also Kozanoğlu 1997, 57–89.

ported Gülen's concept of national identity as Muslim, Ottoman, and Turkish. For many of his followers, to feel one's identify is to experience a religiohistorical emotion, without reifying it. Emotional aspects of identity are not fixed onto a single concept because an emotional state remains a flowing process.

Gülen is first and foremost a Turko-Ottoman nationalist. His nationalism is an inclusive one that is not based on blood or race, but rather on shared historical experiences and the agreement to live together within *one* polity. For him, those "Muslims who live in Turkey, share the Ottoman legacy as their own, and regard themselves as Turks could be considered as Turks."[13] Islam remains the basic criterion of national identity and loyalty. Being a Muslim becomes a sine qua non for being a Turk, and there is no difference between a Bosnian and a Kazak. His first job as a preacher was at the Üçşerefeli Mosque in Edirne, where a large number of Torbes and Pomaks, both Muslim Slavs, live. In his memoirs, Gülen hardly differentiates between ethnic and nonethnic Turks and treats both groups as Turks *and* Muslims. He therefore has a more inclusive notion of identity, shaped by the Ottoman Islamic legacy. Although the Arabs were part of the Ottoman Empire, Gülen is critical of the Arab and Iranian understanding of Islam (Sevindi 1997). He accuses the Arabs of collaborating against the Ottoman Empire and creating a negative image of Islam by reducing Islam to an ideology. Moreover, he differentiates urban Ottoman Islam from tribal Arab Islam and expresses admiration for the Ottoman sultans and Mustafa Kemal. For these reasons, most Gülen schools are either in the Balkans or in Central Asia, and very few exist in the Arab Middle East.

Gülen's ideas fuse the religious community and the national community. In his writings and interviews, he differentiates community (solidarity-based group) from society (interest-based association) and treats Islam as the essential ingredient for community (Can 1996, 23). Community, for Gülen, is a union of believers who share the same cosmic interpretive framework of religion and who have joined together freely for realization of the collective activity of serving both God and nation. The ultimate binding forces of the community are piety, religiously shaped sentiment, and affections. Self-sacrifice provides the foundation for the survival of the Muslim (Turkish) community. Individuals are expected to sacrifice for the sake of the collective and in the service of religion. Gülen's conception of community absorbs the Turkish nation because, for him, the Turks are destined to serve Islam and to lead their region. Indeed, the state in his view is a bridge between religious and national community and an instrument for the realization of these goals. In both Nursi's and Gülen's writings, the

13. Author's interview with Gülen, Philadelphia, 12 Oct. 2000.

shared normative charter becomes the necessary foundation for the public sphere and the workings of civil society.

Islam as Morality and Identity

Islam, for Gülen, means two things at the same time: morality (*kişilik*) and identity (*kimlik*). One might summarize his arguments in the following way: there is no identity without morality and no morality without Islam. Following in Nursi's footsteps, Gülen believes that free and democratic society requires public morality and that this morality cannot be effective without religion. Religion offers the content of moral maximums and renders force to it by stressing divine judgment. The purpose of religion and religious ritual is to internalize the Islamic concept of morality—that is, to learn to live in the presence of God. Gülen constantly refers to a common saying of the Prophet Muhammad that "Islam is about good morals, and I have been sent to perfect the good character." The goal of Gülen's movement is to bring into being morally upright individuals. Islamic morality that is modeled after the life of Muhammad plays a formative role in the construction of self-identity or personality. Gülen presents Muhammad's life story as the grand narrative for Muslims who search for morality and identity (Gülen 2000c). Because human beings define themselves through stories, they never cease to tell foundational stories, so Gülen's sermons and writings constantly bring these stories to the forefront. Gülen utilizes the narratives of Muhammed's life to articulate a moral position.

Gülen as Story-teller: Identity Building by Stories

Gülen does not examine theology in the form of a defense of key Islamic doctrine. His writings always have been a journey of exploration of the key concepts of Islam through stories. He is the best religious story-teller in Turkey. Almost all his lectures and writings entail stories about the first Muslim community. These stories play an important role in the development of the personal identity of Muslims. They help young Turkish Muslims to interpret their present and past life experiences from these perspectives through a shared vocabulary. In short, the stories of the first Muslim community repeated by Gülen's writings and cassettes generate a set of categories with which the present situation can be discussed; people in the Gülen community come together outside the lighthouses because they share the same stories.

The stories of the Prophet Muhammed and the first Muslim community form a dynamic vision and a shared language for the articulation of the "good life." During an interview, Gülen argued that "Islam is not about 'being' but rather 'becoming' a moral person by internalizing the Muslim model of *insan-ı kamil,* a perfect human being."[14] The model of this moral personality is rooted in the stories of the Prophet Muhammad and the first Muslim community. Thus, becoming Muslim means learning the stories of the first Meccan and Medinan communities well enough to interpret and judge one's own life experiences. This interpretation must be communal, and consensus must be respected. In the movement, these shared stories inform personal and collective actions.

In the Gülen movement, there is no single and centralized institution that governs activities, but rather a cluster of associations and individuals who share Gülen's worldview. These religiously rooted social and civic associations take part in and expand the boundaries of the public sphere by incorporating diverse ideas and worldviews into the discussion. For instance, the Journalists and Writers Foundation has been an active participant in the public sphere in terms of its yearly and weekly activities and publications.

Gülen, just like Nursi, seeks to breathe life into Islamic tradition by interpreting it in relation to modern challenges. To avoid reifying tradition and the life story of Muhammad, Gülen turns tradition into a discursive space and treats tradition not as something to be conserved but as a way of making life meaningful and as an instrument of inquiry to articulate a more humane society through Islamic morality. Gülen's conception of identity and morality are interconnected but do not form a self-contained or closed system. Morality translates into identity through conduct and collective action, so acting and engaging in the public and private spheres are part of building the moral self. In short, morality and identity must be put into practice and reinterpreted on the basis of new challenges. "Islam by conduct (*hizmet* and *himmet)*" and "Islam by product (*eser)*" are the two key concepts of the Gülen movement.

Because Islam, for Gülen, is the constitution of morality and identity, he stresses the role of education for the cultivation of the self. His education project is based on three principles: cultivation of ethics, teaching of science, and self-discipline. In his faith-inspired education project, morality and discipline consist of sacrifice, responsibility to others, handwork, and idealism. In fact, this religiously motivated global education movement is a way of bringing God back to one's life through the ethic of self-sacrifice and hardwork. Muslims constantly are reminded that avoiding sin is not enough; rather, engaging to create a more humane world is required. Salvation means not only to be "saved from" sinful activities, but also to be engaged actively in the improvement of the world. Ac-

14. Author's interview with Gülen, Philadelphia, 12 Apr. 2002.

cording to Gülen, moral consciousness toward other cultures can be raised only through participating in an action. In a way, becoming a morally upright person (*insan-ı kamil*) is possible only through morally informed conduct. Those who contribute or take part in this educational activity in fact become a part of bringing the good of Islam to others. In sum, then, Gülen's educational system aims to raise Muslim consciousness, fight against the negative consequences of positivism, and recover collective memory.

Gülen's Ideas of Democracy, Dialog, and Gender Equality

Gülen also believes that the Islamic aspect of Turkish culture has been highlighted more following the 1980 military coup than at any prior time in republican history. He claims, "I am always on the side of the state and military. Without the state, there is anarchy and chaos."[15] His thinking is more strongly shaped by the Ottoman tradition of statehood than by any specific Islamic precepts. His vision for the future of Turkey overlaps with the goal of the 1980 military coup—namely, a symbiosis of Islamic and Turkish national and state traditions and interests. Gülen avoids any form of confrontation with the state. By knowing the way in which the state-centric political culture informs people's understanding of Islamic movements, he wants to develop close ties with the state in order to expand the social base of his movement. Having meetings with politicians and establishing close ties with the Turkish state authorities expand the legitimacy of the movement among non-Nurcu members of the Turkish community. Gülen's main goal is not to reorient the state in terms of Islamic precepts, but rather to promote a state ideology that does not contradict Islamic ethics. He also does not want religious argument in the public sphere to be treated as a rejection of the autonomy of the political sphere.

Along these lines, Gülen is aware of the need to maintain a distance from the particular party that happens to be in power at a given moment. He argues: "We don't support any ruling party just because it is in power. There are ways in which they come to power and leave it. We need to control these ways and doors that play a key to the walk to power. . . . We should respect the government and express our opposition as is done in most developed, Western countries."[16] From various interviews with him, it seems that his ultimate goal is to be a political and cultural bridge between the state, on one side, and the conservative middle class

15. See the Gülen interview in *Sabah*, 27 Jan. 1995.
16. Ibid.

and the upwardly mobile technocrats, on the other. He does not want to be seen as being connected to the antisystem political parties. For example, he argues:

> Democracy and Islam are compatible. Ninety-five percent of Islamic rules deal with private life and the family. Only 5 percent deals with matters of the state, and this could be arranged only within the context of democracy. If some people are thinking something else, such as an Islamic state, this country's history and social conditions do not allow it. . . . Democratization is an irreversible process in Turkey.[17]

Gülen has differentiated democracy and religion, arguing that

> The main aim of Islam and its unchangeable dimensions affect its rules governing the changeable aspects of our lives. Islam does not propose a certain unchangeable form of government or attempt to shape it. Instead, Islam establishes fundamental principles that orient a government's general character, leaving it to the people to choose the type and form of government according to time and circumstances. (Gülen 2001a, 134)

One of the major innovations of Gülen's views of politics and the state is the introduction of the concept of a social contract. He states that "Islam recommends a government based on a social contract" (Gülen 2001a, 136). Although he does not explain what he means by "social contract," his stay in the United States and his readings of the U.S. political system have transformed his thinking on the roles of the state, democracy, and human rights. His writings and interviews from this period mark a "new" Gülen who is more at home with globalization and democracy and also more critical of the state-centric political culture in Turkey.

Since the middle of the 1990s, Gülen's message has evolved to include new concepts of globalization, democracy, and human rights. For instance, in an article examining the meaning of the new millennium, he argues that

> This circulation of the "Days of God," which is centered in Divine Wisdom, is neither a fear nor pessimism for those with faith, insight, and genuine perceptive faculties. Rather, it is a source of continuous reflection, remembrance, and thanksgiving for those having an apprehensive heart, inner perception, and the ability to hear. Just as a day develops in the heart of night, and just as winter fur-

---

17. Ibid.

nishes the womb in which spring grows, so one's life is purified, matures, and bears its expected fruits within this circulation. Also in this circulation, God-given human abilities become aptitudes and talents, sciences blossom like roses and weave technology in the workbench of time, and humanity gradually approaches its predestined end. (2000a, 4–5)

Gülen's immediate concern is not to achieve changes on the macrolevel; rather, he focuses on the spiritual and intellectual consciousness of the individual. He stresses the role that technology and new global networks can play in articulating a newly formed Muslim consciousness, which he feels has a mission to fulfill. He is extremely optimistic about the impact of new information technology in empowering people and consolidating democracy.

Gülen and his movement are open to criticism in four areas: gender relations; silence on the Kurdish question; support for the 28 February 1997 soft coup; and a duty-oriented, noncritical educational system. One also can point out the major gap between his ideas and the practices of the movement. This gap also indicates the movement's multilayered and amorphous nature. Gülen's views on the precepts of Islam are pragmatic and contemporary without being liberal. Although some researchers have presented Gülen as "democratic and liberal," they must be applying these descriptions loosely, given Gülen's writings and activities (Aras 1998). Gülen's notion of politics and activities cannot be considered liberal because he gives priority to the community and the state over the individual. Moreover, as far as gender equality is concerned, there is a gap between what Gülen teaches and how quickly the community adopts his leadership. Gülen argues that the head scarf for women is not an essential issue of faith (i.e., *füruat*), but rather is related to a cultural understanding of Islam and therefore can be interpreted differently. He also argues, "What is in the interest of the state and the nation: education or illiteracy? Each person should decide in her conscience on the issue of the head scarf. As far as I am concerned, she should prefer education."[18] In his speeches, he advocates the integration of women into the workforce but does not clearly articulate equality. The Gülen community itself practices rigid segregation of the sexes and does not permit women to work in high positions in its vast networks or media empire. Gülen himself, however, is more practical and progressive than his community. He is trying to introduce his religiously conservative community to a level of modern

---

18. For Gülen's statement and its implementation in his schools, see *Yeni Yüzyıl,* 16 September 1998; see also A. Ünal 1998.

society. A decade ago this religious community was not willing to allow daughters to go to high schools, preferring instead to send them to Qur'anic courses or to the strictly female İmam Hatip Schools. For years, Gülen publicly and privately encouraged the community to educate all children regardless of gender. Today, there are many schools for girls, and many of their graduates go on to universities. However, as a result of the 28 February soft coup, very few sex-segregated schools remain in Turkey.

Gülen's tolerance and the acceptance of diversity by conservative Turkish society are clearly limited. Further, Gülen and his followers offer little criticism of the oppressive state policies against many independent-minded journalists and human rights workers who are jailed routinely for expressing critical views. It is therefore difficult to consider Gülen's project either liberal or democratic. Rather, it is a hybrid communitarian movement rooted in Turko-Islamic tradition. However, relative to the elitist and socially exclusive nature of Turkish intellectual life, Gülen, as a religious leader, is fairly tolerant of others and is open to dialogue with all groups in order to promote civility in Turkey (see Gülen 1998d). His movement has reconciled itself with democracy and secularism without yet becoming democratic or fully secular.

Gülen's vision of Islam is based on discipline and dialogue. The first precept is stressed within the community, whereas the latter is an external guide for interactions with non-Muslim groups. In order to promote his humanistic interpretation of Islam, Gülen emphasizes the role of dialogue and tolerance, and he has had some success in this regard. He has met with Patriarch Bartholomeos, the head of the Orthodox Fener Patriarchate in Istanbul, and with other leaders of the Orthodox churches ("Diyalog" 1996). He also has met with other Christian and Jewish religious leaders, including Pope John Paul II, in an effort to advance interfaith dialogue ("Fethullah Gülen" 1998). Moreover, the Gülen-inspired Journalists and Writers Foundation has organized a number of conferences on interfaith dialogue.[19]

The Sociohistorical Stages of the Gülen Movement

As a result of the opening and closing up of political and economic opportunity spaces in Turkey in the twentieth century, the focus of the Gülen movement has evolved from building a religious community to creating a global, faith-inspired

19. The foundation organized an international "Abraham Symposium" in Urfa and Istanbul on 13–16 Apr. 2000.

educational system. Three different periods in the movement can be identified. Each period was shaped by structural changes that reproduced a more contextual framing process. In the first period, the religioconservative community-building period from 1970 to 1983, Gülen used the Kestanepazarı Qur'an School to teach and tutor a spiritually oriented and intellectually motivated core group of students with the goal of building an exclusive religious community in İzmir. Summer camps became the spaces of secular education (history and biology) and religious tutoring. In these summer camps, Gülen put his ideas into practice and developed a theology of religious activism. The camps also included male university students. Gülen's knowledge and charisma fascinated these young men and motivated them to use their time and knowledge to bring Islam into public spaces and public debates. In the constitution of this theology of activism, Gülen evoked the life of Muhammad and the classical period of the Ottoman state. The Ottomans, for Gülen, are models to indicate the possibility of becoming "great." They themselves were great because they lived in accordance with Islam. In this view, if Turkey wants to become a "great nation" again, it is necessary to bring God back into life, institutions, and intellect.

During this embryonic period, Gülen wanted to preserve his religioconservative community from active involvement in Islamic political movements, and he treated political activity as a challenge to his attempt to create a dutiful Muslim community. However, owing to the ideological polarization of Turkey, especially the rise of radical leftist movements, the Gülen movement eventually embraced an anticommunist rhetoric and adopted a conservative nationalist position. As a result of the Cold War conditions, neither justice nor human rights but rather the security of the state against the assertive leftist movement became the Gülen community's major concern. The state became as sacred as Islam and even more important for the protection of Islam against the internal leftist and external Soviet enemies.

The movement avoided active politics but created access to educational institutions, media, the market, and other urban public spaces by establishing its own institutions or by using its followers' connections. Informal ties were critical in the evolution and activities of the community-building movement. Owing to state oppression and limited economic resources, Gülen employed informal but tightly knit religious networks—the *dershanes*, but also the lighthouses (*ışık evler*)—to consolidate solidarity and to create a shared moral orientation. He tapped both the personalism and informality of Muslim societies to control the boundaries of religious community. These lighthouse networks mobilized new resources and accumulated powerful social capital to be used in a more conducive social and political environment. They also began to publish the monthly *Sızıntı* science magazine in 1979.[20]

Development of the Lighthouses (*Işık Evler*)

It is helpful to envision the Gülen movement as a web of formal and informal relations that constantly activates its members' loyalty. These relations are carried out within a set of networks in which commitment to the goals of the movement are maintained through informal living spaces—the lighthouses, the dormitories, the summer camps—and through regular fund-raising activities. In these mixed public-private spaces, the participants have the opportunity to bring religious and secular ideas and practices together, to pray together, and to discuss social and political issues. Moreover, the same networks are used to find jobs, housing, and better education for members of the community. In other words, one sees the process of the deprivatization of Islam in terms of bringing Islamic values, agents, and institutions into the public spaces.

The lighthouses play a crucial role in attracting more young people to join the Gülen movement. Gülen treats these lighthouses as the home of Ibn-i Erkam and by doing so seeks to give the same religiohistorical mission to them and to those who live in them as that expressed in the original ideals of Islam.[21] Members of the movement treat these houses as sacred places where private identities and convictions are built and put into practice. Gülen has always focused on the private sphere and private domain more than on the public in defining the constitution of the Muslim community and identity. However, he wants Muslims to transform their private piety into public action by using diverse opportunity spaces in the media, education, and the market. During an interview, he argued that

> Islam is about morality and identity, and these must be instilled in the formative period of childhood. Thus, the family, the private domain, is where Islam must be put into practice. In Turkey, we need similar private shelters for the youth

20. *Sızıntı* articles try to demonstrate the reconciliation of Islam and science. Islamic morality is also a constant theme in its articles.

21. Ibn-i Erkam was one of the first Muslim converts in Mecca and joined Prophet Muhammad in migration to Medina. He turned his private house into an Islamic missionary center. Even Prophet Muhammad lived in Erkam's house and participated in collective prayers and study circles to enlighten the population about Islam. These houses functioned as the moral and intellectual shelters of the first Muslim community.

against disbelief and corruptive influences of the system. These shelters are the lighthouses, and I hope they help each and every young person to create their personality by living together and enlightening their environment with Islamic ideals.[22]

In the Gülen movement, the lighthouses are places where university students stay, study, and develop a sense of identity to protect their Muslim personality from other temptations. In these houses, five or six same-sex students live together within an atmosphere of sincerity and develop a powerful sense of religious brotherhood or sisterhood to protect each other from the excesses of the secular system. Students internalize Islamic values of responsibility and self-sacrifice through collective prayers and regular sessions of reading Nursi's and Gülen's works. In other words, these dormitories are spaces for developing inner consciousness and shelters against such behaviors as drug and alcohol use, premarital sex, and violence. For these reasons, conservative and religious parents encourage their boys and girls to live in the lighthouses in the big cities. It is possible, however, to see the lighthouses as an instrument of social control and as an attempt to create a sex-segregated community with very few cross-gender interactions.

Gülen defines the lighthouses in the following way:

> The lighthouses are places where the people's deficiencies that may have been caused by their human characteristics are healed. They are sacred places where plans and projects are produced, the continuation of the metaphysical tension is provided, and courageous and faithful persons are being raised. Said Nursi himself said that "the men who acquire the true faith can challenge the universe."
>
> It is undoubtedly clear that today the conquest of the world can be realized not on the back of a horse, a sword in hand, a scimitar (*sadak*) at the waist, a quiver on the back like the old times, but by penetrating into people's hearts with the Qur'an in one hand and reason in the other. Here, these soldiers of spirituality and truth raised in lighthouses will pour the light that God has given them for inspiration into empty minds and help them flourish on the way to the conquest of the world in spirit and reality. Thus, these houses are one workbench or one school where these directionless and confused generations who have shaped themselves according to dominant fashionable ideas are now healed and [then] return . . . to their spiritual roots with its accompanying meaningful life. (1997h, 12).

22. Author's interview with Gülen, Philadelphia, 12 Apr. 2002.

These houses, for Gülen, are centers where youth go through a process of "metaphysical tension"—that is, where they revitalize piety through cultivating love, compassion, and hope to shape everyday life. Gülen defines this tension as "inner enthusiasm, the ability to love, the source of inner power and perpetual activity of spiritual sentiments that direct the believer toward religion, worship, and spirit of action" (Gülen 1996b, 145). Human action in the public and private domain stems from a believer's privately formed convictions and beliefs. Spiritual energy formed in the lighthouses translates into action through networks and through individual presence and action in the public domain.

The lighthouses are also very much influenced by Sufi asceticism. Gülen is not a member of a Sufi order but is deeply steeped in Sufi philosophy—involving a constant struggle against the human appetite for power, material possessions, and sex in order to achieve higher moral perfection. This moral perfection is achieved if a believer actively disciplines the self and strips the soul of all forms of appetite. In Gülen's writings, Sufism is not a way of rejecting this world, but rather a way of empowering the believer with spiritual tools and character to help him or her shape and control this world. According to Gülen, if the individual is guided only by egoism, hedonism, and utilitarianism, he or she is less likely to achieve happiness, and the world will become a site of constant conflict. As a solution, individual actions must stem from the religious convictions of love, hope, and compassion.

By utilizing the Sufi model of self-cultivation, Gülen teaches followers to internalize values of tolerance, patience, dignity, self-esteem, and self-sacrifice for the sake of the community. More than any other Turkish Muslim scholar, he also stresses military-type discipline and has made it the key defining feature of the lighthouses. These private spheres of the movement are regulated by teachings that recognize the power of human faculties such as the soul, heart, mind, and body. The constant theme in Gülen's writings is that the private domain of the lighthouses should be used to cultivate faith-based morality and identity. By living together with other members of the lighthouses, students learn and internalize a new cognitive map of meaning and action that entails new schemes of perception, evaluation, and a set of bodily practices that are meant to transform their character.

One of the key concepts that constitute Gülen's cognitive map is love. By *love,* Gülen means self-sacrificing love that initiates action by absolute obedience to God and out of concern for others rather than individual reward or utilitarian calculations for one's happiness (Gülen 1997e, 205–8). This love entails self-sacrifice, abnegation, and the personal conviction to transform life on earth. The second most significant concept in Gülen's writings is hope. By *hope,* Gülen means the birth of the future through the restoration of divine love and human dignity in accordance with the teachings of Islam. His reading of Islam, therefore, is always forward looking and forward moving and is always transforming the present for the realization of the future.

In sum, the lighthouses are religiously rooted, private educational and living spaces where Gülen's ideals and practices are instilled on the unconscious level of personality in the youth who live in them (Kömeçoğlu 1997). This unconscious level of personality gradually evolves into a discursive consciousness as Gülen's followers start to interact with the state or with other sectors of Turkish society to change their social, economic, and moral environment in accordance with Gülen's ideals. Their commitment to the movement is enhanced as they move out of the lighthouses and into everyday life and work. In the everyday competitive business life of Turkey, their discipline, loyalty, and solidarity facilitate their social mobility as members of the movement.

These students' personal piety empowers them to resist cross-gender intimacy and other practices of Western socialization. Fasting, praying, and regular reading sessions are acts designed to build inner conscience for the control of the body and to protect the self against Western tendencies. These privately formed moral orientations very much guide the students' public conduct and positions. They also produce a shared cognitive map of understanding and action. In short, they constitute a religious community that informs the followers' position in the public sphere. Public engagement and discussion also emanate from the religious values and the commitment to expand the boundaries of the Gülen movement. These spaces help to constitute a *şakirt* (contemporary young saint) with three major defining characteristics: religious piety and a communal ascetic life; political conservatism and nationalism; and social success with the mission of living only for the goals of the movement.

The Second Period: The "Education Movement"

The second phase of the movement, from 1983 to 1997, witnessed the loosening of the boundaries of the religious community and the evolution of a market-friendly religioeducation movement. The more the movement spread to different areas and regions of Turkey, the more its organizational structure became decentralized. Owing to a very different political environment in the early 1980s, the Gülen movement put its vision of creating a "golden generation" into practice by utilizing new political, legal, and economic opportunity spaces. Gülen developed close ties with Turgut Özal, then prime minister, and worked closely with him to transform the bureaucracy and the sociocultural landscape of Turkey. The political opening of the system in the 1980s, along with new economic opportunities, enabled the people around Gülen to put locally constructed "trust" into use and thus to form one of the most powerful movements of Turkey.

The movement developed close ties with state institutions and became involved in economic, cultural, and media activities. The entry into social, educational, media, and economic fields also transformed the movement itself. The movement stressed the significance of the media and market economy and tried to become more professional by establishing new broadcasting companies, publishing presses, and cultural foundations. The movement bought out the daily newspaper *Zaman* in 1986. A small community that had gathered around Gülen's ideas in the early 1970s was transformed into a social movement based on a complex web of business networks and control of a large media empire. In addition to *Zaman* and *Sızıntı,* these networks now own *Ekoloji* (an environment-related magazine), *Yeni Ümit* (a theological journal), *Aksiyon* (a weekly magazine), *The Fountain* (an English-language religious periodical), Samanyolu TV, and Burç FM.

The role of the Gülen media networks in the formation of public opinion is different from that of purely commercial media in Turkey. They have to balance the needs and interests of the movement with the commercial conditions in the market, a requirement that has created a more responsible and equitable reporting of news and commentary. The most influential outlets are the daily *Zaman,* Samanyolu TV, and Burç FM. These public outlets are used regularly to bring the movement's ideas and views to the public sphere. In order to preserve credibility and respect among the public at large, they also offer alternative arguments as well. The presence of the movement's media networks in this expanding public sphere has played an important role in diversifying and cross-fertilizing the debates over religious and secular concerns in Turkey.

In its attempts to carve its own space in the public sphere, the Gülen movement carefully avoids confrontation with the state. Over the years, it has gained access to the public sphere through its own institutions as well as through its loyal members and sympathizers. The latter elements are viewed as more important than the former because personal networks are very important in Turkish society. By focusing on putting Islamic values of social responsibility and gender segregation into practice, the movement seeks to moralize the public sphere.

In addition to these media outlets, the movement controls one of the fastest-growing financial institutions, Asya Finans, which is backed by sixteen partners and has more than half a billion dollars in capital. Moreover, a powerful association of more than two thousand businessmen and merchants, İş Hayatı

Dayanışma Derneği (İŞHAD), supports Gülen's educational activities. The movement infrastructure also includes universities and colleges, high schools, dormitories, summer camps, and more than one hundred foundations. Management at all levels of the movement organizes day-to-day activities based on the tenets of trust, obedience, and duty to the community. This management structure is composed of businessmen, teachers, journalists, and students. Gülen is well aware of the opportunities available in a free-market economy. His philosophy, therefore, is very much in tune with this growing business community. According to a prominent Turkish writer, Gülen "reveals the aspirations and desires of the new emerging Turkish bourgeoisie, which [has] internalized modern tastes. The Gülen movement, like the emergence of Protestantism within Catholicism along with the help of European bourgeoisie, is evolving from Orthodox Islam."[23]

A closer examination of interviews with Gülen indicates that in order to develop a valid argument, he constantly cites Western thinkers. This approach indicates that he is a product of print-based rational thinking, that he "is the man who is Muslim by religion and European by thinking, which is what the Republic wanted to create."[24] He stresses education and engagement in the market economy. Such activities are aimed at molding a *cohesive* and *disciplined* community through education, mass media, and financial networks. During the second period, the movement became more alluring to socially and economically high-status groups, those university graduates who were searching for networks with high mobility and an elitist orientation (that is, networks of businessmen, journalists, teachers, academics, and other professionals who act as the entrepreneurs of the movement), and to the "devotees," mostly the university students. There was a competition to join the movement because its benefits were greater than its costs.

After 1983, the most important change in Turkish society took place in the field of education. The privatization of the education system opened it up to competition, and the Gülen movement capitalized on the need and desire to establish a better education system. This was also the period of preparation for a more activist and assertive movement. In 1986, the Turgut Özal government withdrew the arrest warrant issued against Gülen by the military government after the 1980 coup. Gülen started to give public sermons, known as *vaaz,* which became a turning point for him in utilizing the national religious networks to carve a space for himself. Prime Minister Özal played an important role in getting the ban on Gülen's public preaching lifted because he wanted to utilize

---

23. See interview with Atilla İlhan in *Yeni Yüzyıl,* 26 Sept. 1995.
24. Ibid.

Gülen's ideas and activities against more extremist Islamist groups. In short, Gülen was expected to become the "Muslim preacher of liberalism," and he never hesitated to meet that expectation because it also coincided with his own goals.

The combination of mobilized money, knowledge, media, and students has molded the Gülen educational landscape in Central Asia, the Balkans, and Turkey. Gülen relies on merchants, teachers, journalists, and students to enact the realization of his Turko-Ottoman ethos. Anatolian and Istanbul-based merchants and businessmen are the main supporters of these educational activities.[25] Gülen argues that a strong free market is necessary to produce economic wealth, which, in turn, will support a modern educational system to produce and control knowledge. This knowledge then will empower Muslims and the Turkish state.

The movement has founded more than three hundred schools and seven universities in Turkey and other countries.[26] Although the universities are very much at the level of community colleges, the high schools have acquired a strong reputation in the teaching of natural sciences and the English language.[27] Although Turkish is also taught, English is the primary language in the classroom.

Gülen seeks to prevent "emotional alienation" among the Turko-Muslim youth by establishing the missing link between the Turko-Ottoman communities and God. He stresses the role of natural sciences to prevent the fragmentation and alienation caused by skepticism. The Gülen education system, therefore, aims to help students discover the attributes of nature in order to consolidate faith in God. According to Gülen, a lack of religious education creates atheism, but the lack of scientific education results in fanaticism.

The Gülen education networks are closely connected to conservative business circles. The combination of business interests and Gülen's ideas is powerful both inside and outside Turkey. Despite claims of a central organization and a strict hierarchy, the networks are rather loose connections between like-minded Turks, whose similar ideas are a result of their internalization of Gülen's writings. Financial supporters of the schools are invited regularly to visit the schools and to explore investment opportunities in Central Asia.[28] These conservative

25. Not only Muslims but also non-Muslims such as Ishak Alaton and Uzeyir Garih, two influential Jewish businessmen, are among the supporters.

26. For more on Gülen's education networks, see "Fethullah'ın" 1998.

27. For more debate on these schools, see Milli Eğitim Bakanlığı 1997.

28. See further Şen 2001, and Yavuz 1995b. The latter essay examines the microdynamics of the neo-Nur movement in the Fergana Valley, Uzbekistan.

businessmen usually prefer to fund schools in Central Asia because of their commitment to Gülen's Turko-Islamic worldview.

The teachers in these schools usually come from the most prestigious Turkish universities, such as Middle East Technical University in Ankara and Boğaziči University in Istanbul. They believe that they have a mission to fulfill. Unlike true missionaries, however, these teachers are seeking to deliver God along with Turkish culture.

Students in Gülen's high schools in Turkey consistently achieve superior results on university exams. Although these schools do a much better job than state schools, they still stress memorization and conservative values more than critical thinking. The movement's education system is similar to the Turkish state education system in that it does not promote free will and individualism, but rather a collective consciousness and a strict sense of duty to something greater than the self. The schools are thus less likely to encourage self-reflexivity or self-realization of individual potential.

The Gülen movement has been most appealing to the Turks of Central Asia and is dominant in that region, where Gülen's core message is communicated easily. Many Central Asian Turks view the Gülen movement as a national Turkish understanding of Islam. Other Islamic countries such as Iran, Pakistan, and Saudi Arabia have attempted to disseminate their version of Islam in that region, but with no apparent success, with the notable exception of Iran's role in Persian-speaking Tajikistan. There are three main reasons for the Gülen movement's success in Central Asia. First, Islam in the region is not the Islam of the Qur'an, but rather "legendary Islam" based on folk stories and narratives, which Nursi used in spreading his message (Yavuz 1995a, 1995d, 1998). Second, the Soviet legacy of atheism is deep and effective in the region, and religious ideas have to compete with it. The stress the Nurcus put on natural signs and scientific discoveries has generated an Islam that is not in conflict with science and modernity. In Uzbekistan, Nursi's *Risale-i Nur* is referred to as *zamangah,* or a contemporary place to meet modern challenges and "understand our faith."[29] This Sufi-oriented, "softer" Turkish Islam has been more appealing to the Turkic nations than the Saudi version of a rigid Islam. Gülen's schools promote patriotism and a common religiohistorical consciousness for the Turkic youth.

Owing to Gülen's nationalist affinities, most of these educational institutions are in the Turkic republics of the former Soviet Union and the Balkans.

29. Interview with Malik Muratoğlu, *Taşkent,* 24 Jan. 1995; see further *Dergah* 62 (Apr. 1995), 13.

The schools seek to consolidate conservative Islamic and Turkish values.[30] For instance, when I asked a student from Kızılkaya High School in Kyrgyzstan what the main difference was between private Turkish high schools and public schools, he responded by saying that "we [in the private schools] are more patriotic and nationalist than they are." In this interview with the student, one can clearly see the social conservatism and patriotic nationalism among the student body. One also sees the impact of the schools' social conservatism in the segregation of the male and female students. "Patriotism" is a primary goal in boys' schools, whereas "motherhood" is the focus in the girls' schools. Gülen's educational institutions, according to some critics, give the neo-Nurcus a powerful and pernicious domination over the minds of the next generations. His imagined "intellectually able generation" is not likely to become a reality, however, given the conservative nature of the education system.

Gülen's lectures in Valide Sultan Mosque in Istanbul on 6 May 1989 focused on the ethical aspect of Islam and aimed to meet the religious and ethical needs of the middle classes and the new bourgeoisie. He avoided controversial issues and developed an inclusive language, urging people to participate in the economy and in media and cultural activities to create a new and confident Turkey. His emotional preaching style stirs up Muslims' inner feelings and imbues his messages with love and pain. He targets people's hearts more than their reason, an appeal that helps him to mobilize and transform Muslims. Gülen's style is effective and forms a powerful emotional bond between him and his followers. However, he does more than stir up their emotions; he also exhorts them toward self-sacrifice and activism. Thus, he arms his followers with an emotional map to translate their heart-guided conclusions into action. His preaching style also is a way of transforming the self by carving an inner space to resist oppression.

For instance, his nationally broadcast lectures in Süleymaniye Mosque on 19 December 1989 focused on the Muslim community's sins and its failure to act morally. He contrasted this state with the life and ethical personality of the Prophet Muhammed. He constantly examined the hard moral choices the Prophet had to make, stressing the Prophet's activist, loving, forgiving, and caring aspect and the Islamic virtue of social responsibility and coexistence. This language created bridges between secularists, nationalists, liberals, and atheists in Turkey. He acquired a reputation as the moderate, emotional, and caring Hocaefendi of Turkey. Moreover, his inclusive and liberal interpretation of Islam as a

---

30. For example, women can be either teachers or secretaries in these schools, and there are no women teachers in boys' schools. Moreover, students are taught to respect authority.

religion of love, peace, and social responsibility helped him to add new circles to the movement. These newcomers constituted the sympathizer circle within and outside the movement. Because they had different backgrounds and expectations, their presence forced the movement to liberalize further its language and recruitment practice. Gülen had to use more generic and inclusive terms to meet their expectations. In this period, the movement went public and developed inclusive terminology. It gradually shed its religioethnic communalism and anticommunist rhetoric. In short, it evolved into a more moderate and open movement as it participated in all cultural, economic, and social domains, becoming a national civil movement inspired by Islamic ideas of social responsibility.

By the early 1990s, Gülen's movement controlled one of the most powerful media outlets in Turkey. This emphasis on media started the process of making it an audio-visual community as well as a textual community. Thus, the close connection between religious activism and new media technologies offered new opportunities for all groups in Turkey to carve a space for themselves in the public sphere. For instance, the Gülen movement attempted to bring religion into the production of public opinion on issues such as how we ought to live and how we ought to think about how to live. This attempt, in turn, led to the objectification of a religious worldview as an autonomous category to frame social and political issues. The process of going public and trying to communicate within the normative domain of the public sphere in Turkey compelled the Gülen movement to moderate its voice and frame its arguments in terms of reason and interests. This slow yet profound attempt to go public has facilitated the internal secularization of this faith-based movement by forcing the communal networks of the movement to compete with diverse worldviews and to frame their arguments so that anyone can understand them.

The second period of the Gülen movement stressed its becoming a transnational education movement and going public. In effect, the movement shifted from being a Turkish religious movement to being an "Islam as education" movement. It stressed good work, charity, and a just, peaceful society, but without invoking Islamic teachings. This was a period of shifting from *irşad,* open and assertive teaching of Islam, to *temsil,* the persuasion of others regarding the good nature of Islam through good deeds and a moral lifestyle.[31] The latter includes persuasion by example and good conduct rather that by preaching. Thus, the media, the schools, and the lighthouses became channels of representing good deeds and intentions. Moreover, during this period, the movement became a centripetal force that brought diverse ethnic, ideological, and cultural groups

31. See further Gülen 1998e.

together to form a new and inclusive social contract. In particular, it began to absorb the cultural and economic elite into its activities. This attempt to co-opt the elite and incorporate them into the movement was carried out through the Journalists and Writers Foundation, the most powerful civil foundation in Turkey. This effort very much worried the state because it never liked to see the formation of independent power centers.

Gülen's extensive interviews in the dailies *Hürriyet* and *Sabah* in 1995, in which he expressed his views in such a way as to expand the boundaries of sympathizers, turned him into a civic-religious leader.[32] Indeed, he was not only expanding his circles of supporters and sympathizers within Turkey, but also developing close connections with global religious networks by organizing a number of meetings on the "dialogue of civilizations" as opposed to the "clash of civilizations" emphasized by U.S. political analysts ("Medeniyetler" 1996). Within this spirit, Gülen met with Pope John Paul II and other religious leaders. This move to go global became yet another concern for the insecure secular elites of the Kemalist system.

The Gülen movement is a compelling force behind the proliferation of religiously shaped social practices that include shopping at pro-Islamic malls, watching pro-Islamic television programs, becoming involved in the Islamically motivated education system, and consuming popular Islamic literature (Kasaba 1998). In these new public spaces, Gülen's followers carry out their struggle for recognition. In other words, the market economy and the spread of democratization have led to an unprecedented Islamicization of the public sphere. Islamic foundations, associations, and publishing houses in Turkey are urging Muslims to become more involved in social and political activities and to control their own lives. The activities of Islamic groups are establishing new coordinates in the public sphere. Gülen's community is in the forefront of an Islamicization of modern tastes that used to be dominated by the Kemalist establishment. For instance, in the early 1990s, most of the meetings of the Gülen movement began to take place in five-star hotels. There is a full engagement with consumer culture. But the logic of corporate culture and profit making has highlighted internal enmity and division within the Nur movement. The community's increasing power and its transformation into a religiously inspired civic movement further worried the state. Ultimately, its successful attempts to incorporate the elite into its activities and to search for a new social contract prompted hostile forces within the secular state establishment to act against it.

32. Interviews in *Hürriyet*, 23–28 Jan. 1995, and *Sabah*, 23–30 Jan. 1995.

The Third Period: Persecution and Forced Liberalization

The third phase of the Gülen movement began with the 28 February 1997 soft coup by the military and has been marked by both external pressure and an internal opening. The aim of Turkey's military generals, the self-appointed custodians of Kemalism, was to ban virtually all independent sources of Islamic social and cultural expression to prevent a "fundamentalist" Islamic takeover of the state. They banned the Refah/Fazilet Party, restricted the İmam Hatip Schools, severely curtailed the building of new mosques, implemented a dress code outlawing the wearing of head scarves in institutions of higher education, and suspended and imprisoned elected mayors by order of the Ministry of Interior. Gülen publicly justified the military crackdown against the Refah Party and did not oppose the oppression of peaceful Sunni Islamic groups in the country.[33] He has not been very consistent on the issues of democracy and human rights and has sought immunity by promoting his group's interest above the rights of civil society as a whole (Göktürk 1999). He regularly has courted the state by supporting anti-Islamic campaigns against other groups and has excused the military's intolerant behavior. He and his community have tried to present themselves as soft and moderate vis-à-vis other Islamic groups within Turkey. By stressing their "difference" from other groups, they work to gain legitimacy from the Kemalist state.

Certain branches of the state and some secular politicians supported Gülen's activities within and outside Turkey in order to contain more "radical" Islamic forces. Gülen, like many others in Turkish republican history, sought legitimacy as a charitable dispensation from an authoritarian state. Prior to the national elections in April 1999, both President Süleyman Demirel and Prime Minister Bülent Ecevit, the senior leaders in Turkey, defended Gülen's activities and worldview as a "bulwark" against political Islam as represented by the Refah/Fazilet Party.[34]

On 21 June 1999, the military-orchestrated media, prompted by the antireligious Kemalist establishment, launched an organized and fierce attack on Gülen and his activities, calling them "reactionary" and a "threat" to the secular nature of the Turkish state.[35] This confrontation was one that Gülen always judiciously

---

33. In Gülen's television interview, he sharply criticized Refah leader Erbakan and political Islam; see "Hocaefendi'den" 1997.

34. For more on Ecevit's defense of Gülen, see *Zaman,* 14 Mar. 1998, and Ilıcak 1998.

35. For more on the media attack, see various issues of *Milliyet,* 21–28 June 1999; *Sabah,* 21–29 June 1999; and the *Turkish Daily News,* 21 June 1999.

sought to avoid.[36] Uncharacteristically, however, his media outlets met this attack with a sharp and hitherto unprecedented counterattack.[37] For his part, Gülen had learned a painful lesson that obsequiously catering to the center of military power can breed contempt as much as it does forbearance. To be fair, this latest attack on Gülen actually was also meant to erode civilian authority, in particular that of the popular leftist prime minister Bülent Ecevit. Many journalists and members of Gülen's inner circle believed a radical group within the Turkish army was behind this attempt. Nevertheless, some militant Kemalist circles feel very uneasy with Gülen's external connections and cooperation with other religious communities, particularly in the Balkans, the Caucasus, and Central Asia. They see these ties as potential means to undo the authority of Kemalist ideology in Turkey (Khan 1995). The conservative radicals within the army worry that Gülen might use his external connections to pressure the state on human rights issues and democratization. Their other main concern has to do with Gülen's alleged attempts to penetrate state institutions and to co-opt some secular intellectuals.

State officials who are suspicious of Gülen's long-term goals claim that his tactics of vacillating in response to pressures from the state betray his long-term agenda, which is not consonant with that of the country's military-bureaucratic establishment. Even his statements apologizing for the military's draconian edict forcing observant Muslim women not to wear head scarves in public institutions and his liberal and pacifistic understanding of Islam are treated as tactical positions only, rather than the real positions he is alleged to hold. One state official said, "his main goal is to move from the period of the 28 February process with the least damage" and to emerge as the most powerful Turkish Islamic group after the 28 February process.[38] Mehmet Kutlular, leader of the Yeni Asya Nur group, criticizes Gülen for being a tool of the authoritarian state establishment and for not being a sincere follower of Nursi, someone concerned with the issue of human rights even if this concern were to lead to prosecution. Kutlular argues that the state used Gülen against other Islamic groups, and when it felt that it did not need him, it decided to dispense with him and his movement (Çakır 1999).

As the public sphere and social spaces continue to shrink, the boundaries for critical thinking among Muslims expand. This paradox of external diminishment with internal expansion is the major characteristic of post-1997 Turkey. As people are pressured to give up their differences and become one, they become

36. See further Salt 1999.

37. *Zaman,* various issues, 21–27 June 1999.

38. Author's interview with state security officers, Ankara, 15 June 1999.

more sympathetic and supportive of diversity and cultural pluralism. This sympathy for difference is critical for the evolution of liberal thinking.[39] Since the 1997 soft coup, Gülen gradually has moved away from his previous nationalist and statist position to a more liberal and global perspective. This new Gülen has internalized the global discourses of human rights and democracy. He is less political and state centered and more society and market oriented.

During the ferocious anti-Gülen campaigns, Gülen guided the Journalists and Writers Foundation, which became more active in organizing conferences, meetings, and dialogue symposiums to build a new social contract that will include all groups. He has brought many diverse groups together to discuss the problems of Turkey and to present solutions. For instance, the foundation's Abant declarations have identified major divisive political issues within Turkey: the relationship between Islam and secularism (1998);[40] religion and the state (1999); democracy and human rights (2000); and pluralism and reconciliation (2001). The conferences have brought many leading scholars, intellectuals, and policymakers together to discuss these divisive issues and to author consensus-building charters, and they are known as the Abant Bildirisi (workshops). The main points of the 1998 Abant Declaration were: "revelation and reason do not conflict; individuals should use their reason to organize their social life; the state should be neutral on beliefs, faith, and the philosophical orientation of society; governance of the state cannot be based on religion or secularism, but should expand individual freedoms and rights and should not deprive any person of [the right to] public participation."[41] The Fourth Abant Declaration of 2001 examined the subject of pluralism and its political consequences and the question of social reconciliation (Journalists and Writers Foundation 2001). It concluded that "pluralism can be realized only in a democratic and secular regime that takes

39. In my interview with Gülen in Philadelphia, 12 Oct. 2000, he said: "We all change, don't we? There is no exit from change. By visiting the States and many other European countries, I realized the virtues and the role of religion in these societies. Islam flourishes in America and Europe much better than in many Muslim countries. This means freedom and the rule of law are necessary for personal Islam. Moreover, Islam does not need the state to survive, but rather needs educated and financially rich communities to flourish. In a way, not the state but rather community is needed under a full democratic system."

40. For more on the debate over the First Abant Declaration, see Çalışkan 1998. Some scholars criticized the declaration as a sign of the politicization of Islam; see Kepenek 1998. Ahmet Taşgetiren, a prominent Islamist writer, argues that "Gülen is seeking to facilitate the task of the secularists' military establishment by distorting Islam" (1998).

41. For the full text of the First Abant Declaration and debate, see Gündem 1998, 269–72. For other declarations, see Journalists and Writers Foundation 2000a, 2001.

the supremacy of the law as its basis and that is based on human rights. Civil and political freedoms, headed by the freedoms of belief, thought and expression, education, and organization, are the prerequisites of pluralism" (Journalists and Writers Foundation 2001, 316). The Gülen movement wants religion to have a role in the modern world by reimagining religion in terms of modern needs and a shared generic normative charter of the Turkish society.

The three stages of the Gülen movement indicate Islam's remarkable innovative capacity and its ability to renew itself under diverse conditions. The Gülen movement is a social coalition of loose and seemingly disorganized religious and cultural networks. The movement has evolved over time from changing social and political conditions to changing organizational demands. Thus, its ideology and its organizational networks both shape and are shaped by Turkey's ever-changing social and economic context. Although internal aspects of the Gülen ideology—recruiting new followers, giving them a distinct identity that is disposed toward activism, and sustaining a degree of member mobility for activities—have not been changed, the external aspects, such as the shaping of public opinion and the social environment, have changed. The movement has integrated the global discourses of democracy, human rights, and pluralism to communicate with the outside world. Because most of the recruitment takes place through the lighthouses, the youth subculture (composed especially of engineering students) is the most fertile ground of the movement. These lighthouses recruit and offer new personal and social identity to the students by getting them to internalize a set of shared schemata of interpretation that will help them to locate and perceive events in similar ways. The students gradually share the same frames of thought that provide a guide for action. Gülen's group is better organized and more in tune with globalization than politically motivated Islamists, such as the Felicity Party of Erbakan or the Justice and Development Party of Tayyip Erdoğan.

The Gülen movement implicitly argues that Islam is the religion of the nation and should not be reduced to representing the identity of a single party. It both diffuses and absorbs nationalist and market forces and thus has been an instrument of change. Gülen has become the powerhouse among moderate Islamic groups. What differentiates the Gülen movement from other Nur groups is its loyalty to a charismatic leader and its action-oriented culture of community dominated by virtues such as honor, duty, and service to the state.[42] Movement members are Turko-Ottoman nationalists who support a market-oriented econ-

---

42. In Nursi's writings, service to the country is as important as service to the Qur'an, but Gülen stresses the state more than country or nation; see Nursi 1993.

omy, and they are relatively moderate in their interpretation of Islamic dogma. Yet the more the Gülen movement seeks to control sources of power—the market, education, the media—and to transform the world in a religionationalist way, the more it becomes engaged in everyday life and is transformed by the forces it seeks to control.

The proliferation of media, technology, and public discursive spaces helps to prevent any ethnic, religious, or ideological group from establishing a hegemonic position in any state. Moreover, these spaces allow individuals to frame their problems and to communicate with other individuals in order to develop new communities and solidarities. They offer the Muslims of Turkey the opportunity to articulate their own vision of modernity and authenticity. As Turkey moves to a market economy and feels the effects of globalization, its various Muslim communities reimagine their cultural vocabulary within the framework of global discourses. These spaces are instrumental not only in redefining tradition, but also in integrating the cultural periphery. Moreover, multiple public spaces simultaneously lead to a pluralization and fragmentation of groups and the interpenetration of diverse identities and cultures in Turkey. The future of Turkey depends on its ability to integrate hitherto marginalized sectors of the populace into the center.

Said Nursi's main concern was not how to save the state but rather how to save Islamic faith in the face of modern skepticism. He realized that the Kemalist project sought to replace religion, which it viewed as an obstacle to social change, with positivist thought. The neo-Nur movement, unlike the original Nur movement, is struggling to create a new national consciousness by using recently opened economic and communication spaces.

Because Islam is an integral part of Turkish identity and everyday life, most anticenter movements use Islamic concepts and institutions to mobilize the populace. If the current extreme form of Kemalist secularism prevents the integration of Muslims into social, political, and economic life, it will also prevent the pluralization and interpenetration of identities and the democratization of the country. A stable Turkey presupposes a balance between Islamic values and the Kemalist political system; the Gülen movement offers a way to achieve this balance. As the unfolding spiritual embodiment of the new Islam, this movement opens new avenues for the radical reimagination of tradition. As long as alternative public spaces remain open to all groups, there is a good possibility that Muslims can achieve the internal liberalization of Islam.

3

The Gülen Movement's Islamic
Ethic of Education

BEKIM AGAI

> as for man, real life is accompanied by knowledge and education; those neglecting learn-
> ing and teaching, even if they may be alive, can be considered as dead because the aim of
> man's creation consists of seeing, understanding, and teaching the learned knowledge to
> others.
>
> —Fethullah Gülen, *Ölçü veya Yoldaki Işıklar,* vol. 1

INSIDE AND OUTSIDE OF TURKEY, Fethullah Gülen is known among religiously moderate and progressive Muslims for the large number of educational
institutions built and operated by his followers, who constitute a particular sub-
group of the Nurcu movement. This educational work began in the early 1980s
in Turkey; by 1999, his followers were running approximately 150 private
schools, 150 *dershane*s (educational centers that offer additional courses), and an
even larger number of student dormitories. In the early 1990s, this movement
started to expand its activities outside of Turkey; by 1997, more than 250 Gülen-
inspired educational institutions in nearly all parts of the world enrolled more
than 26,500 students.[1] These numbers are impressive, especially if one considers
the short time period involved and the fact that the schools are private. The most
striking point about these schools is that they do not teach religion, even though

An earlier version of this article appeared in the journal *Critique: Critical Middle East Studies,* 11,
no. 1 (spring 2002): 27–47. The journal's Web site is at http://www.tand.co.uk. I gratefully acknowledge permission to offer this revision here. I also thank M. Hakan Yavuz for his continued
support and critical comments on an earlier version of this article.

1. The Turkish media gives very exaggerated numbers with regard to these educational institutions, and even the National Education Ministry does not list all of them, but Yavuz 1995b and
1999c, 599, may serve as an orientation.

religious faith is a primary motive for their creation. Rather, they stress the teaching of ethics *(ahlak),* which are seen as a unifying factor between different religious, ethnic, and political orientations.

Despite the intense activities of the movement, Gülen remained relatively unknown to the nonreligious public until the end of 1994, when the Turkish press began to report euphorically, but not seriously, about him. Interest in the man and his educational projects has remained strong, but after June 1999 media reports about him shifted from a positive to a negative tone.[2] Yet, despite the numerous newspaper articles and several books written about Gülen,[3] very little is known about his ideas and about the people who put them into practice.[4] The reason for this absence of knowledge is the inability of secular circles in Turkey to comprehend how a religious movement can participate in modern education and still remain Islamic.

Participation in the educational sector has some important implications. As recent studies have demonstrated, education is a very important means to create social capital, which, according to Robert Putnam, subsumes the features of social organization such as trust, norms, and networks that can improve the efficiency of society by facilitating coordinated actions. Putnam contends that "voluntary co-operation is easier in a community that has inherited a substantial stock of social capital in the forms of reciprocity and networks of Civil engagement" (1993, 167). Education, in this context, "is one of the most important predictors—usually, in fact, the most important predictor of political and social engagement—from voting to chairing a local committee to hosting a dinner party to trusting others" (Helliwell and Putnam 1999, 1). Education thus can create social capital that is very important in the process of building a civil society and participating in it.[5]

---

2. Prior to June 1999, Turkey's ruling secular elite had not perceived Gülen as part of the "fundamentalist threat" to secularism, but after he and his followers became the focus of the state elite's concerns about religious influence in 1999, Turkey's major media outlets began an anti-Gülen campaign; see Yavuz 1999c, 602.

3. Most of the books are very biased either for or against Gülen. For examples of anti-Gülen books, see Bulut 1998 and Değer 2000. For an example of a pro-Gülen book, see Webb n.d. For more scholarly and objective articles, see Yavuz 1999c, Kömeçoğlu 2000, and Hermann 1996. The only serious study concerning the Gülen schools and the effects of what they teach is Özdalga 2000.

4. For an initial attempt to examine Gülen movement schools and other Turkish schools in Central Asia, see Demir, Balcı, and Akkok 2000. Two dissertations on the schools in Central Asia have been written: Balcı 2000 and Turam 2000.

5. See further Rodrigues 1997.

Social science literature has stressed the importance of education for social change.[6] Many Islamic movements, especially reform-orientated ones, started and took shape in the educational sector by providing knowledge and social capital. The controversy about the Gülen movement in Turkey since 1999 is rooted in the widespread perception of education as means of social change and the fact that the Gülen schools deliver a high-quality education, which is the stepping-stone to a career in all those parts of society that since the 1920s have been reserved for the Kemalist elite.[7]

The goals of Gülen's educational concept derive from the vision of Said Nursi (1873–1960), who believed that through education it was possible to raise a generation both deeply rooted in Islam and able to participate in the modern, scientific world. By following Nursi's educational philosophy, Gülen aspires to use modern education to stop what he sees as a process of decline in the Muslim world. He wants to create an educated elite within the Islamic *umma* (community) in general and within the Turkish nation in particular. Like Nursi, he sees education as a way to create both social capital and a capable community for shaping society. Gülen in effect has produced an Islamic discourse that links Islam so strongly with education that one can speak of an "educational Islamism" that is opposed to political Islamism. His own ideas have changed over time from a very classical Islamic understanding of education to the acceptance of universal values within education. This change has been the direct outcome of the development of structural conditions in politics and the rising level of education inside the movement. His educational philosophy, as demonstrated here, emerged in a particular social context and changes as conditions change. In the case of Turkey, for example, both the political landscape and access to higher education inside the movement changed, helping to transform Gülen's goals and strategies. These internal changes have been possible because the Gülen movement is not ideological, but rather seeks to educate people through flexible strategies.

Educational Institutions and Modernity

The Gülen movement's activities in the field of education are not based on ideology but have developed as Gülen's own ideas evolved as a result of educational

6. See, for example, Reichmuth 1995 and Eickelman 2000, 16–20.

7. Although Gülen has been called a fundamentalist since June 1998, it is possible to buy from Islamic groups in Istanbul books that denounce him as a nonbeliever (*kafir*) because he said that he did not consider a female prime minister as being contrary to Islam.

practice. Understanding this point is very important for understanding the movement. One inevitably may assume that because Gülen's institutions are part of an Islamic educational movement, their focus must be on the teaching of religious subjects. But the Gülen movement, although undoubtedly motivated by religion, has established schools that follow the state curriculum. With regard to Turkey, this practice means that the Gülen schools teach religious courses only one hour per week; in its institutions abroad, they may not teach religion at all. Gülen always has been concerned about creating a "modern Muslim"—that is, an individual both steeped in the ethical values of Islam and possessed of a well-rounded education in all branches of contemporary knowledge and science.[8] By uniting Islam with the idea of universal education, he gave to education a new meaning, which I would call the development of an Islamic ethics on education. By participating in and shaping the educational sector, many of his followers became a part of modern society, from which they previously had been excluded. Consequently, they help shape modern society through their efforts in education, not just in Turkey but in other countries as well.

Gülen's ideas, deeply influenced by the Nurcu movement, evolved in a Turkey that was polarized between religious and secular outlooks. Since the earliest years of the Turkish republic (established 1923), three main positions concerning modernity and the West have existed.

The secular position was shared and promoted by the radical Westernizers who founded the republic and were led by Mustafa Kemal (1881–1938), subsequently known as Atatürk. The Westernizers (later known as Kemalists) had been influenced by the European worldview promoted in the secular *mektep*s and by their studies in European countries, especially France, the most radical promoter of a strictly secular worldview based on materialism and positivism. They used theories such as Darwinism to prove the irrationality of religion and as an argument to push religious authorities out of their influential role in society. Positivism and materialism became dogmas in the process of modernization in Turkey. The Westernizers saw religion, the cognitive patterns shaped by religion, and the lack of modern technology as major causes of Turkey's inferiority and material backwardness in comparison with the West. They claimed that as long as religion and its institutions had a strong influence on society, superstition would predominate over reason, and advancement of society would be impossible (Toprak 1981, 38, 1993, 238). They were convinced that science was connected to culture, so Westernization could not take place just in science but had

8. On Gülen's ambiguous understanding of this change in viewpoint, see Can 1996, 14, and Çalışlar 1997, 36.

to be implemented in all fields of society, including culture and daily life. The Westernizers argued that Europe was like a rose that had to be accepted with its thorns (Özdalga 1998a, 29). During the constitutional reforms beginning in 1923, the impact of religion on society was drastically reduced (Toprak 1987, 223f.).

After Kemal came to power, many religious Muslims adopted the opposing position of traditionalists. Traditionalists held the lack of religiosity as responsible for the decline of the Ottoman Empire. They were highly critical of the republican reforms and saw only negative results emerging from Westernization. Whereas the Westernizers claimed that modern states shared their point of view, the traditionalists took the position that Western science and modernity were against Islam (Toprak 1993, 254). Therefore, the latter refrained as much as possible from contact with the modern state and its institutions, and they did not participate in the new educational system. However, this attitude had the consequence of diminishing their social status and virtually excluding them from modern society. These two opposing positions resulted in a wide gap between the Westernizers and ordinary pious Muslims.

Said Nursi represented a third position that sought to reconcile this gap between the secular and the religious. He clearly understood the importance of science and technology for the future, but he did not agree that modern science belonged only to the West. For Nursi, science and religion were interrelated. He pointed out the dangers of following blindly a positivistic conception of science and developed an indigenous understanding of science for the Muslims. He located the study of science inside religion and clearly opposed the notion that Islam was contrary to science or that science was contrary to Islam. He believed that, from an Islamic perspective, science should be practiced to understand the laws of nature and thus the art of its creator: God. In Nurcu discourse (a Nurcu is one who follows the teachings of Nursi), science is one of four possible ways to understand the existence of God.[9] This position, which rejected neither science nor religion, gave science an appreciated place in religion. Nursi also stressed that having contact with the West and Christianity is not harmful to the Muslim believer, but, on the contrary, even may profit him or her. His position and interpretations moved pious Muslims, who had excluded themselves from technological processes at the beginning of the republic, from the periphery of

---

9. These four ways are: (1) the Prophet Muhammad; (2) the Qur'an; (3) the book of the universe (meaning nature); and (4) the conscience, as in humans' "conscious nature." See further Mermer 1997, 55; other authors mention only the first three points.

modern society right into its center and made the appearance of a person like Gülen possible.

Gülen's Early Activities in the Field of Education

Gülen himself was brought up in the classical Islamic system of education. He was educated at a *medrese* (school for religious training) and visited the *tekke* (dervish lodge). In 1957, he was introduced to Nursi's writings and subsequently became an active participant of his community.[10] His understanding of knowledge before 1980 can be described as orientated toward the classical Nurcu ideals of education: a unity of theological, spiritual, and scientific knowledge (*medrese, tekke,* and *mektep)* (Can 1996, 75). Gülen became concerned that the youth of Turkey might lose knowledge of Islam because it was not taught in the schools. The opportunities to learn about Islam were limited because the state controlled education. Therefore, many Islamic groups imparted general knowledge of Islam in private houses, although children still attended the secular schools for their education in modern science. The religious summer camps that Gülen supervised near İzmir in the second half of the 1960s can be seen as an example of how he tried to solve the problem of instructing school-age children about their faith.[11] Here he taught basic Islamic principles, classical Islamic knowledge, Nursi's writings, and ways to maintain one's Islamic identity in a secular environment.

In the following years, Gülen attracted people who were able to support his ideas with money and their labor. They built community houses where Islamic education was taught on the basis of Nursi's writings and Gülen's teachings. They also built dormitories for students of the Yüksek İslam Enstitüleri (schools educating teachers of religious instruction) (L. Erdoğan 1997, 115). By the end of the 1970s, the teaching of ordinary subjects, in particular science, in the public schools became a major concern for Gülen's supporters because they perceived the educational system as being dominated by antireligious leftists, whom they believed were responsible for social unrest and disorder in society (A. Ersoy 1993, 4).[12] Thus, a new period in delivering religious services (*hizmet)* began in 1978 (Gülen 1997d, 106). Gülen began promoting activities that enabled pupils to attain higher education—for example, by providing dormitories

10. On this period, see L. Erdoğan 1997, 33–78.
11. On the summer camps, see L. Erdoğan 1997, 117–24.
12. The first half of Ersoy's book is dedicated to the issue.

for secondary school students who lived in villages lacking high schools. In İzmir, the first *dershane* (study center) was established to help pupils prepare for the central entrance examination to the university. In 1979, the journal *Sızıntı,* which promoted a synthesis of scientific knowledge and Islam, began publishing.[13] This journal provided Gülen a means to express his views to a broader public because the journal did not remain limited to the Gülen/Nurcu movements, but attracted a large popular readership. During this time, Gülen shifted from an individual-oriented focus to a more society-orientated approach (Barlas 2000). His main goal was to raise a new Turkish elite with both an Islamic and a modern orientation to lead the country.

While Gülen was diversifying his network, he also was breaking away gradually from the Nurcu movement (Yavuz 1997b, 345–48).[14] He initially was part of the vast Nurcu network, but then he began to form his own network, where education played a crucial role. His ways of responding to the conditions of Turkish society differed from those that other Nurcu groups promoted to attain the three major aims of Nursi's project. The differences primarily were connected to Gülen's perception of education and of the effects resulting from engagement in the educational sector.

Post-1980 Coup Activities

Significantly useful for the rise of the movement after 1980 was Gülen's justification of the military coup in that year (Yavuz 1997b, 347). In addition, Gülen continued to stress that schools concentrating on nonreligious subjects could serve religious needs and that Turkey needed elite secular schools run by religiously motivated, conservative teachers who would stress Turkish Islamic values that would provide stability and social peace. This message became significant and timely because the military favored private investment in the educational sector. The first step toward the development of an Islamic ethics of education emerged in Gülen's movement during this time. Gülen did not want to confine his education ideals to Islamic circles only, but wanted to deliver them to the entire society. For him, it was very important to educate a new elite in secular schools influenced by his ideas. He believed that only such an educated elite would be able to come into positions for shaping society through their activities. That is, he believed a bureaucrat or a businessman could do more to change society than could a preacher because the purely religious part of society was so

---

13. The journal can be read on the Internet at http://www.sizinti.com.tr.

14. Yavuz explains the different factions inside the Nur movement.

marginalized that people with solely religious knowledge were not in position to influence society.

The new political climate was suitable for the propagation of Gülen's ideas about a Turkish Islamic synthesis.[15] In fact, the new moderate religious conservatism propagated by the government and the state elite made it possible to introduce religious courses into the school curriculum, thereby guaranteeing a basic religious education. But the new political climate also raised new problems. For example, it was possible for devout Muslims to attain positions they never would have dreamed of prior to 1980. Nevertheless, the government and the Istanbul business community continued to recruit employees mainly from private foreign schools, a practice that pious Muslims strongly criticized (M. Ersoy 1989, 53). However, because the postcoup governments permitted private educational institutions to operate, Gülen urged the building of such institutions as a contemporary form of Islamic activity.[16]

Gülen argued that pious Muslims should be engaged in modern Turkey and help to shape its institutions. He saw high-quality education combined with Turkish Islamic values as the means to generate well-integrated, but still pious Muslims willing to serve their country. Accordingly, his movement took advantage of the new regulations by establishing numerous private schools, dormitories, *dershane*s, and even colleges (Akyüz 1999, 324). Their Islamic, very nationalistic, and pro-state discourse fitted into the political climate of the 1980s. During the 1990s, Gülen was able to reach wider parts of society by transforming his religious discourse into a universal discourse that stressed the ethical dimension of Islam. His supporters argued that this style of education was the answer to the question of how Turkey could maintain its identity in a globalized world. Gülen himself saw that Turkey could benefit and gain influence from opening itself to the world, although he also pointed out the danger of being absorbed by other countries culturally and religiously. In this context, he saw and presented education as a cure for resolving identity conflicts, as a bridge between the people inside and outside Turkey, and as the basis for an interreligious dialogue. The movement argued that one who has a firm sense of identity based on knowledge does not fear contact with others. Thus, a solid national and religious

15. Gülen draws a clear distinction between the Turkish and Arabic versions of Islam. He has always been a strong opponent of communism and a defender of state order, even when this order was directed against him. See Can 1996, 54; Gülen 1997l, 49; and Özsoy 1998, 64.

16. Gülen says that *hizmet* and *davet* (the call for Islam) are not something fixed, but that they must be practiced in relation to time and place. This view is what distinguishes his position from a fundamentalist's approach. See Gülen 1995b, 67.

identity was not a contradiction to participation in the process of globalization (Can 1996, 43; Gülen 1997d, 214). The Turkish state encouraged such views as well as private investment in education, a sector the government had been neglecting for decades.

The new Gülen schools were justified with a national and a religious rhetoric, depending on the audiences.[17] On the one hand, the universalization of the movement's discourse broadened its framework to act and brought it wider recognition in the public sphere. On the other hand, it reduced the room to act independently.[18] The movement's dependence on the state grew significantly, which became problematic in the mid-1990s, when many antireligion laws were introduced. Gülen felt compelled to justify these laws and thus was in danger of producing a negative effect on the schools by a false statement.[19]

Changes in Gülen's discourse had effects on the social structure of his followers. A review of three decades of the movement's participation in education clearly shows that the foci of that education changed with regard to its concepts, content, and regional involvement. In a certain way, the movement became the product of its previous work. The educational environment of the 1970s taught religious pupils that science is not against Islam and that studying at secular universities is not synonymous with becoming an unbeliever. Gülen liberated science from the connotation of being opposed to Islam. In addition to a rise in the educational level of pious Muslims, the movement's efforts resulted in a growth in the number of religiously committed teachers of modern science. The educational institutions of the 1980s provided for many graduates the opportunities to take up careers at universities, in the economy, in state institutions, or in schools. These developments supplied the movement with money, contacts, and qualified teachers who were able to understand the secular context of society, to articulate their overall aims in this environment, and to stress that their Islamic aims were to a large extent universal ethical values. This generation of followers also was able to act on an international level.

17. At this time, all levels of Turkish society were dreaming of the twenty-first century as the Turkish century, but in different respects. See Gülen 1997j, 109; Özsoy 1998, 53; and Yavuz 2000c, 195. Here he speaks of the people of Central Asia as "people of our nation." The educational institutions he presents as a modern adoption of *ma'bet, tekke,* and *mektep.* Here we see the mixture of motives for the activities.

18. Barlas sees the schools as the reason why the media near to Gülen did not criticize the 28 February 1997 coup.

19. He justified the closure of the Refah Party, did not criticize the state measures against veiled students (although most of his female religious followers are veiled, and most of the male followers see veiling as an Islamic duty), and did not oppose the 28 February coup.

Modern Muslims as the "Golden Generation"

Gülen, just like Nursi, tries to fulfill three major goals: (1) to raise Muslims' consciousness; (2) to reexamine the connection between science and religion in order to refute the dominant intellectual discourses of materialism and positivism; and (3) to recover collective memory by revising the shared grammar of society, Islam (Yavuz 2000a, 7). His key concepts on education are the means to achieve these aims and the overall aim of creating a "golden generation" armed with the tools of science and religion. The metaphorical concept of a "golden generation" or a "new generation" (*yeni nesil, altın nesil*)[20] is Fethullah Gülen's description of a future generation that is educated in all respects and that forms the basis for the perfect future, the "Golden Age." This generation will be educated "representatives of the understanding of science, faith, morality, and art who are the master builders of those coming after us" (Gülen 1998k, 128)—that is, the movement's teachers. Combining knowledge and human values, this new generation will solve the problems of the future. It will incorporate all the ideas Gülen has taught since his first summer camp in Izmir. Because Gülen does not employ definitions systematically, I concentrate here on major characteristics of the "golden generation he has described.

One main characteristic is faith, which shows believers their purpose and teaches them responsibility for their deeds. Faith, according to Gülen, leads one to the absolutely beneficial (Özsoy 1998, 22). Gülen believes that only with faith can science be applied in a beneficial way to humankind because faith teaches humans what is good and what is wrong. Other characteristics of the generation are love resulting from faith and embracing everything that is created (Can 1996, 87), idealism, and selflessness (Gülen 1998g, 87). The generation should transform its combination of moral values, science, and knowledge into action (a possible field of action is education) because the solution to all problems is linked to knowledge (Özsoy 1998, 47). Here we see the idea that formed the basis for the activities of Gülen's supporters after 1980. They created an infrastructure to ensure the Islamic, moral education of their children, but they also observed that only in combination with knowledge—that is, secular education—could society benefit from their religious principles because it is secular education that enables the follower to shape society.

According to Gülen, the establishment of educational institutions is the result of the desire to see this generation realized. A member of this generation will be able to overcome the ideologies of the past. In fact, says Gülen, "the West

---

20. Though the names of the generation may differ, general traits of character are the same.

and the East cannot chain his feet or capture him. Also the 'isms' that are against his soul's origins will not change the direction of his path or even touch him" (1997l, 158). This "new man" will fill science and technology with spiritual values, something that has been neglected in the West and among Turkey's Westernized elite (Sevindi 1997, 9). He will not just participate in, but even shape modernity. It should be noted that just as Gülen's teaching concept transformed from a Turkish Islamic ideal into a universal one after 1990, so too did his understanding of the golden generation evolve from an isolationist Turkish one to a global one.

The golden generation concept can be seen as a kind of counter ideal critical of the Kemalist secular ideal. It seeks to demonstrate that it is possible to be modern in the "Islamic way"—or, if we want to observe the Gülen movement in the Nurcu context, to be modern in the "Nurcu way" (Yavuz 2000a, 7). This generation embodies Gülen's major aim: pious Muslims making use of science without adopting materialism and positivism and with a firm Islamic identity that unites them with ordinary people in Turkey. The implicit critique here is that the Turkish republic did not succeed in creating such persons. Rather, by diminishing the role of religion and imitating the West, it created a gap in language and lifestyle between the Westernized elite and the ordinary people (Gülen 1997k, 41).

Prior to 1990, Gülen envisioned the golden generation as saving Turkey, but subsequently his view evolved to one of seeing the golden generation as the sign of hope for the world as a whole. This change occurred at a time when Gülen and important people around him got to know the West and realized that they had much more in common with many Europeans than they did with the Westernized elite in Turkey. It also was a time when the discourse of globalization became popular; this discourse helped to show that an isolationist solution to Turkey's problems was impossible and that other countries suffered the same problems.

Teaching as a Holy Duty (Kutsi Vazife)

In achieving the aim of building the metaphorical golden generation, teachers have the most important role. They are the ones who lead pupils to be good and therefore to serve Islam. Teachers have the duty to fill science with wisdom so that it will be applied usefully to society (Gülen 1997c, 99). It is a general assumption in the Gülen discourse that a pure materialist and positivist understanding of science is to blame for wars and the destruction of the environment because scientists who have this understanding do not feel responsible for the effects of their work. Providing education and especially teaching in this context becomes a holy duty, and the teacher is a blessed person (A. Ersoy 1993, 93; Gülen 1997c, 101).

With this rhetoric, Gülen was able to direct to his schools the money that traditionally was donated for mosques. With reference to the Qur'an, he argued that the whole earth was given to man as a mosque (Gülen 1998b, 17); therefore, the Muslim community was not in urgent need of mosques. For a deeper religious understanding of the creation, however, humans need knowledge (Gülen 1997g, 250), and such knowledge can be given only in schools. This argument has put education right at the center of Islamic activities. During his involvement in education, Gülen discovered that it was possible to bring people from different backgrounds together, which aided his efforts to solicit contributions to build schools and to train teachers to instruct the future golden generation.

Because Gülen ascribes very Islamic attributes to the teacher, being a dedicated teacher becomes a kind of religious merit and a way to ensure that individual's religious salvation. This double justification becomes a strong motive for people to choose this profession. From Gülen's point of view, the teacher gives "guidance" (*irşad*), implementing it in a flexible way according to the circumstances (Gülen 1997b, 166). To give guidance generally is accepted as a worthy Islamic merit, but Gülen extends this connotation even to teaching in secular schools. Through teaching, the teacher can save the souls of others as he or she shows the pupils the right way. For Gülen, this is the highest merit an individual can achieve in Islam and also for his or her own soul.[21] Thus, the teacher performs one of the highest duties in Islam, *hizmet*. *Hizmet* is a key term for Gülen because it implies both religious and national service.[22]

Work as a Holy Duty

Hizmet for Gülen implies that a person devotes his or her life to Islam, serving for the benefit of others, which is beneficial for life after death. Gülen is a very restless person who is always asking himself if he might do more for God (Gülen 1997g, 33).[23] Death is always present in his preaching to his followers (Gülen 1997a, 90), and the fear of judgment day is the motivation to work hard.

---

21. The director of the Turkish educational institutions in Tirana in March 2000 said to me that if he shows pupils the right path, their good deeds will be attributed to him after his death.

22. For the different understandings, compare L. Erdoğan 1997, 55, and Gülen 1997c, 168.

23. For a more detailed elaboration of Gülen's notions of *hizmet* and work, see Özdalga 2000, 88.

Work becomes a religious act. Working incessantly for the cause of Islam is a religious norm for Gülen (Gülen 1995a, 131f). One who works hard will earn more money that he then can give to the cause of Islam. Thus, ordinary work is Islamized. In addition, hard work is presented as a purifying act because the individual who works hard does not have time to think sinful thoughts (Gülen 1998f, 63ff).

Because the schools and the work done at them have a religious aim, giving money to them becomes an Islamic deed. Gülen has always argued that it is not enough to save one's own soul, but that one must help others (Gülen 1998f, 110). Working in or contributing to schools is a way to help others. Gülen is a very impressive preacher who convinces people of the truth of this argument. In his sermons, one finds the reason why people work for the schools as teachers and why they donate money:

> Man of service, for the sake of the cause to which he has given his heart, must be resolved to cross over seas of filth. . . . His voice and each breath are spent in the glorification and magnification of God, the Sublime Creator. . . . He knows himself first of all to be responsible and answerable for work left undone. . . . So rational and sagacious that he admits in advance that this path is very steep. . . . So faithful to the cause to which he has devoted his life that, deeply in love with it, he can sacrifice his life and all that he loves for its sake. So sincere and humble that he will never bring to mind all that he has accomplished. (1998f, 52)

This "ethics of vocation" statement and the activities of Gülen's followers resemble the ideal type of Max Weber's "inner-worldly asceticism": "In this case the world is presented to the religious virtuoso as the assigned duty. The ascetic's task is to transform the world in accordance with her/his ascetic ideals." The inner-worldly ascetic does not seek "flight from the world," but rather he or she attempts to demonstrate his or her religious qualification within the world through work. "Hence, as the object of this active demonstration, the order of the world in which the ascetic is situated becomes for her/him a 'vocation' which s/he must 'fulfill' rationally." Rationalism in the daily work becomes very important because the inner-worldly ascetic is a rationalist who "rationally systematizes his own conduct of life" (Weber 1980, 329).[24] This is why Elisabeth Özdalga has described the conduct of the Gülen movement as "pietistic activism" (2000, 88).

24. For these quotations from Weber, I used Fischoff 1963 for translation. An on-line edition is available at: http://www.ne.jp/asahi/moriyuki/abukuma/.

The one who performs *hizmet,* the holy duty, can be described in Weberian terms as the person of inner-worldly asceticism who sees his or her occupation as given from God (Weber 1991, 72; see also Gülen 1998g, 27). For Gülen, doing the work in the best way, devoting it to God, is a religious duty. Gaining money in this context is not negative; only spending it for luxury is perceived as bad (Gülen 1998c, 71; Weber 1991, 167). Life is too short to spend it for amusement because there are always more important and religiously worthwhile things one can do (Weber 1991, 168).[25] "Gülen calls this ideal *aksiyon insanı* [man of action]. Such an *insan* is one who is inclined to work his or her best until this world is turned into paradise, and also is one who in struggle for a better world is stopped by nothing except death itself" (Özdalga 2000, 89).[26] One can find statements by Gülen saying that the person who performs *hizmet* sleeps three hours, reserves one or two hours for other necessities, and devotes the rest of the time for *hizmet,* with its various facets—a program resembling very much the Protestants' "ethic of vocation," which Weber describes in his work (Gülen 1995a, 87). In the Gülen version of the "ethic of vocation," derived from Islam, we find the reason for the strong emphasis on work and discipline inside the movement. The educational sector profits from this discipline in two ways: (1) people of the movement working outside the educational sector earn money that they invest in the educational sector; and (2) teachers do their work with devotion even under very unfavorable circumstances because they perceive it as a duty to God.

Knowledge Is Power: Islamizing Secular Knowledge

To understand why people deeply motivated by Islam teach in schools that do not have a religious focus, it is important to understand Gülen's notion of knowledge in Islam. His own writings unquestionably are influenced deeply by Nursi's writings—for example, the idea that knowledge taught in secular schools can function as the basis for a scientific way of thinking, which is the only means to gain certainty in belief through reflective thought (İrfan Yılmaz et al. 1998, 114).[27] But Gülen and his followers consider that the way in which this knowledge is taught together with materialism and positivism in Turkey's schools is harmful to belief. Gülen used to argue that a combination *medrese*s and *mektep*s

25. Followers of Gülen write whole chapters on time management from a religious perspective. See Aydın 1996, 3–46.

26. Özdalga presents this attitude in a more detailed way.

27. To get an introduction into the universe of Said Nursi with its many facets, I suggest reading the special issue of *The Muslim World* on him: *The Muslim World* 89, nos. 3–4 (1999).

ought to be established as the ideal type of educational institution that would offer both religion and science (Can 1996, 72, 77; Gülen 1995a, 11). Although he still believes in this ideal, he recognizes that there is no place for such institutions in Turkey or in most countries abroad. Furthermore, because Islamic education is available everywhere to those who want it, he and his followers acknowledge that even without teaching Islam explicitly, their schools serve Islam because they deliver knowledge. From Gülen's perspective, knowledge itself becomes an Islamic value when it is imparted by teachers with Islamic values who can show students how to employ knowledge in the right and beneficial Islamic way (Gülen 1997c, 53).

Given this interpretation, it is not surprising that the Islamic public supporting Gülen's views accepts the work of his teachers as *irşad,* or moral guidance, in an Islamic sense. For the teachers, it is not a problem if they teach their understanding of knowledge to non-Muslims (as is done in many Gülen schools outside Turkey) because they believe that knowledge will make the pupil a better person and will provide the basis for a future understanding of Islam. However, only Muslims with knowledge can serve Islam, for Gülen believes it is impossible to perform moral guidance without knowledge (Gülen 1998e, 9): whereas "the one who has knowledge is useful, the one who does not have knowledge is harmful" to Islam and society (Şahin 1992, 58). Teachers with knowledge, then, act as models for their students. Through their own persons, they show how to combine Islam with science, and by being good teachers they teach others, including non-Muslims, that Muslims are good persons, and they thereby serve Islam. Parents appreciate this ideal and trust the teachers as pious Muslims who teach their children knowledge in a manner that is not perceived as contrary to Islam.[28]

The fight against *cahillik* or *cehalet,* usually a term for religious ignorance, has attained an ethical value in Gülen's writings (Gülen 1997c, 98). Teachers proclaim that they fight ignorance by teaching science from their perspective and therefore serve Islam, even when they do not teach it to Muslims, because what is beneficial to humankind is also beneficial to Islam. This way of interpreting the relationship between Islam and knowledge is the reason why an Islamic-motivated movement was able to merge into the secular educational system. Depending on the observer's perspective, this phenomenon can be called either the universalization of Islamic principles or the Islamization of secular institutions.

---

28. Gülen, like the rest of the Islamic part of the Turkish public, is a strong opponent of materialism, Darwinism, and positivism. A book such as *Yeni bir Bakış Açısıyla İlim ve Din* (İrfan Yılmaz et al. 1998) shows how his movement adopts modern science without these theories.

Together with the transformation of the Turkish Islamic discourse into a universal, ethical discourse, this combination of Islam and knowledge has been the basis for the Gülen movement's global activities.

Teaching Nationalism for Participation in the Globalized World

How can a movement that emerged under very nationalistic premises become engaged in global educational activities that encourage the national identities of the countries in which it is operating institutions? Although Gülen sees himself as the supporter of a Turkish Islamic identity (Türkiye Müslümanlığı), his notion of this identity has changed significantly. Until the late 1980s, this identity was based to a large extent on a nationalistic, Islamic chauvinism,[29] but it changed totally during the 1990s. Gülen used to see the solution to Turkey's problems as raising Muslims' consciousness in order to overcome the dominance of Westernized cognitive patterns and to restructure a shared grammar in Turkey based on Islam. He perceived the United States as bad and as destructive as the Soviet Union (Gülen 1998a, 200). But perhaps influenced by supporters who had become engaged in global activities owing to their education, he began to see that isolation was not the solution to Turkey's problems; rather, he realized that the reasons for these problems were to be found in Turkey itself. Gülen wrote that ignorance comes from within society and compared it to blood cancer or a Trojan horse (Gülen 1997c, 60); education was a cure for this illness. At the same time, he came more and more into contact with the West. Owing to this experience, he began to praise the United States for the way it made coexistence among different ethnic groups possible (Sevindi 1997, 35). He even accused the Westernizers of not bringing to Turkey the moral values that constitute the West.

To understand why devoted Turkish Muslims leave their country to work abroad teaching foreign pupils, it is important to examine Gülen's changed understanding of nationalism. To Gülen, Islam is a universal religion with different local and national traits (Can 1996, 201). He attributes a positive meaning to national identities, which consist of values shared in one country and which give individuals a frame of reference. These national identities form the basis for

---

29. Today most of his followers do not want to speak about his previous statement on nationalism, which included such ideas as Turkey being surrounded by enemies, Europe wanting to destroy Turkey by Christianizing it, Jewish philosophers and scientists destroying the religious spirit in Turkey, enemies within Turkey wanting to destroy the Islamic identity of the Turks, and the United States being a bad influence. Although Gülen has changed his ideas, the old books with these ideas are published still.

peaceful interactions between countries. Although each country has its own identity, all countries have shared values, one of the most important of which, according to Gülen, is knowledge (Gülen 1997d, 194). However, people who do not know themselves or their origins do not have a national identity; thus, they cannot see the shared values between different nations and will react to contact with hostility.[30]

The modern world, in Gülen's view, needs an exchange of ideas, but the individual needs a national identity. Gülen sees globalization and national orientation as interdependent. In the Turkish context, this interdependence means that Turkey has to open itself to the world, but also maintain its national identity.[31] He hopes that by following this path, Turkey will be capable of becoming a global player (Özsoy 1998, 53). To Gülen, national orientation is a universal value and is not opposed to Islam. People who are patriots in Turkey also may support an Albanian sense of national identity. They do so to the benefit of their own country and of Islam because they are creating strong ties between countries. Such a development is beneficial for Turkey and also overcomes religious prejudice, which again is good for Islam.[32] The preservation of national and religious identities through contact with others justifies participation in the process of globalization. This is why and how globalization and national orientation go hand in hand inside the Gülen movement.

Tolerance and Dialogue

During the second half of the 1990s, two key words have dominated the Gülen discourse: *tolerance* and *dialogue*. Like many other Islamic modernists, Gülen sees Medina at the time of the Prophet as proof that there is room for other religions and even for nonbelievers to coexist with Islam. Regarding the Ottoman Empire, he says that by practicing a tolerant Islam, 10 million Turks were able to govern 250 million people living on three continents (Özsoy 1998, 23). In his view, charity, the basis for tolerance, is a duty toward God, and he considers it to be a Turkish value. As an example of tolerance in early Turkish Islam, he quotes the Turkish poet and mystic Yunus Emre: " 'We love the created for the sake of

30. Compare the quotation by Yunus Emre given later.

31. To solve their problems, the people of the world have to work together. There are no solutions for just one country. Compare Can 1996, 16.

32. For the economic importance of Central Asia, see Özsoy 1998, 110.

the Creator' " (Gülen 1999b, 104). After 1994, Gülen engaged in dialogue based on his understanding of tolerance, acting as a model for his followers to do the same in their institutions. For him, dialogue rests on the premise that all kinds of humans share values because they have the same Creator; dialogue is able to show these shared values.

Gülen tries to stress that those shared values are Islamic and universal ethical values. That is why his movement's schools are worthy projects from an Islamic perspective (Sevindi 1997, 76). He understands tolerance as cooperation among different societal groups and as cooperation on the international level based on shared values. Some differences will remain, of course, so people have to practice tolerance. He describes tolerance as a main attribute of Islam in particular and of the Turkish nation as whole; it encourages dialogue with others and acceptance of their differences (Sevindi 1997, 78).

Although many Islamic leaders talk of tolerance in Islam, it may be problematic to put it into practice. Gülen himself has shown that he has no fears of meeting leaders of other religions, including the pope and the representative of the Jewish community in Istanbul. He also crossed the borders of Islamic discourse to meet with important persons in Turkish society who are atheists. These activities were not easy from a religious perspective because Islam in Turkey has definite boundaries and does not appreciate close ties to the leaders of other religions and to nonreligious persons. Also, his support for the Alevis was not very popular among most Sunni Islamic groups (Çalışlar 1997, 42).

But Gülen's tolerance does not lead to his seeing values as relative. Despite all their readiness to accept different religious groups, the teachers in the Gülen schools remain pious Muslims, with a firmly Islamic national identity serving as the basis for their tolerance. To clarify this attitude, Gülen quotes Mevlana Rumi, who said that man has to be " 'like a pair of compasses, with one end in the necessary place, the center, and with the other one in the seventy-two nations [*millet*]" (Sevindi 1997, 99), an allusion to the different *millet*s in the Ottoman Empire and the way they lived together. Thus, the teachers with their strong sense of Turkish Islamic identity and their activities in so many parts of the world may remind us of Mevlana's compasses. This attitude allows the movement to act under very diverse circumstances because others' differences are not a problem so long as members can remain true to their own values. This attitude and the movement's ability to unite Islamic aims with an ethical discourse are the reasons why its teaching activities are acceptable to many governments outside Turkey.

Gülen Schools in Albania

It is very interesting to observe how the Gülen ideal, consisting of Islamic and Turkish values, is put into practice outside Turkey. In Albania, for example, the movement's activities started in 1992 with the opening of one primary school. Albania is particularly interesting because it formed its national identity in opposition to the Ottoman Empire. Its population is composed of Sunni Muslims, Bektashi Muslims, Roman Catholics, and Greek Orthodox Christians. The Albanian state, well known for its nationalistic outlook, wants to see neither Turkish nationalism nor Islam promoted in these schools. As discussed earlier, the aim of the Gülen movement schools is to teach values and modern sciences, not religion per se. By providing a quality education, they have won support from the government and the public. Thus, by 1999, the movement operated in Tirana one kindergarten, a primary school for boys, a primary school for girls, a secondary school for boys, and one for girls. These institutions provided education for nearly two thousand pupils. They follow a curriculum based on the Albanian and Turkish curriculum, which allows the graduates to study in both countries; lessons are taught in Albanian, English, and Turkish, with English being especially important to teach science.

The goals of the Gülen schools in Albania are to teach their pupils discipline and to raise them by providing guidance.[33] As one teacher said, they hope to deliver a vision of humanity to the students because Albania lost the human dimension during its communist era. For example, they brought their pupils together with the physically disabled and with people living in poverty to teach them the "joy of giving." In such activities, one can see how Gülen's ideals are constructed around local needs. In effect, Gülen's religious values are transformed into a language of ethics, for his supporters believe in the existence of a shared ethics of what is morally right and wrong. Because of their education, they have seen that others who do not accept Islam as their system of reference nevertheless may have the same aims and values as Muslims. It is this belief in shared values that prompted Gülen's efforts at dialogue. His followers share this position and know how to translate their Islamic values into the local language of ethics. For example, among themselves they justify in a very Islamic way their helping another nation to develop its educational system. But when they want to communicate to a nonreligious environment, they may say that they serve out of common humanist reasons. They have learned that one who does not know

---

33. Information in this and the following paragraphs is based on my interviews with staff and teachers of the schools in Tirana, Albania, Mar. 2000.

Islam cannot understand Islamic principles if they are conveyed in an Islamic language. Relying on Gülen's premise that "the road of reason is one" (Sevindi 1997, 42), they have adopted a vocabulary that can be called an Islamic ethics because it can be understood by both Muslims and those sharing another reference system. Again, these supporters resemble the ideal type of Max Weber's inner-worldly ascetic who is "a rationalist, not only in the sense that he rationally systematizes his own conduct of life, but also in his rejection of everything that is ethically irrational, whether esthetic, or personal emotional reactions within the world and its orders. The distinctive goal always remains the 'conscious,' methodical mastering of one's own conduct of life" (1980, 329).

In interviews with me, the teachers in Tirana described their advantage, in comparison with other schools, as having a very good reputation regarding both their technical skills and their moral qualities. The parents appreciate teachers who neither smoke nor drink. The teachers from Turkey do not come just to earn money. They are persons willing to make sacrifices (*fedakar*). In this sense, they see themselves as influenced by Gülen's ideas. They perceive their work as Islamic because they work for their own religious benefit and because they provide guidance and teach ethics. In addition, they are educating an Albanian youth who will be beneficial for Albania because of the schools' high standard of education and morality—as proven by the many awards that the students win in international contests. Furthermore, their teaching and testing methods are oriented toward the U.S. system, which allows the pupils to study in English-speaking countries, a stepping-stone to holding high positions in society in the future. Interestingly, the materials used to promote the Albanian schools adapt Gülen's discourse regarding a "golden generation": "with a vivid past and science to a happy future."

The interviewees described their work as *hizmet,* with the aim to save others (*kurtarmak*) and themselves because the results of good deeds continue even after death. Here we see how they perceive Gülen's ideal of work in the educational sector as religious worship. They find in the schools an environment in which others share their moral values; thus, their own religious morality is reinforced.[34] They see their work as Islamic because it promotes moral guidance (*irşad),* serves religion (*hizmet),* and fights ignorance (*cehalet).* I observed great mobility among the teachers. Some of them came from the movement in Turkey, went to many countries abroad before or after working in Albania, and finally returned to Turkey to work for the movement again. The most striking point is

---

34. Gülen sees doing work that is devoted to an Islamic cause and to the community as a powerful means to lead an Islamic way of life. For the importance of community, see Gülen 1997j, 186.

how they can translate their own Islamic motivation and values into ethical values that they can share with people from so many countries.

Islamic Modernity

With his teachings, Gülen has laid a foundation for his followers, who apply his ideas in the field of education in different environments. In this context, education has always been seen as a means to ensure one's own salvation and the salvation of others. The movement developed its own work ethic around the field of education. First of all, Gülen encouraged his followers to support the religious education of youth. During the 1980s, by emphasizing the importance of knowledge to Islam and to Turkey, he encouraged them to invest in the educational sector in Turkey. The 1990s was characterized by the expansion of these ideas onto an international level. During this time, Gülen propagated education as a means to deliver ethical values. His supporters in the institutions agreed with the new part of his discourse and implemented his ideas in different environments. They continue to act out of a deep Islamic motivation, and, wherever they are, they form a pious environment around themselves. They combine their individual efforts to work for Islam in accordance with the needs of different communities. The movement has responded to the social and economic issues of the modern world, a response they perceive as crucial. They try to find a place for Muslims in a globalized world. By building educational institutions, Gülen and his movement have answered the question of what Islam means in the modern context. They are not antimodern; they want to be a part of modernity, but they also want to contribute their religious and ethical ideals to it. With these attitudes, the movement appeals to many Muslims in Turkey who ask the same questions as Gülen. The universal aspect of his aims in the field of education also appeals to people of other nations and religions. Because the movement accepts the political and cultural diversity in Turkey and in the world as natural and normal, members have no problems in adapting themselves to very different surroundings. Through education, they want to educate a special class in Turkey that will unify Islam with the requirements of the modern world. They have found their version of Islamic modernity in the work they do in all parts of the world: delivering ethical values to others. Therefore, they form one of the many modernities possible in a world of multiple modernities.[35]

---

35. On the issue of multiple modernities, see Eisenstadt 2000.

4

Fethullah Gülen as Educator

THOMAS MICHEL

I MUST CONFESS at the outset of this essay that I arrived at the topic back-wards. Rather than having studied the writings of Fethullah Gülen on education and pedagogy and then trying to see in a deductive approach how he has put his principles into practice, I instead first became acquainted with his movement's educational institutions. This practical knowledge led me in turn to study Gülen's writings to discover the rationale that lies behind the tremendous educational venture that has ensued from his educational vision and that of his colleagues.

It is necessary initially to be precise about Gülen's relationship to the schools that often and loosely are called "Gülen schools" or "schools of the Gülen movement." Gülen describes himself primarily as an educator, and members of his movement generally refer to him as Hocaefendi, a title of respect given to re-ligious teachers in Turkey.[1] However, he is careful to distinguish between educa-tion and teaching. "Most human beings can be teachers," he states, "but the number of educators is severely limited" (1996a, 36). He also has tried to make clear that he has no schools of his own. "I'm tired of saying that I don't have any schools" (qtd. in Webb n.d., 106), he affirms with a bit of exasperation. Never-theless, a circle of students, colleagues, and businessmen, first formed about Gülen in Izmir during the 1960s, had founded by the late 1990s more than three hundred institutions—elementary schools, high schools, college preparatory institutions, dormitories, and universities—associated with his name in fifty dif-ferent countries (Gülen 1998h, ii). These schools have been established in accor-

---

1. Gülen has had to defend his movement from accusations that the title *hocaefendi* indicates a kind of sect, quasi-Sufi *tarikat,* or Ottoman revivalism. The term, he says, has no hierarchical sig-nificance or official connotation but is simply "a respectful way of addressing someone whose knowledge on religious matters is recognized and acknowledged by the general public" (qtd. in Webb n.d., 80).

dance with individual agreements between the countries in which they are located and educational companies set up for this purpose. Each school is an independently run institution, but most of the schools rely on the services of Turkish companies to provide educational supplies and human resources. In addition, they maintain links of coordination and training, and they share a common pedagogic vision, similar curriculum, and human and material resources.

Personal Encounter with Gülen Schools

My first encounter with one of these schools dates back to 1995. I was in Zamboanga, on the southern Philippine island of Mindanao, when I learned that there was a "Turkish" school several miles outside the city. As I approached the school, the first thing that caught my attention was the large sign at the entrance to the property, bearing the name "The Philippine-Turkish School of Tolerance." This name is a startling affirmation in Zamboanga, a city almost equally 50 percent Christian and 50 percent Muslim, located in a region where for more than twenty years various Moro separatist movements have been locked in an armed struggle against the military forces of the Philippine government.

I was well received by the Turkish director and staff of the school, where more than one thousand students study and live in dormitories. As I learned from the Turkish staff and their Filipino colleagues, both Muslim and Christian, the school's affirmation of their school as an institution dedicated to the formation of tolerance was no empty boast. In a region where kidnapping is a frequent occurrence, along with guerrilla warfare, summary raids, arrests, disappearances, and killings by military and paramilitary forces, the school offers Muslim and Christian Filipino children an excellent education and a more positive way of living and relating to each other. My Jesuit colleagues and the lay professors at the Ateneo de Zamboanga confirm that from its beginning the Philippine-Turkish School of Tolerance has maintained a deep level of contact and cooperation with Christian institutions of the region.

Since that initial visit, I have had occasion to visit other schools in the Gülen network and to discuss educational policy with the teaching and administrative staff. In Turkey, I have visited several institutions in the Istanbul area and in the city of Urfa. In Kyrgyzstan, a former Soviet republic in Central Asia, I had the opportunity to examine at length about half the twelve Sebat schools, including the new Atatürk Alatoo University—all inspired and founded by the Gülen movement. I can state without qualification that I find these schools to be among the most dynamic and worthwhile educational enterprises I have encountered in the world.

The strength of their programs in the sciences, information sciences, and languages is shown in their students' repeated successes in academic olympiads. In a junior high school in Bishkek, I addressed a group of seventh-grade Kyrgyz children for about a half-hour. At the end of my talk, the teacher asked the students to identify those elements of pronunciation and vocabulary that showed that I was speaking an American rather than a British form of English, and to my amazement the children had no difficulty in doing so. Although English was the language of instruction in this school, as is usual in the Gülen schools outside Turkey, the students seemed equally competent in Russian and Turkish in addition to their native Kyrgyz. The teachers' dedication and esprit de corps give evidence that they are conscious of being engaged in an exciting educational venture. Nowhere did I encounter any signs of the malaise and apparent confusion that so often afflicts schools in developing countries.

Aware that these schools are a manifestation of religious commitment on the part of some Muslims, I had expected to find a more explicitly Islamic content to the curriculum and the physical environment, but this was not the case. When I asked about the surprising absence of what to me would have been an understandable part of a religiously inspired educational project, I was told that because of the pluralist nature of the student bodies—Christian and Muslim in Zamboanga, plus Buddhist and Hindu as well in Kyrgyzstan—what they sought to communicate were universal Islamic values such as honesty, hard work, harmony, and conscientious service rather than any confessional instruction. In the Sebat International School in Bishkek, students from Korea, Turkey, and the United States appeared to be studying comfortably with those from Afghanistan and Iran.

These encounters led me to study Gülen's writings to ascertain the educational principles and motivation that undergird the schools and to try to find Gülen's own techniques, which have made him into an educator capable of inspiring others with his vision. The answers to these questions occupy the remainder of my essay. I concentrate mainly on the Gülen schools as the central expression of his educational policies. In doing so, I must pass over in silence the educational aspects of other ventures Gülen has promoted to advance interreligious dialogue and understanding—such as the Samanyolu television network, *Zaman* newspaper and other publishing projects, the scholarship program for needy students, and the efforts of the Journalists and Writers Foundation.

The Educational Vision of Fethullah Gülen

The focus of Gülen's views regarding education seems to be what he sees as a fundamental crisis in Turkish society. Analyzing the factors that have contributed to bringing about this societal crisis, he concludes that an element one cannot dismiss is the lack of integration[2] among the various types and systems of education. He regards the development of education in Turkey throughout the twentieth century as an unhealthy competition among mutually exclusive systems that have produced graduates who lack an integrated perspective about the future and perpetuate the existing divisions in society. He states: "At a time when modern schools concentrated on ideological dogmas, institutions of religious education [*medreses*] broke with life, institutions of spiritual training [*tekkes*] were immersed in sheer metaphysics, and the army restricted itself to sheer force, this coordination was essentially not possible" (Gülen 1996d, 11).

Modern secular schools, he holds, have been unable to free themselves of the prejudices and conventions of modernist ideology, whereas the *medreses* have shown little interest or capability to meet the challenges of technology and scientific thought. The *medreses* lack the flexibility, vision, and ability to break with the past, to enact change, and to offer the type of educational formation needed today. The Sufi-oriented *tarikats*, which traditionally fostered the development of spiritual values, have lost their dynamism and, as Gülen puts it, "console themselves with virtues and wonders of the saints who had lived in previous centuries" (1996d, 11). The educational training offered by the military, which in previous times had been the representative of religious energy and activity and a symbol of national identity, has devolved into an espousal of attitudes of self-assertion and self-preservation.

The challenge today is to find a way in which these traditional pedagogical systems can move beyond regarding each other as rivals or enemies so that they can learn from one another. By integrating the insights and strengths found in the various educational currents, educators must seek to bring about a "marriage of mind and heart" if they hope to form individuals of "thought, action, and inspiration" (Gülen 1996d, 12). An integration of the interior wisdom that is the cumulative heritage built up over the centuries with the scientific tools essential for the continued progress of the nation would enable students to move beyond the societal pressures of their environment and provide them with both internal stability and direction for their actions. Gülen states: "Until we help them through education, the young will be captives of their environment. They wander aimlessly, intensely moved by their passions, but far from knowledge and reason. They can become truly valiant young representatives of national

---

2. I believe that the term *integration* conveys Gülen's intent better in English than *coordination,* the term used in English translations of his writings.

thought and feeling, provided their education integrates them with their past, and prepares them intelligently for the future" (1996a, 59).

The last phrase is important and appears to be Gülen's answer to an ongoing debate in Turkey. *"Integrate them with their past and prepare them intelligently for the future."* Many observers have noted that one of the characteristic features of the modern Republic of Turkey has been its concerted effort to *break* with the Ottoman past. Many of the laws enacted by the Turkish government since 1923 consciously have sought to break with the Ottoman past as a way of modernizing the nation. Examples include the change of capital from Istanbul to Ankara; the abolition of the caliphate/sultanate; the orthographic reform in which Arabic script was replaced by Roman letters; the language reform in which Arabic and Persian terms were substituted for words with Turkish roots; the legal reform in which the Swiss civil code and Italian penal code were adopted in place of shariah law; the establishment of Sunday as the weekly day of rest; the enforced use of surnames and the replacement of the Persian *-zadeh* by the Turkish *-oglu* suffix; and the prescription of Western dress along with the prohibition of characteristic Ottoman clothing such as the fez and turban. All these reforms were aimed at breaking with the Ottoman past in an effort to modernize Turkey (Lewis 1969, 268–89).

In the decades since the establishment of the Republic of Turkey, many Turkish Muslims have criticized the modernization program undertaken by the government, in particular for blindly adopting the best and worst of European civilization. They see secularization as not merely an unintended by-product of the modernization process, but rather as the conscious result of an antireligious bias. They contend that underlying modernizing reforms is the unspoken ideological conviction that religion is an obstacle to progress and thus must be excluded from the public sphere of society, economics, and politics if the nation is to move forward. The battle lines drawn up during the decades since the establishment of the republic in 1923 and reinforced by the mutually competitive systems of education have made the religion-secularization debate in Turkey one in which every thinker is expected to declare his or her allegiance.

One of the reasons why, in my opinion, both the "right" and "left" and both the "secular" and "religious" in Turkey have often attacked Gülen is precisely that he has refused to take sides on an issue he regards as a dead end. Instead, he is offering a future-oriented approach by which he hopes to move beyond the ongoing debate. His solution is to affirm the intended goal of modernization enacted by the Turkish republic, but also to show that a truly effective process of modernization must include the development of the whole person. In educational terms, this process must take the major concerns of the various existing threads of education and weave them into a new educational style that will respond to the changing demands of the contemporary world.

This objective is very different from reactionary projects that seek to revive or restore the past. Gülen denies that the education offered in the schools associated with his name is an attempt to restore the Ottoman system or to reinstate the caliphate. He repeatedly affirms that the schools are oriented toward the future. He cites an ancient Turkish adage, "If there is no adaptation to new conditions, the result will be extinction" (qtd. in Webb n.d., 86).

Despite the necessity of modernization, he holds that there are nevertheless risks involved in any radical break with the past. Cut off from traditional values, young people are in danger of being educated with no values at all beyond those of material success. Nonmaterial values such as profundity of ideas, clarity of thought, depth of feeling, cultural appreciation, and interest in spirituality tend to be ignored in modern educational ventures that are aimed largely at mass-producing functionaries of a globalized market system (Gülen 1996d, 16).

Such students might be prepared adequately to find jobs, but they will not have the necessary interior formation to achieve true human freedom. Leaders in both economic and political fields often favor and promote job-oriented, "value-free" education because it enables those with power to control the "trained but not educated" working cadres more easily. Gülen asserts that "if you wish to keep masses under control, simply starve them in the area of knowledge. They can escape such tyranny only through education. The road to social justice is paved with adequate, universal education, for only this will give people sufficient understanding and tolerance to respect the rights of others" (1999a, 4). Thus, in Gülen's view, it is not only the establishment of justice that is hindered by the lack of well-rounded education, but also the recognition of human rights and attitudes of acceptance and tolerance toward others. If people are educated properly to think for themselves and to espouse the positive values of social justice, human rights, and tolerance, they can be agents of change to implement these beneficial goals.

The crisis in modern societies arises from decades of schooling that has produced "generations with no ideals" (Gülen 1996d, 51–52). Human ideals, aims, goals, and vision are the source of movement, action, and creativity in society. People whose education has been limited to the acquisition of marketable skills are unable to produce the dynamism needed to inspire and carry out societal change. The result is social atrophy, decadence, and narcissism. He states: "When [people] are left with no ideals or aims, they become reduced to the condition of animated corpses, showing no signs of distinctively human life. . . .

Just as an inactive organ becomes atrophied, and a tool which is not in use becomes rusty, so aimless generations will eventually waste away because they lack ideals and aims" (1996d, 51).

The societal crisis is intensified by the fact that, in Gülen's judgment, the teachers and intelligentsia, who should be the guides and movers of society, have allowed themselves to become perpetuators of a restrictive and nonintegrated approach to education. Rather than raising their voices in protest against the elimination of humane values from the educational system and campaigning for a pedagogy that integrates scientific preparation with nonmaterial values studied in the disciplines of logic, ethics, culture, and spirituality, the educators themselves too often have "readily adapted to the new low standard" (Gülen 1996c, 16). He finds it difficult to understand how intellectuals can prefer the spiritually impoverished and technologically obsessed modern culture to a traditional cultural foundation that grew in sophistication and subtlety over the centuries.

It follows that if educational reform is to be accomplished, teacher training cannot be ignored. According to Gülen, "education is different from teaching. Most human beings can be teachers, but the number of educators is severely limited" (1996a, 36). The difference between the two lies in that although both teachers and educators impart information and teach skills, the educator is one who has the ability to assist in the emergence of the students' personalities, who fosters thought and reflection, who builds character and enables the students to interiorize qualities of self-discipline, tolerance, and a sense of mission. He describes those who simply teach in order to receive a salary, with no interest in the character formation of the students, as "the blind leading the blind" (1996a, 36).

The existence of competing and mutually antagonistic educational systems gave rise to what Gülen calls "a bitter struggle that should never have taken place: science versus religion" (1996a, 39). This false dichotomy—which during the nineteenth and twentieth centuries exercised the energies of scholars, politicians, and religious leaders on both sides of the debate—resulted in a bifurcation of educational philosophies and methods. Modern secular educators saw religion as at best a useless expenditure of time and at worst an obstacle to progress. Among religious scholars, the debate led to a rejection of modernity and to a view of religion "as a political ideology rather than a religion in its true sense and function" (Gülen 1996a, 20). Gülen feels that through an educational process in which religious scholars have a sound foundation in the sciences and scientists are exposed to religious and spiritual values, the "long religion-science conflict will come to an end, or at least its absurdity will be acknowledged" (1996a, 39).

For this reconciliation to come about, he asserts that a new style of education is necessary, one "that will fuse religious and scientific knowledge together with morality and spirituality, to produce genuinely enlightened people with hearts illumined by religious sciences and spirituality, minds illuminated with positive sciences," people dedicated to living according to humane qualities and moral values, but who are also "cognizant of the socio-economic and political conditions of their time" (1996a, 39). Having as a school's educational goal the integration of the study of science with character development, social aware-ness, and an active spirituality might appear to critics to be a highly idealistic, possibly quixotic endeavor. The only adequate test of the feasibility of this edu-cational philosophy is to examine how successful Gülen's associates have been in establishing schools on these principles. I return to the matter of verification later in this essay.

Several terms appear repeatedly in Gülen's writings on education and need to be clarified lest they cause misunderstanding. For example, consider the terms *spirituality* and *spiritual values*. Some people might read these terms as code words for "religion" and think Gülen employs them perhaps to counteract prejudices toward religiosity in modern secular societies. However, it is clear that Gülen uses the terms in a broader sense. For him, the term *spirituality* includes not just specifically religious teachings, but also ethics, logic, psychological health, and affective openness. Other key terms in his writings are *compassion* and *tolerance*.[3] It is the task of education, he feels, to instill such "nonquantifiable" qualities in stu-dents, in addition to training them in the "exact" disciplines.

Gülen also often speaks of the need for *cultural*[4] and *traditional* values (see Gülen 1996a, 44–45, 1996d, 16). Critics have interpreted his call for the intro-duction of such values in education as a reactionary call for a return to prere-publican Ottoman society. Consequently, he has been accused of being an *irtica*, which, translated in the Turkish context, means "reactionary person" or even "fundamentalist." Gülen has denied this accusation. In defense of his position, he states:

3. Gülen's studies of Muhammad's life and mission focus repeatedly on the qualities of com-passion and tolerance. See Gülen 1998h, 3–4, 7, 11, 87, 94, 100, and passim; and 1998i, 1: 118–19, 179, 2: 96, 123, 131, and 150. At the 1999 Parliament of the World Religions held in Cape Town, South Africa, Gülen stated: "The Prophet, upon him be peace and blessings, defined a true Mus-lim as one who harms no one with his or her words and actions, and who is the most trustworthy representative of universal peace" (Gülen 1999a, 20).

4. Cf. "Little attention and importance is given to the teaching of cultural values, although it is more necessary to education. If one day we are able to ensure that it is given importance, then we shall have reached a major objective" (Gülen 1996a, 35).

The word *irtica* means returning to the past or carrying the past to the present. I'm a person who's taken eternity as a goal, not only tomorrow. I'm thinking about our country's future and trying to do what I can about it. I've never had anything to do with taking my country backwards in any of my writings, spoken words or activities. But no one can label belief in God, worship, moral values and purporting matters unlimited by time as *irtica*. (qtd. Webb n.d., 95)

In proposing cultural and traditional values, Gülen seems to regard Turkey's past as a long, slow accumulation of wisdom that still has much to teach modern people and that is still quite relevant to the needs of contemporary societies. Because of this collected wisdom, the past must not be discarded. However, any attempts to reconstruct the past are both shortsighted and doomed to failure. One might say that although Gülen rejects efforts to break with the Ottoman past, he equally rejects efforts to reestablish or re-create premodern society.

Gülen regards the tendency among some modern reformers to break free of the shackles of the past as a mixed blessing. Those elements of the heritage that were oppressive or stagnant or had lost their original purpose and inspiration no doubt have to be superseded, but other liberating and humanizing elements must be reaffirmed if new generations are going to be able to build a better future. The challenge, he states, is "to evaluate the present conditions and make good use of the experience of past generations" (Gülen 1996a, 45). It is clear that his thinking is not limited by internal debates about political directions in Turkey or even about the future of Islamic societies. His educational vision is one that embraces societies "throughout the world" and the role of religious believers in shaping that world. He states:

> Along with the advances in science and technology, the last two or three centuries have witnessed, across the world, a break with traditional values and, in the name of renewal, attachment to different values and speculative fantasies. However, it is our hope, strengthened by promising developments all over the world, that the next century will be an age of belief and moral values, an age that will witness a renaissance and revival for believers throughout the world. (1996d, 103)

Gülen's main interest in education is the future. He wants to form reformers— that is, those who, fortified with a value system that takes into account both the physical and nonmaterial aspects of humankind, can conceive and bring about the needed changes in society. Well-rounded education, by its very nature, thus must involve a personal transformation in students, who must be accompanied and encouraged to move out of restrictive, particularistic ways of thinking and to interiorize attitudes of self-control and self-discipline that will enable them to make a lasting contribution to society.

> Those who want to reform the world must first reform themselves. In order to bring others to the path of traveling to a better world, they must purify their inner worlds of hatred, rancor, and jealousy, and adorn their outer world with all kinds of virtues. Those who are far removed from self-control and self-discipline, who have failed to refine their feelings, may seem attractive and insightful at first. However, they will not be able to inspire others in any permanent way, and the sentiments they arouse will soon disappear. (Gülen 1999a, 30).

To the extent that the crises in society are owing to a lack of coordination among rival educational systems and philosophies, the new Gülen style of education is aimed at responding directly to the root causes of the crisis. In doing so, he claims, it offers a sound hope for building more stable and harmonious societies. Educational reform is thus a key to development and progress in nations. If national and private school systems are oriented solely toward the acquisition of material knowledge and mastery of technological skills, they cannot offer a way out of tensions and conflicts in society or offer a solution that can lay the basis of a better future. Because Gülen sees educational reform as the key to positive societal change, he calls for a type of education that seeks to develop both the material and spiritual needs of the students: "The permanence of a nation depends upon the education of its people, upon their lives being guided to spiritual perfection. If nations have not been able to bring up well-rounded generations to whom they can entrust their future, then their future will be dark" (Gülen 1996a, 56).

Criticisms of Gülen's Educational Philosophy

Gülen's proposal for a new style of education, as put into practice in the network of schools associated with his name, has not been accepted universally, particularly in his native Turkey. Some critics have regarded his educational philosophy as an intellectual cover for forming cadres who conceivably might pose a threat to the established secular order in Turkey. Gülen continually has had to defend the schools from this type of criticism. Secular critics claim that by means of the many schools erected in Russia, Central Asia, the Caucasus, and the Balkans, Gülen is attempting to build a "Green Belt" around secular Turkey.

Accusations of brainwashing are likely to be leveled against any form of education that seeks to shape students' feelings, values, and attitudes. Gülen has not been spared this accusation. Critics in Turkey (see Webb n.d., 135) have claimed that even though there is no direct religious training carried out in the schools, religion and politically oriented Islamic teaching are inculcated in the students by example and by informal relations between students and teachers.

In response to these accusations, Gülen notes that the schools established by his movement employ the program and curriculum of the Turkish Ministry of Education. He notes further that the schools are inspected continually not only by the ministry, but also by the intelligence agencies in those additional countries where the schools have been established (Webb n.d., 107). The inspectors have found neither any evidence of brainwashing nor the inculcation of politically activist or antigovernment sentiments either through formal teaching or informal contact. By now, he claims, the schools have been operating long enough so that their graduates are working in all sectors of Turkish society, and they have never raised a complaint about undue influence being exerted on them as students. The same is the case, he states, of official visitors: "Two presidents of our country, premiers, ministers, members of parliament, scholars, high-ranking retired officers, journalists and thousands of others from every view and level have gone out and seen these schools and have returned. There has been no complaint of the kind referred to from the countries where the schools are found. Without exception, they mention them with praise" (qtd. in Webb n.d., 105–6). In the final analysis, such categories as "breaking with the past," "defending the past," or "restoring the past" are irrelevant in attempting to understand Gülen's educational vision because the schools inspired by his movement are conceived in terms of a humanism rooted in a particular historical context but always aimed at transcending that context. The schools established in countries as diverse as Turkey, Kyrgyzstan, Denmark, and Brazil are necessarily very different from one another, but they all are inspired by the same humanistic vision.

Gülen describes this vision succinctly: "A person is truly human who learns and teaches and inspires others. It is difficult to regard as fully human someone who is ignorant and has no desire to learn. It is also questionable whether a learned person who does not renew and reform oneself so as to set an example for others is fully human" (1999a, 5). Into this humanistic vision fits the study of science, humanities, character development, and spirituality—the latter understood, as mentioned earlier, in the broad sense. Thus, it is not surprising that students of these schools have scored high consistently in university placement tests and produced champions in the International Science Olympics in fields such as mathematics, physics, chemistry, and biology.

It is the concern for human formation, however, that distinguishes these schools from the thousands of other prep schools around the world. Gülen understands the school as a laboratory where students not only acquire information and skills, but also begin to ask questions about life, seek to understand the meaning of things, reflect on the particular contribution they would like to make to life, and understand life in this world in relation to the next. In some of his writings on education, he even speaks of the school in quasi-religious terms, as a holy place where sacred activities take place: "The school . . . can shed light on vital ideas and events and enable its students to understand their natural and human environment. It can also quickly open the way to unveiling the meaning of things and events, which leads one to wholeness of thought and contemplation. In essence, the school is a kind of place of worship whose 'holy persons' are teachers" (1996d, 98).

Fethullah Gülen as a Teacher of Islam

The focus of this essay thus far has been on Fethullah Gülen as an educator. His role as religious scholar and teacher (as underscored by the traditional honorific *hocaefendi*) is a topic that deserves careful examination, as does the study of his religious thought arising from his role as a modern interpreter of Islam. These important topics, however, are outside the scope of this essay. Nevertheless, a brief look at his writings about Islam is merited because many of the accusations leveled against the educational ventures inspired by him are owing precisely to his accepted status as a scholar and teacher of Islam.

Of Gülen's more than thirty books, the majority deals explicitly with Islamic topics. Some are compilations of talks and sermons that he delivered to students and worshipers. Others are responses to questions that students put to him at one time or another. They range from studies of the Prophet Muhammad's life,[5] to a basic introduction to Sufism,[6] to a treatment of questions traditionally raised in the science of *kalam*,[7] to elaborations of essential themes of Islamic

5. Two of these works have been translated into English: *Prophet Muhammad as Commander* (Gülen 1996c) and the two-volume work *Prophet Muhammad: The Infinite Light* (Gülen 1998i). Relying on sound hadith reports and the early *sira* or biography of Muhammad by Ibn Hisham, Gülen seeks mainly to outline the qualities displayed by Muhammad as a model to be imitated by modern Muslims.

6. His work *Key Concepts in the Practice of Sufism* (Gülen n.d.b) is a basic introduction to *tasawwuf*, where he analyzes in turn each of the *maqamat* (stations) and *ahwal* (states) on the Sufi path.

7. Gülen's *Asrın Getirdiği Tereddütler* (1997a, 1997b) is a wide-ranging work of four volumes, the first volume of which has been translated into English as *Questions This Modern Age Puts to Islam*

faith.[8] These studies are directed not toward specialists, but toward a more general audience of educated Muslims.

In seeking to present the faith and practice of Islam in a way that responds to the needs of modern believers, Gülen can be said to carry forward the tradition of Bediüzzaman Said Nursi. Gülen's relationship to this eastern Anatolian religious leader continues to be a matter of controversy in Turkey, where Nursi and his followers have remained under government suspicion in the decades since Nursi began to teach. Gülen often has been accused of being a Nurcu—that is, a follower of Nursi. When questioned about this accusation, Gülen does not deny that he has benefited from studying Nursi's writings, just as he has profited from reading the works of many other Muslim thinkers, but he rejects the claim that he is a follower of Nursi in any sectarian sense:

> The word *Nurcu,* although it was used a little by Said Nursi, is basically used by his antagonists to belittle Nursi's movement and his followers and to be able to present it as a heterodox sect. In life, everyone benefits from and is influenced by many other people, writers, poets, and scholars. In my life I have read many historians and writers from the East and West, and I've benefited from them. Bediüzzaman Said Nursi is only one of these. I never met him. On the other hand, I've never used suffixes like *-ci, -cu* [meaning *-ist*] that refer to a particular group. My only goal has been to live as a believer and to surrender my spirit to God as a believer. (qtd. in Webb n.d., 96)

Nevertheless, some observers see the Gülen movement as being one of the transformations that have occurred as Nursi's thought is reinterpreted and applied in evolving historical situations. Yılmaz notes that

> Nursi's discourse "has already weathered major economic, political, and educational transformations." . . . Today, the Gülen movement is a manifestation of this phenomenon. The movement spreads into daily life activities at two levels. First, it uses collective identity structures by producing meanings over time and history, reason and submission, love and worship, faith and rationale, science

---

(Gülen 1998j). The work covers theological topics such as the revealed character of the Qur'an and the nature of revelation, and it presents an interesting treatment of the possibility of the salvation of non-Muslims (149–60).

8. Gülen 1997i takes up matters related to creation and causality, eschatology, the resurrection of the body, the unseen world of angels, *jinn,* and Satan, and it concludes with a study of *nubuwwat,* the prophethood of Muhammad, and the question of science and religion in relation to the study of the Qur'an.

and revelation, divine being and natural order. At the second level the movement tries to influence major patterns of societal institutions, like high schools, foundations, universit[ies], insurance companies, finance houses, sport clubs, television and radio channels, newspapers and magazines. (2000, 2)

What can be said about Gülen's personal approach to interpreting Islamic sources and tradition? The first thing that strikes the reader of his works is his emphasis on morality and moral virtue, which he appears to stress as more central than ritual practice to the religious élan inspired by the Qur'an. Although affirming the need for ritual, Gülen regards ethical uprightness as lying at the heart of the religious impulse. "Morality," he states, "is the essence of religion and a most fundamental portion of the Divine Message. If being virtuous and having good morals is to be heroic—and it is—the greatest heroes are, first, the Prophets and, after them, those who follow them in sincerity and devotion. A true Muslim is one who practices a truly universal, therefore Muslim, morality." He buttresses his point by citing a hadith from Muhammad in which he states: "Islam consists in good morals; I have been sent to perfect and complete good morals" (1996d, 30).

The various aspects of the Islamic way of life—the shariah, creed (*aqıdah*), ritual obligations (*ibadât*), economic affairs (*mu'amalat*), principles of government (*siyasah*), regulations of family file (*al-ahwal al-shakhsiyya*), and moral instruction (*ahlâk*)—are meant to work together to produce the honorable, ethically upright individual. In this broad sense of Islam, or submission of one's life to God, it can be said that the schools established by the Gülen movement have as their inspiration an ethical vision rooted in Islam but not limited in its expression to members of the *umma* (community). When Gülen speaks of forming students who are dedicated to living according to humane qualities and moral values, and who adorn their outer world with all kinds of virtues, he is proposing a kind of universal ethical code that he as a Muslim has learned from Islam. It is equally obvious that he does not consider virtues, humane qualities, and moral values to be the exclusive possession of Muslims; the schools welcome non-Muslim students, and no attempt is made to proselytize.

With this strong ethical sense at the heart of his understanding of Islam, Gülen's many writings on the life of Muhammad affirm Muhammad's role as the Prophet who brought the Qur'anic revelation, but they emphasize even more strongly the figure of Muhammad as moral exemplar for Muslims—Muhammad as the first hearer of the Qur'an whose life preeminently was shaped by its message. Particularly in his two-volume work *Prophet Muhammad: The Infinite Light* (1998i) Gülen shows his central concern to be Muhammad as a role model for the contemporary Muslim. This concern leads him to concentrate on Muhammad's moral qualities as manifested in his personal relationships with his companions, wives, and enemies, and in the qualities of leadership he showed in being Commander of the Faithful. What Gülen finds of special importance in the life of Muhammad are personal qualities such as piety, sincerity, generosity, modesty, determination, truthfulness, compassion, patience, and tolerance, as well as leadership characteristics such as realism, courage, a sense of responsibility and farsightedness, and a readiness to consult, delegate, and forgive (Gülen 1996c, 122–23).

Gülen thus understands the religion of Islam as a "way leading a person to perfection or enabling one to reacquire one's primordial angelic state" (1998i, 153–54). If Islam is a path to moral perfection, one must consider the development of *tasawwuf* as natural and inevitable within the Islamic tradition. Gülen suggests an ethical definition of Sufism as "the continuous striving to be rid of all kinds of bad maxims and evil conduct and acquiring virtues" (Gülen n.d.b, 1). He praises the Sufis in Islamic history as being spiritual guides who have shown generations of Muslims how to follow this path to human perfection:

> [They] have illumined the way of people to the truth and trained them in the perfection of the self. Being the embodiments of sincerity, Divine love, and purity of intention, the Sufi masters have become the motivating factor and source of power behind the Islamic conquests and the Islamization of conquered lands and peoples. Figures like Ghazali, Imam Rabbani and Bediüzzaman Said Nursi are the 'revivers' or 'renewers' of the highest degree, who combined in their persons both the enlightenment of sages, knowledge of religious scholars and spirituality of the greatest saints." (1998i, 154)

Such a positive reading of the mystical Sufi tradition inevitably has led to accusations that Gülen has created within his movement a type of neo-Sufi *tarikat*. Although denying that he ever has been a member of a *tarikat,* much less set up his own quasi-Sufi order, Gülen asserts that to condemn Sufism, the spiritual dimension of Islam, is tantamount to opposing the Islamic faith itself:

> I have stated innumerable times that I'm not a member of a religious order. As a religion, Islam naturally emphasizes the spiritual realm. It takes the training of the ego as a basic principle. Asceticism, piety, kindness and sincerity are essential to it. In the history of Islam, the discipline that dwelt most on these matters was Sufism. Opposing this would be opposing the essence of Islam. But I repeat, just as I never joined a Sufi order, I have never had any relationship to one. (n.d.b, 102–3)

Gülen's educational vision sometimes appears to be the sort of highly idealistic "mission statement" that many educational projects have been declaring for more than a century. The real test remains whether the many schools associated with his movement and consciously established on the basis of this idealism are successful in providing the kind of education Gülen advocates. The answers will be as various as the expectations of those who evaluate these schools. Some schools are likely to be more successful than others owing to differences in the teachers and administrators' individual talents, in government support or interference, in financial arrangements, and in the students' capabilities and backgrounds.

In quantifiable aspects of the educational process, such as generalized examinations, academic olympics, and entrance into high-quality university programs, the schools in the "Gülen network" so far have verified Gülen and his associates' expectations. Moreover, they are greatly sought after by parents. For example, I visited a secondary school in Bishkek, Kyrgyzstan, where 5,000 applicants had sought entrance although only 250 places were available.

It is in the unquantifiable aspects of educational formation, precisely those aspects meant to distinguish the schools in the Gülen-inspired network from the many other prep schools, that evaluation is most difficult and necessarily subjective. Have the schools been producing graduates who display "a marriage of mind and heart," as Gülen puts it—individuals of "thought, action, and inspiration"? Do the students who emerge from these schools go on to become "valiant young representatives of national thought and feeling"? Do they give evidence of the "profundity of ideas, clarity of thought, depth of feeling, cultural appreciation, and spiritual values," the instilling of which Gülen sees as the primary goals of education? The ongoing answers to such questions—which only the graduates themselves and those who know and work with such graduates can give—will form the ultimate criteria of evaluation by which the success of Gülen's educational philosophy can be judged.

5

Following in the Footsteps of Fethullah Gülen

Three Women Teachers Tell Their Stories

ELISABETH ÖZDALGA

THE NEO-NURCU FETHULLAH GÜLEN community is one of the most influential revivalist Islamic groups in modern Turkey. Fethullah Gülen started out as a preacher (*vaiz*) in Izmir in the late 1960s, but it was not until the early 1980s that his community developed into a nationwide movement. Owing to its loose structure, there are no reliable figures as to the numbers of supporters[1] of this community, but its influence may be measured in the number of schools set up under the inspiration of Fethullah Gülen's ideas. Today, approximately three hundred such schools exist, half of them in Turkey, half in other countries (mainly in Central Asia). The establishment of new schools peaked in number during the first years of the 1990s.[2]

Fethullah Gülen's ethic can be summarized in a few key directives or recommendations, such as remaining awake to your image of death and to your existential broods; doing good deeds (*hizmet*); and practicing humility, sacrifice, and self-criticism. His philosophy, based on a combination of activism and pietism, is readily accessible in his own books and in the vast number of widely distributed videotapes. Gülen's writings and the physical expression of his activism (building schools and establishing economic enterprises) have also been the subject of several books and articles.[3]

1. To use the term *member* would wrongly imply a kind of formal organization, which does not exist.

2. For further information about the distribution of schools and other activities in Turkey, see Yavuz 1996b, and in Central Asia, see Balcı 2002.

3. See, for example, Armağan and Ünal 1999, 2001; Can 1996; M. Erdoğan 1999; Özdalga 2000; Şen 2001; Soydan 1999; Yavuz 1999b.

A less-explored aspect of this movement, however, is what it is like to live under the spell of Fethullah Gülen. How is his philosophy transformed into principles of guidance for daily life? How is his activist pietism reflected in the life of those who have chosen to follow in his footsteps?

The objective of this chapter is to shed light on these questions. For that purpose, I carried out in-depth interviews with women teachers in two major urban centers in Turkey during the early spring of 2001.

Fieldwork Experiences

The Gülen community is a rather closed community. This characteristic may seem paradoxical, given the objectives of the movement to spread the message of Allah's universal, transconfessional love. Notwithstanding that message, it is very difficult for an outsider to approach this movement. An important—and obvious—reason behind this reserve is the fear of persecution of the sort that already has affected the Gülen *cemaat* (community), especially after the beginning of 1997, when the Turkish military started to impose stronger control of Islamists.[4] Since then, the schools and economic enterprises supported by Gülen's movement have been under increasingly strict control.

Control and intimidation from the secularist establishment, however, are not the only reasons for the reticence characteristic of this movement. Such reticence also is embedded deeply in Gülen's own worldview. Humility and self-awareness—in the sense of being aware of one's deficiencies and shortcomings—are basic to his teachings. One is supposed to work God's will in silence. *Temsil,* which means being a good example through one's deeds, therefore is preferred to *tebliğ,* which means open declaration or persuasion through preaching or both.

Another obstacle relates to sex. The Gülen *cemaat* is quite conservative on the relationships between the sexes and tries to keep up an old tradition of segregation between men and women. Until a new law was instituted in 2000 enforcing mixed education, the Gülen schools were separated by sex. An overwhelming majority of the schools were boys' schools, with only a small number of girls' schools. As a result of these practices, it was rather difficult for a woman researcher to establish anything other than formal contacts with teachers and other staff at these schools.

To be a participant in organized visits to the so-called Gülen schools both

4. The notorious *"28 Şubat kararları,"* or decisions of 28 February 1997, led to the government of the Islamist Necmettin Erbakan being forced from power a few months later.

within and outside Turkey is not difficult. I have taken part in several such tours in Turkey as well as in Turkmenistan and Uzbekistan. However, when trying to establish those closer contacts needed for further and deeper information about what it is like on a personal level to be part of this community, I was met with a friendly face but most often with firm resistance. To minimize the distance that arose from my being a woman, I decided to concentrate this part of my research on women teachers. The result is presented here in the form of three life stories of women who are active as teachers in Gülen schools in two large cities in Turkey.

Methodology

The interviews were conducted in Turkish in the interviewees' respective schools, lasted one and one-half to two hours each, and were structured rather loosely. My main objective was to obtain the interviewees' life stories, including childhood, adolescence, schooling, university education, professional life, and marriage. Within this life-story, I especially wanted the interviewees to elaborate on certain areas of daily life, such as their religious experience, communal relationships (especially within the Gülen community), professional commitments, intellectual achievements, and concerns about private (family) life. Depending on which of these areas the particular individual emphasized, a cluster of values and ideas crystallized for each of them. In this way, three individual portraits emerged, with similar and different characteristics. I titled each story according to what I found to be its most striking feature. I have changed the interviewees' names, the school names, and some locations to protect the participants's identities.

Zeynep: Yearning to Become a Nameless Hero

Zeynep works in Zafer Lisesi in Istanbul. This school is situated in one of the many distant suburbs and is approximately one hour's drive from the city center. This suburb is a lower-middle-class neighborhood that is poorly organized and that lacks integration and a settled urban structure. You get the feeling of being in a new settlement, even though people have been living there for several decades. En route there, you realize how huge the hardly more than nominally unified urban conglomerate Istanbul in fact is.

This lyceum used to be a boys' school, but from the fall of 2000 Turkish law has imposed coeducation, as already mentioned.[5] As a result of this decree, at the time of this research only around thirty girls were at the school, all in the first year. The total student body was around 450 students.

The staff includes only two women teachers.[6] One of them is Zeynep. They have at their disposal a rather large teachers' staff room, where they receive the girl students during the school breaks. It is likely that the girls also perform their daily prayers in this room.

The room gives the impression of being very big and very empty because its furnishings are meager—only two desks and a few chairs—and the acoustics are so poor that even the slightest sound rings out piercingly.

Zeynep is dressed in a white uniform (long jacket) and has a very neat hairstyle, which I learn later during the interview is a wig. Because the authorities have become increasingly rigid in outlawing head scarves over the past few years, and because Fethullah Gülen's community is very anxious to do nothing illegal, all women working in these schools either uncover their heads or wear a wig.[7]

She is open and outspoken and is therefore easy to interview. She is confident and, as her interview reveals, is a very conscious and devoted follower of Fethullah Gülen. Her husband works for a computer company set up by the same religious community and situated in another quarter of the city.

Zeynep's working-class family had immigrated to Germany before she was born. Although her family continued to live there after she was born, she spent her first four years in school in Turkey, living with her paternal grandmother. When she was about eleven, her parents took her to Germany, where she continued to study until she reached the final class of middle school (the eighth year of education). At that point, she insisted on being sent back to Turkey. She did not feel comfortable as a foreigner, and, as she notes in the interview, her family is very nationalistic. Back in Turkey, she finished high school in a public vocational school (Yalova Lisesi) for girls in her family's hometown, Balıkesir. She wanted to attend a "normal" lyceum, but her parents insisted on sending her to vocational school. This decision placed her at a disadvantage when she sat for the university entrance examinations, but, as she described it, she struggled hard

5. The empirical study on which this study is based was carried out during the early spring of 2001.

6. I use present tense in describing the contents of the interviews in order to create a greater sense of immediacy.

7. For a later visit, Zeynep was wearing tight head gear in the form of a *tülbent* (she had probably just performed her *namaz*). On that occasion, it was quite embarrassing for me when I realized that I had not recognized her in this different gear.

to succeed even in the face of the lack of support from her family. Thanks to her own purposefulness and persistence, she managed to get into the university, more specifically the Department of Turkish Literature at Ankara University.

Zeynep was born in 1971, which means that she was admitted to the university at the very end of the 1980s. This was a time of relative economic prosperity and political stability in Turkey. It was also significantly a period of comparative lenience toward Islamist groups. Therefore, the fact that Zeynep started to wear a veil during her second year at university did not create a great problem for her in the sense that she had to quit or delay her education. During her years at Ankara University, she lived in a private flat with friends—that is, neither with her family (they were in Germany) nor in a dormitory.

Zeynep met her future husband when she was in her fourth (last) year of university, and they were married when her university education came to an end. She relates in her story how she did not marry for love, but because she and her husband shared a certain religious outlook. Thus, she acted out of her religious convictions in choosing her future husband.

I chose my husband because he had a certain religious outlook. I did not marry him because I had fallen in love with him. He represented my ideals, and, based on that, I married for convenience.

Zeynep is the one person among the interviewees in this study who speaks most openly about her strong commitment to Fethullah Gülen. She came across Gülen and his ideas when she just started at the university. This discovery triggered more serious inquiries and led to extensive studies of certain religious sources. Soon thereafter, she started to dress the Islamic way (that is, according to *tesettür*).

After getting married, Zeynep chose on her own initiative (she especially stresses the role of her own free will) to stay at home as housewife for three years. Her reason for doing so was that it would give her a kind of spiritual breathing space.

I wanted to learn more about religion. Until then I never had a chance to do so because I never had any formal religious education.

During this period, she also had her one and only child, a girl. Her role as housewife came to an end when an attractive work opportunity opened up following the establishment of girls' schools within the Gülen community. She apparently had been reluctant to work among people who would not respect her Islamic identity. Because this identity entailed covering her head, she preferred to work in a milieu where women's and men's spheres truly were separated. This separation could be maintained easily within the work environment of a girls' school.

Discourse Based on Peace, Love, and Humility

Zeynep articulates her "philosophy" (her expression) mainly in relation to two fields of social action: the communal and the religious. In the communal field, she is concerned about the quality of relationships within the religious community of which she is a part, but also within society at large. In the religious field, her outlook includes, on the one hand, a certain code of ethics and piety, and, on the other, ideas about important elements of worship. It is also possible to discern a third field, the intellectual, even if it does not play a very prominent role in my interview with her.

Community Relationships: National Identity

Because Zeynep lived in Germany for some years, she knew what it was like to be perceived negatively.

There, I experienced what it was like to be a second-rate citizen.

[*Was that related to religion?*]

No, religion was no problem there. On the contrary, I had the chance to learn something about their religion, which was a good thing.

[*How about your German?*]

I speak German well. No, you see, Turks are second-class citizens there. In addition to that, the social status of my family was not that good. That was the reason.

[*Did you feel this discrimination especially in school?*]

Yes, in school, but also outside school.

[*How about friends? Did you make any German friends?*]

There were not that many Turks where we were living. Yes, I had German friends, and I did not experience any problem in entering into a dialogue with them. No, the problem I had was more related to my inner self. I had started to question the way I was living. Ever since I was small, I had said to myself that if I ever go to Germany, I would not go there as a worker. If I go there, it has to be in order to learn something and acquire a profession. A desire had been born in me to achieve better aims in life. This brought me back to Turkey.

Her negative experiences as a young girl in Germany had certain effects on her opinions.

I am strongly against any kind of human discrimination. Because I lived through these degrading experiences, I also started to love my own country in a different way. It made me critical of all kinds of illegal oppositional activities, such as street demonstrations and the like. I love my own country, so the kind of religious outlook I was to choose had to be such that it did not cause my country any harm.

Peaceful Relationships

The best way to protect the country's interests is through peaceful relationships. It is at this point in Zeynep's story that Gülen comes into the picture. She
was about eighteen or nineteen years old when she was affected by his message
and appearance. She also relates how at this time she constantly was asking herself about both her aim in life and her social relationships.

*No, political commitment was out of the question. At this time, I looked into many differ-
ent groups, but I did not like any of them or their political preferences. But then one day I came
to listen to one of Fethullah Gülen's Friday sermons [vaaz], and there he said something like
. . . yes, there he said that he looked upon the whole of humanity with the same eyes. Allah is
the creator of all human beings, irrespective of religion and language. He also talked about
having equal respect for all believers. You know, just as in Christianity, within Islam there are
also a large number of different groups and sects that are fighting each other. And here he said
that we should learn to pay equal respect to all of them. . . . These ideas went right to my heart.
After that, I started to read his books and listen to his videocassettes regularly.*

*It may be that people have good intentions with their actions, even if they take to the streets.
Groups with opposite ideas from yours may very well have good intentions. But I believe that as
Muslims we have to avoid conflict and chaos. As good Muslims, we have to give something, but
when doing so we have to make sure that it does not do any harm to society.*

Zeynep believes that young activists should refrain from open street demonstrations because the uneducated masses may not understand their real objectives and misinterpret such actions as being political. Religion, in contrast, is the
real source of their commitment and comes closer to philosophy than to politics.

*We were not born to fight with each other. Until the end of my life, I will spread the mes-
sage of peace.*

Conflict Avoidance

In Zeynep, the wish to play a peaceful role in society seems to have developed into an exaggerated, almost phobic anxiety to avoid any kind of conflict.

*I have decided that wherever I meet people who do not share my ideas, I will refrain from
criticizing them.*

*For example, at the time when I was sharing a flat with my friends from the university, we
used to read books together. Now if it so happened that we came across a passage related to veiling, and there were friends who did not veil in the group, then we would omit that part in our
reading. In particular, there were two friends in the group who did not wear a head scarf: one
was studying law, the other went to a school of education. We were of the opinion that veiling*

was an issue that should be left to everyone's individual discretion. Imagine then reading a text that decreed veiling! Such a thing might easily have hurt these two friends' feelings. So the best thing was to skip over that part.

The aim behind this urge to avoid criticism and conflict is that a believer should refrain from hurting other human beings and thus indirectly hurt Allah. Human beings owe their value to the fact that they are the greatest miracle, the highest creation of God.

Humanism, Universalism, and Equality

Zeynep believes in human equality. She bases this belief on the concept of universalism—that equality is transcultural or transconfessional. Closely inter-woven with this belief is a profound humanism. Human beings represent the crown of the creation.

Every act carried out for the good of human beings is sacred. Love must be universal, and human beings have to see it as their mission to work for the good of humanity.

The urge for equality also is seen in the relationships within the Gülen *cemaat.* There is no person in the position of sheikh in the community, but everybody has the right and the authority to speak and take part in religious conversations (*sohbet*). With regard to studies of religious texts, the individual makes her or his own choice. Where people choose to study some texts together, they decide among themselves what to read, how much, and so on. Every person is therefore his or her own master.

No, no one among us would play the role of leader or hoca. *But let's say that I have been part of this movement for twelve years, and there is another friend who has been here for only three years; well, then it is natural that I would start the conversation. But it does not have to be like that. Let's say that we have chosen the topic "wastefulness." It does not necessarily have to be the elder, but may well be the other, less experienced friend who introduces the topic.*

We decide among ourselves how many pages to read before the next meeting. There is no rule that we have to follow, but we set an objective together in order to control each other. Let's say I have a very good and close friend. Together with her, I may decide on a one-month program. But this is not like having a program set by a hoca, *sitting as a superior to us. This is also what is written in the* Risale-i Nur [by Said Nursi]—*namely, that our time is not a time for* tarikats,[8] *but for communities: that is to say, a time for simply getting together.*

[But do not people come together also within tarikats?]

No, when saying that our time is not a time for tarikats, *he* [Said Nursi] *did not mean to*

---

8. Sufi lodges, often built on an authoritarian relationship between *mürşit* (master or sheikh) and *mürit* (disciple).

criticize Sufism [tasavvuf düşüncesi—Islamic mysticism]. *As you know, during late Ottoman times the word* tarikat *acquired a very negative and degraded connotation. It was those kinds of corrupted groups that the master* [üstad] *was criticizing. His aim was to oppose the exploitation* [of uneducated people's ignorance]. *As a matter of fact, even today one has to guard against such sullied groups.*

Good Manners

When asked about the difference between Nursi and Gülen, Zeynep answers: *Said Nursi sermonizes about belief* [iman], *about fate, and about the thoughts and objectives of Allah, whereas Fethullah Gülen teaches more about Islamic history, about the life of the Prophet, about how a practicing Muslim should live in daily life.*

Zeynep also stresses the importance of living a decent life by avoiding smoking and drinking and by being faithful to and responsible toward your family. She derives great happiness from teaching these values to her students and to other young people.

Religion: Ethics and Piety

Zeynep's religious commitment is closely related to the experience of individual responsibility. Even though the *cemaat* means much to her, her religious belief does not come from without, but from within. Religious commitment is an expression of decisions made individually and independently, but they are anchored firmly in a social context.

Love and Responsibility

Love toward everybody, toward every human being, is central to Zeynep's message. This is a universal value. It is love, irrespective of religion, language, or social status. Love also brings with it responsibility toward others.

What we lack is a universally extended concept of love. The whole of humanity should embrace this idea and pledge itself to it. You find it in the West. . . . Yes, there is a real need for such an idea in today's world. In order to spread this idea, one should go out to other parts of the world.

[So that other people also become Muslims, you mean?]

Well, I do not want to deny that we would like to see other people becoming Muslims, that is true, but the main objective is not to convert others to Islam, but to carry the message of peace and dialogue further. No, I do not want to be misunderstood on this point: when our friends go to other parts of the world as teachers, the main objective is really not to spread our religion.

When they go to places like Russia, for example, the circumstances may be such that it is not even appropriate for them to carry on with their own prayers [implicitly, much less to teach other people these prayers]. *They even have to sacrifice this part of their own lives when they go to such places.*

This is also the desire of Hocaefendi [Gülen], that we should spread the message of love to other people.

The fact that universal love plays such an important role in Zeynep's worldview sits well with her admiration of the master of Sufism in Turkey, Mevlana.

Mevlana is like a great, big heart. It is big enough to embrace the whole world. As a matter of fact, I was more affected by Mevlana than by Said Nursi. That is because of the universal message found in Mevlana's poetry. So there has always been a place for Mevlana in my life. Hocaefendi comes after Mevlana for me. And then, after becoming acquainted with Hocaefendi's books, I also developed an interest in Said Nursi's writings.

Love for other human beings gives rise to endless responsibilities. Within the concrete school context, these responsibilities include dealing with the smallest details of students' problems.

To deal with other human beings outweighs everything. It is our conviction that if it is a question of another human being, to help him or her take just a tiny little step forward is enough. Imagine that you invest five years of energy in the education of one single student. If this helps him or her to improve ever so little, at the end of the day this small improvement is still worth the effort.

The *hizmet* owing to other human beings is endless. This is the consequence of the concept of love espoused and practiced by Zeynep and those like her.

Sacrifice

Love, thus understood, also means considerable, even endless sacrifice. This concept of sacrifice is reflected in Zeynep's way of evaluating *zekat* (alms giving), one of the five pillars of Islam. There is no rule as to how much to give from your salary. This decision is left to the individual's conscience.

In our community there is no such thing [that a fixed amount should be paid]. *If I give 50 million* [out of a salary of 350 million lira], *that is my own decision. It could be 100 million or nothing. I have friends who do not give anything. But we believe in Allah's justice. He does not leave anybody totally deprived. Let's say that I am very good at writing poetry. Then somebody else may be very good at embroidery. If sharing with others is important for me, other characteristics may be important for someone else.*

Humility

With regard to how life changes when one becomes part[9] of the Gülen *cemaat,* Zeynep says:

First of all, you become a slave [kul], *that is, you start to criticize yourself.*

[*Is self-criticism a very important dimension?*]

Yes, of course: reserve, humility, getting away from being egocentric. This is at the very foundation of religion, and Hocaefendi represents a very good example for us in this respect. A human being who takes these beliefs seriously becomes like an angel.

The gentleness I have encountered in this community has made me gentle also.

Religion as Worship

Prayer means a great deal to Zeynep. In discussing which one of the five pillars is the most important one, she says:

Namaz [prayer] *is very important. In our religion,* namaz *is more important than anything else.*

[*Do you pray five times a day?*]

Yes, of course, without exception. Often I pray more than five times a day. There are prayers that you take on personally, like praying at night. I try to say these prayers, too.

To study and teach science is also a form of worship, according to Zeynep.

Science is also a kind of worship.

[*What do you mean by that? Do you mean that studying Said-i Nursi's texts related to science is like worship?*]

No. Of course, reading his books is something that nourishes our worship. But I mean that to study physics or chemistry, to read about atoms and their particles, that is also a kind of worship. To study biology, for example, is to learn how intricate and complicated is the construction of the human body. To learn this is also to get an idea about the greatness of Allah. Here heart and reason work together in order to praise Allah.

Consciousness (the Intellectual Field)

Zeynep, like the other women interviewed, often stresses that she is a conscious believer, whereas her mother and father or other relatives of the older generation believe out of habit or tradition.

---

9. *Part,* not *member.* Zeynep rejects the latter concept: "The term *member* is not the correct expression."

[*What does being part of this community express for you?*]

It means that you realize that your life has to be built around one all-embracing philosophy. It should be a philosophy that is not only valid for me or for Turks or for Arabs or for Muslims, but for all. Religion, or the choice of religion [a specific confession], *comes after that. This philosophy should permeate our whole existence.*

This means that she sees religion as a rational or value-rational (Max Weber's term) choice. An inquiring person is supposed to study many different religions and then decide which one is more true or logical. This line of reasoning is very common among those Islamists I have met in Turkey; in other words, at the beginning of their religious experience they explore different religions, and only after that do they choose Islam. Thus, their choice stands out as a rational, conscious choice. This mode of reasoning reflects the crucial importance of individual responsibility and autonomy in the religious experience, according to the Gülen philosophy.

To Become a Nameless Hero

Idealism and heroic activism is an important ingredient in Zeynep's discourse.

At the end of a long day at school, it sometimes happens that I have to call my husband to tell him that one of the students is having a problem with her course work, and I have to stay in school to help her. This means perhaps two or three hours of overtime because I take the student back and forth between school and her home. I do all this because I do it in the name or Allah or for the sake of Allah. I see this as a kind of worship.

[*Do you think that actions like yours based on strong belief may have a positive effect on history?*]

Zeynep prefers to answer by expressing an ideal:

Do you mean me personally, as Zeynep? Well, rather than playing an important role in history and becoming a name in the history books, I would like to have a seat with Allah in heaven. That is to say, I would rather become what they call a nameless hero. That is my objective, even though, to be honest, I do not feel I have fully reached that stage yet. But that is what I desire, to reach that [level of self-denial] *and then die.*

Ayşe: Choosing Teaching—the Profession of the Prophet

Ayşe works in Edirne Lisesi. She is only twenty-two years old and is in her first year as a practicing teacher. She teaches hygiene, acts as counselor for the newly enrolled girl students, and is slated to teach biology when her class (first-year lyceum students) starts to take that course. Edirne Lisesi (just like Zafer Lisesi, where Zeynep teaches) used to be a boys' school, but because of the new governmental decree of fall 2000 that all schools must be coeducational, it now includes a small group (around thirty) of first-year girl students.

Ayşe comes from a lower-middle-class family. Both her mother and father have only the obligatory five years of elementary schooling. Her parents were born in Bolu, the mountainous area situated between Ankara and Istanbul, but came to Istanbul with their respective families in the early 1960s. Ayşe is the second of five siblings (two boys, three girls).

Ayşe's family lives in Kasımpaşa, a central part of Istanbul, not too far from Taksim Square. She went to a middle school in that neighborhood, but as a high school student studied in a public lyceum for girls in another part of the city. She has her university degree from a community college in a midsize Anatolian town.

Profession

In speaking about the reason for her choice of profession, Ayşe answers:

To be a teacher means that you instruct and educate others—that you have a chance to share with others what you have learned. These are perhaps trivial [self-evident] *things, but that's it. As for biology, well, the reason for that is the subject itself, which I find quite intriguing. From the micro- to the macrolevel of the universe, everything is so interrelated. Everything is held together in a fantastic system. Biology is based on a mixture of curiosity and discovery. It is open to new discoveries all the time, and you constantly learn new things. The fact that everything is so interrelated appealed to me. In addition to that, I liked it because it is a science about living things with offshoots into our daily life as well. In this respect, it is not like mathematics, for example, or like physics. I really liked it.*

Regarding whether she would have wanted to enter the medical faculty and thereby study for a more prestigious profession if her university entrance grades had been good enough, Ayşe admits that medicine had always been her dream, but that she changed her mind later on. According to her, an influential figure in her choice of biology was her lyceum teacher in that subject.

Teachers often influence their students' choice of profession, and I liked my biology teacher very much. She was a good instructor and made all of us like biology very much.

[*What was so special about her?*]

Well, apart from being very engaging, she was also our class teacher, so we had a very close relationship. And the way she instructed us never bored us. You may think that a subject like biology is solely based on rote learning, but as a matter of fact much reasoning and logic go into this subject. If you approach it with the purpose of committing everything to memory, then it becomes very boring. But when you approach it from the point of view of its own systematic relationships, then it really appeals to your imagination.

Considering that the question of evolutionary theory is emphasized in biology, which is a controversial issue among many Islamists, I ask Ayşe if she has experienced any difficulty with her teachers in this respect. She states that she has encountered two different types of instructors: her lyceum teacher was an evolutionist who encouraged her students to read Darwin's books; her university instructor in biology, on the other hand, was a creationist, critical of evolutionary Darwinism. Neither of them, however, tried to impose their views on their students. She feels that the students were sincerely presented with both perspectives and allowed to evaluate this controversial issue for themselves. Even though each teacher's personal view was clear to the students, Ayşe did not experience any pressure in this or that direction. She declares that as a teacher she will present both views and leave the decision to the students themselves. By referring positively to Western scientists' recent criticisms of evolutionary theory, she demonstrates clearly a preference for the creationist view (to be sure, she offers her special, Islamist interpretation of this critique), but she is by no means fanatical about it.

Veiling

Ayşe's biology teacher from the lyceum had yet another important influence, this time negative, on a significant decision Ayşe had to make in her life—namely, whether to veil.

I started to veil when I was in the third grade in the lyceum. In doing so, I was influenced by a group of friends in my class who were already veiling. Our biology teacher, the one who was in favor of evolutionary theory, used to treat those students really badly. My friends usually put their head scarves on in the women's restroom before leaving school. She was very angry with them because of this and reacted very harshly. So even though she was my favorite teacher, I did not like it that she tried to frighten my friends in this way. After all, they covered because of their beliefs and not as an act of opposition. What else could have been possible? At one point, I even suggested taking her to see The Danish Bride.

Ayşe here speaks of a film that influenced her greatly. A young Danish girl falls in love with a young Turkish man living in Denmark, and in order to marry him she converts to Islam. But after a while she starts to question her decision, saying to herself that if she has become a Muslim, she should also take her new religion seriously. She studies Islam and starts veiling, which causes her difficulties with her Turkish husband and his family.

I saw this film on TV—now I don't remember which channel—and it was just that kind of persecution our teacher was engaging in. She went as far as to threaten to beat the students.

She did not do it, but she threatened to do so, and that roused my feelings. So, mainly to be obstinate, I also started veiling.

[*You wanted to support your friends?*]

Yes, it was out of solidarity with them. It was not such a conscious [religious] *decision, after all. It was rather because that film had affected me a great deal. After I started to cover, I looked into the reasons for doing so. That was how I became more conscious about the reasons behind veiling.*

Religious Experience

Ayşe's interest in religion did not start at that point. She already had started to recite regular prayers during her first year of high school. The person who initiated her into these practices was her paternal grandmother, who was living with the family.

We were living as an extended family. My grandmother was living with us, so I was affected by her and started to pray regularly. But I was just saying my prayers. It was not until later that I started to veil.

[*How many times a day did you pray? Once or twice?*]

No, I prayed five times a day. Sabah, yatsı, akşam, öğlen, ikindi. *I liked to do it.*

[*But what about the hours when you were in school?*]

Well, I said my prayer in the morning; the noon prayer I would miss, but I performed that as kaza [compensation] *after school. The other prayers took place after I had come back from school anyway.*

[*How about your parents?*]

They are very kind people, they really are, but they do not take their religious obligations that seriously. So it was my grandmother who taught us religion, what was good about it and why we should recite our prayers. It sounds perhaps childish, but I started to pray during my years at the lyceum in order to ask for good results in school. You know, you pray to Allah in order to ask for His help in getting better grades at school. That is how I started my religious practices.

There was a group in Ayşe's class with whom she could share these experiences. Her acquaintance with Gülen and his writings came later, but exactly when is difficult to tell from the interview. She relates, however, that before she started to read his books, she had read other things—for example, a book by Turan Dursun, which seems to have had a strong effect on her.

Before reading Hocaefendi's book, I had come across books by Turan Dursun, but these books terrified me. I was terribly terrified.[10]

10. Turan Dursun was a former imam who became a journalist extremely critical of Islam, which he came to interpret as nothing but a form of reactionary superstition. He was killed in Sep-

[*Why were you so frightened?*]

He told everything as if it was all about hobgoblins. It was like if you do not perform your prayers, you will be burning in hell. He was talking about hell all the time. I was quite young at that time, and I said to myself: "No, I do not want these things." So I burned his book, and then I did not read anything for many years to come.[11]

[*You burned the book!*]

Yes, indeed, I did.

[*How did you do that?*]

I burned it in the iron stove at home. No, that kind of book was nothing for me.

[*Were you on your own when you burned the book?*]

Yes, I was alone. I guess I was in the second grade in the lyceum at that time. I was so scared. He mentioned dragons. And he also said that if you do not recite your prayers in an accepted, proper way, you would burn in hell. Really, it was so frightening. So after this experience, reading books by Hocaefendi was comforting and soothing. Later on I learned that Turan Dursun's ideas were not that sound anyway.

Gülen comes into Ayşe's story as a rescuer from these frightening ideas about religion.

What was so good about Fethullah Gülen's books was that he did not convey a harsh message. It is a question of character, perhaps: I cannot stand too much of that kind of atrocious stuff [like Dursun's work].

[*Why?*]

It is perhaps because it hurts my feelings [gurur], *or for some other reason. Well, I do not know really; anyway, it was offensive. But Fethullah Gülen's books appealed to me a great deal.*

At first, I had difficulty in reading his books. His language was difficult and heavy, with a lot of Persian and Arabic words. But as I read, I started to understand better and better. He was conveying a message that one should try to be on good terms with everybody. He was men-

---

tember 1990, and after that sensational event his books sold in tens of thousands. In a book from 1971, he criticizes the Nurcu movement in very harsh terms and indicates that Said Nursi's *Risale-i Nur* is nothing but "rubbish." He systematically compares Nursi's interpretations of the Qur'an with the Qur'anic texts themselves and notes that Nursi distorts the texts beyond recognition (see Dursun 1996). Dursun's crushing critique of Nursi may explain Ayşe's strong aversion to him; otherwise, his interpretation of the Qur'an in relation to prayer does not seem to be as exaggeratedly austere or horrific as Ayşe herself suggests (see Dursun 1998).

11. Ayşe's way of relating to time is rather confusing. The period during which she became a practicing Muslim and started to believe in Gülen's ideas coincides with her three years at the lyceum. What probably took some months, perhaps at most a year, is related as taking several years.

tioning love and indulgence. I have to admit that in the beginning I did not understand very much of what he was writing because his message was so different. This was also during my early adolescence, when I was easily affected by all kinds of things taking place around me.

Apart from the peaceful message conveyed by Gülen, Ayşe also points to other ideas that appealed to her.

He was always mentioning beautiful and pleasant things. And then he also taught that to tell what you know to others is also a good deed [sevap]. *He emphasized that one should choose the middle road, neither totally withdrawing from action and responsibility nor doing things to extremes. The best thing, he would say, is to worship on a low but continual level.*

When I started to read his books, I did not know about any cemaat *connected to his person. I did not know about his videocassettes at that time, for example. I was very young then, and I think that his community was not that well known at that time.*[12] *Not like now, in any case.*

It was not until later that I started to watch his videocassettes. At first, I did not understand why he was weeping.

[*Perhaps you found his weeping repugnant?*]

No, not repugnant, because I found it sincere, and there was nothing that seemed simulated in it, but I simply could not comprehend it. No, it was not fake, but where did all this suffering he exposed come from? But then, by listening over and over again, I started to understand his message better. How is it possible, he wanted to say, for us Muslims [that is, believing Muslims] *to sit back, even to sleep, when the Islamic world looks like it does and people are not aware of their true Muslim character? We have to tell of Allah to all those who have not yet achieved insight into their real purpose in life.*

After that, after I had understood why he was weeping, I started to weep myself as well. Really moving.

[*Do you still weep when you watch his videocassettes?*]

Yes, I do, and as recently as yesterday I watched one, and I wept again.

Ayşe complains about all the negative propaganda in the press about Hocaefendi and adds:

He really is not like that. I like him very much, and he has assisted me in increasing my love of religion. Especially after my having read Turan Dursun's book, Hocaefendi showed me the truth, the sensible face of religion. This was how I also learned about the life of the Prophet and the purpose of our life on earth. I was thinking a lot about questions having to do with the real objective of life. At night, I would ponder about who I am, who my parents are, what is the reason behind Allah's sending us into this world, and so on.

12. This was, according to Ayşe, around 1993–94. Obviously, she was too young to follow the debates in the press at that time. Gülen has been a hot topic in the media since the beginning of the 1990s.

Conquered Discourses Versus Life Projects (Zeynep and Ayşe)

In the interview with Zeynep, the communal, the religious, and the intellectual fields of discourse (with special stress on the first two) are particularly emphasized and consciously defended. Zeynep is twenty-nine years old and already has several years of *cemaat* and professional experience behind her. She has already formed an identity consisting of a certain combination of fields of discourse. She embodies a form of life that she is eager to safeguard.

Ayşe is different, however. She is at the very beginning of her professional career, and her story is not so much about defending certain already defined discourses as it is suggestive of certain life projects. Her story reveals three such projects for the future—namely, becoming a teacher, mastering religion, and becoming a modern individual.

Each of these projects contains in itself different combinations of preferred courses of action and therefore may be considered a prototype for more structured discourses in the future.

The Teaching Profession

Science has almost religious attributes in Ayşe's worldview. She considers teaching science a special mission. Because science steadily develops, it also requires constant renewal on the part of science instructors.

On the question of how important the teaching profession is in relation to other professions, Ayşe says:

All professions are important, but teaching is the profession of the Prophet [Peygamber mesleği]. *That is what I have learned. The duty of prophets is to teach. It is true that people who have other professions, such as trades and the like, also can read books and develop themselves and then teach what they have learned to others. But to do so they divide their attention, and they cannot read and teach all the time. For a teacher, it is different, however, because all his or her working hours are dedicated to teaching.*

[What is more important, to teach Fethullah Gülen's ideas or to teach a science course?]

This is what we have learned [from Gülen], *and it is a really great thing: for a Muslim, studying or learning science is equivalent to worship. The same is true of teaching science.*

[Especially science?]

Yes, sciences such as physics, biology, chemistry, and mathematics—that is, the positive sciences. To teach these subjects is equivalent to worship. And that is also the reason we have to teach these courses very carefully: because science is essential.

Ayşe praises the teaching profession so emphatically because: it is the profession ascribed to the Prophet Muhammed himself; it means learning and conveying knowledge; the knowledge at hand is science oriented and thus has a sacred dimension; and it involves conveying sacred knowledge to others, which means doing good deeds. The teaching profession, thus conceptualized, is based on a combination of intellectual considerations (learning and teaching) and religious considerations (the ethics of giving). Gülen and his followers emphasize this entangled relationship between the religious and the intellectual with regard to the project of becoming an active believer.

Becoming an Active Believer

For Ayşe, reading and studying—that is, achieving knowledge—became a very important part of her religious venture. Thus, the intellectual dimension overshadowed other aspects of her becoming a practicing Muslim.

She tells of the diversity in the kinds of books she read during her years at the lyceum:

We were around forty in our class at the lyceum. All kinds of tastes and inclinations were represented and different groups developed. There were those who adored Heavy Metal, and there were those who, thanks to their parents' political inclinations, were communists. We also formed a group like that. I think we came to influence each other in a positive way. Yes, we competed among ourselves over how much we were able to read. The discussion would go like this: "I have read these and these books, which ones have you read?" and that kind of thing. We tried to sleep less in order to have more time left for reading. We read an enormous number of books. As a matter of fact, we read seventy books in five months.

[Did you say seventy books in five months?]

Yes, we completed with each other like that. We also were doing well at school. The school we went to was demanding. Those who did not work hard enough were not able to pass. Now it is not considered to be such a good school anymore. It changed later on.

[Did you do all this reading together?]

No, no, but we would try to sleep less in order to have more time for reading. We would sleep for maybe five or six hours.

Obviously, Gülen influenced Ayşe and her friends about the importance of reading extensively.

Hocaefendi always has said: "Read a lot. If your glass gets filled up, you always can empty it out."

[What do you mean?]

Well, an empty glass does not contain anything to be given to others. But as you learn more and fill up your glass, you also will have something to give others. The teaching profession is exactly like that. You have to renew yourself all the time in order to have something to give to the students. And in order to have something to give to the students, you have to learn and know a lot of things. The important thing is to proclaim the importance of science.

Ayşe means that children at the age of fourteen or fifteen are full of energy. Other students in her class spent their energy on futile, sometimes destructive activities and therefore brought many problems upon themselves.

So, I think that for ourselves [her group of six or so friends] *it was very good that we channeled our energy into reading and not into other things like being obstinate and aggressive with our families.*

I found Ayşe's testimony that she and her friends had read seventy books in five months quite astonishing, so I returned to that subject.

[What kind of books did you read? Was Said Nursi's Risale-i Nur *among these books?]*
Yes, we read them a lot.
[But that is really a lot of reading! Thirteen volumes!]
Yes, it is a series of books [külliyat]. *I read through them all.*
[But how is that possible?]
We used to read maybe sixty pages a day. We competed with each other. Still, we did not ignore our schoolwork. And, as I said before, we tried to sleep less. And our mothers did not ask us to do very much housework. Concerning television, we did not spend any time on that: we did not watch the news programs because we did not understand very much about politics, and we were too old for the animated films.

Ayşe admits that reading the *Risale-i Nur* was very difficult in the beginning.

Yes, his language is very dense. But instead of approaching the text sentence by sentence, I started to read it paragraph by paragraph.

[Did anyone tell you to read his books that way?]
No, I discovered that method by myself. So I started to read his texts paragraph by paragraph and tried to understand the meaning of the paragraph as a whole. In the beginning, I did not understand very much, but after reading it once, twice, three times, I started to be able to interpret the text. It is not enough to read it only once. You deepen your comprehension as you read. The more you read, the more you come to understand. And you also see different things in the text each time you read it. The second time is not like the first, the third time you understand something else, the fourth time again something different, and so it goes. But you have to read his work continuously. If you do not do that, your mind becomes dull. Let's say you have not read anything from his books for three months, then when you start reading again, you no longer will understand what you were able to comprehend three months ago.

[What is so fascinating about his work?]
At the point of belief [iman], *this text addresses both my reason* [akıl] *and my heart* [kalp].

As if underlining the idea that her venture is intellectual as well as religious, Ayşe brings up an old dream of hers:

We [students] spent all our money on books, and our greatest dream was to be able to set up a library, a great big library.

[Did you get that idea from Hocaefendi?]

No, it was our own idea.

Becoming a Modern Individual

Ayşe obviously deepens her religious commitment as part of a project of greater enlightenment. Her devotion to science and her ideal of becoming a widely read person are closely intertwined with her religious outlook and bear witness to this project. A few other details from the interview emphasize her modern, reflexive mind: her predilection for psychology, her therapeutic approach to problems encountered in her role as counselor, and her way of looking at herself from the outside.

Concerning the therapeutic dimension, she often refers to her own experience as a young teenager and to her own lyceum students in the terminology of a professional psychologist:

Adolescence is a process that is not like anything else. Young boys and girls set themselves up against their families; they think that nobody loves them, and peer groups become more important than the family. They live through all kinds of problems. And I am very happy to be able to help the students through these problems.

When I was that age, there was nobody at school to approach us in this way. Our parents did not have any knowledge as to what was going on in our minds, so they did not bother themselves with us very much, but left us to ourselves.

This kind of comment implies that Ayşe and her colleagues know that they now possess better (more scientific) knowledge with which to approach, and perhaps even prevent, the problems among the younger generation of students. The protective mentality implicit here is associated with modern forms of control that Foucault advocates in his writings.

Toward the end of the interview, I ask her about her way of conceiving death. Ayşe gives a classic answer to that question, saying that life on earth is like a testing ground for the afterlife:

I feel myself to be a guest. After this visiting period, we will pass to the other world, and in order to go there one has to pay attention to certain rules: for example, one has to do this, one has to avoid that. If one does things this way, it will be bad. If one does them that way, it will be good. We have to know all these rules intimately.

And she adds:

It is like a play in the theater, and we are playing a scene where everybody is given roles. You have to watch your steps so that you play your role as well as possible because after the play is over, the curtain will fall.

[How do you feel you play your role?]

Well, with the help of the books we read, the cassettes we either listen to or watch, we try to raise our consciousness. Yes, we for sure will be held responsible one day for our deeds, and the good and the bad deeds will be weighed against each other on a scale.

There is nothing new or modern about the ethical responsibility Ayşe is talking about here. The theater analogy, however, may bear witness to the fact that she has adopted a mode of looking at herself and at all action (including, perhaps, the rules themselves) from the outside, which is reflexive in a more individualistic way.

If the communal and the religious dimensions are prominent in Zeynep's case, the major fields of discourse discernible in Ayşe's story about her life projects are the professional and the intellectual. In her worldview, scientific knowledge and the ideal of wide reading, symbolized in the dream of a huge library, constitute the foundation stones. What is this if not an expression of an ongoing project of enlightenment?

Hatice: Belonging to a School to Which You Can Bring Your Own Children

Hatice is thirty-two years old. She has been a mathematics teacher in a girls' lyceum in Izmir for seven years. When we meet, she is just about to leave her position because her husband has obtained new employment as a teacher in a small and relatively new community college in a midsize historical Anatolian town. Hatice comes from Çanakkale Province, more exactly from a famous holiday resort on the Aegean coast, a small town called Ege. She has been married for about ten years and has two girls.

The lyceum where Hatice works is situated on the outskirts of the city in an area up in the hills and named after the observation tower set up there in the 1940s. It takes a good half-hour to get there from the center of the city by car. The five-story lyceum glows bright pink and green against the backdrop of a low-class *gecekondu* area of dull, earthen color. Together, these different styles of architecture form a postmodern image.

The atmosphere inside the building, however, is impressive and more sterling. The school building is brand new—only one year old. The director of the school, a young man in his early thirties, shows me around during my first visit. Everything shines. The classrooms are spacious, and the equipment in the science laboratories is of high quality. In addition to the science laboratories, there are a computer lab with at least twenty-five computers and language labs for English. On the lowest floor, the dining-hall accommodates 350 people. Lunch is served to all staff and those pupils who have signed up for it. All eat at the same time.

Classrooms and labs fill three floors. The dormitory is situated on the top floor, with space for approximately 150 students. On the top floor, there is also a sports hall big enough to house a basketball arena. Students gather on this floor during the breaks. The top floor also opens out onto a huge terrace overlooking the city. During the interview, I learn that there is space on the top floor reserved for a daycare center for the children of staff.

Erzurum Lisesi is a new school, but is at the same time the continuation of another school, the Fatma Hanım Lisesi, which closed and moved here when the new building was finished. Fatma Hanım Lisesi was a girls' high school, and so was Erzurum Lisesi until the school year 2000–2001, when coeducation was imposed. In that year, about 30 boys were included in a student body of about 450.

The working conditions for the teachers in this school are very different from those in Zafer Lisesi in Istanbul, which originally was (and still basically is) a boys' school. Whereas the two women teachers from Zafer Lisesi, where Zeynep teaches, more or less are confined to their "common room," with the space outside being reserved for the male majority, Erzurum Lisesi belongs to its women staff. Thanks to these circumstances, there is an open, stimulating, and supportive working atmosphere for women in this school. The major focus of the interview with Hatice is, therefore, working conditions. However, I also summarize and reproduce our discussion of her religious experiences.

Religious Experiences

Hatice repeatedly comes back to the importance of telling the truth and being sincere. She laments the lack of sufficient trust in other people. Transparency between human beings is one of the most important values to be taught to the young generation of students. The desire for such an ethic has followed her since she broke away from her own hometown, which she found disturbingly narrow-minded.

The reason I wanted to get into the university was that I wanted to get away from Ege. I could not get along with the local people. They were too simple and vulgar, I thought. The only thing they did was gossip, fight, and be unsupportive toward each other. Their topics of conversation were so simple and boring that for a long time it was on my mind to get into the university, to get a chance to study and develop my thinking. I thought I had to improve myself in such a way that I would be of help and benefit to other people. Just to sit back home watching TV for hours, change the furniture, and take part in women's tea parties was not enough for me. So I struggled on and got into the Middle East Technical University in Ankara.

Hatice got into the Department of Education and studied math as her major subject. She was initially disappointed in her desire to find friends with whom she could share her concerns about some higher values in life.

I watched my roommates in the university dormitory, but I found them too earthy and utilitarian. I did not find the kind of sincerity I was looking for. My friendship relations remained on a superficial level.

People tell lies for no reason at all. For example, I once went back to my hometown for vacation together with another friend. Now, in the bus she was talking to the lady next to her, and the woman asked her where she was studying and things like that. This friend was studying in the Department of Psychology, but to the lady on the bus she said that she was studying in the Department of Public Administration [political science]. *Afterward I asked her why she had said this. What if this lady for one reason or another found out the truth? Wouldn't she feel very bad about not having told the truth? No, she did not seem to be disturbed about that at all. According to her, there was no risk that this fellow traveler would find out the truth, anyway. But what was good about lying about such petty and unimportant issues? I really disliked this kind of attitude, and perhaps it was experiences like these that made me approach religion.*

Still, if Hatice is critical about many things in her own childhood environment, she is also grateful that her parents sent her during summer vacations to the mosque to do some Qur'anic reading. Her parents were not fervent about religion, but they paid attention to the main traditions of Islam, such as fasting during Ramadan, joining the prayers in the mosque on special festive days, and so on. Hatice's idea was that when she reached their age, she would follow their example. Her attitude toward religion always has been benevolent.

It may sound funny, but I even dreamed that the man I would marry should be a person with whom I could share these feelings.

Then, as she continued to ponder her identity and future, she came to know a student who did not appear to be particularly religious, but who nonetheless performed her *namaz.*

[*Do you think she was trying to hide her commitment?*]

She just did not tell anybody about it. She affected me. Her father was a military officer and her mother a teacher. She really had a very nice mother. The fact that this girl was performing her prayers also affected me. Praying really gives you inner peace. So thanks to this friend, I became acquainted with the practice of praying. Later on I lost contact with her.

Hatice was in her third year at the university when these events took place. Adopting the habit of praying regularly led to her veiling one year later, when she was in her last year at the university. Regarding whether becoming a conscious believer changed her life in any way, Hatice is a little ambivalent. She denies it in terms of her daily life practices, but admits to it in terms of an inner bearing:

No, I never have tried to change my life in any direction. Just like other friends of mine, I go on vacation together with my husband, I take the children along to the movies, we go together to the shopping mall, we celebrate the holidays like most other people do. No, there is nothing in our life that sets us apart from most other people.

I did not become a different person. But, still, I think that I found [a rationale for] the way I wanted to live. As a practicing Muslim, one should not lie, one should take on responsibility for others, one should not exploit others, and so on. I felt comfortable with this way of living. Perhaps it is part of my personality. . . . But, yes, in thinking about it, my attitude to life changed in at least one way: even when reading a single exam paper, I do it with the caution of one who knows she will be responsible for this at the last judgment [ahirette].

In this way, Hatice is convinced that she has become a more conscientious person, something that she thinks influences her to do a good job and to be a fair and just teacher. Her religious experience requires of her that she read the exam papers very carefully, sometimes again and again.

She carefully points out that if her religious commitment is to be reflected in her work at all, it should not be in the name of any specific religious interpretation (that is, of any specific sect or community), but as a universal and humanistic ethic.

I think that religious believers essentially are carriers of universal values. That is also perhaps the reason parents prefer to send their children to our schools.

Erzurum Lisesi as a Work Environment

A major part of the interview with Hatice centers on what makes a school such as Erzurum Lisesi attractive as a workplace.

Because this school is a private school, teachers do not have to worry about job placement. By contrast, public school teachers in Turkey may be placed in any part of the country, which can upset their family lives and even make it impossible for a woman teacher to continue her professional career.

The Ministry of Education rotates the teachers, which means you might end up being sent to the eastern parts of the country. So my intention was not to work, but then a friend of mine told me about this school, and I ended up being appointed here.

Teachers in this and other private schools usually are better paid. In this school, the staff also is provided with daycare facilities for their young children.

What attracted me to this school was that the administration also took responsibility for the children. I liked their attitude, saying that mother and child are one inseparable unit. I have two children, and I have raised both of them in this school; I was even able to breastfeed both of them while at the same time carrying on my job. This is great good fortune for me. Just think about it! That is also what has tied me to this school.

What I like most about this school is that it is possible to combine being a mother with being a teacher. I never had to leave my children with a stranger. I feel very much at ease right now knowing that my child is upstairs. I brought her in the morning and left her with the attendant at the daycare center. In-between lessons or whenever I have time off, I can go up there and see my child. In this way, my child does not have to be away from me. A colleague of mine left her child in a private daycare center in the city. One afternoon her child was left sleeping, and the people working there forgot her inside when they locked the place and went home. Just imagine what that child felt when it woke and there was no one around. . . . No, I really do not want to leave my children with someone I do not know. Also, I am not sure how much the childminder and I would agree on the norms and values to be taught to the child. I do not want to let anybody else impose what is good and what is beautiful. The values I want my child to take on I teach much better myself.

In addition to a fairly good salary, staff members in this school also have other advantages, such as very low-cost bus service and free lunches. They are also free to say their prayers. They usually get the kind of class material they ask for, such as books, videos, photocopy services, and so on. In exchange for such advantages, they are expected to work very hard, often sacrificing several hours after work and over weekends. But even if the work is demanding, they feel it is also stimulating.

One afternoon each week all department instructors get together after school to check with each other on how much progress they have made against the schedule. Such meetings give them a chance to discuss problems with individual students both concerning the learning process and discipline. Every other week one representative from each department attends a meeting to compare the problems of the different departments.

It happens fairly often that a teacher has to make appointments with weak students on the weekends in order to help them catch up with difficult parts of the course. The school administration is also eager to arrange further education for instructors. For example, Erzurum Lisesi offers a computer program course every so often. This course occupies teachers over several weekends because such activities are not given at the expense of the normal curricula.

These programs and extra tasks are really an advantage, I think. All instructors are being motivated in this way, and we carry out the program together. Let's say that one teacher has difficulties in explaining a certain problem or theory to students. We hear this quite often from the students—that, oh, "we do not understand what our teacher is saying, she does not explain clearly enough for us to understand." Well, in a situation like that, we do not leave the teacher to her own devices but keep up an open, cooperative dialogue until all the students really get the same instruction. We also work in coordination with the other schools [sponsored by the same company, Asya Şirketi]. *It is really stimulating to work that way.*

My husband, who is just about to take on a university position, has looked with envy at our way of working and thinks he should try to introduce a similar work discipline and ethic into the university department where he is going.

Hatice is of the opinion that the reason they have to work so hard at Erzurum Lisesi is that the school is private. It has to compete in the market, so it has to maintain high educational standards. This pragmatic argument seems to outweigh the more romantic idea of performing a duty for some higher authority. However, she is also aware that it takes a rather devoted idealist to cope with such a demanding work schedule. She does not understate the influence of her religiously influenced ethic on her own conscientiousness, but has no dreamy illusions about the economic forces involved in the demanding work discipline.

The Role of Religion in School

Hatice's general attitude to the role of religion in these schools is rather sober.

The parents of our students do not ask for a certain [religious] *worldview. What they want for their children I know very well for myself because I am not just a teacher, but also a mother of a pupil. What I want for my child is, first of all, good-quality education. Then I also want my child to learn good manners, good judgment of what is right and wrong, how to behave toward older people, the importance of doing things that are good for society. This is what I would expect, and I do not think that other parents think very differently. I also think that to bring up the question of religion with children of that age* [fourteen to seventeen years old] *is too early. There is no intention of imprinting such ideas on the minds of children at an early age because that often results in a backlash. The best thing you can do is just to set a good example. If I as a teacher behave in a decent way, and if this means that the students gain respect for me and think that they want to be like me, then that is all right. But to impose my own religious outlook on the children . . . no, I would not want to do that.*

Religion is a different kind of experience about which the individual has to decide on her own. So, with respect to that question, we do not have anything to give as teachers.

Family Concerns

In Hatice's case, the private sphere, or the family, is essential. The main issue for her, therefore, is how to combine family and professional life. These two fields of action constitute the core of her life story.

The other fields of action—the communal, the intellectual, and the religious—play a secondary role. Hatice's general approach is neither discursive, as in Zeynep's case, nor project oriented, as in Ayşe's, but is more a relaxed attitude of listening to what life offers and then accepting it without too much objection or resistance or too much rationalization. Her personality is marked by a kind of peaceful *tevekkül,* or acquiescence, based on deep trust in God.

That the family plays an important role in her life can be understood from the fact that she is just about to leave her position as teacher in the school for a life (most probably) as a housewife in a midsize Anatolian town. In addition, her job satisfaction at the Erzurum Lisesi is very much owing to the fact that she has been able to bring her children with her to work. She has accepted work there on the premise that the unity between herself and her children would not be broken. Her warm devotion to her family probably is related to the fact that she seems to have a harmonious relationship with her husband. During the interview, she repeatedly emphasizes that they share not only their religious outlook (which was a precondition for marrying him in the first place), but many other attitudes relating to daily practicalities.

When evening comes and we rest back at home, I want to share what I read with my husband. If I am tired or feel sorry about something, I want to be able to share these feelings with him. Just think about living with someone who does not like the things you like. Even if it is a question of such simple things as food, to share likes is very important. I even like to go shopping together with my husband, so very often we go together.

The importance of the family is also seen in Hatice's evaluation of her profession. According to her, teaching is the ideal profession not primarily because it is the profession of the Prophet (as Ayşe believes), but because it is relatively easy to combine with family duties.

When the students ask me about my profession, I answer them that teaching is an ideal profession, especially for women because they will also become mothers and wives.

Hatice also stresses the moral dimension of being a teacher, but in much less exalted terms than the other women in this study:

Being a doctor means that you help other human beings physically. It is different for a psychiatrist, of course. But a teacher plays a very important role in the life of children.

Concerning the intellectual dimension, Hatice does not have much time for reading.

I try to set certain objectives for myself. For example, last Ramadan I decided that I should read the Qur'an with a group of friends. But, to be honest, I did not have time, so I ended up reading it by myself at home. I go to work in the morning, and when I get back home at night, I am too tired. The children also need their time, but if there is any time left after I have finished my house chores, I try to use it for reading.

She seems to reserve reading for more special occasions:

Especially after the earthquake of 17 August 1999, I was feeling terribly anxiety-ridden because of the agony of death. Then I read Said Nursi's books, and they really helped me to overcome my depression.

However, Hatice read a great deal in earlier years, reading that now gives her a certain self-confidence in relation to the great variety of books on Islamic issues that overwhelm the book market. She is proud of reading not just one type of book, but also books representing different ideas and worldviews. This is what she also recommends to her students: to read a great deal and to read widely.

Concerning the religious field, Hatice keeps a low profile. The same is true of the communal field, especially with respect to relationships within her *cemaat.* Zeynep, in contrast, is much more outspoken on issues related to her *cemaat.* The communal dimension enters Hatice's story in a more abstract way. It is not missing from her story, but it is related more to society at large and to certain solidarity values that she finds missing in contemporary society.

As noted earlier, she is very preoccupied with the problem of sincerity and honesty. People tell lies even when they cannot benefit from them. The desire that young students should learn certain basic and universal norms and values is related to Hatice's concern to secure some kind of "precontractual solidarity" (Durkheim 1961; see also Collins 1982). It is possible to see this desire on her part as an objection (perhaps without really being conscious of it) to a society in which people cannot trust each other and that therefore does not function very well other than on the level of family and patron-client (corporative) relationships. The foundation for a society based on rationally organized associations and institutions is an ethic of honesty. Without that, the whole modernization project will be delayed or spoiled. By emphasizing the need for honesty, Hatice calls not only for a religiously relevant ethic, but also for values that are necessary for the greater civilization and the modernization project.

Secrecy and Autonomy

The stories end here. The limitation of the interview as a source of information is in the narrative, the discourse itself. However honest, open, and benevolent the interviewees, the stories reproduced here reflect the interviewed teachers' own self-images. What about the rest of the picture? In order to get an idea about the social practice of the adherents of the Gülen community, a different method based on participant observation is required. The status of the interviewees' stories may be likened to the door of the dormitory on the upper floor of Erzurum Lisesi. When I was walking through the big and impressive building, the doors to classrooms, labs, dining hall, sports arena, and offices were hospitably opened. The door to the dormitory, however, remained closed.

Owing to the methodological tools available, many questions cannot be answered within the framework of this study. For example, how much did Ayşe and her friends in fact read? How did they read and with what benefit? What about Turan Dursun's book? What was the real reason why she burned it? Did Ayşe really read Dursun before she became acquainted with Gülen's books or ideas? How much did she act on her own initiative? What was the actual time perspective in her story? In Zeynep's case, what was the *namaz* regime in her school really like? And as for Hatice, what did the children's daycare center and the dormitory on the top floor of the school look like?

This study does not rise above the level of discourse; that is, it does not contain information about the social practices of the Gülen community. In spite of this limitation, the contention I advance here is that the interviewees are faithful followers of Fethullah Gülen. Regarding love (encompassing the whole of humanity), pietism, humility, self-criticism, professional (not political) activism, they all have studied their Gülen catechism very thoroughly. But, at the same time, this urge to follow in Gülen's footsteps answers a voice within themselves that genuinely is their own and that has not been forced on them through communal pressure. Once within the magnetic field of the Gülen community, however, collective pressure may work differently for different persons. This study offers examples of both those who are strongly attached to the community, such as Zeynep, and those who are much less tied to it, such as Hatice. The fact that Zeynep is strongly committed to the *cemaat*, however, does not mean that she is enslaved by it. On the contrary, my impression is that she is high up in the moral hierarchy within the community. In addition, the much younger Ayşe does not lack self-confidence and, especially in light of her age, stands out as a remarkably independent individual.

Becoming part of the Gülen community, therefore, does not mean that individuals are turned into passive tools in the hands of an authoritarian leadership. The Gülen ideology is strongly conservative, it is true, but that is not the same as saying that the principles of its organization are authoritarian or by any means totalitarian. I have seen examples of strong hierarchical relationships within the community, too, but more often among men at the top than among women in the lower echelons of this community (which, of course, shows the gender hierarchy of the community).

At the level where Zeynep, Ayşe, and Hatice are working and acting, there is room for self-reflexivity as well as for individual initiative and autonomy. The media through which this individualism is transmitted are the privacy and the activist piety taught by Fethullah Gülen.

6

Fethullah Gülen's Search for a Middle Way Between Modernity and Muslim Tradition

AHMET T. KURU

ARE THE CONSTANT and allegedly transcendental principles of religion compatible with ever-changing human experiences?* This question has been at the center of the debates about the relationship between religion and modernity, in general, and between Islam and modernity, in particular. Many modernists answer in the negative. Modernization and secularization theorists claimed that religion was a traditional phenomenon that would eventually wither away (Inkeles and Smith 1976, 27–28). According to these theorists, there was a dichotomy between modernity and Muslim tradition (Stark and Finke 2000, 1–82). Therefore, Muslims should choose "Mecca or mechanization" (Lerner 1958, 405).

Two developments recently have challenged modernization theory, however. Religion emerged empirically as an important public issue in many modern and modernizing countries (Casanova 1994; Kepel 1991). A group of social scientists launched a theoretical debate on "multiple modernities,"[1] rejecting modernism (Heffner 1998, 2000, 22).[2] The supporters of the idea of multiple modernities, despite their influential challenge to the modernists, have not specified yet what they actually mean by multiple modernities, in general, and by Islamic modernity, in particular. Their arguments have remained by and large speculative.

Nilüfer Göle, the leading scholar on this issue in Turkey, has tried to overcome this problem by examining social examples as "snapshots of Islamic modernities" (2000a, 2000b). She has made a significant and insightful contribu-

*I thank Joel Migdal and Zafer Çetin for their helpful comments on earlier drafts of this essay.
1. See the special issue of *Daedalus* on multiple modernities, 129, no. 1 (2000).
2. On reconciling modernity and various religions, see Heft 1999, Yu and Lu 2000.

tion by collecting individual and social stories that combine modern and Islamic lifestyles to show the existence of Islamic modernities. Her cases, however, are ad hoc examples that do not explain how agents synthesize Islamic and modern values on a coherent basis.

In this chapter, I investigate the idea of Islamic modernity in an empirical example that has a coherent theoretical basis. I explore how a Muslim thinker, Fethullah Gülen, searches for a middle way between modernity and Muslim tradition. Gülen is worth analyzing because his ideas have inspired a movement that has opened more than three hundred schools and six universities in almost fifty countries, in addition to establishing both media and business networks.[3] I begin with the analysis of Gülen's understanding of the "middle way." Then I examine Gülen's ideas about the relationship between four features of modernity and four aspects of the Muslim tradition: (*a*) modern science and Islamic knowledge; (*b*) reason and revelation; (*c*) the idea of progress and conservation of tradition, and (*d*) free will and destiny.

A Middle Way?

Scholars long have debated the meaning, origin, causes, and results of modernity. The words *modernity* and *modern* represent relative evaluations rather than absolute meanings. The term *modern* was first used in the late fifth century to define the Christian present vis-à-vis the pagan and Roman past (Habermas 1997b, 39). Modernity may be defined as "a form of civilization characteristic of our current historical epoch" (Inkeles and Smith 1976, 15). We can view some historical trajectories—such as the Renaissance, the Reformation, the Enlightenment, the French and American Revolutions, the Industrial Revolution, and globalization—as way stations in the long march of modernity. The West is the main place where modernity originated and with which it is still associated because "In every era of human history, modernity . . . has meant the ways, norms, and standards of the dominant and expanding civilization" (Lewis 1997, 129). Modernity has various definitions. For Marx, the essence of modernity is capitalism; for Durkheim, it is industrialization and division of labor; and for Weber, it is rationalization and bureaucracy (Giddens 1990, 10–12).

In this chapter, I focus exclusively on four features of modernity: modern science, rationalism, the idea of progress, and individual free will. Extreme modernists and religious fundamentalists ironically agree that these four fea-

---

3. Gülen frequently emphasizes that his own position is more like an inspirational and guiding thinker rather than a formal leader of a social movement.

tures of modernity are incompatible with four aspects of Muslim tradition: Islamic knowledge, revelation, a conservative understanding of time, and the belief in destiny. Gülen, in contrast, refuses such an incompatibility between modernity and tradition. He sees it as a false dichotomy and tries to take a moderate position.

Many scholars have pointed out Gülen's moderate point of view. According to Göle, Gülen shakes the dichotomist perception of modernity and Islam. He tries to end the Western monopoly on modernity and aims to add an Islamic set of meanings to it. Göle emphasizes that Gülen works to domesticate excessive rationalism with Sufism and love, and to reconcile individualism and humbleness (1996c, 206). Similarly, Hakan Yavuz stresses that Gülen seeks "to synthesize reason and revelation, religion and science, individuals and community, stability and change, and globalization and nationalism" (2000b, 32). Ahmet T. Alkan notes that the summary of Gülen's ideas is a search for the middle way. He claims that Gülen's emphasis on the middle way is the reason for his public popularity and that Gülen's understanding of the middle way is not an instrumental strategy: "To follow the middle way in an intellectual environment like Turkey, which is full of the obsession of dichotomies, is not 'compromising,' but an honorable and reasonable way of 'arguing.' Despite the general expectation, today 'the middle way' is amazingly empty" (1996, 203).

Although these comments on Gülen are insightful, they are not detailed analyses. This chapter makes two contributions to the discussion: one is a detailed and analytical exploration of Gülen's ideas; the other is a specific analysis of the debates on modernity and Islam by means of focusing on the four supposedly dichotomous features of modernity and Muslim tradition.

According to Gülen, an extremist understanding of modernity may be in tension with an extremist understanding of Muslim tradition. The moderate understandings of these two concepts, however, are compatible and, furthermore, complementary. Gülen's idea of a middle way does not depend on compromise, but on his understanding of Islam. He argues, "Islam, being the 'middle way' of absolute balance—balance between materialism and spiritualism, between rationalism and mysticism, between worldliness and excessive asceticism, between this world and the next—and inclusive of the ways of all the previous prophets, makes a choice according to the situation" (1995d, 200–201).

Gülen's understanding of the middle way is to a great extent similar to Aristotle's. Aristotle criticized the Platonic "virtue versus vice" categorization and classified phenomena in three groups, two of which are vices (excess and deficiency) and one of which is virtue (the mean or the middle way). In this perspective, the appetite's excess is licentiousness, its deficiency is frigidity, and its middle way is moderation. Anger's excess is rage, its deficiency is cowardice, and its middle way is courage. Reason's excess is demagogy, its deficiency is ignorance, and its middle way is wisdom (Aristotle 1996, 268–71).

The middle way is also an important concept in Islam. The Qur'an defines the Muslim community as the *ummeten vasatan,* or the community of the middle way (2:143). Alija Izzetbegovic (n.d.), for example, wrote a book to reveal that Islam is the middle way between materialism and spiritualism. By the same token, Gülen interprets the important Islamic concept of *sırat-ı müstakim* (the straight path), which is recited in a Muslim's prayers forty times a day, as the middle way between *ifrat* (excesses) and *tefrit* (deficiency).[4]

Gülen's understanding of the middle way has been affected mainly by Bediüzzaman Said Nursi (1873–1960), the author of *Risale-i Nur* (The epistles of light) (1994).[5] Nursi, in addition to being a prolific writer, was the founder of the faith-based Nur movement. He tried to reconcile science and Islamic faith and employed a modern scientific perspective to prove the existence and names of God from the universe and nature. He was eager to establish a university that would combine modern sciences and Islamic knowledge. The understanding of the middle way was crucial in Nursi's ideas, as it is in Gülen's. According to John Voll, "In [Nursi's] writings and teachings, there is repetition of the term that Islam is a middle way, a path of moderation, rather than extremism. . . . Nursi frequently would discuss two opposing positions and then define the truly Islamic way as the middle way between the two" (1999, 254).

Gülen's middle way arguments may face harder times while being applied in practice than when they were simply ideational articulations. Gülen tries to solve this problem by emphasizing two factors. First, the context, including time and space, is crucial to the interplay between ideas and actions. He stresses that Islam is not just an abstract set of ideas, but also includes deliberated and systematic behaviors (1998l, 22). He emphasizes that his own ideas, after being constructed briefly in the abstract form, evolve in-depth through action. He attaches importance to the realities that bind ideals, instead of to utopian projects. In other words, he sees theory and practice as indispensable and mutually constitutive (Can 1996, 14–15).

Second, Gülen attaches importance to the human agency that has eminent impact on theory and practice, as well as on the interplay between them. For that reason, he has focused on the education of a "golden generation" that will learn the theoretical aspects of the middle way and will bring it into practice. This gen-

---

4. Gülen's taped series of sermons, *Ahlaki Mülahazalar,* vols. 1–14 (1980) (Istanbul: Nil Aş).
5. For Nursi's perception of the middle way, see Nursi 1994, 613.

eration is supposed to absorb and represent both modern and Muslim identities through its mind and its behaviors.

Since the 1960s, Gülen has tried to educate an idealist, activist, disciplined, and tolerant youth (L. Erdoğan 1997, 124). He has described the eight characteristics of this new generation as: faith; love; a balanced view of science; a reevaluated view of humans, life, and the universe; free thinking and respect for freedom of thought; a habit to counsel and collective consciousness; mathematical logic; and appreciation for art (Gülen 1996d, 4–12). The new generation is expected to reconcile four fragmented, and even polarized, institutions in Muslim societies: modern science of the public schools, Islamic knowledge of the *medrese*s (Islamic schools), spiritual life and feeling of the *tekke*s (Sufi lodges), and the discipline of the barrack (Can 1996, 77). It is natural to ask about the extent to which the schools of the Gülen movement have been successful in educating such a golden generation. Further research is necessary to answer this question, however.

In the next section, I analyze the crucial pillar of Gülen's understanding of the education of the golden generation: the relationship between modern science and Islamic knowledge.

Modern Science and Islamic Knowledge

Although postmodernists have challenged the metanarratives of science and its monopoly on knowledge (Lyotard 1997, xxiii), science still dominates the modern worldview. The rise of modern science created a duality in the late Ottoman society between the graduates of the Western(ized) schools and those of the traditional institutions, the *medrese*s and the *tekke*s (Mardin 1991a, 124; Rahman 1982, 43–83). In modern Turkey, although this duality ended to a great extent, the status of Islamic schools (i.e., the İmam Hatip Schools and theology departments in universities) and Qur'anic education is debated passionately still.

Gülen avoids taking a clear position in this debate. He sees scientific education and Islamic education as compatible and complementary. Although he was educated in traditional institutions, he has urged his sympathizers to open modern schools rather than traditional *medrese*s. He even has advised opening schools instead of mosques. Gülen tries to educate the young generation in Islamic knowledge through informal publications and sermons, rather than through official curriculums at schools. He attaches specific importance to Nursi's statement on the interdependency of modern science and Islamic knowledge in an ideal education:

The light of the intellect is scientific knowledge while the heart of the spirit derives its light from religious [knowledge]. Scientific knowledge without religion
usually causes atheism or agnosticism, while religious knowledge without intellectual enlightenment gives rise to bigotry. When combined, they urge a student
to research, further and further research, deepening in both belief and knowledge. (Gülen 1997i, 320).

The schools opened with Gülen's encouragement have become the elite high
schools in Turkey. Their students have won several medals in the International
Science Olympics and the top rankings in the nationwide university entrance examinations. The Gülen movement also has opened schools and universities in
many other countries, especially in the former Soviet republics and in the
Balkans.

For Gülen, there are two reasons for the so-called dichotomy between scientific and Islamic education. The first historical and institutional reason is the exclusion of natural sciences from the *medrese*s. Between the ninth and eleventh
centuries, when science was part of the *medrese* curricula, Muslims accomplished
significant scientific developments (Gülen 1998l, 40–45). However, in the era of
the Seljuk Empire (1040–1194), philosophy and natural sciences were expelled
from the *medrese*s, resulting in the decline of scientific research in the Muslim
world. The influential Islamic scholar al-Ghazzali (1058–1111) opposed some
Muslim philosophers who offered views against the Islamic creed, an opposition that was misunderstood and used to legitimize this expulsion of the sciences (Can 1996, 75).

Second, the historical tension between science and the medieval Catholic
Church was mistakenly attributed to science and Islam, although Islam's attitude
toward science has been different. Because Muslim modernists completely emu-
lated the Western model, they applied the dualities between modern and
Catholic values to the Muslim world, ignoring the peculiarities of Islam (Gülen
1997i, 23).

In Turkey, the debate between faith and scientific understanding of causality
continues to occur frequently. After the 1999 earthquake, for instance, the media
discussed whether God created the earthquake or it was a natural accidental
event. Gülen does not accept such a dichotomy. On the one hand, he attaches
importance to the laws of causality functioning in the universe, even in social
events (I. Ünal 2001, 23–24). His interpretation of the Qur'anic verse "But no
change will you find in Allah's way of dealing, no turning off will you find in
Allah's way of dealing" (35:43) emphasizes the principle of continuity in natural
events and the regularity of natural laws (Gülen 1998l, 42). On the other hand,

however, he stresses that God is omnipotent and that nature has no efficacy independent of Him (Gülen 1997i, 310). He quotes Nursi to stress that people call God's creation "natural laws. . . . God manifests His Names through veils, although His absolute Unity demands that we attribute the effects directly to His creative Power. His Transcendence, Grandeur and Majesty require natural causes to veil His acts, so that people not ascribe to Him the things and events that seem unacceptable to them" (Gülen 1995d, 128). In this perspective, one may attribute a death, for example, to a material cause (e.g., an illness), to the Angel of Death, *and* directly to God, simultaneously and without any contradiction (Nursi 1994, 121–22).

Gülen wrote a long foreword to the book *Science and Religion from a New Point of View* (in Turkish), which some of his sympathizers wrote to emphasize the compatibility of science and religion (İrfan Yılmaz et al. 1998). Two magazines put out by the Gülen movement, *Sızıntı* and *The Fountain,* also frequently publish articles on this issue. It is possible to see Gülen's middle way in his interpretation of the Muslim concept of *takva* (*taqwa* in Arabic). This term is crucial in Muslim life, as this verse stresses: "Verily the most honored of you in the sight of Allah is (he who is) the most advanced in *taqwa* among you" (41:13). In Gülen's interpretation, *taqwa* gains a second meaning in addition to the traditional first one:

> Derived from *wiqaya,* meaning protection, *taqwa* means to be in the safe-keeping or protection of God. This has two aspects. The first is that a man fears God and obeys Him by performing His commands and refraining from His prohibitions. The second aspect of *taqwa* is that, by studying nature and life and discovering God's laws controlling them, people find scientific knowledge and order their lives. The establishment of sciences depends upon the discovery of these laws. In order to be under the safe-keeping of God, the true religion and sciences should be combined, for they are two faces or two expressions of a single truth. (1995d, 160)

The twentieth century was an era of science for Gülen, and he believes that science also will be dominant in the twenty-first century. Muslims' weak interest in science is a source of regret for Gülen, who claims that to read the universe as a book constitutes half of a Muslim's responsibilities (Gülen 1995d, 76). In his own words, "the universe, where God's laws issuing from His attributes of Will, Destiny and Power are operative, is 'the created Qur'an,' and the Qur'an, which is the collection of the Divine laws issuing from God's Attribute of Speech, is 'the composed universe' or the universe in the words" (1995d, 160). Although many Muslim intellectuals accept the significance of natural science, they generally are suspicious of the social sciences because of the influence of Western paradigms. Gülen, however, also emphasizes the importance of social sciences, arguing that they will be much more important in the future.

Given the hegemony of positivist science, some Muslim modernists have tried to explain miracles through the lens of science or have denied them because they seem contradictory to natural laws.[6] Gülen, however, differs from positivist modernists by recognizing the limitations of science and its inability to explore religious and metaphysical issues, including miracles. He argues that science and technology cannot explain the meaning and the purpose of life, and they may be harmful for humankind if unjust and irresponsible people manipulate them. Science can neither provide true happiness nor replace the role of religion. Moreover, he emphasizes that the development of physics in the twentieth century shook positivist science:

> It is true that science has been the most revered "fetish" or "idol" of modern man for nearly two hundred years. Scientists once believed that they could explain every phenomenon with the findings of science and the law of causality. However, modern physics destroyed the theoretical foundations of mechanical physics and revealed that the universe is not a clockwork of certain parts working according to strict, unchanging laws of causality and absolute determinism. . . . Experts in atomic physics say that no one can be sure that the universe will be in the same state a moment later as it is in now. (1997i, 309–10)

Gülen ontologically accepts that there is an absolute truth; therefore, he opposes extreme social constructivism: "Truth is not something the human mind produces. Truth exists independently of man and man's task is to seek it" (1997i, 308–9). Therefore, in the search for the truth, science can address the question "How?" *while* religion addresses the question "Why?" The true civilization may emerge as a result of the cooperation between science and religion (Gülen 1996a, 49).

Reason and Revelation

Scientific development and mass education encouraged rationalization of individuals and societies; therefore, rationalization of social structure became an important pillar of modernity (Lichbach 1997, 268). Rationality implies, on the one

---

6. Sayyid Ahmad Khan and Husayn Ahmad Amin are examples of this modernist group. See Majeed 1998 and Abu-Zahra 2000.

hand, coherence and consistency, which results in regularity and orderliness in social life, and, on the other hand, efficiency based on the rational selection of the best available means to clearly formulated ends (Gellner 1994c, 22). Although there is no clear emphasis on rationalization in Gülen's works, his attention to this concept is implicit in his speeches and writings. His emphasis on efficiency and division of labor, for example, is one of the sources of success for the Gülen movement. He encourages the ability of systematic thinking as a feature of an ideal Muslim: "Every attempt to make progress which has not been authorized by reason and science is condemned to futility" (1996a, 44). Elizabeth Özdalga explains his activism as a rationalization process: "The perspective taught by Gülen is based on activism, stirred up, as well as controlled, by pietism. This 'activist pietism' (or Weber's 'in-worldly asceticism') describes, I argue, a new feature in Turkish religious life. . . . [T]he general effect of Gülen's similar 'activist pietism' has been the direction of a rationalization of social relationships" (2000, 87).

Gülen is against the kind of rationalism that focuses on egoistic self-interest and pure materialistic cost-benefit analysis. Rational choice instead should take into account the Day of Judgment. Gülen criticizes the Enlightenment movement for being based on only the enlightenment of reason. Ethics and moral principles, he argues, are crucial for the real enlightenment of humans. To maintain harmony, peace, and happiness in human life requires the realization of both mental/rational and heart-based/spiritual enlightenment. Therefore, rationalism should not negate the spiritual aspects of humans:

> Neglect of the intellect . . . would result in a community of poor, docile mystics. Negligence of the heart or spirit, on the other hand, would result in crude rationalism devoid of any spiritual dimension. . . . It is only when the intellect, spirit and body are harmonized, and man is motivated toward activity in the illuminated way of the Divine message, that he can become a complete being and attain true humanity. (Gülen 1995d, 105–6)

Rationalization of a Muslim society has generally been accepted as difficult because of the perceived tension between reason and revelation in that society. Orientalist and fundamentalist essentialisms have claimed a dichotomy between reason and revelation in the Muslim world (Al-Azmeh 1996, 179). Gülen argues that reason and Islamic revelation are not only compatible, but also complementary: "All principles of Islam, being a revealed religion originating in an All-Encompassing Knowledge, certainly can be confirmed by reason" (1995d, 128).

Gülen pioneered the creation of the Journalists and Writers Foundation, which has organized the Abant Workshops to discuss the relationship between reason and revelation, in addition to some other related issues (Gündem 1998; Journalists and Writers Foundation 2000a, 2001). According to Gülen, one of the historical bases of the false dichotomy between reason and revelation is the degeneration of the Muslim *medreses*. He is critical of *medreses* because of their weaknesses in science and logic, even on the eve of the twenty-first century (Can 1996, 72–73).

On the issue of dogmatism, Gülen stresses that the Islamic understanding of revelation, which seeks a balance between spiritualism and materialism, is far from dogmatic (Can 1996, 50–51). He argues that the Qur'an clearly opposes scholasticism, rumor, and irrational imitation, while attaching great importance to reason, thinking, and interpretation. To have the ability to reason is the main requirement to be a Muslim (Gülen 1998l, 43–44, 46). Gülen seeks a middle way between reason and revelation. He accepts the Qur'an as the eternal and perfect words of God, while recognizing the role of reason to understand and interpret the Qur'an.

The Idea of Progress and the Conservation of Tradition

The traditional conceptualization of time in many European and Muslim societies throughout the Middle Ages was based on a static and passive mentality (Pattaro 1976). This understanding aimed to preserve the status quo (generally justified by religions), while accepting change as a deviation from the stable natural condition. One of the reasons for this passivity in Europe, according to Benedict Anderson, was the understanding of Messianic time—the waiting for Christ's second coming, or the end of the world, an event that might occur at any time (1998, 23–25).

With the rise of the capitalist market economy and secularization, this mentality underwent a transformation. Change and progress became glorified vis-à-vis the status quo (Gellner 1994c, 22). The idea of progress resulted in competition and development, as well as in an "insatiable desire for growth" (Bermann 1988, 35). The linear, evolutionary understanding of history maintains the legitimacy of modernism and claims to downplay tradition. Although the postmodernists challenge this understanding through a relativistic perspective (Inglehart 1997, 23), the idea of progress is still the source of motivation for modern life.

"The idea of progress is not entirely alien to Muslim thought" essentially and historically (Hasnaoui 1977, 52). Nevertheless, the reconceptualization of time inspired a debate between the idea of progress and the conservation of the tradition in many Muslim countries. Turkish modernists accepted the idea of progress as one of their three main objectives, *akıl, bilim, ilerleme* (reason, science, and progress). The major modernist party in the late Ottoman era, for example, is named the Committee of Union and Progress.

On the one hand, Gülen appreciates the importance of cultural and scientific progress throughout history, but, on the other hand, he emphasizes that this development did not make religion obsolete because the essential pillars of humans' character, needs, and desires did not change. In other words, he accepts change in conjunction with continuity throughout history. He argues that history pursues cyclical ways even though it results in progress, and thereby it has a kind of spiral path (Kömeçoğlu 2000, 174).

Gülen criticizes passivity and the conceptualization of Messianic time in medieval Europe (1998l, 29–31). In some of his speeches, he reminds Muslims that submissively waiting for a *mehdi,* or a messiah, is against Islamic mentality. Instead, he tells them to be dynamic and spend their time efficiently by disciplining their lives with daily schedules and long-term projects. According to Gülen, even if the conditions are not conducive to action, Muslims should wait actively. For example, a holiday means a shift from one work to another, not the cessation of work (2000b, 397). Up until one's death, activity has to continue because no one has a guarantee of salvation, and good deeds are the only capital for the hereafter. This perception provides a religious motivation for worldly activism. As Özdalga puts it,

> According to Gülen, everyone has only one life, one opportunity, to accomplish anything in the service (*hizmet*) of God. . . . Gülen's urgent nervousness is caused by his desire to get people to choose between seizing this opportunity and gaining eternal life, or else being deprived of everything.
>
> To serve God is without limits. . . . One never can sit down, satisfied he or she has done enough or finished what is expected; as soon as one work is done, one has to rush to the next project. The question "Oh, my Lord, what else can I do"? . . . summarizes this understanding of a never-ending urge to work and to serve others.
>
> Gülen calls this ideal *aksiyon insanı* [man of action]. . . . The human being . . . identified with this ideal is one who is never satisfied with existing conditions. Such an *insan* is one who is inclined to work his or her best until this world is turned into a paradise; and also is one who in the struggle for a better world is stopped by nothing except death itself. (2000, 88–89)

Gülen believes that the opportunities provided for a particular period of time should be seized immediately. Every event has its own time of scattering seeds, cultivation, and harvest. If a person misses even one of these steps, he or she cannot reap the final result. Gülen claims that Muslims must be proactive. If they remain reactive and passive decision *takers* (as they were in the nineteenth and twentieth centuries), then they cannot make a contribution to and play a key role in the era of globalization (2000a, 7–8). It may be because of this emphasis on dynamism and activism that a prestigious news magazine in Turkey linked with the Gülen movement is named *Aksiyon* (Action).

The role of time and the linear progress of history in the interpretation of Islamic principles have been contentious issues among Muslims. Some scholars stress the importance of time while interpreting Islam,[7] whereas others reject this approach. Gülen stresses that the Qur'an is the eternal and perfect words of God, but he also points out that time makes one of the best interpretations of the Qur'an, helping people to understand better its multidimensional meanings (1993, 100–101).

For Gülen, it is not necessary either to discredit the past or to glorify it. A critical evaluation of tradition is crucial to peel away the heresies and reveal the real core of religion. The previous *ijtihad*s (interpretations of Islamic principles), based on the custom and convention of preceding societies, require revision to accord with the customs and conventions of contemporary societies. Not only Muslim theologians but also Muslim academics and experts in other fields have to contribute to the new *ijtihad*s (2001b, 141). Gülen emphasizes the necessity of seeking a "balance between the constant and changing aspects of Islam" (Ünal and Williams 2001, 53). Because of his middle way understanding, he appreciates both Muslim tradition, especially based on the Prophet Muhammad's "Time of Happiness," and the ongoing progress of civilization.

Individual Free Will and Destiny

Modern mass education has provided—to some extent—equal access to resources and social mobility, liberated modern individuals from traditional ties, and enabled them to reach for self-awareness (Taylor 1999, 55–56). The role of individualism in modernity is a controversial issue, however. For example, Alain Touraine points out that modernity depends on the interaction and tension between reason—which is connected to rationalization, collectivism, and the sys-

---

7. Abd al-Karim Soroush, for instance, encourages "dynamic *fiqh*," which is forward looking; see Cooper 1998, 43.

tem—and the subject—which is associated with subjectivism, individualism, and the agent. In this regard, throughout the modern era, the pendulum of history has been swinging between collectivism and individualism, according to Touraine (1992, 410).

Individualism generally has been defined as the opposite of collectivism. Ali Bulaç, a Turkish pro-Islamic writer, for example, criticizes modern individualism for demolishing communal ties and for making the atomized individuals weak vis-à-vis the state.[8] To Gülen, individualism defined as opposed to collectivism is the most alien feature of modernity. His ideas on this issue, however, seem to be an eclectic collection of individualism and collectivism rather than a middle way.

Gülen often stresses the necessity of and importance for individuals to be members of a collective and social group. Collectivity needs to be based on the individual's voluntary participation. Once that individual has participated, however, the role of free will is not so clear. Despite his overemphasis on community, Gülen also attaches importance to the individual by emphasizing that humans, being the main addressee of God, are the most honorable and perfect of creatures, and an individual is equal to a whole species. Therefore, the rights of individuals cannot be sacrificed for the sake of the society (2000a, 8).

Nevertheless, Gülen has been criticized for supporting community at the expense of individuals. In a *Milliyet* article, M. Hakan Yavuz (1997a), for example, defines the Gülen movement as a "beehive," which is based on action-oriented obedience. In another article, he adds, "Gülen's educational system does not necessarily promote free will and individualism, but rather promotes a collective consciousness" (1999c, 598). Given these kinds of criticisms, Gülen has stressed the necessity of encouraging the development and flowering of Turkish individuals despite the communitarian Turkish culture.[9]

Another aspect of modern individualism is based on the individual's productive power and efficacy in shaping the course of social and historical events (Taylor 1985, 275–76). This aspect also relates to the dynamic conceptualization of time because it challenges the passive submission to destiny (Sadri and Sadri 2000, 56). "[T]he modern man's sense of efficacy would express his confidence in his ability . . . to organize his life so as to master the challenges it presents" (Inkeles and Smith 1976, 22). Some Muslim scholars oppose such an individualism, which they believe depends on humans' ability to determine their social and natural environments (Tibi 1995, 8), arguing that this ability contradicts the Islamic belief in destiny and the practice of humility toward God. They claim that

---

8. For Bulaç's critique of modern individualism, see Çınar and Kadıoğlu 1999, 62.

9. Interview in *Yeni Yüzyil,* 6 Aug. 1997.

the modern human and *Homo islamicus* are incompatible. The former is the complete master of his or her own destiny and the earth, living in a profane historical time, lacking a sense of the sacred, and being responsible to no one but himself or herself. The latter, on the contrary, is both God's slave and God's vicegerent on the earth (Nasr 1980). Some other scholars, however, reject the changeless definition of the *Homo islamicus* and his or her opposition to the modern human. These scholars attach importance to the context rather than to the text while interpreting Islam (Al-Azmeh 1996, 178).

Gülen does not deal with the discussion about the contradiction between the so-called modern human and *Homo islamicus*. He attaches importance to individual free will, saying that if a good thing happens without deliberated and willed action, the individual cannot gain *sevap* (the pleasure and rewards of Allah) (Özsoy 1998, 55). He quotes the Qur'anic verse "A man has only that for which he makes effort" (53:39). In this regard, success in worldly affairs is based on endeavor and in harmony with natural laws, which are neutral to individuals whether they are Muslim or not. Because God orders the natural laws, to respect those laws is to respect God. On the one hand, Muslims should be successful in worldly affairs (Gülen 2001b, 159), but, on the other hand, their success should not prevent them from having humility vis-à-vis God.

Individual efficacy is very important for Gülen, who was born in a small village in eastern Anatolia that lacked any political, economic, or social sources of power. He has become influential by his own individual efforts. In other words, he represents the success of human agency despite inconvenient socioeconomic and political conditions. According to this perspective, Gülen describes his ideal generation as the "new people" who "will never be reactionary. They will not go after events, for they will be the motors of history that initiate and shape events" (Ünal and Williams 2001, 105).

Gülen claims that the middle way in the relationship between free will and destiny in Islamic creed is provided by the Maturidi school of faith. There have been three main schools of faith in Islam: Mutezile, Eş'ari, and Maturidi. The Mutezile School argues that man creates his own deeds independent of God, and it places an excessive emphasis on rationality. The Eş'ari School emerged as a reaction to the Mutezile and emphasizes destiny at the expense of free will and causality. The third school, the Maturidi, has sought balance between free will and destiny. According to Gülen, the Islamic universities in the Seljuk Empire (Nizamiye Medreses) tended to embrace the Eş'ari as a reaction against the Mutezile. The Eş'ari preserved its influence on the Muslim societies throughout the Ottoman era and does so even today. Although Turks overwhelmingly have claimed loyalty to the Maturidi, they have been under the subconscious influence of the Eş'ari. Gülen stresses the necessity to revitalize the Maturidi point of view, which pursues the middle way (Gülen 1995c; I. Ünal 2001, 207).

Gülen sees individual free will and the belief in destiny as compatible because "God Almighty has endowed man with the power of choice—free will—and, taking into account his choices in life, (pre)determined his life down to its smallest details" (1997i, 131). In other words, "man wills and God creates" (1997i, 136). Because humans are the *halife*s (vicegerents) of God upon the earth, they have the right to intervene in nature for good reasons. In this perspective, a person who believes in God and in her own destiny can gain an infinite power and issue a challenge to the whole universe on behalf of her Lord without any fear or worry. Therefore, optimism, self-confidence, and dynamic understanding of *tevekkül* (submission to and trust in God) should be the main pillars of a Muslim worldview. By the same token, Gülen emphasizes the role of human agency in the determination of social and historical events:

> Islam . . . sees humanity as the "motor" of history, contrary to fatalistic approaches of some of the nineteenth century Western philosophies of history such as dialectical materialism and historicism. Just as every individual's will and behavior determine the outcome of his or her life in this world and in the hereafter, a society's progress or decline is determined by the will, worldview, and lifestyle of its inhabitants. The Quran (13:11) says: "God will not change the state of a people unless they change themselves [with respect to their beliefs, worldview, and lifestyle]." In other words, each society holds the reins of its fate in its own hands. (2001a, 135)

Gülen points out that the particular role of destiny or free will in a specific event cannot be clarified and known exactly. He quotes Nursi to show the middle way on this issue by referring to destiny for the past and for disasters, but to free will for the future and sins: " 'whatever is (including misfortunes) should be considered in the light of Destiny, and what is to come and sins . . . should be attributed to humans' free will' " (Gülen 1997i, 124). Gülen's understanding of the middle way opposes both fatalism and the denial of destiny. For him, a Muslim can possess self-confidence about his or her own individual efficacy and productive power, while still believing in destiny and preserving his or her humility toward God.

At the beginning of the chapter, I promised to analyze the idea of "Islamic modernities" through an empirical example that has a coherent theoretical basis. I believe I have fulfilled that promise through a textual analysis of Gülen's ideas.

I did not give a contextual analysis because other chapters of the volume offer details about Gülen's biography and the activities of his movement.

I disagree with the essentialist claim that modernity and Islam have inherent incompatibilities. My analysis of Gülen's ideas is helpful in disproving this essentialist argument for two reasons. First, Gülen pursues an inclusive middle way between fundamental features of modernity and the Muslim tradition—science and Islamic knowledge, reason and revelation, progress and conservation, and free will and destiny—accepting them as two faces of the same reality. Second, he provides historical-institutional reasons (e.g., the degeneration of the *medrese*s and *tekke*s), rather than essential dichotomies, to explain the alleged problems of modernity and Islam.

Gülen does not try to create an eclectic or hybrid synthesis of modernity and Islam or to accommodate to the hegemony of modernity by changing Islamic principles. What he does is reveal a dynamic interpretation of Islam that is both compatible with and critical of modernity and Muslim tradition. His understanding of the middle way is not a purely abstract set of ideas, but a conception that interacts with practice. He generally pursues a practical common sense, avoiding overly abstract discussions and polarities, and focuses on what one should keep in mind as principles to operate in a certain time and space. Gülen attaches particular importance to human agency in bridging theory and practice, so he aims to educate an ideal youth.

Actually, neither Gülen's nor anyone else's search for a middle way can provide a fixed and stable guideline for future generations. The middle way is not something to be found out once and for all and then applied perpetually. It might change with regard to the new conditions of life. Today's middle way may turn into an extreme (either excess or deficiency) in tomorrow's conditions.

7

Diaspora and Stability

Constitutive Elements in a Body of Knowledge

YASIN AKTAY

ONE CONVENTIONAL WAY of portraying a person intellectually is to look at his or her intellectual works, the references he or she has made, where he or she studied, and the figures that inspired him or her. This method, however, usually results in the reduction of that person to his or her formative components and neglects the creative role an individual plays in his or her own composition and production of specific knowledge. Especially in the case of Fethullah Gülen, it would be a mistake to reduce such a man to the books he has read, the schools where he studied, the religious or intellectual influences on his thinking, and so on. Many others undoubtedly have read the same books, have received a similar education, have traveled to the same locations, or have been influenced by the same people, but no one else became the same person as Gülen.

Indeed, a hermeneutical point, which I pursue in this chapter about the sources of Gülen's knowledge, stresses uniqueness in the formation of one's body of knowledge. Specifically, in this pursuit, I apply the ideas of Hans-Georg Gadamer, who treats this dimension of understanding in terms of the role of prejudices in the process of reading a text and in the analysis of the historically effected consciousness. Gadamer understands prejudices not (as is usual) as negative elements in understanding, but as positively contributive elements in the constitution and reconstitution of one's own body of knowledge; they work as a preunderstanding of a text, stimulating the process of understanding (1991, 341 ff.) Consequently, not only Gülen's knowledge but also all personal knowledge, including the reader's creative performance, should be considered unique. That is, knowledge is not there to be appropriated in an objective way. It is always subject(ive) to the reader's preunderstanding, which in turn is determined

131

mostly by the reader's general history and particular biography. Furthermore, the reading process and the formation of a body of knowledge are determined mostly through an aesthetic dimension, which includes the creative performance of the knowing subject. Of course, a simple conclusion of this formula is that different persons may, and usually do, work the same collection of knowledge resources in completely different ways.

I concentrate mainly on two historical elements that can be considered constitutive in the formation of Gülen's body of knowledge: diaspora and stability. Since the establishment of the Turkish republic in 1923, the diasporic element has operated in a special way in the consciousness of Islamist generations. Social scientists employ the term *diaspora* as a way to explain some modern experiences of migration or mobility in a wider sense, especially the social mobility created by wars and massive migrations in the modern world. Even modernity has been considered a state of exile because it often results in the nonbelonging to a place, the drastic rupture from a space, and permanent movement over the world.[1] In this sense, modernity can be understood as an existential moment through which everyone feels himself or herself exiled from his or her homeland.

I employ the word *diaspora* to conceptualize some aspects of the Islamist discourse in general and of Gülen's discourse in particular. From the destruction of the Ottoman state onward, a strong and peculiar kind of diasporic theme has dominated Islamist discourse in Turkey. The peculiarity of the theme stems from the fact that it is a diaspora produced discursively without a geographical base. It is characterized by the phrase "being a stranger and pariah in his own homeland," as expressed by Necip Fazıl Kısakürek in one of the most prominent Islamist poems. This kind of diaspora is maintained through identity-making literature, which defines the position of the Islamist Subject with relation to the political power. Focusing on the diasporic theme provides grounds for considering several aspects of the mechanisms of making the political identity of the Islamist subject.

The second constitutive element considered here is the quest for stability as a characteristic element of the traditional Islamic ulema, a quest that produced a correspondent ideology of obedience to the state. This ideology is articulated in special ways by Gülen's characteristic nationalism, which distinguishes itself from the other parts of Turkish Islamism.

Of course, I do not reduce all of Gülen's knowledge to these constitutive elements; rather, I distinguish diaspora and stability in outlining his political theory. Although concentrated on intellectual and educational projects, Gülen's

1. See, for example, Papastergiadis 1993 and Ahmed 2000.

individual or communal movement also has much to do with politics. The evidence for this relevance is the movement's program of raising new generations through education, which is a completely political ideal. No less important is a conception of the political that superficially narrows the sphere of its content, reducing it to a formal competition for attaining control of the government apparatus. In this special usage, negative significations are assigned to the political. It is something "bad" to take part in or to think of taking part in the political struggle. By their own set of actions, however, Gülen and his community not only are taking part in the political sphere, but also—and more important—are demonstrating the best example of a new orientation of political action. Since the 1970s, society in Turkey has "reinvented" the civil possibilities of the political sphere as a "subpolitics" [2] that is separate from the struggle for attaining control of the formal governmental apparatus. However, the new possibilities of politicization and Gülen's political theory are the subjects of another investigation. Here, in order to locate Gülen's epistemological resources, I map the intellectual heritage of Turkish Islamism, which produced a strong diasporic mood along with a corresponding peculiar political action.

Diasporic Discourse in Turkish Islamism

Since the foundation of the Turkish republic as a replacement for the Ottoman Empire, the Turkish state has been a symbol of disembodiment for Islamists. Its foundation displaced a political body, the caliphate, which embodied all Muslim political ideals for the early Islamists, such as Mehmed Akif Ersoy, the poet of the Turkish national anthem; Elmalılı Hamdi Yazır, one of the last prominent Ottoman ulema; Mustafa Sabri, the last *sheikh-ül-islam,* who escaped to and spent the rest of his life in Egypt; and Said Nursi, Gülen's predecessor and the author of the collection *Risale-i Nur* (The epistles of light). Despite several criticisms these men made about the late caliphate, they were not at all content with its end. In fact, most Islamists actively or passively protested the secular reforms of the 1920s.

Looking at some of the various forms of these protests may help us understand the immediate effect of abolishing the caliphate. For example, Yazır sequestered himself in his home in order to avoid the social reforms and devoted himself to growing roses. This reaction is illustrated in the novel *Gül Yetiştiren Adam* (The man who grows roses) by Rasim Özdenören, one of the most im-

---

2. Beck (1994) describes the subpolitical development as the process of reinventing politics.

portant Islamist literary figures,[3] and exemplifies the attitude of a significant number of the ulema. For them, the world outside had become irrelevant because of the disembodiment of the Islamic political existence; an Islamic political body was in many respects what made Islamic life possible. Modern Turkey had become "like a transgendered body with the soul of one gender in the body of another."[4] These Islamists conceived of their religion as a blueprint for social order and the caliphate as the sine qua non for the existence of a Muslim society; the absence of the caliphate seemed to create a radical sense of estrangement in them. Özdenören's story shows how "the man who grows roses" has nothing else to do once his society is abolished; he even loses the language through which he could communicate with the society embodying the new dominant foreign soul. Therefore, the only communication he can develop is with the roses he grows, which is easier than communicating with any modern person. In the novel, a child comes to take some informal lessons from the man. That is the element of hope within almost all stories of this kind, the best symbolic possibility of consolation under the diasporic conditions.

Mehmed Akif Ersoy, another writer of diasporic literature, went to Egypt for the rest of his life after the absolute decline of the Ottoman body politic. He ceased to write poetry after the foundation of the republic. His silence was thought to have produced the most meaningful symbolic message. Although he wrote the poem "Nightingale" ("Bülbül"), in which the bird is silent forever because of the absolute absence of hope, in response to the false news that the Greeks had invaded Bursa, it subsequently played a very significant role in articulating the diasporic sentiments of the Islamists in modern Turkey. He compares his condition with that of the ever-crying nightingale:

> You have a partner, a nest, a spring to be waited for;
> Why is this uproar, o nightingale, what is paining you?
> You ascended an emerald throne, founded a divine kingdom
> Your land won't be invaded even if all lands in the world are involved
> . . . Then, while the strangers [*na-mahram*] walking in the intimate places of Islam
> Silent o nightingale! It is mine, not yours, the right to mourn.
>
> (M. A. Ersoy 1989, 435–36)

---

3. Özdenören 1979; on Özdenören, see Meeker 1991.

4. Yavuz (2000b) uses this metaphor for depicting the image of modern Turkey's transition from the Islamists' and the Kurds' point of view.

In his later poems, Ersoy reflected deeper anxieties and mourning: "I'm stupefied, o God! Where is your light, where is your blessing? Should my separation [*hicran*] make a hell walk on my horizons?" (M. A. Ersoy 1989, 452).

Of course, it was not only the abolishment of the caliphate that made the late Ottoman intellectuals feel they were in a diaspora, but also the other reforms the new republican regime made to abolish all remaining religious institutions. For example, along with the caliphate, the Ministry of Shariah and Evkaf also was abolished in 1924. The implementation of the Unification of Education Law in 1924 closed all *medrese*s, the only Islamic institutions for higher learning, or transferred them to the jurisdiction of the Ministry of Education. This action cut off the supply of religious trainees almost completely, thus making it difficult to reproduce an Islamic leadership. With the abolition of the Faculty of Divinity as part of the general University Reform Law in 1933, higher religious studies in Turkey effectively ceased. A 1925 law banned the Sufi (dervish) orders, confiscated their properties, and made illegal all religious practices, rites, and titles connected with them. In effect, virtually all manifestations of religion became illegal, the objective seeming to be the elimination of any civil possibilities for Islamic socialization (Stirling 1958, 396–97). With these measures, most religious functionaries lost their positions and withdrew from public space, and the official propaganda devalued and humiliated them in the eyes of the masses. For many years, words such *medrese, imam, ulema, türban,* and *sheikh* stimulated for many people in Turkey complex feelings between fear and irony.[5]

Other laws affected personally not only the religious elite but also the mass of believers. For example, many Muslims viewed the Hat Law, also known as the dress reform, as the appropriation of individual bodies to make them carriers of the soul of the "other." Therefore, they met this law with resistance. In the 1926 legal reform, secular laws replaced the religious laws that had corresponded to the notion of the unity of an Islamic identity. Islamic laws governing land holding, marriage, inheritance, incest, parental authority and responsibility, and a host of other personal matters were dropped in favor of new laws based on the Swiss Civil Code. The 1928 alphabet reform decreed that Turkish, heretofore written in the Arabic script, be written in a specially adapted Latin script, ostensibly to effect a rapid mobilization of collective literacy. This change in the writing of Turkish had a shocking effect on the minds of the literate, effectively making the majority of them illiterate in their own language in a very short time.

The aim here is not to give a detailed history of the republican reforms con-

---

5. For good depictions of this process, see Aktay 1993, 45–46, and Güngor 1981, 208–9.

cerning secularism, but rather to highlight those measures that contributed to the disembodiment and decaliphatization of the Turkish society and thus began the diasporic experience. All of these reforms dissolved an Islamic political embodiment that made everyday life relevant for the believers. They also came to elaborate all parameters of a diasporic consciousness. Islamism in modern Turkey ought to be understood within the context of such a diasporic history, which is peculiar to Turkish Islamism.

It is important to point out that the majority of people did not have the same experience. One needs to distinguish, for example, between the attitude of the masses and that of the Ottoman Islamist elites during the early years of the republic. As Paul Stirling indicates, the masses were even "less clear about the distinction between loyalty to Turkey and loyalty to Islam" (1958, 399). In fact, some of the reforms required an appropriation and instrumental employment of the Islamic vocabulary for making the new nation. That is, an alternate aspect of these reforms was the obvious quest for a national religion that could serve as a source of vocabulary for Turkish nationalism. However, although Islamists could not justify or tolerate such a pragmatic and instrumental approach to religion—Islam depends on a relative universalism—the masses adopted and legitimated this approach. This process deepened the diasporic situation of the Islamist intellectuals because they seemed to lose their social support and became alienated from the rest of their society. In discourse, however, the Islamists never admitted this reality; rather, they always claimed to represent and to address 99 percent of that society. What was alien for the Islamists was the existing political body that represented Western values and that had ignored the hopes and expectations of the masses, who indeed remained innocent and helpless. Nevertheless, the republic either gained the consent of the masses or created a sufficient mass out of Turkish Muslim society to support the new regime, so the Islamist intellectuals were more likely to be estranged from the rest of society under these circumstances.

In assessing the effect of secularization on the late Ottoman intellectuals, Şerif Mardin argues that they had to situate themselves as persons who communicated with an abstract public:

> Modern Turkish litterateurs like Necip Fazıl felt a sense of disequilibrium both because their traditional status as intellectuals had been restructured while remaining equivocal and also because they had lost a guiding pattern for the elaboration of the self. Nevertheless, they established a new link with the Turkish population at large through the new audiences built by mass media. This new re-

lation may be described as ideological and was a new input into Turkish society. (1994, 211)

The "disequilibrium," the equivocality, and the loss of "a guiding pattern" are associated with the self-narrative of the Turkish Islamist intellectuals, who at the time described themselves as "alienated in their own country," employing vocabulary such as *gurbet* (estrangement), *garip* (stranger), *pariah, homecoming,* and so on. An example of this narrative is Kısakürek's "Sakarya Türküsü." Kısakürek reveals his characteristic poetical personality in the title he gave to the collection of his poems, *Çile Sakarya* (Suffering Sakarya), about a major river in Turkey that has historical significance because one of the most important battles in the Wars of National Liberation was fought on its shores. In the poem, the Sakarya River symbolizes the country, the essential sons and daughters of the country, with whom Kısakürek declares a joint fate:

> But Sakarya is different, it climbs uphill!
> As if a burden made of lead has been charged on its foamy body . . .
> O Sakarya was this burden charged upon you
> This suit is despised, this suit is orphan this suit is great . . .
> There is not but a bitter morsel, from the food cooked with poison
> And a separation, from your mother, your country and friend . . .
> Equal to compunction, o Sakarya, boil! boil!
> You are a stranger in your own home, a pariah in your own country!
> O Sakarya the pure son of the innocent Anatolia
> We remained alone in the way of the God.
>
> (Kısakürek 1988)

The feelings of being a pariah in one's own country and estranged in one's own home bring an unusual dimension to a diaspora: the diaspora need not be a geographical displacement from a homeland, but can be experienced *in* one's home. Such a movement obviously has to be realized by an elaborate discursive effort. Therefore, apart from some individual cases that may be associated with a spatial change, the movement in the Turkish case usually takes place at a discursive level. The new Islamist intellectuals have elaborated this discourse since the foundation of the republic. Not only in "Sakarya Türküsü" but also in most of Kısakürek's poetry, we can see such themes as the sense of estrangement from one's own country, a condition that makes life insufferable and meaningless.

One feature common to all these intellectuals is that they all are very reclusive. This aspect of their personalities is the subject of various anecdotes told about them.[6] Furthermore, in much of the writings of Eşref Edip, Sezai Karakoç, Nuri Pakdil, and other Islamist intellectuals, one can see the elaboration of the same themes. Karakoç's literary movement, for example, takes the name Diriliş (Resurrection), which implies the death of the mission owing to the series of interventions that forced Muslims to live in diasporic conditions. His audience is designated as the generation of resurrection (Diriliş Nesli). In all his writings, he emphasizes the diasporic condition of the Muslims under the rule of the republic, which has meant the disembodiment of Islamic ideals. Not surprisingly, he gives a central place to the *hijra,* the Prophet's migration from Mecca to Medina, in his narrative of Islamic history, but he takes it as a symbolic movement to encompass all Islamic existence. For Karakoç, all Muslims live in a state of *hijra.* That state signifies all moments of a Muslim's existence so that he can see the ultimate reality: he is in a diaspora in the world.[7]

Despite the composition of Karakoç's audience, Diriliş and several themes in his writings suggest a kind of hope. Of course, this hope is similar to that which an ideology always requires for creating an identity and for convincing its adherents to think of themselves as Subject (with a capital S). This hope does not contradict a sense of diaspora, but on the contrary supplements the total condition. The diasporic discourses are elaborated mostly for their higher value in producing such energy. In a similar way, Nietzsche shows that even the discourse of victimness and of oppressedness is (mostly) another expression of the "will to power": the more one can demonstrate being treated unjustly and being wronged, the more one can claim power.[8] Therefore, although the diasporic discourse may be the result of real conditions, appeals to it usually are associated with an implicit or explicit claim for power. Furthermore, like most such discourses, these appeals indeed are more involved in politics than their formal language may suggest.[9]

It must be stressed that Turkish Islamism's diaspora is a discursive rather than a spatial movement. It creates a sense of estrangement through words—that is, literature and poetry. Thus, it represents a different diasporic experience, a diaspora within one's own country. This conception of country, or rather of

6. For a good analysis of Karakoç's personality, see Özdalga 1997, 33.

7. Karakoç tries to interpret all moments of the Muslim's daily life in terms of the *hijra.* See Karakoç 1968, 24–26, and Aktay 1997.

8. For psychoanalysis of the discourses of some Turkish Islamists, especially Necip Fazıl Kısakürek, in Nietzschean terms, see Açıkel 1996.

9. In Nietzsche 1968 and 1995, see aphorisms against the quasi-humble, otherworldly, and seclusion discourses of the Christian priests.

"home," has determined the form of participation in Turkey's social contract. For a long time, the Islamists of Turkey considered the existing body politic as a foreigner that, by its rule, had estranged them from their own home. Of course, the apparent paradox in this situation has created several complexities in their political participation and discourses.

Indeed, many problems related to political life in Turkey arise from this deep problem of mutual legitimization. This reciprocal requirement of legitimization has characterized modern Turkey's history of secularization. Although the secular state has based itself on opposition to some religious elements, it also has been in a quest for legitimization at the religious level. This latter effort has resulted in the state's devising several religious policies, most prominently a unique Turkish Islam. At the same time, the Islamists have been in a mood of diaspora—that is, feeling that the state has treated them unjustly—but they also have been in a quest for legitimization at the state level. Undoubtedly, the most important sources of this tense relation are the lack of a social contract, the ambiguous conditions of citizenship, and the painful process of replacing the Ottoman body politic with the republican regime. Despite the lack of consent (from the political elite), however, Islamism survived and was revitalized by the objection to such a configuration of the body politic.

Until the Refah Party came to power in 1996, it had relied on a complex conception of the body politic. For a significant number of people, however, Refah's governmental experience brought about a decrease in the diasporic discourse. They saw that the existing system—that is, the current tacit or implicit social contract—indeed did include sufficient possibilities for others than the political elite to represent the national body politic of Turkey. From the Islamists' point of view, this realization presented some peace with the existing political apparatus that had been injurious to them since the 1920s. This moment of peace, which Refah usually referred to as the "peace of the nation and state," again was ruptured by the army's 28 February 1997 intervention in the political sphere.[10] A strong mood of diaspora subsequently reemerged among the Islamists because in that year the constitutive definition of the state and body politic was revised again to eliminate all public Islamic elements and to strengthen the secularist element. The secular courts shut down the Refah Party, and its successor, the Fazilet Party, awaits a similar fate; secular leaders abolished the İmam Hatip Schools (for training religious leaders), which they accused of being gardens for the cultivation of backwardness. And the state has been enforcing the prohibition on veiling in public because secular authorities view the

10. For a more detailed analysis on this process, see Yavuz 2000b.

wearing of head scarves by women as a political symbol of antisecularism. Protests for and against veiling have led to the occurrence of very dramatic scenes. The details of these scenes identify a strong channel for the outflow of diasporic discourse: the estrangement of citizens from the body politic.[11]

A Symbolic Geographical Journey: From Erzurum to Izmir Through Edirne

Fethullah Gülen was born in a village in Pasinler, a district of Erzurum Province in eastern Turkey. The city of Erzurum and his father, a mosque leader (*hoca*), were the first two determinants of his intellectual world. Erzurum is unique in eastern Anatolia, known as having a culturally conservative and highly pious population. Piety probably remained strong there owing to the widespread religious institutional possibilities, the presence of leading religious personalities, and the informal educational courses in *medrese*s. Although under the University Reform and Unification of Education Laws of 1924 Turkey banned all religious educational activities outside the limited number of İmam Hatip Schools (which very soon were closed completely),[12] religious figures and institutions not recognized by the state did not disappear, but rather retained a wide network of *medrese*s throughout eastern and southeastern Anatolia. These *medrese*s taught various modern sciences and philosophy and to some extent Islamic sciences such as Qur'anic exegesis, hadith (prophetic traditions), *fiqh* (Islamic jurisprudence), and Arabic. The *medrese* network had been broken up or forced to go underground during the one-party regime of Turkey from 1923 to 1946, but it never completely disappeared. In this period, the underground experiences of the *medrese*s, which offered the only possibility of transmitting Islam or Qur'anic scholarship, created popular narratives of escaping or hiding from state operations. State officials prosecuted those who read, learned, or taught the Qur'an secretly in Arabic because as part of the reformers' policy of nationalizing Islam, the use of Arabic in religious texts had been prohibited. This prohibition was unacceptable for the majority of people, who saw it as a direct attack on Islam,

---

11. For a good analysis of the veiling issue in Turkey, see Özdalga 1998b.

12. This closure was the first closure of these schools in the republic. The İmam Hatip Schools reopened in 1949 to educate enlightened and secularist religious men to cope with religious backwardness. For more on the İmam Hatip Schools, see Akşit 1991, Aktay 1993, and Jäschke 1972. For a good sociological analysis of these schools following the eight-year obligatory school reform, see Özdalga 1997.

and it prompted the pursuit of conservatism in the remaining institutions, even at the underground level.[13]

Although no formal education was available outside state institutions, Gülen left school in the middle of the elementary level and began receiving an informal education. This process constitutes the early phase of the diasporic experience, an important determinant not only in Gülen's life but also in the life of almost all Turkish Islamists. His mother, who profoundly influenced him, secretly taught the Qur'an to the girls of the village, and Gülen learned his first lesson this way (L. Erdoğan 1997, 25). Indeed, this circumstance, together with the general conditions of the country, was enough to create a sense of himself as the "other" in relation to the dominant policies. Of course, these lessons were not the only informal education Gülen received. His grandfather was also very influential in the formation of his personality and education. He was the hero of Gülen's early life, his heroism exemplified by his insistence on not wearing a hat, as decreed by the government, but instead always wearing a turban. He thus made a contrast to villagers who wore hats in fear of the government soldiers (L. Erdoğan 1997, 43). Another important figure in Gülen's early life was Alvarlı Hoca. Alvarlı seems to have given Gülen his elementary education, as well as an education in personality. Under Alvarlı's supervision, Gülen committed the Qur'an to memory and studied the elementary lessons in Arabic, *fiqh,* and exegesis. Thus, Erzurum, like many other eastern Anatolian cities, played its characteristic role in resistance against the modern educational reform.

Despite its opposition to republican cultural policies, Erzurum also has been an important center for defending Turkish nationalist ideology. This ideology is imbued with statism, even its authoritarian aspects. Erzurum's special kind of conservatism is characterized by the *dadaş* culture, an "identity . . . characterized by the culture of frontier conditions, which stresses security over other concerns. Due to this geographic frontier position and the presence of immigrants from Caucuses [*sic*], the cultural identity of the region has always been highly politicized" (Yavuz 1999c, 594; see also Yavuz 1999b, 121). In Turkish popular culture, *dadaş* connotes traditional virtues such as honor, generosity, manliness, and loyalty, as well as a frontier kind of nationalism. A *dadaş* culture takes up the protection of the Turkish Islamic frontier against attacks that come from "the East." Here the East is a very sensitive concept because it makes *dadaş*ism work as a defense against threats from inside Turkey, rather than from the outside. What makes a threat from the external East an internal danger is the possibility

13. For a literary depiction of this mood, see Kısakürek n.d.

of its finding supporters inside Turkey. In this sense, Russian communism formerly posed a threat because it found support among the Turks. During the
1970s, for example, when the rightist-nationalist and leftist-communist movements divided Turkish society, the *dadaş* culture demonstrated its strength as
being the most zealous defender of Turkish nationality against all challenges. In
fact, Gülen mentions in his biography that one of his earliest political activities
was leading the Turkish Association for Struggle Against Communism in Erzurum.[14] Later, Iranian Islam was perceived to be a political threat that *dadaş* Islam
in Turkey should counter, and subsequently Gülen began to recruit ideological
support against this external movement as well.[15]

Thus, Erzurum was not a passive site of residence for Gülen but played a
crucial role in developing his deep convictions. In addition, Gülen points out
that his origins via his grandfather go back to Ahlat, a district of another eastern
Anatolian city, Bitlis. According to Gülen, the most prominent aspect of Bitlis is
its historical role. It served as a gate to Anatolia for Turks and Muslims coming
from the east and south and as a refuge for the descendants of the Prophet who
fled from the oppressions of the Umayyad and Abbasid dynasties. Thus, Ahlat
became a meeting point for Turkish and Islamic cultures and provided a haven
for a significant number of prominent men (L. Erdoğan 1997, 14).

Of course, the emphasis placed on both features of Ahlat in Gülen's self-
narrative illuminates a constitutive element of his personality and his consciousness.[16] His choice of such features gives us some clues to the nature of his
identification. Here, we can distinguish the shelter quality of the city in question.
In fact, a shelter is a temporary place. It is a stopping point, where one prepares
to continue his journey. Although Gülen's ancestors had to flee from Ahlat, altogether these journeys had a strong impact or in turn were employed in constituting a diasporic consciousness. A diasporic discourse prominently marks Gülen's
body of knowledge.

Indeed, this discourse corresponds to the reality in Gülen's biography more
so than is the case with any other Islamist figure. He went to the other frontier
city in western Thrace, Edirne, where he felt very much a stranger because
Edirne is more secular than Erzurum. He was a mosque leader there for four

14. This was the second branch office of the organization, which was based in Izmir, a western Anatolian city where Gülen resided after moving from Erzurum. See L. Erdoğan 1997, 78.

15. Despite Gülen's efforts, it is difficult to say that he showed the same degree of sensitivity
toward Iranian Islam as toward communism. However, his manner of reacting to Iranian Islam is
comparable to his earlier reaction against communism.

16. A self-narrative is a story that works as a method of making a political identity; see further
Laclau 1995.

years, fulfilled his military duty, and then spent one more year at another city in the same region. Although the secular cultures of these cities made him feel like he was in another country, he never ceased to propagate his own ideals. In 1966, the Turkish Directorate of Religious Affairs appointed Gülen to İzmir, another frontier but also the third largest city in Turkey. While preaching in various mosques of the region, he experienced legal problems, and since the late 1960s he has been the subject of legal prosecutions for Nurcu activities. Following the military coup of 12 September 1980, he had to evade state prosecutors for six years. Only after 1986 could he appear publicly, although in a very cautious and prudent manner. Although all these characteristic behaviors may be related to his mystical dimension, one is inclined to see Gülen more as a personality who avoids confrontation. In fact, despite all his attempts at reconciliation and legitimization, he is now in exile from his country.

The Sources of Gülen's Diasporic Mood and His Quest for Overcoming It

One of the best ways to understand Gülen is to situate him within the context of the Islamist history of diaspora, to which he brings a peculiar solution and interpretation. Indeed, Gülen's biography, which describes many moments of terrible conflict with existing laws, clearly exemplifies the diasporic experience. He was prosecuted, sentenced, and imprisoned numerous times because of his religious activities. Nevertheless, he seems to have undertaken almost all of his activities under the pressure of the legitimization problem. Indeed, offering explanations for the true meaning of his actions seems to be one of his most common activities, and his interview with Latif Erdoğan (1997) is filled with such anecdotes. Enduring such experiences appears to have had a deep effect on him.

Furthermore, Gülen seems to have inherited the diasporic discourses of his predecessors. He often refers to Ersoy's poems, which make a powerful impact in a sermon, and to Kısakürek's writings and poems. In his youth, Gülen organized conferences to which he invited Kısakürek, and he organized groups to read and even to distribute Kısakürek's publications, mainly Kısakürek's major periodical *Büyük Doğu Mecmuası* (L. Erdoğan 1997, 54 ff.). Gülen also treats Sezai Karakoç in the same way, reading and distributing his works. Of course, the most important figure in this diasporic context is Said Nursi. Thus, Gülen grew up within the context of Turkish Islamism, inheriting a strong political identity based on diasporic grounds. Nursi's contribution to the development of Gülen's consciousness and to the diasporic mood, as one can see in the rich material of

Nursi's biography, was very important. After the founding of the republic, Nursi, who died in 1960, spent most of his life under prosecution or in exile. Most of his books were written and distributed secretly in Barla, Isparta, and Eskişehir, places where he lived as an exiled man after being arrested several times and questioned for some of his ideas. He was tried in the courts on numerous occasions, although he was acquitted each time. These times in his life have been described as the days of secrecy, and they led to the social actions of his followers, the Nurcus.[17]

Earlier disciples and the most important carriers of the Nurcu movement, including Gülen himself as a youth, grew up during these years in which Nursi was exiled and prosecuted. Indeed, Nurcu political action was influenced deeply by this mood of diaspora and feeling of being wronged. Furthermore, this mood also deeply impacted Nursi's approach to various intellectual issues. For example, he refused to accept the opening of the gate of *ijtihad* (interpretation in Islamic jurisprudence) with respect to these diasporic conditions. According to Nursi, although the gate essentially is not closed, *ijtihad* should not be used while Islam is under collective attacks by its enemies.[18]

One very easily can identify in Nursi a higher level of diasporic mood expressed both ontologically and politically. According to Yavuz, Nursi "always felt himself in *gurbet* (estrangement) and explain[ed] how he overcame this sense of isolation through dynamic belief, trust and patience" (1999a, 199). Yvonne Haddad (1999) distinguishes the term *gurbet* (Arabic, *ghurba*) as a paradigm for Muslim life. She explores its deep influence in Nursi's life but also shows how it is a mood that should be conquered by practicing such inner strengths as *sabr* (patience) and *tawakkul* (trust in God). Nursi's life, for Haddad,

> provides an example of how it is possible to conquer the profound sense of loneliness and alienation experienced by the immigrant in an alien and hostile environment. It sets a paradigm for survival, for seeking solace and affirmation from God by attempting to dwell in His presence. In the process, the experience of *ghurba,* estrangement, is transformed into *uns,* companionship. Nursi described his life in exile as one of profound pain, of being alone and separated from all peers, loved ones and relatives, deprived of all things dear to him, exiled from his native land, and enveloped with a profound sense of estrangement from himself. (1999, 309)

17. For the details of Nursi's life and his experiences in exile, see Mardin 1989 and Nursi 1987.

18. For the effect of the diasporic mood on Nursi's approach to several issues, see Aktay 1997, chap. 5.

Although exile is an objective reality for an individual, *ghurba* is a mood, a consequence of this reality that one can overcome by psychological will power. Although Haddad tries to show how Nursi overcame the *ghurba* mood caused by the objective conditions of his exile, his mention of these conditions in his biography effectively is a passage through a diasporic mood.

Having been influenced deeply by this legacy, Gülen, too, undoubtedly passed through similar phases. Although he came from the Nurcu tradition, he differed from the mainstream movement by supplementing his views with diverse sources of knowledge in addition to Nursi's *Risale-i Nur*. In effect, he developed a separate branch within and outside the general Nurcu movement. Although he never departed completely from Nursi, sharing with him a strong mood of diaspora, he also differed from Nursi in developing a peculiar way to overcome the diasporic conditions. This way is Gülen's different approach to politics and the state apparatus. His approach, as shown previously, was to effect a reconciliation with the foreign body politic.

Since the beginning of the 1990s, Gülen has been a strong ally of various state policies in exchange for state tolerance of his activities. For example, he has taken an active role in the Central Asian countries, opening schools and motivating his clients to invest there. This activity, which has brought him to the center of attention, derived from an ideology that evolved easily out of the existing configuration of the Gülen movement. Former president Turgut Özal, in an interview just before his death, said that Gülen's supporters represented the pioneering conquerors of the neo-*akıncı*[19] movement of a new Turkish imperial era (Çandar 1993–94).[20] This alliance with the state symbolizes Gülen's reconciliation with the existing political body. At this time, one can see in Gülen's discourses a shift in the diasporic mood from political to ontological and mystical. This shift required an ascetic conception of the world, one that could motivate his supporters to go abroad and work hard for low wages. They have undertaken such activity for the sake of a higher moral value that transcended the physical values and is symbolized by the employment of a rich vocabulary of the Islamic ethics of hard work, self-sacrifice, and self-devotion. Terms such as *gurbet, hijra* (migration), *ghazi* (holy warrior), *fikir akıncısı* (the Ottoman frontier of ideas), and so on are prominent examples of this vocabulary. The books put together from Gülen's sermons and speeches (and regularly distributed by the daily newspaper *Zaman*) are handbooks for his students and contain texts that very suc-

19. *Akıncı* were the (very often) irregular frontier warrior groups in Ottoman society.
20. Gülen explains his task in the Central Asian countries in Can 1996, 53 ff. Cf. Yavuz 1995b.

cessfully motivate people to share such values and to participate in the activities that demonstrate these values.[21] These books combine modern science with traditional religious knowledge and try to solve the exaggerated science-belief conflict on behalf of religious claims. They employ terms such as *hijra* and *ghurba* and others in the diasporic vocabulary in an aesthetic manner to mobilize community members to go out of the country to work voluntarily, even in the worst conditions, in the movement's educational network. The ultimate purpose of this *hijra*, however, now is defined in terms of Turkish Islamic nationalism.[22]

The shift in mood also required a sort of nationalism that could be reconciled with a religious universalism, for, above all, the employment of the Turkish frontier movement required association with an idealistic concept. Although Gülen's intellectual and ideological background was ready enough to provide such a concept, in critical times the alliance required more than a voluntary engagement in nationalism. In the process begun by the 28 February 1997 "soft coup"—a campaign against the Islamist movement being led by the Refah Party—Gülen took the side of the state and blamed Refah for creating tension with the Turkish nation. He appeared several times on national television, where he declared his differences with "other" Islamists and made references to "tolerance," "Turkish Islam," "cultural Islam versus political Islam," and so on. He permitted the state-dominated media to portray him as an alternative to the political Islam led by the Refah Party—that is, as a characteristically cultured, enlightened,[23] national, and indigenous religious man.

Nevertheless, the same media and state forces always remained suspicious and reserved about Gülen because his past was filled with speeches and declarations implying his differences with and hostility to the existing political body. Indeed, in a process like the one through which Gülen had passed, he really may have changed. However, the state, in its violent campaign against Islamic formations, in the end could not accept that Gülen's movement had revised its stance against republican authorities and values. Consequently, the Gülen movement's diasporic discourse increasingly has been transformed into an actual diasporic condition. In fact, the movement is under permanent legal persecution, and Gülen is out of his country. The Institution of Higher Education has chosen the

21. Gülen rarely has written books. Most of his writings are essays published in the monthly journal *Sızıntı,* which he directs, and edited collections of his speeches, sermons, and interviews. These collections include essays on Qur'anic exegesis, Islamic mysticism, and modern problems and their Islamic solutions.

22. For Gülen's views on *hijra,* see Gülen 1997g, 43.

23. The "enlightened religious man" has been the ideal target of Turkey's educational policies since the establishment of the republic.

university Gülen advised—one noted for its high academic standards, ranking fifth among more than eighty universities in Turkey—for gradual closure. For these reasons, not just Gülen himself but also his followers have fallen into the same mood of diaspora. In such a context, one really cannot measure true intentions. The only available logic is that a diaspora implies nothing but a distorted condition of communication, as Habermas explains it (1979, chap. 1).

From Modernity as Diaspora to a Religious Existential Diaspora

Although Gülen did not receive a modern formal education, he represents a highly modern ideology in many respects.[24] Take, for example, the experience of the modern world as an exile or as a diaspora. One way of reading modernization is to see in it the feeling of strangeness. What characterizes this sense of diaspora is above all the higher mobility that modernity brings about. No less important is the diaspora that results in the distance between corresponding ideologies that define authentic ideal life worlds and actual reality. The imagined and idealized world always has to be out there in exile; it cannot be present because the possibility of its presence naturally puts an end to the working of the ideology. What makes the modern world a diasporic one is the domination of this distance, the nonpresence or the *différance* in Derridean terms.[25]

In its early stages, modernity made people believe in the possibility of closing this distance, but, over time, this belief had to be replaced by a sense of hopelessness, which corresponded to a discourse of diaspora, or exile. Communists are exiled from their idealized world; almost all nationalists are distant from their original countries or the ideal country they hope to reach. Whereas political ideologies rely on the maintenance of the distance of the idealized world and the existing realities in experiencing their diaspora, religions rely on their conceptions of a "Golden Age." The tradition of Islam, like all other religions, provides a rich vocabulary for such a conception. Believers, for example, still use such famous prophetic sayings as the following: "man is in exile in this world"; "the best people are those who live in my time, then come their successors, then theirs"; and "the world is the hell of the believer." The terms *ghurba,* (estrangement, being away from one's home) and *garib* (alien and strange) are used to describe the strangeness of a believer in the worldly life. A huge discourse exists in Sufi

24. Gülen's movement even may be considered as representing a postmodern condition in terms of its motivations and its orientations regarding faith, science, and recruitment of students; see further Laćiner 1995.

25. See Derrida 1978 and Zizek 1989.

literature elaborating the implications of *ghurba*.[26] However, this discourse also has proliferated and produced such sayings as "a Sufi is a child of the time" (*ibn al-waqt*) and descriptions of the Sufi as resisting ongoing realities. Whereas the general religious discourse of exile usually implies a conflict with the on-going realities, the Sufi discourse usually is employed to accommodate that resistance. These double aspects constitute an interesting perspective in Gülen's discourse.

In Gülen, one can see a strong appropriation of both aspects of these traditional elements. In various speeches, he emphasizes his strangeness in this world. The days, even the years, he spent in Edirne, Kırklareli, and İzmir made him feel such an actual distance from his home, but he has been very adept in reading and accommodating to changing conditions. This accommodation, of course, takes a form of "understanding the contemporary place to meet modern challenges and 'understand our faith' " (Yavuz 1999c, 597). His community's performance in synthesizing its Islamic ideal with global conditions is striking. Furthermore, the political reconciliation articulated by the dialogic discourse of the community, although maintaining some traces of double-speak, seems to indicate the same performance as stimulated by a sense of diaspora.

The Accommodative Effects of Diaspora

Perhaps this is the proper place to review some parallel aspects of the original experience of diaspora by the Jews. Indeed, as mentioned earlier, diaspora has been a general discourse of social displacement or unsettlement in the global context of our time and so has been disassociated from its Jewish context. However, as a conceptual model, it should serve well enough for a comparative outlook. As S. Sayyid notes, "The Muslims do not have a Zion—a place of redemptive return. Also the universalistic urge within many Muslim discourses makes it difficult to locate a unitary point of origin, and so there is no homeland, imagined or otherwise. . . . It is for this reason, therefore, that the notion of diaspora seems an unlikely metaphor for describing the Muslim umma" (2000, 41).

Therefore, if we insist on using this metaphor with regard to Muslims, it should correspond to some specific discourses of some specific Muslims. In that case, those specific Muslims should be considered deviants from the "universalistic urge" of the Islamic way. Another way of insisting on the metaphor is, as Sayyid also admits, to reconceptualize it "from demographic to political"

26. These poetic words by Gülen, written during his journey to the United States, probably represent more than a longing for his own country. See, for example, his poem in Sevindi 1997.

(2000, 41). Indeed, our description of the diasporic elements in the specific Muslim discourses tries both ways. We find there a deep and fragile sense of the world and a quest for accommodating to conditions, probably the result of a defensive reflex. Such a reconceptualization would help us understand the development of a will to the stability of conditions, even those under which one is suppressed. What makes one desire the stability of conditions under which one is oppressed? This question can be answered best through a reconstruction of the diaspora concept. We read from Mircea Eliade's *A History of Religious Ideas* about the Babylonian Talmud, which appeared in the diaspora period and

> played a decisive function in the history of the Jewish people: it showed how the Jews should adapt themselves to the different sociopolitical environments of the Diaspora. Already in the third century, a Babylonian master had formulated this fundamental principle: the legislation of the regular government constitutes the only legitimate law, and must be respected by the Jews. Thus the legitimacy of local governmental authorities receives a ratification of a religious order. In matters which concern civil law, the members of the community are obliged to present their litigations before the Jewish courts. (Eliade 1985, 3: 155)

Of course, it would not be proper to try to find strict parallelisms between this Jewish experience of diaspora and Gülen's experiences. However, the rough parallels we can find are inspiring enough to help us understand how diasporic feelings or discourses usually lead to accommodation rather than to conflict. Although Gülen's statist vision might sincerely be motivated by his nationalist worldview, it also must be influenced significantly by a search for security. Indeed, in Gülen's appeals to anticommunist movements and to political Islamism articulated by the Refah Party tradition, such a concern is evident. Moreover, it is very difficult to distinguish sincere nationalism from a clientele relation with the state. The special characteristic of diasporic experiences is that they raise a communal solidarity among the believers in exile. This solidarity may take the form of defense against the challenging dominant forces, as in many examples of ethnic or religious minorities. Protestant believers have exemplified such solidarity on various occasions.[27] It also may take the form of ambitious desire to gain positions in social, economic, and political spheres for the sake of the group. In any

---

27. I believe the Protestants' contributions to the development of capitalism were their diasporic feelings, which seem to have created a high level of solidarity in face of the threat of Catholicism, rather than their ascetic calling for working hard. See Aktay 1999, 120 ff.

case, such diasporic experiences create higher-level social capital, even in a foreign society.

An Aporia in Such Usage of the Term Diaspora

Nevertheless, if an aporia (irreconcilable paradoxes; see further Derrida 1974, 60–61) would be sought in this conception of the diaspora—that is, the diaspora in one's own home—it would be found in the dissimilarity of the original purposes and conclusions of a diaspora. In the original experiences of diaspora (that of the Jewish people), the main purpose of diasporic activity was to flee from enemies or from various pressures or from both. In fact, the diaspora always meant relative freedom, compared with life in the departed places. What makes diaspora painful is the separation from home, the estrangement in the new countries—an estrangement that can be overcome. In my employment of the term, however, the pain is permanent under the conditions of modernity; diaspora continues the pressures, prosecutions, and the undesired conditions. In fact, a true diasporic experience should mean a relative emancipation. Under what conditions should it be desired, then? What is diasporic in the experiences of the Turkish Islamists in general and of Gülen in particular?

Indeed, a significant amount of freedom can be found in relations with the imagined original country, with the literal meanings of the texts, or with the idealized conditions. That is, the pressures themselves provide the liberating conditions of a diaspora. Feeling estranged in one's own home paradoxically provides an additional legitimacy to feel free of the charge of conducting an Islamic ideal life. Everything can be delayed or even abolished because of the dominant evil conditions. One even can violate one's main principles because the conditions make their application impossible. Such discourse of diaspora thus fulfills its function in articulating a liberal way of life associated with a rightist or conservative ideology. It mobilizes a strong discourse of accommodation to the real conditions, while also basing its reason of existence on the hopes and intentions of changing the world, intentions that now have to be delayed because of the impossibility of closing the great gap between them and the ongoing world. Indeed, Leonard Binder (1988) has demonstrated how some radical movements paradoxically may result in strengthening the liberal mode of life owing to the constant gap between ongoing reality, on the one hand, and the ideal world and their usually anachronistic conception of the social world, on the other.[28] Al-

---

28. Max Weber (1976) also discusses this paradox in his analysis of fundamentalist religious movements in Europe.

though this gap initially may create tensions in society, in time a greater level of accommodation to reality replaces it, perhaps contributing to a relatively more civil society based on communal solidarity.[29]

In various Gülen speeches and interviews since 1997, one can see admissions of political withdrawal in his ideas and practices. He declared, for example, that an Islamic state is not necessary because it would constitute just a small portion of the total Islamic life. Even the interviews that made Gülen a public figure centered on how to create a strong Turkish country and society and how to make Turkey powerful among other nations. This clear identification of the Islamic community with the national body politic occurred even in the heyday of the state- and media-led political campaign against the Islamist movements. Of course, from the expression of such ideas only, one cannot deduce a liberal tendency in Gülen's political philosophy and practices. On the contrary, these practices include a prominent authoritarian manner. Rather, the liberal effect appears in their relationship with the religious texts and with their application to the real world. "Thus the legitimacy of local governmental authorities receives a ratification of a religious order. In matters which concern civil law, the members of the community are obliged to present their litigations before the Islamic courts" (Eliade 1985, 3: 155). That is the diasporic effect on the observation of religious belief in a liberal way.

The Legacy of Islamic Political Philosophy: Stability Versus Anarchy

The ideological basis of such an accommodation relies on Islamic terms, and one cannot see Jewish references in either Gülen's or any other Islamic movement's discourse. Diaspora is only a metaphor to conceptualize the conditions of Turkish Islamism in terms of its being deprived of any focus of decision, of a leader, of a political body. That is, it is a condition of decaliphatization, a condition reflected in the discourse of being estranged in one's own home. Gülen's predecessors exemplified such a discourse. He, however, tried to overcome this condition that separated the political body and individual Muslims. Although Gülen has been influenced by his predecessors and inherited a strong theme of diaspora from them, he also articulates a special way of closing this gap with the state. His characteristic solution has been to change the interpretation of the relationship between the state, on the one hand, and the national and religious identities, on the other.

His interpretation has an important origin within Islamic political practice

---

29. See Yavuz 1999c.

because it was shaped during the Umayyad, Abbasid, and Ottoman periods. The establishment of a legitimate caliph or leader always has posed an important problem for the practice of an Islamic life. Beginning with the creation of a sultanate as a model for leading Islamic society and policy, the caliphate's legitimacy has been under question. Although the first four caliphs were considered fully legitimate as successors of the Prophet, the ones thereafter usually were questioned because of the sultanate nature of their rule and succession. In fact, the first major schism in Islam, between the Sunni and Shia sects, came about because of the conflict over the definition of a legitimate caliph. Whereas the Shias insisted on a leader fully legitimated through descent from the Prophet, the Sunni ulema preferred a realistic way of basing the legitimacy of the caliph: on his ability to apply the compulsory religious principles of Islam. Then, the Muslim ulema condemned armed revolt against an established government and required obedience from all subjects. This obedience was limited only in the sense that the individual should refuse to disobey a command of God. Otherwise, Islamic scholars such as al-Ghazzali held that obeying rulers, even tyrannical ones, was better than resistance that could lead to civil war and anarchy. Although these fears were realistic, the pressure of political necessity actually led Muslim jurists to accept any established government as legitimate and to put aside their insistence on the supremacy of the religious leader—the caliph—over the political ruler (Lapidus 1988, 183).[30] Even Ibn Taymiyya (1985), despite his fundamentalist tendency, admitted the desirability of a stable administration versus conditions of anarchy under which religion could not be applied.

Gülen's predecessor, Nursi, relied on such reasons in rejecting Sheikh Said's call to revolt against the newly established Republic of Turkey in 1925. Sheikh Said justified his revolt because the republic had abolished the caliphate and substituted a national identity that divided and discriminated against groups within the Islamic *umma*. Thus, for Sheikh Said, the state had destroyed the only principle holding the Turkish and Kurdish peoples together in a unified country. Although Nursi, too, was a Kurd, his response to the situation represented both the characteristic attitude of the ulema regarding anarchism and justice and the interesting discourse of religious nationalism. He said, "I cannot revolt against a nation whose ancestors for centuries led the Islamic movement in the world" (qtd. in Şahiner 1979, 254–55). He then improvised a special discourse against anarchism, even within the secular state, because of the worse conditions of instability.

Apart from the complications of Gülen's special experience of a diasporic

---

30. On the debates in Islamic political philosophy about this problem, see Rosenthal 1962.

condition, this fear of civil war or anarchism seems to have influenced his political philosophy and attitude toward the existing system. The state "has an essential value even in a context of relativity" (Sevindi 1997, 43). For Gülen, the existence of a state or a system of law is essential. It would be good, of course, if the state were administrated by a just ruler and even better if the rulers were good caliphs, but in their absence even the worse ruler should be obeyed because the absence of a state leads directly to anarchy, which is always the worse alternative. Anarchical conditions make the application of even the simplest Islamic rituals impossible. As Eyüp Can explains it,

> The absence of a state is an immediate anarchy. Statelessness means instability. It also means the excess of the hostility against every kind of idea. For a while assume the absence of a state, even of a socialist state in Turkey. You would see blood flow in the struggles between factions, religious sects, orders and groups. The mosque communities would each be like the Anatolian principalities of the Ottoman times. One skilled preacher would arise and influence a crowd of people and lead them in the streets. In tolerating the conditions of democracy, sometimes we see such occurrences. (1996, 134–35)

The fear of anarchy and civil war and their threat to the existence of even the simplest Islamic body politic leads Gülen to favor stability over complete justice, just as Sunni ulema did for centuries. Furthermore, he charges upon himself the defense and legitimization of Turkish state policies concerning international relations and cultural identity. This ideological service includes the promotion of an Islam with a Turkish character, versus political Islam and the Islamic models of other countries such as Iran, Pakistan, and Afghanistan. In his various speeches, Gülen has declared the superiority of Turkish Sunni Islam especially to the Iranian Shia Islam. His comparisons portray Turkish Islam as more humanitarian, tolerant, intimate, and plausible, while describing Shia Islam as intolerant, insincere, and reactionary (Sevindi 1997, 7–52). Gülen articulates the Turkish popular and official opinion of Iranian Islam, and for this reason the state in the early 1990s promoted him as an "enlightened and cultured" figure. Through his educational network, he replies positively to the notion of service in making the new Turkey. Thus, he promotes the Turkish language as a world language (Sevindi 1997, 55–58), strengthens cultural Islam vis-à-vis political Islam, denounces terrorism in the name of Islam (Sevindi 1997, 83 ff.), and raises a new type of citizen required by a Turkish state that seeks to be a new superpower in the region (Sevindi 1997, 97 ff.). Gülen's manner of overcoming the diasporic mood that resulted from the great gap between his ideas and the realities in Turkey is expressed through accommodation and appropriation of the existing world. In turn, it is articulated easily and strongly with a rightist and conservative ideology because of the burden imposed by his tacit cooperation with the dominant political forces.

The Hermeneutical Context

The Islamic literary men employed the diasporic condition as metaphor to represent Turkish Islamism with the widespread usage of phrases such as "stranger in one's own home" and "pariah in one's own country." This essay has shown how Gülen inherited and shared such a metaphor and how it determined the formation of his body of knowledge. It relies on a hermeneutical assumption that literature or certain knowledge cannot be appropriated objectively. On the contrary, it is appropriated in mediation of the constructive reading of an individual or a community. A historical principle works in this constructive reading, of course, but the ontological and aesthetic dimensions hold sway, and certain knowledge flourishes and is manifest in numerous ways. The historical conditions of a particular community, certain persons' special commitment to a political and communal identity, quests for religious and political (dis)embodiment, and corresponding tensions and conflicts are important in understanding Gülen and his aesthetic contribution to the constitution of a body of knowledge. Apart from these conditions, depicted through a diasporic vocabulary, several approaches have played a considerable role in Gülen's and his community's development: his aesthetic performance, his special rhetorical skills in addressing his audiences (such as crying and using metaphors, allegories, and small historical anecdotes), and his establishment of communication channels to spread the message. By taking these communication channels into consideration in understanding how Gülen and his community have configured a certain body of knowledge, one can find a hermeneutical context.

The aesthetic dimension is very prominent in the formation of a peculiar personality. Gülen's oral and written texts function in an aesthetic way rather than in merely cognitive or argumentative ways. These texts—spread through videotapes, cassette recordings, and printed material—have a semireligious mood, and their reproduction and consumption are very important in configuring a body of knowledge.

In this context, the employment of diasporic elements in the discourse has much to do with the constitution of a political identity and with the relationship between the body politic and the political body—that is, between the society and the political apparatus. The more the diasporic mood increases, the more the unity of a society and the integrity of a political body decrease. This process is related very closely to the development of the definitions of citizenship in Turkish political life. Gülen's body of knowledge represents a characteristic moment in the unstable process of forming this concept.

8

Fethullah Gülen

A Sufi in His Own Way

ZEKI SARITOPRAK

FETHULLAH GÜLEN is one of the most influential and impressive Muslim Turkish scholars of the last decades of the twentieth century. Despite this, no published work about him has studied his school of religious thought adequately. In this chapter, I explore his Sufism. After a preliminary introduction of Sufism, I focus specifically on Gülen's attitude toward Sufism and his own spirituality.

What Is Sufism?

There are many definitions of Sufism, as well as several theories regarding the origin of the term. Delving into the details of definitions and theories is beyond the scope of this chapter, but a brief look is possible. Some scholars say the term is derived from the Arabic word *suf,* which means "wool," but others say it is from *safa,* which means "purity." The latter seems to be more relevant to the context and aims of Sufism. The person who follows Sufism is called a Sufi. A well-known Sufi in North Africa, Ahmad al-Alawi, describes the essence of Sufism: "It is an Islamic way of transcending one's own soul, that is, of letting one's spirit rise above oneself. And it is where human self ends and the heavenly mysterious begins" (qtd. in Lings 1993, 34). In other words, Sufism means abandoning one's physical form in order to gain a spiritual nature. This transformation is expressed in the phrase "annihilation in God's presence." Through annihilation, one realizes oneself in God. The principle of annihilation has been formulated by a Nakşibendi sheikh as follows: "Four things are necessary in the Nakşibendi order: Abandoning the world, abandoning the hereafter, abandoning the body, and abandoning this 'abandoning' " (Nursi 1992, 511). It should be noted that

156

reaching this level is a long process for a Sufi. In his invocations, the poet Khawajah Abdullah Ansari illustrates fully the aim of the Sufi path:

> The heart inquired of the soul
> What is the beginning of the business?
> What its end and what its fruit?
> The soul answered:
> The beginning of it is
> The annihilation of self,
> Its end faithfulness,
> And its fruit immortality.
>
> (Singh 1939, 42;
> cited in S. H. Nasr 1991, 34)

Sufism is grounded in the powerful spiritual message of the Prophet of Islam. Even before the revelation of the Qur'an, the Prophet used to go to the cave of Hira and isolate himself from the worldly life in order to focus on his spirituality. Then, one day, the angel Gabriel appeared unto him. This was the spark of the Prophet's long spiritual journey. The revelation of the Qur'an came verse by verse and encouraged the Prophet and his companions to follow a spiritual path of life. The freshness of God's words dominated their spirits. They commenced a profound glorification of God's names. Starting from the very beginning of its revelation, the Qur'an has been promoting and encouraging piety and purification of the heart. The Qur'anic concordance records 133 different variations of the term *qalb* (heart; Turkish: *kalp*). For example, it describes the Prophet Abraham as one who had a "peaceful" heart (37:84). However, it describes others with the phrase, "There is a sickness in their hearts" (2:7). Sickness and peacefulness are not physical traits here, but rather spiritual attributes. Hundreds of verses in the Qur'an deal with similar issues. For instance, the Qur'an posits a different kind of seeing and hearing. Describing nonbelievers, it says, "they have eyes, but they don't see, and they have ears, but they don't hear" (7:179). It also recounts the Prophet's experience with the unseen or the invisible world, one that average humans cannot see—that is, the realm of angels. A clear example of movement in this unseen world is the Prophet's mysterious night journey, which is mentioned briefly in the Qur'an and treated more extensively in the hadith. The Qur'an states simply that the Prophet took a night journey from Mecca to Jerusalem. According to the hadith, the Prophet ascended from Jerusalem to the heavens, accompanied by the archangel Gabriel, and finally met God in the realm of the unseen. The Qur'an calls the level that the Prophet reached *kab qawsayn* (the space between two eyebrows) (81:23), where the physical world separates from the eternal one.[1] Sufis frequently use this term to indicate their closeness to God. Through his ascension, the Prophet opened a way for Muslims to the world of the unseen, *alam al-ghayb*. The Prophet brought back with him from this world the gift of the five daily prayers for his community. This story indicates that believers, through prayers, are able to follow the path of spirituality taken by the Prophet. The Prophet said, "the servant's nearest position to God is when he is in prostration."

The Qur'an emphasizes that this worldly life is a deceptive toy and that the real life is that of the hereafter: "This worldly life is but a test of time and a game. Lo, the home of the hereafter—that is life, if they but knew" (29:64). The Prophet asked his followers to be ascetics, saying, "Be in this world as a stranger or as a passer-by." He asks them to purify their hearts in order to reach the level of perfection. In the hadith, when Gabriel asks the Prophet about *ihsan* (perfection), the Prophet replies: "Pray to God as if you see Him; although you don't see Him, He sees you." The term *ihsan* later became one of the key terms of Sufism.

The generation of believers who came after the Prophet explored the areas of Qur'anic spirituality and asceticism that constituted a paradigm for later Sufis. They borrowed key terms from the Qur'an, which they applied to their spiritual experience and teachings. Terms such as *qalb* (heart), *tawba* (repentance), *khawf* (fear of God), *baqa* (abiding), *barakah* (blessing), *rida* (contentment), *dhikr* (remembrance of God), *haqq* (the truth), *reja* (hope), *ikhlas* (sincerity), *marifa* (mystical knowledge), *sabr* (patience), *qurb* (nearness to God), *tawakkul* (trust), and *yaqin* (certainty) constitute the heart of the Sufi tradition. At the same time, the later Sufis borrowed negative terms from the Qur'an to describe the temptations with which they struggled, terms such as *nafs*[2] (ego-self), *ghafla* (ritual lapse), *riya* (self-display), and *shirk* (associationism).

Early Sufis—such as Hasan al-Basri (d. 728), the famous woman saint Rabia al-Adawiyya (d. 801), Harith al-Muhasibi (d. 857), Abu Yazid al-Bistami (d. 874), and Junayd al-Baghdadi (d. 910)—used the terms of the Qur'an and the sayings of the Prophet in their teachings and practices. They developed a spiritual basis for the later institutionalization of Sufism. The process of articulation began with Al-Qushayri (d. 1074) in his *Risale* (Treatise). Feriduddin Attar (d. 1230) and his contemporaries Ibn al-Arabi (d. 1240) and Jalalu'ddin Rumi (d. 1273) further

1. On Ibn Hisham's account of this event, see Cells 1996, 54–56.

2. For example, in discussing the term *nafs* and how humans can take refuge from its inclinations, al-Muhasibi refers to the famous verse from the Qur'an in sura al-Yousef (12:53). This verse later became the foundation for the Sufi understanding of the term. See Cells 1996, 176–79.

articulated Sufi thinking in the early period.[3] The Sufi tradition became a way of life that Sufis practiced even in the public sphere. Even before the institutionalization of Sufism, people began to call those who followed the path of certain saints after the names of these saints. In the second phase of its development, innovations and practices such as dance and music (especially that elaborated by Rumi) penetrated into Sufism and caused the ulema to take a stand against it. Therefore, a debate ensued among the scholars of Islamic law (shariah) and the practitioners of Sufism.

One arguably can say that by the thirteenth century Sufism was a reaction to the formalism of the ulema, whom Sufis called the *ulama-i zahir* (scholars of the outward), meaning they judged external actions. Similarly, in the Sermon on the Mount, Jesus said that he had come to breathe spirituality and soul into Hebrew law in order to retain the spirit of the law (Matt. 5–8). One can say that Sufism was to Islamic law what Jesus was to Hebrew law. In time, some Sufis went too far, underestimating and even neglecting some basic religious law, which resulted in the emergence of extreme, esoteric movements. The debate continues between fundamentalist Wahhabi Muslims and Sufis even today.

This period also marked the establishment of the major Sufi orders—namely, the Nakşibendi, Qadiri, Chisty, Suhrawardi, and Shadhili orders.[4] Scholars believe that the most influential Sufi order is the Nakşibendi, named after the famous fourteenth-century Sufi Bahauddin Nakşibend (d. 1389). Many branches of this order remained powerful in India, Central Asia, the Middle East, and Europe throughout the nineteenth and twentieth centuries.[5]

Initiation into the Nakşibendi Sufi order continues to follow traditions developed several generations ago.[6] It may be useful to review this initiation rite, which is similar to that practiced in other orders. When a person intends to become a member of the Nakşibendi order, first he visits the sheikh (master). He takes his sheikh's hands, kisses them, and then the master takes the novice's hands, reciting formula words calling for the repentance of all the sins the novice has committed in his life. The novice repeats the words and promises never to make the same mistakes again. He then accepts the master as his spiritual guide, verbally promising that he will be a member of the order from that

3. Some ideas in Sufism suggest the influence of Jewish and Christian tradition, Gnosticism, neoplatonism, Hinduism, Buddhism, and Zoroastrianism. See Politella 1963.

4. See Shah 1968, 120–75. On the Shadhili order, also see Lings 1993, 57.

5. On the influence of Khalidiyya branch of the Nakşibendi order, see Hakim 1990. For a brief history of the Nakşibendi order, see Algar 1990.

6. The account here is based on the author's interview with a novice who was initiated into the Nakşibendi order in southeast Turkey, 30 April 1994.

moment on. After this ceremony, he leaves the master and takes a shower, symbolizing the cleansing away of spiritual dirt. On the next day, the novice tells the master what, if anything, he saw in his dreams. Then, according to the novice's capacity, the master gives him some spiritual duties, such as reciting the name of God, "Allah," five thousand times a day. The sheikh increases this number up to one hundred thousand in accordance with the novice's ability. If the novice continues to manage what the master asks, depending on his spiritual level, the sheikh may choose him as his successor, or *khalifa,* in certain regions. Then the "novice" may become a prominent Sufi and his fame may surpass that of his master. In short, this is the way a person comes to be a Sufi.

As mentioned, the early Sufis had neither orders nor formal organizations. For example, famous Sufis such as Rabia, Junayd, Muhasibi, Bishr, al-Ghazzali, Feriduddin Attar, and even Rumi did not belong to a *tarikat.* From the perspective of institutionalized Sufism, their Sufism might be problematic because none of them had a spiritual master. In the Sufi tradition, he who has no a sheikh finds Satan as his sheikh. However, current Sufis consider this general principle as nonapplicable to the earliest Sufis, and no member of any Sufi order would claim, for example, that Junayd's sheikh was Satan. These early Sufis, who were not attached to any specific order but practiced and even elaborated the principles of Sufism, simply constitute a different category of Sufism. Hujwiri, an eleventh-century Sufi of Lahore (in modern Pakistan), considered the Prophet's companions and their successors as real Sufis. He wrote: "In the time of the companions of the Prophet and their successors this name [Sufi] did not exist, but the reality thereof was in everyone; now [meaning his time] the name exists, but not the reality."[7] This statement by one of the great Sufis in history indicates that the reality of Sufi thought and practice is much more important than the name Sufism. In fact, Islamic history is replete with Sufi practitioners who did not belong to any Sufi orders. A famous twentieth-century example is Bediüzzaman Said Nursi (d. 1960), the Islamic scholar in Turkey, whom many perceive as Fethullah Gülen's predecessor.

Gülen's Doctrinal Sufism

The basic sources of Gülen's Sufism are the Qur'an, the Prophet's words, and the various Sufi texts, specifically Nursi's seminal work, the *Risale-i Nur* (The epistles of light). We may consider the latter text as the warp on which Gülen has woven his ideas. Basing himself on Junayd, Shibli (d. 946), and other early Sufis,

7. From Reynold A. Nicholson's translation of *Kashf al-Mahjub* and cited in Lings 1993, 34.

Gülen defines a Sufi's way as "the path followed by an individual who, having been able to free himself or herself from human vices and weaknesses in order to acquire angelic qualities and [conducting himself in a manner] pleasing to God, lives in accordance with the requirements of God's knowledge and love and in the resulting spiritual delight that ensues" (1999c, xiv).

In his definition, Gülen focuses on a path by which one can overcome weaknesses by oneself rather than with a guide. The individual must live in accordance with the requirements of the Qur'an and follow the example of the Prophet. Therefore, a Sufi's path must accord with the teachings of the Qur'an and with the sunna of the Prophet. All Sufi practices have to be measured by these criteria. According to Gülen, in order to purify one's heart, "strict observance of all religious obligations, an austere lifestyle, and renunciation of carnal desires [are] required" (1999c, xv).

Gülen divides Sufis into two categories: "Those who stress knowledge and seek to reach their destination through knowledge of God (*ma'rifa*), and those who follow the path of yearning, spiritual ecstasy, and spiritual discovery" (1999c, xxv). In his interpretation, he favors the first group of Sufis. I would argue that the first category also is divided into two subcategories: those who are attached to a Sufi order and those who are not. For example, al-Ghazzali was a Sufi and simultaneously a scholar of Islamic law, but he did not belong to any Sufi order.

Gülen does not differentiate between Sufism and Islamic law (shariah). They are like two departments in a university, each seeking to teach their students the two dimensions of Islam so that the students can practice them in their lives. These two departments are not in opposition; rather, they complement each other. One teaches how to pray, how to fast, and how to give charity, while the other concentrates on what these actions really mean. Sufism in particular teaches how to make worship an inseparable part of one's life and ultimately how to elevate oneself to the rank of a universal and perfect being (*al-insan al-kamil*) (Gülen 1999c, xix-xxx). Sufism helps a novice to gain a deeper understanding of Islamic law (Gülen 1999c, xix). For Gülen, "Sufism is the spirit of Islam" (1998g, 24–27).

Gülen uses Sufi terminology, adding his own understanding by means of a thorough analysis of the technical terms. In his book *Sufism,* he interprets fifty key words of the Sufi path, and his interpretations are consistent with the path of early Sufis such as al-Muhasibi and especially al-Ghazzali. In the case of some terms, it appears that Gülen has elaborated on Nursi's understanding of them. For example, in his interpretation of the term *tawadu* (humility), Gülen quotes from the Qur'an, the hadith, and specific Sufis—particularly from Nursi. The

Qur'anic verse he quotes says: "The servants of the All-merciful are those who walk on the earth in modesty, and if the impudent offend them, they continue their way saying 'peace' " (25:63). After elaborating on the verse, he gives an example from the Prophet's hadith that says: "Whoever is humble, God exalts him; whoever is haughty, God humiliates him."[8] To support his approach further, he also quotes from Muhammed Lutfi Efendi, who said about humility, "Everybody else is good, but I am bad," and from Nursi, who said, "Do not see anything or anybody else other than God as so much greater than you as to deserve adoration or servanthood. Do not boast of yourself in a way to see yourself as greater than another." Finally, Gülen describes humility in his own terms: "Humility is the portal to good conduct or being characterized by the qualities of God (such as generosity, mercy, helpfulness, forgiveness, and so on), it is also the first and foremost means of being near to both the created and the Creator. Roses grow on the earth, and humanity was created on the earth and not in the heavens" (1999c, 76–80). As this example illustrates, Gülen's writings on Sufi concepts share the same features of the early Sufis' work.

In order to examine his concept of Sufism more thoroughly, we can look at how Gülen has elucidated other Sufi terms such as *tawba* (repentance), *zühd* (resistance against desire), *muhasaba* (questioning oneself), *tafakkur* (meditation), *sayr ila Allah* (journey to God), *hudur* (divine presence), *qalb* (heart), and *ihsan* (perfection).[9] According to Gülen, the first step in the Sufi path is *tawba,* or repentance, a Qur'anic command. His definition of this term is larger than the traditional Sufi one. In the traditional understanding, repentance is done by words. However, Gülen adds repentance in motion, in thought, in imagination, and with regard to behavior committed against the will of God (1997e, 14). He is quite explicit in this matter, dividing repentance into three levels, a division also found in early Sufi thought. The first stage is the *tawba* of common people. The second stage is *inaba.* If *tawba* is the journey to God, *inaba* is a journey in God. The third stage is *awba,* which is a journey from God. In other words, *tawba* is refuge in God; *inaba* is annihilation in God in order to maintain the spiritual levels that one has attained; and *awba* is to be closed to everything except God.[10]

Resistance against bodily and mental desires is called *zühd* in the Sufi tradition. According to Gülen, *zühd* is an important moral value. It always has had an important place in Islamic Sufism since the Prophet Muhammad and his life de-

---

8. The hadith mentioned is in the collection of al-Haythami, *Majmau'zzawaid,* 10: 325.

9. I rely on the Turkish version here, but refer to the English translation as well.

10. For the origin of these stages in the Qur'an, Gülen refers to verses 24:31, 39:54, 38:44, and 50:33.

fined its meaning and spirit. *Zühd* should be a significant virtue of every Muslim, especially in this present age of materialism, when it can be very difficult to resist the lures of reputation, money, career, and so on. Yet the principle of *zühd*, an ascetic way of life, requires this resistance. In a softened tone, Gülen says, "The first step in asceticism (*zühd*)] is the intention to avoid what has been forbidden (*haram*) and to engage only in what has been allowed. The second and final step is being extremely careful even when engaging in what is allowed (*halal*) (1999c, 42).

Gülen believes that one who follows the path of Islamic spirituality—which all Muslims are supposed to do—must question oneself every day and even every moment, comparing one's good deeds to one's bad deeds. Gülen calls this *muhasaba-i nafs*, a term that basically is grounded in the Prophet's saying, "O people, question yourselves, before being questioned." In essence, one must discover oneself within one's inner depths. On this matter, Gülen completely reflects al-Ghazzali's ideas about self-knowledge, as expressed in his *Kimya-i Saadat* (The alchemy of happiness) (al-Ghazzali 1991, 5–15). Self-knowledge is the key to knowledge of God: "He who knows himself knows God."

On the subject of questioning oneself, Gülen refers to a verse in the Qur'an: "Verily those show piety, who when a phantom from Satan touches them, recollect themselves, and, lo, they see clearly" (7:201). Accordingly, they are always alert to the satanic phantoms. Gülen describes this self-questioning as the presence of an inner preacher who distinguishes between good and bad. He also refers to the tradition of the Prophet that says, "If you only knew what I knew, you would laugh a little and weep much" (Al-Bukhari, al-Kusuf, 2). The people who are aware of this Sufi way always think of the Qur'anic verse "To God belongs all that is in the heavens and on Earth. Whether you show what is in your minds or conceal it, God calls you to account for it" (2:284). Gülen says: "While it is difficult for everyone to achieve this degree of self-criticism, it is also difficult for those who do not do so to live today better than yesterday, and tomorrow better than today" (1999c, 9). In other words, Gülen wants to emphasize that whoever does not question himself or herself will make no progress, and his or her future will not be better than the present.

In Gülen's opinion, meditation is the light of the heart, the sustenance of the spirit, and the spirit of knowledge. He likens meditation to lifeblood, in accordance with Islam. For those who have this sense of meditation, the universe is a book to be read; it does not require a specific time and space or a definite position. The Qur'anic verse on meditation refers to those people who contemplate, mentioning their specific postures: "those who celebrate the praises of God, standing, sitting, and lying down on their sides, and contemplate the wonder of creation in the heavens and the earth" (2:191).

Gülen defines the Sufi term *sayr,* the spiritual journey, as "a journey from creature to Creator" —in other words, from shadow to reality and from a single drop to the ocean of His mercy. The verse "Hasten you then to God" (51:50) constitutes and shapes the idea of the Sufi journey. The term *hudur* (divine presence), for Gülen, means the feeling of being with God, of being filled with Him, and of finding Him in one's conscience. By continuously maintaining this feeling, one comes into His light. Although the feeling of divine presence emanates from God, Gülen says it changes according to one's personal level and abilities. He views attaining the higher level of *hudur* as having spiritual taste (1995a, 25).

As mentioned earlier, *qalb,* or "heart," is the most distinguished term in Sufism, and it is of paramount importance in Gülen's teaching. Anyone even slightly familiar with Sufi tradition knows the importance of *qalb.* By this term, Gülen does not mean the physical organ of the human body, but the spiritual one, the heart that is the place of faith and the mirror of God. He articulates the matter of heart in his writings through examples from Qur'anic verses, prophetic traditions, other prophets mentioned in the Qur'an, and previous Sufis such as Rumi. In fact, the Turkish title of his book on Sufism is *Kalbin Zümrüt Tepeleri,* (The emerald hills of the heart) (Gülen 1997e).

According to Gülen, *qalb* is a subtle and divine essence that Sufis call "the reality of humanity." The spirit is the ineffable essence of the divine, and the biological soul is its vessel. *Qalb* is a central feature of Sufi teaching in accordance with the Prophet's saying, "God does not look at your appearance, but He looks at your heart" (Muslim, Birr, 33). The heart is the fortress of reason, science, intention, faith, wisdom, and knowledge of and proximity to God. The life of these vital senses is connected to the life of the heart; if the heart is alive, then these others are alive and vice versa. Gülen quotes the prophetic tradition on this point: "Oh, there is a part in the body that, when it becomes good, the whole body becomes good, and when it becomes bad, the whole body becomes bad. Oh, that part is the heart" (Al-Bukhari, Iman, 39). Hence, just like Ahmad Sirhindi, the founder of Mujaddidi Nakşibendi *tarikat,* Gülen holds that the miracles and mysteries of the Sufi path are considered toys of the path. Real Sufis do not ordain such miracles as their target.

It is true that the aim of all Sufi practices is to reach the level of *ihsan,* of being a perfect human. Gülen holds that love is the vital condition of perfection. If there is no love, there is no perfection. Souls without love cannot be elevated to the horizon of human perfection. Even if such people live hundreds of years, they can make no advance on the path of perfection. Those who are deprived of love become entangled in the nets of selfishness, are unable to love anyone else, and die unaware of the love deeply implanted in the very being of existence.[11] These several examples of Gülen's approaches to the Sufi terms are explicated in his books on Sufi concepts.[12]

In the Qur'an, there is an emphasis on the paramount importance of certainty in faith. Believers are encouraged to have certainty in their belief in the hereafter (2:3–4). In further expressing this idea, Gülen states that certain steps are necessary to reach that level of certainty: above all, the believer has to surrender to God and pray sincerely to Him.[13] Gülen describes eleven principles as pertaining to this process:[14]

reaching true belief in God's divine Oneness and living in accordance with his demands;

listening to the word of God and comprehending His power and His will in the physical world (the law of creation);

overflowing with divine love of the truth and seeing the universe as a "cradle of brotherhood";

acting in accordance with the idea of preference, *ithar*—that is, putting others' needs before one's own;

giving priority to the will of God and realizing that through annihilation one can never be separated from God;

being able to discern what is in hearts or minds through facial expressions, the inner, divine mysteries, and the meanings of surface events;

being open to love, spiritual yearning, delight, and ecstasy (*wadjd);*

visiting those places that remind one of the eternal life and intending holy migration (*hijra);*

being content with permitted pleasure and not transgressing against the will of God;

struggling continuously against the desires (longing) of worldly life and being constantly aware that it is transient;

11. On Gülen's teachings about love, see Ünal and Williams 2000, 362–64.

12. In addition to his work *Sufism* (Gülen 1999c), Gülen addresses the subject further in Gülen 1996a, 1996d, 2000c, and 2000d.

13. Gülen says it is unfortunate that many are led away from spirituality by the influence of positivism and thus are deprived of the fruits of Sufism. Those who do not believe in the spiritual life and its results will not be able to reach certainty.

14. Hazrat Inayat Khan, a contemporary Pakistani Sufi, condenses the teachings of Sufism into ten principles, each focusing on a different dimension of Sufism; see "The Sufi Message of Hazrat Inayat Khan, Part 1, ch. 1," cited in Politella 1963.

remembering that there is no salvation without certainty *(yaqin)*, sincerity *(ikhlas)*,[15] and contentment *(rida)*

It must be noted that the concept of *wahdat al-wujud*—the notion that there is no being but His being, formulated as the doctrine of ontological monism—engendered a bitter debate between Sufis and the ulema, especially the scholars in the school of thought founded by Ibn Taymiyya (d. 1328). Gülen's discourse on the subject in his book *Asrın Getirdiği Tereddütler* (Gülen 1998b, 47–60) deserves attention. Referring to Qur'anic verses and prophetic traditions, Gülen accepts that there are some verses that apparently deny the function of human will (8:16, 48:10) and identify God with humans. In the tradition of "My servant becomes so much close to me until I become his eyes, his ears, his hands, and his feet," Gülen delicately distinguishes the difference between the doctrine of *wahdat al-wujud* and pantheism. He argues that the first is a joyful spiritual experience, whereas the second is a mere philosophical theory. In general, he favors the creed of the majority of Sunni scholars that creatures are the signs of the existence of God; therefore, one has to accept the physical realities. The particles of the world cannot be parts of God; because the Qur'an mentions creatures as signs of the existence of God, one must accept the reality of things. Also, there will be an end for everything, so we have to ask, "How can something unreal come to an end?" The eternity of matter is not accepted by consensus (Gülen 1998b, 47–60). Accordingly, Gülen believes that the idea of oneness of being has some Qur'anic and prophetic references; however, those references should not be taken literally. What prominent Sufis such as Ibn al-Arabi and Rumi wrote on the doctrine are the result of their spiritual observations and little understood by those who have not reached that level of spirituality.

The Practical Aspect of Gülen's Sufism

Gülen's way of practicing Sufism is different from that of the Sufi orders. As a devout, celibate[16] person, his life is very simple. He prays five daily prayers, almost without exception, with the congregation and with his followers. Although

15. Gülen criticizes those who pray to God to get a reward of paradise, quoting from Junayd, who says, "They are the servants of Paradise, but not God." "Therefore," Gülen says, "Pleasing God must be the only aim of prayer. One should not pray to God for the sake of paradise, or for the fear of hell" (1998b, 82).

16. Regarding his predecessor's celibacy, Gülen describes how when Nursi was asked whether he ever had thought of marriage, he gave an interesting answer: "The suffering of the Islamic community is more than enough. I haven't found a time to think of myself" (Gülen 1995b, 140).

Sufis are concerned about prayers, in many cases litanies (*awrad*) come before prayer. For Gülen, prayer is the most important part of his life. He wakes up very early and reads his *dhikr* or *awrad*. Because he knows the Qur'an by heart, for him a devotion to constant recitation of the Qur'an is significant. Therefore, he recites and asks his followers and his community to recite. Supplication to and recitation of the Qur'an and application of the verses in his own life have influenced both his interpretation of those verses and his approaches to a variety of faiths. This fact sets him apart from other Sufis. For example, he believes that dialogue is Qur'anic teaching. Accordingly, he seeks to establish good relations with scholars and spiritual leaders of diverse religious groups.[17] To a certain extent, he follows Rumi in pursuing the path of love, opening his arms to people of all religions.

Some Sufis cite this attitude to justify their criticism of Gülen. They think he has no spiritual master. They also criticize him for abandoning the sunna of the Prophet, for not growing a beard, and for not getting married. Gülen, however, believes that having a master is not necessary and that the master does not have to be human. For him, the Qur'an is a superior master and guide. He holds that the way of contemplation is drawn from the Qur'an, and it is not necessary to be confined by a specific Sufi order. Abu Ubayda, one of the prominent companions of the Prophet, is famous for a saying that fully illustrates Gülen's contemplative way: "I have never looked at a single thing without God being nearer to me than it."[18] In this teaching, everything from atoms to stars reflects God according to its level.

It might be useful to picture a day in Gülen's life, a life surrounded by four walls. As mentioned, he wakes up very early, reads his litanies, recites his regular daily Qur'anic reading, performs the morning prayer, and then recites his *awrad*. After having breakfast, he speaks to his students or visitors for half an hour. He responds to questions or discusses religious topics. He then edits his books and articles. He takes a nap before noon and then performs noon prayer. After lunch, he again talks to the people around him and recites some of his daily *awrad* until the afternoon prayer, *asr*. He performs the *asr* prayer and recites and reads some of his regular *awrad*; then, following his doctor's instruction, he uses an exercise bicycle. He performs the *maghrib* prayer. After dinner, he responds to

17. He has met with Pope John Paul II; Leon Levy, former chairman of the Conference of Presidents of U.S. Jewish Organizations; Abraham Foxman, executive director of the (Jewish) Anti-Defamation League; and other spiritual leaders.

18. Quoted from Arberry's translation of al-Kharraz, *Book of Truthfulness,* and cited in Lings 1993, 128.

questions and reads. Finally, after performing the evening prayer, he goes to bed, to wake up for night prayer, *tahajjud*. He sleeps for only a short time. One might say that Gülen's life is filled with three things: prayer, recitation, and reading. His life is full of the awareness of God. Just as Jesus said, "My kingdom is not in this world," Gülen believes that the reason why humankind comes to this world is to prepare for the hereafter, where God has prepared for his servants something "no eye has seen, no ear has heard, and no heart can conceive."

Gülen never calls himself a Sufi. One is not a Sufi in name, but rather in spirit and heart. As Rumi asks, "What Makes the Sufi? Purity of heart, not the patched mantle and the perverse lust of those earth-bound men who steal his name. He in all things discerns the pure essence."[19] In short, Gülen understands that one may annihilate oneself in the rays of the existence of the Truth through knowing one's own impotence, poverty, and nothingness.

The Gülen Community

If Gülen does not promote any Sufi order, then what should one call his gathering of followers? What keeps this large community together?[20] This question has been the source of some confusion and controversy. The Turkish media, in general, call Gülen's community a Sufi order, perhaps intentionally because Sufi orders are prohibited by law in Turkey. The most appropriate term seems to be *Gülen community*. In this community, there is no registration or membership, no verbal promise. The community has an inclusive character, which reflects diversity. The supporters of the community are a diverse group from Jewish businessmen to the *müftü*.[21]

The ties that bind the people of Gülen's community differ from those of the Sufi orders. Sufis share a sheikh and an order. The people of the Gülen community share the same values and understand that these values are conveyed via modern mass communications—books, cassettes, journals, and educational institutions. Nursi's interpretations of the Qur'an and Gülen's writings and videocassettes comprise the main sources of the community's teachings.[22] These teachings and the Qur'an constitute the main connective links between individ-

---

19. Rumi 1990, 24, verse 355–60, cited in Politella 1963.

20. There are no reliable statistics about the number of people in the community. It is believed that the numbers range from between 2 and 4 million (for the numbers of the schools, reading circles, foundations, and active businessmen, see Yavuz 1999c).

21. *Müftü* in modern Turkey are the highest-ranking official religious persons of the city.

22. For textual sources of the community, see Yavuz 1999c.

uals in this community, but Gülen's spiritual influence on those who meet with him also constitutes a very important tie that brings them together. A student in Turkey who sent an e-mail message to the Rumi Forum in Washington, D.C., is a good example of how people are influenced by Gülen's teachings: "I am a student in Turkey. I am very happy that you are organizing a program about Mr. Fethullah Gülen. I have read many of his books and listened to many of his seminars. His ideas, which come from Islam, have changed my life." One can hear similar views from thousands of people in Turkey. An American newspaper correspondent has referred to the Gülen group as a "loosely-knit Islamic Community" ("Turkish Court" 2000).

The people of the Gülen community choose to become active participants in their society and to perform public service by establishing schools and hospitals. The community's enthusiasm for establishing secular schools in both the Muslim and non-Muslim world, specifically schools serving people of all faiths and nationalities, is unprecedented among Sufis. Instead of being isolated from the society, they try to reconcile their spiritual life with their worldly one, following Gülen's advice. Gülen does not have a problem with material prosperity, although he possesses no personal wealth himself.[23]

Gülen's way of Sufism cannot be confined by the framework of a specific Sufi order. Although somewhat following the path of the early Sufis, he also encourages his followers to take an active part in the community, thus differentiating himself from previous Sufi traditions. He has a strong place in the heart of literally millions of people. Their intense support, dedication, and commitment demonstrate the strength of his spiritual presence. History will look at him as one of Islam's greatest figures.

Strictly speaking, Gülen is not a Sufi. However, in light of Hujwiri's definition quoted earlier, Gülen is a Sufi in practice, if not in name. The companions of the Prophet and their successors also were real Sufis, although they were not called Sufis. Given all of the matters discussed here—his dedication to Islam, his interpretations according to Sufi belief, and his ascetic lifestyle—it is clear that Gülen can be called a Sufi, albeit a Sufi in his own way.

23. A Turkish prosecutor, Nuh Mete Yüksel, investigated Gülen's wealth in 2001 and proved that he had none.

9

The Making of Enemy and Friend

Fethullah Gülen's National-Security Identity

HASAN KÖSEBALABAN

FETHULLAH GÜLEN and the movement he established and leads comprise two of the most important actors in Turkish social and political life. The movement retains its power by means of hundreds of schools it manages inside as well as outside the country, as well as by an unofficially affiliated media web that includes widely circulated national daily newspapers, magazines, and television and radio channels not only in Turkey but also in many other countries. Gülen, who now resides in the United States, continues to air his views to his followers directly through interviews and private video recordings. These materials provide sufficient data to analyze how he and his followers perceive the world around them. Their perceptions suggest the ways the movement would like to see Turkish foreign policy oriented.

This chapter provides an overview of Gülen's ideas on issues central to Turkish foreign policy, such as European Union (EU) membership, the hegemonic position of the United States, the relationship with Iran and the Arab world, and the status of the Balkans and Central Asia. The working assumption of this chapter is that the identity of the Turkish state emerges out of a process of identity conflict at the domestic level. Kemalism, nationalism, and Islamism—the latter including Gülen's movement—are important players in this conflict. Although Gülen's movement belongs to the Turkish Islamic identity at large, it is different in significant ways, reflecting the rich diversity within the Turkish Islamic movement. As this chapter shows, his vision of an ideal Turkish foreign policy differs from that held by other segments of the Islamic movement. The construction of the Other—or rather, of multiple Others—in Gülen's national-security identity contrasts sharply not only with Islamists in general, but also with other identity groups in Turkey. His ideas, despite a number of complications and contradictions in them, directly influence Turkish foreign policy and certainly would bring some vivacity to that policy if put to practical application. Rejecting a confrontational attitude toward the West and building a bridge with the East, Gülen offers a dynamic and multidirectional foreign-policy vision. His open antagonism toward Iran and to a lesser extent toward the Arab world, two important centers of power in the Middle East, indicates the limits of his inclusiveness, however.

International Relations and Social Actors

Fethullah Gülen is the leader of a formally apolitical social movement who nevertheless has influenced Turkish political debates, including those related to international relations. International-relations scholarship does not offer much theoretical guidance in understanding the influence of such movements on international politics. Security perceptions of movements like his largely are overlooked in the field, mainly because of the hegemony of structural realism, which perceives the state as the only actor in international politics. States' policies are assumed to be made to maximize national security in an anarchic environment where the meaning of both *security* and *anarchy* is static (Waltz 1979). The constructivist challenge to realism has questioned these assumptions successfully. For constructivists, each state defines its security environment subjectively through the influence of national identity. However, for others, the state continues to be the main unit of analysis; states are the actors in international politics and construct their national identities through interaction with other states; domestic politics remain a distinct area of interest (Wendt 1999). Yet the Turkish case suggests that states do not construct their identities independent of a domestic political environment. Social actors in Turkey have influenced foreign policy by directly participating in policy debates with their national-security identities loaded with their own distinct perceptions. State policies are not constructed solely as reactions to the outside world, but also as reactions to domestic politics. In other words, foreign policy comes as a product of state-society relations wherein "the identity of the state and of social actors . . . could be understood only as mutually constitutive" (Jepperson, Wendt, and Katzenstein 1996, 51).

Alexander Wendt, criticizing realism's monocultural interpretation of anarchy, argues that anarchy can have at least three cultures—namely, Hobbesian, Lockean, and Kantian. These cultures are based on three different social roles—

enemy, rival, and friend, respectively—that dominate the international system (Wendt 1999, 247; see also Wight, Wight, and Porter 1991).

Although Wendt's discussion concerns interstate interaction, perceptions of enmity, rivalry, and friendship are by no means limited to state identity and can be applied equally to social actors' identities. In the case of Turkey, different social groups have different perceptions of the Turkish security environment, and thus in their minds the three social roles are attached to different nations. Each social actor subscribes to a distinct culture of insecurity that informs the actor's perceptions of national-security threats. As Jutta Weldes explains, "insecurity is itself the product of processes of identity construction in which the self and the other, or multiple others, are constituted. . . . [T]hey can all be seen as resting on the assumption that identity and insecurity are produced in a mutually constitutive process" (1999, 10—11). In contrast to the view that in international politics the state is a unitary actor that can construct an identity through interaction with other states, the Turkish case suggests that each social actor produces its own culture of insecurity. The material base comprised of history and geography in which identity construction takes place is the same for all social actors. However, their subjective interpretations of history and geography produce entirely different sets of security perceptions. For instance, many Turkish groups are able to link the process of Turkey's EU membership with the experience of European occupation of the country following World War I. They fear that the membership process will lead to a similar loss of national integrity. Many others, including Gülen, do not share this culture of insecurity and regard membership as an opportunity rather than a challenge for Turkish national security. State policies often are made through a dynamic interaction of these different interpretations. In other words, culture and identity exert influence on foreign policy via domestic politics.

Three Layers of Gülen's National-Security Identity

Among other Turkish social groups, Gülen and his movement adhere to a distinct security identity formed around a set of security perceptions and multiple "Others." Gülen's national-security identity is shaped by three perceptions of the Other or by varying degrees of separation: (1) a strong degree of common identification with the Turkic world, (2) a lack of common identification with the West but a desire to integrate with Western institutions, (3) a strong lack of common identification with Iran. With regard to the Turkic world, including Central Asia, he constructs a Kantian Other in which the distinction between the Self and Other is weak, where the Self perceives the Other as part of its own group. His perception of the West, however, is different. He does not totally internalize the West as part of his identity, but he does not view it as a security threat to Turkey or to Islam. This perception approximates the Lockean Other, where the Self perceives the Other as a peaceful rival. This view contrasts sharply to his perception of Iran, which is marked by a feeling of mistrust and insecurity. Gülen views Turkey's relations with Iran in terms of a Hobbesian culture of anarchy in which not only the distinction between Self and Other is clear, but also the Self perceives the Other as an imminent security threat. On the issue of relations with Iran, he probably shares a similar culture of insecurity with many Turkish secularists, but not with political Islamists.

The Turkic World: The Kantian Other

In spite of his religious and conservative background, Gülen adheres to a remarkably unusual perception of Turkish national interests and security—that is, unusual with respect to most other Islamists. Such differences can be traced to his realistic understanding of the global political landscape and of his Turkish Islamic identity. In contrast to many other Islamists, Gülen appears to see the hope that Turkey will play its natural leadership role in the Islamic world as just a distant dream. Instead, he suggests strong integration with Western institutions such as the EU and defends the continuation of close relations with the United States. He is deeply aware of the political weight the West has in international relations and tries to avoid any conflict with it. As for the Islamic world, Gülen strongly distances himself from the Arab world and Iran. Whereas the conventional map of the Islamic world takes the Middle East as its center, his cognitive map perceives Turkey to be at the center of a region comprised of the Balkans, Caucasus, and Central Asia. Yet he carefully avoids words that would suggest Turkish political leadership in this region.

Although the Turkish world is a vibrant theme in Gülen's identity, he does not sacrifice his realism to any idealistic notion of Turkish leadership. His pragmatism does not allow him to support the cause of Turkish minorities in Western Thrace, of Uigur Turks in China, or of Turkic minorities within Russia. His group does not have any educational activities in these problematic spots on the Turkish Islamic political map because he fears that such activities may draw reactions from the Greek, Chinese, or Russian regimes:

> While trying to establish a presence for us in Greece, we should not support [the cause of] Western Thrace, because they [Greeks] see it as a bleeding wound. If

we touch on this sore spot of theirs, then we would be not able to do anything in any part of Greece.

Similarly, we cannot keep ourselves busy with East Turkistan or Xinjiang. We cannot meddle in sensitive issues in any country. Otherwise, we would become a source of problem from the start and be unable to do anything. (Sevindi 1997, 43)

Although these lines clearly are informed by a pragmatic wariness, they also indicate the realistic limits of Gülen's idealism in embracing the Turkish world. For the sake of doing "more" in other parts of China and Greece, he practices caution. However, this reticent attitude contrasts sharply with his attitude about Iran.

He also attributes the lack of Gülen schools in the Arab world to the difficulties presented by Arab regimes. However, in the cases of Iran and the Arab world, he appears to have given up any hope of influencing a change of policy on their parts and has adopted a harsh rhetoric against them. He points out that deep cultural, political, and historical differences separate the Persian and Arab world from Turkey. Accordingly, he excludes that world from his notion of *us* (Sevindi 1997, 32). Gülen insists that the Islam practiced in Turkey is culturally different from that practiced in the Arab world. He embraces the phrase *Turkish Islam* to indicate this difference, and he is very sensitive about the Turkish character of religion. As M. Hakan Yavuz argues, the element of nationalism is very strong in Gülen's interpretation of Islam, reflecting his *dadaş* spirit (1999, 53). Gülen is from the city of Erzurum, located in a historically frontier region between Russia, Iran, and Ottoman Turkey. In modern Turkey, the eastern borders have been vulnerable to influences from both the former Soviet Union and Iran, provoking strongly nationalist and statist reactions. Gülen began his political activity in Erzurum by establishing the Turkish Association for Struggle Against Communism. This sense of nationalism is coupled with a high degree of statism in Gülen's mentality. Reflecting the Ottoman and Sunni political culture, Gülen perceives Islam and the state as woven together in a conception of "father state" (Akman 1995). Ahmet İnsel (1997) explains that Gülen's statism is purely political rather than economic because Gülen is an ardent supporter of the free-market system and offers a version of Protestant Islam. His support of the free-market system is a reflection of the group's sociopolitical base in a highly mobile upper middle class and of his strategic thinking that the group will gain power through economic activities.

This view is in sharp contrast with other Turkish Islamists' views on the Muslim world. The Muslim *umma* (community) is a constant theme in general

Turkish Islamist rhetoric, reflecting a sense that Turkish Islamists are leaders of the Islamic world. Necmettin Erbakan, Turkey's first Islamic-leaning prime minister, is remembered for his attempts to forge close relations with non-Turkish Muslims. In 1997, he initiated the Developing Eight (D-8) group that included Turkey, Iran, Egypt, Nigeria, Pakistan, Bangladesh, Malaysia, and Indonesia. His selection of countries representing the Muslim world is peculiar because it does not include any Turkic nation, a point for which he was widely criticized. D-8 generally reflects Erbakan's as well as Turkish political Islam's perception of the Muslim world, and it rekindled their hope for Turkish leadership in that world. Gülen, however, subscribes to a remarkably different interpretation of the Muslim world and realistically draws the boundaries where Turkey can play a leadership role. He did not regard D-8 optimistically and considered it Erbakan's cheap message to his constituency. Such initiatives are, for Gülen, quite adventurous and risky, and therefore a waste of time (Sevindi 1997, 33). Instead, he advocates a leadership role in the Turkic-speaking world based on a distinct Turkish interpretation of Islam (Yavuz 1999c). This argument holds that although Islam does not accept nationalist interpretations, one still can talk about a Turkish Islam specific to the Turkish sociocultural milieu. It needs to be mentioned, however, that Gülen's nationalism is not based purely on ethnicity. He does not exclude from his definition of nationality non-Turkish Muslims such as Bosnians, Albanians, and even Kurds, although he has maintained a persistent silence on the Kurdish problem.

His Turkish world is defined more culturally than ethnically and comprises the primary focus area for his educational activities: "I always thought about and cried for rescuing Asia and bringing Asia to [our] nation's line" (qtd. in Özsoy 1998, 46). His feelings reveal a strong positive identification with the Turkic people of Asia, most specifically Central Asia. Integration within the Turkish world will take place in "feelings, ideas and faith," through "a road from heart to heart" (qtd. in Can 1996, 61). In other words, this integration is a not a strategic partnership based on interests, as he sees Turkey's relations with the West. The distinction between the Self and the Other loses its meaning in integration with the Turkic people, and the Other becomes an integral part of the Self's ideational world. Gülen views the people of Turkey and the Turks of Central Asian as "milk brothers" who were nursed by the same mother. He considers the dream of visiting Buhara and Samarkand (Uzbekistan) as dear as that of entering paradise (Can 1996, 57). He believes that integration with Central Asia is a precondition for Turkey's acceptance by the West as an important partner. This integration also should come before any attempt at integration with the Islamic world because Turkey first should prove its ability to integrate the Turkic world (Can 1996, 59).

The West: The Lockean Other

Gülen always has been a strong supporter of economic and political integration with the EU. Gülen's pro-Western attitude has played a key role in the domestication and softening of other Islamist groups' anti-Europe and anti-U.S. positions. Although many Islamists eventually came closer to embracing this idea, a majority of them initially criticized Gülen for his pro-Europe views. He was one of the first Islamic leaders to embrace the idea of EU membership and at a time when Islamists in general regarded it as a threat to Turkish security and Islamic culture. He supported Turkey's entry to the European Customs Union. He argued that the Turkish stance on the Customs Union should be based on a strategic evaluation of economic costs and benefits of this agreement rather than on a fear of cultural assimilation (Çalışlar 1995). He approaches the case of Turkey's EU membership with a similar degree of confidence:

> We should be comfortable in our outreach to the world. We will not lose anything from our religion, nationality and culture because of developments like globalization, customs union or membership in the European Union. We firmly believe that the dynamics that hold our unity are strong. Again, we also firmly believe that the Quran is based on revelation and offers solution[s] to all the problems of humanity. Therefore, if there is anybody who is afraid, they should be those who persistently live away from the invigorating climate of Quran. (2003)

He does not view EU membership as incongruous with the ideal of Turkey's being a leader to the Islamic world, if this ever has been an aim for him at all. It is clear through his speeches and writings that Europe or the West does not represent a threat to his Turkish Islamic identity. He believes that the goals of building relations with Europe and assuming a natural role of leadership in the Islamic world are not necessarily contradictory. For him, "it cannot be imagined that a devout person would be against the West," as the West became supreme following universally applicable rules and principles (*şeriat-ı fitri*). Hence, embracing the same principles through a material Westernization will not harm Islamic principles. Rather than seeing integration with Europe as a threat to Turkish Islamic culture, Gülen expresses his hope that in the future Islam will come to Europe, citing Nursi's similar foresight ("Ahir Zaman'da" 2002).

According to Gülen, Turkey is both European and Muslim at the same time and should pursue a foreign policy that acknowledges this fact. Political and economic integration with Europe will make it easier for Turkey to play a leadership role in the Islamic world (Sevindi 1997, 24). As noted earlier, Gülen is not optimistic about this role; for him, it is a distant dream at best. Therefore, it is natural that he focus attention on relations with what he sees as Turkey's natural sphere of interest, the Turkish world of Central Asia, while continuing to be engaged strongly in Western political institutions.

In Gülen's view, the United States is in control of all affairs in the world. He adopts a realistic view on this hegemonic power, arguing that it is imperative to maintain a friendly relationship with the United States in order to do any "work": "If voluntary organizations are opening schools in different parts of the world for the sake of global integration, these projects would not be possible if they are in conflict with the United States. America is still the nation at the helm of the world leadership" (Sevindi 1997, 39). What he refers to, of course, is his educational activities in different parts of the world, in particular Central Asia. In addition to these pragmatic pro-American views, Gülen also is concerned about the weakening of U.S. hegemony because it might cause the rise of other powers, notably Russia and China. As he sees the situation, U.S. hegemony is preferable for Turkish national interests, a view that is in line with official Turkish foreign policy. It is also interesting to note that Gülen chose the United States for his extended medical treatment, which many political analysts interpret as a voluntary exile term given the state court trial process against him in Turkey. He talks positively about his experiences in the United States (İ. Ünal 2001).

Gülen also has tried to forge close relations with Western religious institutions, the Vatican in particular. His group managed to organize a meeting between him and Pope John Paul II. The symbolic nature of the meeting between a religious leader in Turkey and the pope seems to have agitated the Turkish political establishment, however, especially given the fact that Turkish official religious authorities (the Diyanet İşleri Başkanlığı) were not able to obtain an appointment with the pope for a long time. Gülen also has established friendship with Orthodox Christian and Jewish religious authorities in Istanbul, including Patriarch Bartholomeos and David Aseo, chief rabbi of the Jewish community in Istanbul. Interestingly enough, some of these leaders defend Gülen against the Kemalist accusations that he is trying to destroy the secular republic. Georgi Marovistch, general secretary of the Turkish Catholic Community Spiritual Leaders Council, acted as a "defense witness" in the case against Gülen in the Turkish state security court. He denied hearing about Gülen's wish to form an illegal organization with the goal of replacing the secular regime with a theocratic one ("Catholics Act" 2001). This testimony was a noteworthy demonstration of cooperation by leaders of different religions against the secular nationalist regime.

Gülen's perception of the West as a partner rather than as a security threat is in line with his advocacy of globalization and with his universalist interpretation of Islam (Yavuz 1999b). It is a widely distributed tale among his followers that he once asked his assistants to replace an Ottoman map hanging on his office wall with a world map because the Ottoman map allegedly narrows his vision. The educational activities he inspires are spread throughout most of the world, with the notable exceptions of Iran and the Arab world, as explained previously. He tries in particular to forge close relations with the West and its leaders. He offers a broad interpretation of Islam by arguing that "everything in the universe is Muslim," as all obey God by submission to His natural laws. Even those who disobey God's ethical commands obey Him, and hence they are "Muslim as far as their bodily existence is concerned" (Gülen 1996c, 18). This inclusive understanding can be contrasted sharply to many Islamic movements' confrontational arguments in regard to the West and gives clues to his vision of the world. Yet, in Gülen's weltanschauung, the dominant reference is still Islam. In other words, when he views the non-Muslim world, he does not depart completely from his Islamic references; he embraces everything in the universe as being Muslim. The coexistence of two apparently conflicting perceptions of the world in Gülen's mind illuminate his views on war and peace.

In accordance with Nurcu teachings, Gülen strictly defends a nonpolitical line. In an interview given to *Aksiyon* magazine, he defines jihad in a very broad sense as "an effort to reach the level of perfect man [*insan-ı kamil*]" and "to discipline human desires and negative feelings." However, in that same interview, he does not rule out the option of war altogether if need arises: "battle by sword is only an exceptional situation that can be resorted to only in defense" ("Interview" 1998). In his book entitled *Prophet Muhammad as Commander,* Gülen offers a comprehensive definition: "Jihad denotes, literally, doing one's utmost to achieve something. It is not the equivalent of war, for which the Arabic word is *qital.* It has a wider connotation and embraces every kind of striving in God's cause" (1996c, 20). Here Gülen explains the greater jihad using a hadith of Prophet Muhammad that says, "We are returning from the lesser jihad to the greater jihad." Greater jihad connotes "fighting against superstitions and wrong convictions and also against carnal desires and evil inclinations" (Gülen 1996c, 29) On the other hand, he argues that an Islamic goal can be achieved only through Islamic means and methods. In other words, the means and methods employed can render one's political purposes religiously unjustified, as "neither Islam nor Muslims directed toward their real targets through diabolic means and methods" (Gülen 1996c, 9). In accordance with these views, Gülen was one of the first Muslim scholars to denounce the 11 September 2001 attacks in the United States.

Iran: The Hobbesian Other

Gülen and U.S. president George W. Bush ironically may share a similarity in their perceptions about an Iranian threat. Gülen's reaction to Iran apparently is influenced by a multitude of factors, including his own understanding of Islam as a social movement, Turkish and Islamic political history, and his realistic opinion of Iran's position in the world.

Islamic political involvement always has been an anathema to the Nur movement in general, to which Gülen in part belongs. For the Nurcus, social change through educational activities always precedes political change. Gülen holds that politicization of religion creates a false image of Islam, which only helps critics of Islam (Birand 1997). In this regard, the 1979 triumph of political Islam in Iran never appealed to Gülen's social Islamic identity. He argues that the Iranian desire to export revolution provoked regimes in other parts of the Muslim world, making things difficult for Islamic movements there (Gülen 1997a, 17–18).

In an explicit attempt to avoid association with Iran, Gülen's followers have not shown any interest in establishing a presence in Iranian territory. Gülen cites the lack of authorization by Iranian officials as the primary reason for not setting up schools there: "The [Iranian] regime did not give [us] the permission. We insisted [on] opening a school in [Iranian] Azerbaijan in the name of Turkism. They made an odd suggestion: 'if you have that much money and would like to help, give it to us and we can open [that school]' " (Sevindi 1997, 50).

However, in many other countries where it was not possible to open formal schools, Gülen's group has established language schools or cultural centers. As discussed earlier, the movement has been extremely careful not to annoy officials in risky areas such as China or Russia. Like Iranian officials, the officials of these countries have similar reasons to be suspicious of any Turkish educational efforts in their lands, but Gülen's group carefully manages such fears by refraining from any activity involving Turkish minorities. In the case of Iran, however, it has shown a different strategy, which exposes his desire to distance himself from this country. This voluntary abstinence might be attributed to Gülen's realization that Iran is a source of resentment both for the Turkish state and for the international system under the hegemony of the United States. Kemalist circles within Turkey widely accuse Gülen of practicing *takiyye,* a practice rooted in Shia Islamic tradition. They believe there is a hidden Khomeini behind Gülen's modern attire. These accusations may have affected his stance. His stance on Iran similarly might be considered an attempt to gain American approval for his activities in many parts of the world, which he considers crucial. However, if all his views and statements against Iran are tactical, Gülen is not terribly uncomfortable with this position. In other words, his strategic mentality is not without a purpose. The Turkish nationalist and sometimes Islamic rhetoric often singled out Iran as a source of anger. Reflecting Gülen's frontier nationalist identity, his perceptions of Iran are rooted deeply in historical and religious cleavages in Islamic and Turkish history and are strongly internalized by members of the movement:

> There are two things about Iran that we have to be [mindful of]. First, an attempt to export a fanatical Islam and sect under the name of religion and Islamic revolution. They prioritize their own sect and interpretations before real religion. If somebody is not Shia, then he is nothing. Second, the love of Ali is only a pretext to give color to their mentality. In fact, what keeps their unity is not the love of Ali, but hatred of Abu Bakr and Omar. They misuse Ali in order to base their false belief system on a religious ground. (Sevindi 1997, 49)

The threat of Iranian influence is a constant theme in Gülen's rhetoric on the Middle East and Central Asia. He spares his harshest criticism for Iran, which he sees as a security threat to the entire region. Although Iran was a key member of the D-8 group and the Erbakan government tried to foster close relations with this country by signing a multi-billion-dollar gas deal, Gülen does not hide his poor opinion of this important neighbor of Turkey. His negative perception of Iran apparently is informed by his perceptions of it as a security threat to the region: "Today there is a danger of Persian expansionism as well as a strong Iranian historical rivalry with us. It doesn't look like Iran will remain idle in the region. I am worried because there is a significant Shia population in Iraq" (Sevindi 1997, 49). In an effort to curb this influence, he supported adoption of a Turkish-style Latin alphabet in Central Asia to replace the Cyrillic script. The Arabic alternative would be undesirable because it would pave the way for Iranian as well as Saudi influence (Çandar and Akyol 1998; Sevindi 1997, 69). Gülen is not optimistic that Turkish relations with Iran can be improved because "the history of our relationship with Iran is a history of problems and cleavages" (Sevindi 1997, 49). For him, Iran is "a sick part of the body of Islam," which has preferred throughout its entire history "to wage a war against the Sunni world within Islam rather than direct its attention outside of Islam" (Gülen 1997a, 17–18, and 1997b, 137–138) In other words, his animosity toward this country is rooted both historically and religiously, reflecting his Sunni Turkish background and informing his strategic mentality.

Gülen's Ideas in Practice: Multiple Orientations in Turkish Foreign Policy

Gülen's success as a Muslim leader in establishing a strong presence in many parts of the Muslim world and in the West through dialogue with high-ranking leaders of other religions, including Pope John Paul II, offers some insights for Turkish foreign policy. Turkey, which has attempted to strip itself totally of its Islamic identity, finds itself in the awkward situation of being accepted by neither the Islamic world nor the West. In contrast, as discussed earlier, Gülen suggests that strong integration with both regions simultaneously is absolutely necessary for the success of Turkish foreign policy. There are some strong indications that Turkish foreign-policy elites recently have begun to realize this fact.

Foreign ministers of the countries that are members of the EU and of the Organization of Islamic Conference (OIC) came together in a historic summit meeting in Istanbul on 13 February 2002. The meeting, accompanied by a series of intellectual panels on civilizational dialogue, highlighted a significant change of orientation in Turkish foreign policy. Both European and Islamic leaders and scholars welcomed the meeting and Turkey's leading role in its organization. For the first time, Turkey accepted and brought two of its conflicting identities together, an obvious contradiction to radical secular ideology. Through this meeting, Turkey emphasized the Islamic aspect of its national identity and had European leaders endorse it. Although the architect of this historic meeting was former Turkish foreign minister İsmail Cem, member of Bülent Ecevit's Democratic Leftist Party, it remains to be seen if this Islamic identity will be endorsed by influential circles within the Turkish state establishment who not only firmly oppose Turkey's active involvement in the Islamic world, but also resist implementation of political reforms required for EU membership.

The leading Turkish media, in particular the Islamic-leaning ones, supported the EU-OIC summit. Most commentators noted that such a meeting can be organized by Turkey because it can claim both Islamic and European identities at the same time. They questioned unilateral policy orientation leaning toward either side, arguing that it is in Turkey's best interests for the country to portray itself as both European and Islamic. A few made references to Gülen's intellectual contribution to this reconstitution of official identity. Gülen was one of the first Islamic scholars and leaders in Turkey to endorse Turkey's participation in the process of European integration. He also defended the argument that for the success of this integration, it was necessary for Turkey to integrate itself first with the Islamic world. In fact, Gülen's own group claims credit for the Istanbul summit. Hüseyin Gülerce, a columnist in *Zaman,* argues that Gülen prepared the groundwork for this meeting: "The first steps that required courage were taken by Mr. Fethullah Gülen, who established the infrastructure of intrareligious dialogue. Mr. Gülen destroyed taboos on this issue, widened the horizons of our people and country, creating waves of dialogue and tolerance with his patient and persistent efforts. We can even claim that the meeting of civilizations in Istanbul is the result of these waves" (2002). Of course, Gülen's definition of the Muslim world includes primarily the Turkic world and excludes Iran and to some extent the Arab world, which constitute a central part of the Islamic world in others' views. However, his acceptance of the two Turkish identities—European and Islamic—as complementary rather than contradictory was innovative at a time when both secular and Islamist identities totally rejected this duality. Gülen's national-security identity encourages Turkish foreign-policy decision makers to remain fully on track with EU membership. As a leader of a significant Islamic movement, he gave his approval to this policy goal. Many Turkish Islamists joined him later, unloading the Islamic element in the anti-EU camp. Yet Gülen also defends the argument that the success of Turkish diplomacy in the West lies with its success in the East. The reverse also can be said.

Turkish national identity, or any national-security identity for that matter, is not static. Different social groups have their own interpretations of the national-security environment in which Turkish foreign policy is made. There is no single definition of what constitutes national interests or threats to them. Kemalism as the official state ideology in Turkey has lost its appeal to the country's dynamic population in the age of globalization. Its dictates on foreign policy have come to be viewed as reflecting yesterday's realities, when securing national independence was Turkish leaders' primary concern. Today's realities require active involvement in regional integration processes for which a reconstitution of national identity is necessary.

As an important and influential participant in the Turkish public debate on national interests and security, Gülen offers an alternative vision of foreign policy. He tries to fulfill his vision through his extraordinary educational network as well as through his active dialogue with leaders of other religious traditions. He has risen to a level of influence beyond his career as humble mosque preacher and in doing so has caused an uproar among radical secular circles. However, his success is an indication that a confident Turkish foreign policy cannot be made without the recognition of Turkey's rich religious and historical traditions. The West, in particular the United States, thus far has perceived radical secularism as its principal working partner in Turkey, and many argue that modern Turkey can present a model for the Islamic world. However, the primary condition for being a model is its chance of being accepted. The Turkish model, with its radical interpretation of secularism in confrontation with religion, does not have a strong chance of being accepted other than as a Western Trojan horse in the Islamic world.

Only through a project of national-identity reconstitution that bridges the gap between the West and Islam can Turkey offer an appealing model. It needs to work toward the peaceful coexistence of its Western and Eastern identities, as well as of its past and future in this project. Only through this identity, which is at peace with both religion and history, can Turkey present a viable alternative to destructive radicalism. In the aftermath of the carnage of 11 September 2001, tension and mutual dislike seems to be rising between the Islamic world and the West, as rhetoric of the "clash of civilizations" has gained currency. This dangerous trend can be reversed only through conciliatory approaches that call for a dialogue among civilizations. Turkey is the only nation that is in the unique position to play a historic role by serving as the stage for this conversation.

10

National Loyalties and International Undertakings

The Case of the Gülen Community in Kazakhstan

BERNA TURAM

THE LIMITED SCOPE and narrow focus of social research on the religious parties—Refah and its successors—have prevented a fresh look at the emergent realities of a particular form of fast-growing nationalist Islam in Turkey. This focus specifically has obscured the increasing influence and effectiveness of a leading Islamic movement, the Gülen community,[1] which since the early 1990s has been extending its activities outside Turkey to the Turkic-speaking countries of Central Asia. Rejecting the reductionist generalization of Refah and its successors as the main representatives of modern Islam in contemporary Turkey, I show in this chapter how the Gülen community actually fulfills this representative role. Interestingly, although the Turkish state successively banned religious parties and still maintains its suspicion about the contemporary religious party in power, the Justice and Development Party, the Gülen movement has continued its rapid rise and success not only at the national level but also at the international level. Political openings for Islam usually seem to fail in integrating with or challenging the system, but the Gülen movement continues to expand its scope of influence. In sharp contrast to other Islamic groups, which are perceived as threats to democracy and the republic, it presents the image of a civil society organization.

What makes the Gülen movement so distinct from other Islamic movements and organizations? Like other Islamic groups in Turkey and Middle East, it arose

---

1. The scholarly work of M. Hakan Yavuz about the Gülen movement is an exception. See further Yavuz 1999b, 1999c, and 2000a, 14–15.

in a context of tension and erratic clashes between the state and Islam. In addition to the ban on religious parties, the state implemented repressive policies such as banning the wearing of head scarves at the universities. The Gülen movement's distinction in this ambivalent context, however, is its commitment to its *hizmet* (service): the reconciliation of Islamic culture and identity with the secular republic. One might say that it aims to revitalize faith *in* secular regimes and not *against* them. With this point in mind, I focus on two central questions: What makes a nonconfrontational Islam possible? And why should this particular form of Turkish Islam be recognized as a civil society organization?

Despite an ongoing unresolved theoretical clash over Islamic revival, little empirical research has been done on this burning issue. Empirical evidence collected in the sites of the Gülen community since 1996 challenges both pessimistic and optimistic theories of the compatibility between Islam and civil society. The broader purpose of this chapter is to invite a culturally sensitive thinking of conventional approaches to civil society. On the basis of extensive findings, I suggest a shift away from both optimist and pessimist theories of compatibility. Both camps in the debate highlight several presumed characteristics of Islam to argue whether Islam contributes to or undermines civil society. In doing so, they tend to deal with some ideal characteristics of both Islam and civil society, characteristics that exist mainly in abstract thinking rather than in everyday life. Owing to the ethnographic nature of my research, this study captures emergent Islamic sensibilities with respect to ethnicity and the nation at the level of the everyday. Analyzing what is "out there," rather than what should be there to be qualified as "civil," the study invites critical thinking about civil society in a non-Western context. Specifically, it explores the role of the nation and nationalist sentiments in understanding the relationship between Islam and civil society.

Pessimistic spokespeople make various claims about the alleged incompatibility of Islam and civil society. First, they argue that Islam is resistant to secularization and therefore an enemy of secular political rule (Gellner 1981, 1994a, 15). Accordingly, Islam fails to qualify for the main premise of the originally Western ideal and institutional framework of civil society, which is secularism. Islam is viewed as a threat to secular states because of its distrust of politics (Gellner 1981; Lindholm 1996). Political instability and lack of trust cannot make a cozy home for a civilized social world (Hall 1995; Tocqueville 1955). Second, pessimists anticipate a civilizational clash between Islam and the West (Huntington 1996), which reinforces the Western perception of Islam as a threat. Third, they regard Islamic mobilization as a pan-Islamist or fundamentalist antistate activity or both, rather than one associated with the nation-state. In other words, pessimists argue that Islam is blind to national feelings and ethnic affiliations and thereby cannot recognize the nation-state, but only the unity of *umma,* or community (Gellner 1981, 1994b, 22 and 28).

My study challenges these arguments of incompatibility between Islam and civil society through its analysis of the Gülen movement's strong national loyalties and the related ethnic politics that it pursues in Central Asia. I argue that this new Islamic conception of nation and ethnicity is the key to exploring the Gülen movement's distinctness from other Islamic groups. Specifically, I inquire into the difference these loyalties make in the movement's organizational abilities as a civil society entity.

The opposing optimistic view in the scholarly literature argues that Islam and civil society are perfectly compatible. Several spokespeople for this view highlight that Islam refuses hierarchies and thereby enforces equality before God (Esposito and Piscatori 1991; Esposito and Voll 1996). This egalitarian heritage, they argue, qualifies Islam as a propellant of democracy and civil society. Still others point to the strength of civil society in the Muslim context as the existence of a civic culture and community life (White 1996). This broad definition of civil society embraces a wide-ranging variety of religious organizations, which create voluntary participation at the local level. The solid community and strong reciprocal relations in Islam are regarded as perfect grounds for civic participation and community-based action. According to the optimists, Islamic ways of life and political culture are conducive to egalitarian values and civic participation (Lindholm 1996). Similar to studies of the Refah Party, my findings support several of the optimists' arguments. My data show how Islamic faith may successfully trigger cross-class cooperation. Put differently, followers of the community come from various class backgrounds and participate in the same cause; faith facilitates voluntary self-sacrifice for the common good and encourages charity by the capital owners. Further support for the optimistic camp comes from the evidence on the ground, which shows that the Gülen community derives enormous power from its communal ties and civic participation. However, these definitions of civil society have some problems, too, unless the term is qualified further.

A definition of *civil society* that overstresses communal solidarity may miss some legitimate liberal concerns. Disagreeing with communitarians,[2] many liberals express suspicion of the primacy of community because of its potential to limit individuals' autonomy (Gellner 1994a; Hall 1995, 1998a). Moreover, an exclusive emphasis on the civic culture and informal associations may underem-

---

2. See further Taylor 1989, 1992; and Walzer 1983.

phasize, if not discard, formal organizations and political institutions. Because civil society represents the general quality of social life, often coupled with civility, its relevancy cannot be reduced to a particular sphere of the social world. What takes place in the local communal life is as relevant as what occurs in the impersonal realm of institutions and politics.

Another related problem associated with optimistic accounts is the view that regards Islamic movements mainly as contributing to pluralism in the public sphere. This view of the public sphere highlights diversity and cohabitation of differences as the main propellant of civil society (Göle 2000b).[3] However, it is important to question whether the mere existence of a variety of autonomous groups may be taken for granted as civil society. If we do not adopt a narrower definition of *civil society,* the term easily can become too elastic and even may run the risk of embracing terrorist and anarchist groups, which are indeed nongovernmental, informal, voluntary, and autonomous. Hence, the mere existence of either communal solidarity or public diversity cannot be regarded as an assurance of civil society. These critical remarks call for critical analysis of the *nature* of both diversity and homogeneity within the Gülen community.

First, my findings reveal an interesting blend of both uniformity and differences in the Gülen movement. On the one hand, it displays a striking homogeneity in its inner core, which consists of devout followers who often serve the community unconditionally. Boundaries are fixed, rigid, and often rule based there. On the other hand, the Gülen movement accommodates a diffuse network of associations that not only tolerates differences but also celebrates the pluralistic quality of public life. The associational life in the community entails fuzzy boundaries and different forms and degrees of attachment. This seemingly paradoxical mixture is an important key to analyzing the movement's claims for being a civil society organization.

Second, my findings demonstrate that the followers of the Gülen community aspire to reconnect Central Asians with their Turkic origins by spreading Turkish Muslim culture and morality to that region. This form of ethnic politics in Central Asia is realized largely through Gülen's "civil society projects" of education—schools, dormitories, summer camps, and so on—as well as through business and trade networks inside and outside Turkey. It is important to examine to what extent the community's educational projects in Central Asia can be considered as propellants of civil society. If the Gülen schools have a religionationalist agenda to Turkify or Islamicize the region or both, do they not contradict the ideals of civil society?

3. For theories of the public sphere and the politics of difference, see Calhoun 1992.

The Paradox of Fellow Feeling: Constructing the "Natural"

More than three hundred schools—not only high schools, but also seven universities—have been founded in the name of the Gülen community all around the world (Yavuz 1999b). More than one hundred of these high schools and one university are located in Turkey.[4] Faithful followers and sympathizers of the community participate in educational projects, such as the opening or financing of new schools, dormitories, *dershanes* (private centers devoted to preparing students for national scholastic exams). The schools offer relatively higher academic standards, science, and secular curricula, all of which have proved to be successful, as measured by the graduating students' accomplishments.[5] The intended social engineering of these schools is to create scientifically competitive future generations who also will be faithful believers. In other words, the schools' primary goal is to overcome the perception of conflict between science and Islam.

Outside Turkey, however, the schools have broader cultural and political agendas. The schools abroad, in particular the ones in Europe, attract Turkish families who prefer to raise their children in the "Turkish way." In the underdeveloped or developing countries, they appeal to students owing to their better technology and better standards of education. Finally, and perhaps most important, the high concentration of Gülen schools in Central Asia constitutes a major part of the pan-Turan ethnic politics that Gülen pursues in that region.

Among the many countries where the Gülen movement has opened numerous schools, Kazakhstan stands out in terms of both the quantity and quality of schools. Gülen's followers have founded twenty-seven schools in Kazakhstan, five of which are located in Almaty.[6] The majority of students are Kazaks, selected in a nationwide competitive exam, while a small minority is Russian and Turkish students. The quality and popularity of the Gülen schools prepared the grounds for a large-scale accommodation of Turks in Kazakhstan and for extensive business interaction between Turkey and Kazakhstan. The Gülen com-

4. Although people who are part of the Gülen movement provide most of the financing for these schools, Gülen does not own schools; rather, he serves as the mentor, leader, mobilizer, coordinator, and source of ideas. For a detailed series of reports on the Gülen schools abroad, see *Yeni Yüzyıl,* 14, 21, 28 Jan. and 2 Feb. 1998.

5. It is important to note that acceptance into these schools in Turkey and in the Central Asian countries is highly competitive. See further ibid.

6. There are two secondary schools for girls, two for boys, and a coed university in Almaty. The basic language of instruction is English, but the schools also teach in Turkish and Kazak and offer courses in the Russian language.

munity's central organization in Almaty, the Kazak-Türk Eğitim Vakfı (Kazak-Turk Education Foundation), or KATEV, is the cornerstone of the resident Turkish community. KATEV is an efficient hierarchical organization supported by charities operated by private Turkish companies, the devout of the Gülen community, and businessmen in Almaty. Thus, it is not merely a community organization for Gülen's followers, but also a community center, and it attracts a diverse constituency of Turks. The teachers in the Gülen schools are devout followers of the community. Some of these followers coordinate the community's schools with other work on the KATEV agenda.

KATEV not only coordinates and supervises the schools, but also serves as a public-relations agency, a community association, and sometimes a coffeehouse for a vibrant Turkish community in Almaty. One of its primary duties is to coordinate and organize events, such as hosting guests from Turkey—helping them to find accommodations, to make immediate connections (with businessmen, schools, entrepreneurs, local politicians, and so on), and to find their way in the city—and initiating and facilitating intercultural programs. In other words, KATEV is the social, cultural, and economic center that organizes international connections, with a heavy emphasis on education and trade.[7] In fact, within Turkey, Almaty is known as the "Turkish center" in Central Asia. One legitimately may ask how a domestic Islamic organization has succeeded in creating a Turkish center abroad? Is KATEV's goal the Islamicization or Turkification of Kazakhstan? How do the local people feel about Gülen's exposure in Almaty?

Gülen has played an important role in creating a particular kind of ethnic politics in Central Asia. In Kazakhstan, the ethnic politics emphasize pride in Turkicness, proudly celebrating—and to some extent inventing—commonality between Kazaks and Turks. The Gülen community's exposure to Central Asia seems to be more emotion laden and nostalgic than politically driven. Gülen aspires to reconnect Turks with their "ancestors" and Kazaks with their Turkic origins. In Kazakhstan, one often hears the affirmative sayings of this celebrated commonalty: "we have the same roots" (in Kazak), "the same mother nursed us" (in Turkish), "we are blood bothers" (in Turkish). Expressions of commonalties facilitate relations with the local people, especially with students in the Gülen schools, with their parents, and with local businessmen and politicians. Along with fostering warm ties, the Gülen community triggers and transmits a new Islamic sense of nationhood. Gülen's followers inherit this attitude in part

---

7. KATEV's records in Almaty, to which I was provided access in 1999, contain the curricula of the schools, lists of the courses, bulletins on the cultural events, and copies of various handouts.

from the nationalist characteristics of the Nur movement, which stressed an ethnic consciousness of Turkish Islam. However, Gülen's followers diverge from earlier Islamic movements, including the Nur, in the distinct way they *nationalize* their *hizmet* outside the Turkish borders. In this way, they appeal to a variety of Turks from different political and even religious orientations and enlist their cooperation in their agendas for Central Asia. Unlike other religious groups, they also successfully *internationalize* their *hizmet* owing to Gülen's alertness to broad geopolitical transformations, such as the post-Soviet adjustments in Central Asia.

Commitments to Gülen's projects are highly diversified. Communal and national loyalties seem to work together in these projects. For example, in Kazakhstan, I met more Turkish ultranationalists and even self-defined fascists than Islamists; they all were benefactors of the Gülen community's schools. This discovery was less surprising than finding Turkish Jews, respected businessmen in Turkey, opening schools in Asia in the name of the Gülen community. Furthermore, I also met several secular and nonreligious businessmen who provided support to the schools in Kazakhstan in the name of the nation. This wide-ranging participation in Gülen's educational project indicates not only prioritization but also politicization of national affiliation. In this sense, Gülen represents a pragmatic Islam, which is a product of the national culture, the culture of the nation. An emerging Turkish Islam is actualizing a network at the international level on the basis of its primary loyalties to the nation. It is extremely important to understand the nature and implications of Gülen's ethnic politics in Central Asia because this ethnic politics provides important clues about the interplay between modern nationalism and Islamism.

Almaty offers generic and implicit references to a common folk culture, symbols, myths, and memories between Turks and Kazaks in everyday life. The claims to a common past are expressed through several shared symbols, such as the similarity between the Kazak and Turkish language, customs, food, and drinks such as *kımız*. Often, the comparisons amount to physical similarities between Central Asians and Turks, thus acquiring a racial tone in addition to the ethnic and cultural characterizations of similarity. All these symbols of belonging are celebrated because they can be cited as the tangible proofs of Turkic roots.[8] These characteristics, the features of an *ethnie* in Anthony Smith's term

8. During fieldwork, my Turkish female student hosts took me to a big open market in Almaty, where I was amazed at the frequent use of broken Turkish by the rural people selling their goods. The way they bargained, joked with us, and even mothered the girls was loaded with familiarity, warmth, and sharing.

(1986, 16), create a sense of warm solidarity and brotherhood between the Turks and Kazaks in Almaty. The explicit reference to a common ethnie goes back to premodern times and to the geographical space, Central Asia, which is called the "homeland of Turkish blood." The followers of the Gülen community and other Turks in Almaty genuinely believe that the Soviet regime repressed "Turkic ways of lives." Very often people insist that Soviet rule could not destroy all of the "Turkic ways," however, so some of those features still survive.

Despite wide-ranging differences of religious and political orientation among the Turks in Almaty, ethnic politics automatically assumes and induces the "natural" feelings of membership in a definite whole with undeniable and genuine boundaries (Hedetoft 1995). Hedetoft correctly underlines this presumption of a natural bonding—namely, the postulate of a natural will behind the feeling of fellowship:

> There is the assumption of a priori, deep-rooted commonalty between various sections of a given population, semi-automatically welding into a unity across various rifts and differences of interest and standing. Ideally, such commonalty is embedded in the nature of each citizen, and thus on his or her own will, whether (s)he is aware or not. The discursive construction of national identity thus claims the existence of that oxymoron, a natural will, in the social-anthropological make-up of citizens. (1995, 23)

Hence, it should not be surprising that Gülen displays different boundary maintenance inside and outside of Turkey. Within the national boundaries, the social composition of the community's followers does not presume any "inherent" or fixed quality. In contrast to the community's "fuzzy boundaries" in Turkey, affiliation with the Gülen community outside the national borders takes on a much more obvious form. Owing to the presumption of a "natural will" among the citizens, the fuzzy boundaries symbolically are transposed to "real" boundaries of nationhood. In Kazakhstan, the borders of "we," the fellow Turks, are regarded as natural. This transposition takes place on the basis of the fellow feeling—that is, "we" versus the others. Fellow feelings create communal warmth and thereby comfort in and around KATEV. They foster interpersonal ties and networks of trust. Therefore, they have a certain attraction and appeal for the local Kazaks, who may want to be part of this warm collectivity.

Does this collectivity embrace an ethnoreligious community,[9] which conveniently would welcome and incorporate other Turkic Muslims in Central Asia?

9. See further Smith 1999.

Indeed, ethnic politics aspires to include the so-called "Kazak Turks," who, according to the followers of the Gülen community, merely need education and self-awareness to realize their Turkic origins. An implicit pride in Turkic roots motivates the Gülen community to socialize Kazaks into "Turkish ways of life" through education. Similar to its effective mobilization of a diversified constituent in Turkey, the Gülen movement attracts an ethnically, culturally, and politically diverse people in Kazakhstan. Maintaining the broader goal of the development of a Muslim civil society, Gülen aims at the revitalization of the forgotten Muslim-Turkic identity in Kazakhstan. Ironically, Gülen's diversity-friendly image conceals an ethnic agenda, which calls for the realization of Turkic homogeneity in Central Asia. It is this ethnic politics that makes Gülen an effective international actor and that positions the Gülen movement quite differently than other Islamist movements and organizations in relation to the nation and the state.

Is this ethnic politics merely an imagination of a shared belonging or a revitalization of historically undermined factual commonalties? In fact, for the purposes of the present study, it is not important whether these commonalties are factual or imagined. The issue of concern here is descriptive: owing to the emergent Islamic conceptions of the nation and ethnicity, Gülen appears as a legitimate international actor recognized not only by the Turkish state but also by the Kazak state. The nature of ethnic politics suggests explicit aspirations of homogenization and contradicts the apparent diversity in the Gülen centers (for a theoretical analysis, see Yack 1999, 115). It is often believed that these diversity-friendly attitudes make the community a civil society entity. However, Gülen's appeal to a heterogeneous audience is much more complicated than several advocates of multiculturalism have theorized in other contexts.[10] I argue that the movement's success is its appeal to warmth of community and homogeneity, while it maintains tolerant and diversity-friendly public sites outside its kernel. Here, it is important to note a quality of modern nationalism: the intermingling of the political and cultural communities as well as the integration of the political and cultural identities (Yack 1999, 114). Specifically, through ethnic politics, a faith-based movement can create the international platforms for permeation between citizens and "their" nation and thus indirectly between citizens and the state of the nation (Hall 1998c).

As one highly respected pro-Gülen entrepreneur and benefactor of the schools stated, "The schools represent and belong to the Turkish nation and nothing else. Naming the schools Islamist or anything else is an attempt to pro-

---

10. See further Taylor 1992.

voke cleavages and camps. We all are Turks and are very proud of it."[11] The KATEV officers and the teachers often asked me not to mention to the students and their parents that the schools are associated with an Islamic group. Their concern was mainly that they not lose their credit as Turkish schools because of lingering Soviet-inflicted negative feelings against religion. However, they also feel proud to represent the nation by presenting their schools as "Turkish schools." Interestingly, a recent state-funded publication in an academic journal referred to and represented the Gülen schools as Turkish schools (Demir, Balcı, and Akkok 2000).

The followers in Almaty anticipate or perceive a tension between their internationalist orientation and their Islamic inner selves. This undeclared uneasiness is in part owing to their self-perception and in part to the state's ambivalent attitude toward Islam. As Craig Calhoun observes about recognition in general, "It is not just that others fail to see us for who we are . . . or repress us because of who they think we are. We face problems of recognition because socially sustained discourses about who it is possible or appropriate or valuable to be inevitably shape the way we look at and constitute ourselves, with varying degrees of angst and tension" (1994, 20–21). Hence, it is not surprising that the Gülen followers downplay their Islamic identity because they are afraid that it will be perceived as in contradiction with their international identities and undertakings.

In contrast to the discomfort with the Islamic identity, they assume the national identity to be natural because it is shared comfortably and legitimately with all Turks. Moreover, it is widely believed among Turks in Almaty that this comfort also might be shared with other Turkic people. In other words, they aspire to extend fellowship to an imagined "pan-Turkic" community. Obviously, the nationalist identity feels at home with the international undertakings, more so than does the Islamic identity. Hence, outside Turkey, the Gülen community has developed a more efficient and effective national identity, manifested in national organizations such as KATEV, rather than an Islamic one. This identity is explicit in the name of the foundation, the Kazak-Turk Education Foundation, which excludes the name of the specific community and thereby simply emphasizes an international bridge between Turkey and Kazakhstan. Contrary to what I found in the domestic sites of the community, in Almaty I rarely heard mention of the Gülen movement, its Islamic vision, or its mission.

In Kazakhstan, the Gülen schools were presented to me simply as "Turkish schools." In other words, the schools' national affiliation was emphasized in everyday use, whereas their community affiliation was practically omitted. Simi-

---

11. Author's interview with the owner of a chain of food factories, June 1999, Almaty.

lar to the followers' identities, KATEV's identity was under continuous reconstruction in the international domain of the community. In my interviews, the followers in *hizmet* explained their efficiency in terms of their devotion to their nation. If it was not for the nation, most of the teachers stated, the difficulties they faced would have been impossible to overcome. They presented their devotion to the cause and their willingness to sacrifice themselves in the name of the nation. The non-Turkish students in the schools and their parents knew only that the schools were Turkish, extremely successful, and competitive, and that the main language of instruction was English. The students and parents with whom I spoke were not informed about the Gülen community and its Islamic association.

The Gülen community also aspires to appeal to the Turkic community. Hence, its taking part in the continuous reconstruction of Turkish national interest seems almost natural. It is extremely important to note that the followers' usage of the term *millet* (nation) in the interviews usually could be interpreted as being interchangeable—or almost identical—with *ulus-devlet* (nation-state) or sometimes simply just *devlet*, the state. They strongly identified the nation and the state with each other (Gellner 1994c; Hall 1998b). This is exactly why and how national culture and political community are strongly attached; it also explains how the political community is nationalized and the nation is politicized as an ongoing process (Yack 2000). Hence, it is not a coincidence that the uneasy domestic interactions between the Gülen community and the state in Turkey were transformed into smooth cooperation and proud affiliations in the international realm. Indeed, the Gülen community is outspoken about its immediate educational agenda. However, the long-term *intended* outcomes of the schools and the educational projects are overshadowed by the *unintended* immediate outcomes of these projects—for example, Gülen's unexpected positioning with respect to "the state of the nation."

In Almaty, Gülen's *hizmet* is integrated into a national mission of "returning to the ancestors." Therefore, it does not seem to be defined independently from the national interest. Paradoxically, however, the strong national affiliation does not reduce KATEV's autonomy. KATEV fits the definition of a civil society organization because it has the "capacity to organize itself without being organized by the state" (Calhoun 1994, 309). This capacity may seem contradictory with its self-definition as the servant of the nation, rather than of the community. However, there is no contradiction. The Gülen community's new Islamic approach to the nation strengthens its loyalties to the state of this nation. This emergent loyalty, in turn, enables Gülen to organize autonomously at the international level. Hence, the community expands its sphere of influence and power outside the national borders *because* of its national loyalties, not despite them. The primary identification with the nation qualifies the community as a civil society organization.

Making a Good Homogenous "Turkic World": Order and Discipline

The followers who serve in KATEV are teachers, experts in education, coordinators of teaching and education in schools, principals, and heads of the dormitories. They are fluent in Kazak as well as in English, the main language of instruction. The educational project they created and implemented is actualized on the basis of networks between the teachers, parents, graduates of the schools, and businessmen and entrepreneurs who financially support the schools and provide scholarships to students. Although KATEV appears like an all-encompassing public-relations organization, its main function and responsibility is the coordination of education and the management and financing of the schools. All of the schools are considered to be high-prestige schools that are difficult to enter: KATEV gives a nationwide exam in order to select the best students in Kazakhstan. Moreover, during orientation week (the first week before classes formally start), they eliminate the students who have difficulty with adaptation or discipline problems.

The curriculum does not privilege Islam or Turkey. The education is secular. There is no religious teaching, except for a general course on the history of world religions. Hence, it may seem far from obvious in which ways these schools promote the national interest, let alone the community's *hizmet*. However, although the followers acknowledge English as a universal medium of education and science, their goal is to make Turkish an international means of communication. The teachers with whom I spoke highlighted the importance of teaching fluent Turkish and making it a widespread medium in Central Asia. The principal of the boys' high school in Almaty stated that their students graduate with a proficiency in Turkish. During my fieldwork, I met several graduates who work for the community. They all were fluent in Turkish. They not only work for Turkish companies in Almaty but also have become closer and friendlier to Turkish culture. As the principal proudly put it, the graduates are "the bridges between Kazakhstan and Turkey." Obviously, Gülen's success in teaching Turkish in Central Asia is not merely educational: it is primarily political (Hobsbawm 1996, 1070). It is an important part of the ethnic politics in Central Asia. The similarity between Central Asian languages is seen as the most tangible reason for ethnic unity in the so-called "Turkic world."

The students compete in the International Science Olympics and so far have won several awards. Schoolbooks are imported from the West. Relatively better equipment and opportunities are offered to the students as a result of the collaboration of two states and the Gülen community (mainly businessmen and entrepreneurs) in Almaty. Although the Kazak state provides the buildings and infrastructure, the Gülen community appoints teachers, education and counseling specialists, administrators, and principals from Turkey. The parents usually pay for meals. It is important to note how Gülen's educational projects create a culture of cooperation, which is the main propellant of civil society. In addition to the wider cultural yet fluid outcomes, Gülen's undertakings have more concrete and immediate implications for the yearnings of civil society in Kazakhstan: some of the community's schools have started to charge tuition based on their proven success. As a result, the standards of Kazak education have been raised by a considerable degree. What, then, is the interest of the Turkish nation in this international project? How exactly is this national interest pursued?

KATEV's educational projects are professionally conducted. They have multiple dimensions: it is a hierarchical organization with two basic departments, *eğitim* (education) and *öğretim* (teaching). The teaching department coordinates the courses, schedules, and the curriculum—that is, the scientific orientation—in collaboration with the Turkish and Kazak states, whereas the education department is oriented toward socialization and cultivation. Hence, KATEV's agenda includes applying the curriculum and educational objectives not only during the school hours but also at all other times by requiring students to live in dormitories. The schools offer mandatory extracurricular activities, which aim to discipline and educate students by socializing them. After school, the students are taught "practical" manners such as hygiene, bathing, clothing, and so on. Some of these lessons may even interfere with the students' private and personal habits. The students become familiar with Turkish customs, traditional values, cultural codes and sanctions, and the meaning and importance of the national days of Turkey, which they are invited and encouraged to celebrate. The broader goal is to spread the morality and culture of Turkish Islam to Kazak children, who are viewed as the offspring of a society morally corrupted under the wicked Soviet rule (Durkheim 1961). Discipline is an important issue in the schools: the aim is to eliminate the remnants of the immoral and antireligious Soviet past. It is important to note the double mission in the schools. The scientific competitiveness at the international level is combined with a moral education, discipline, and cultural training. As my interviews with the teaching staff and officers in KATEV reveal, the ultimate aim is to create a morally superior and scientifically competitive Turkic world. This agenda is explicitly pan-Turanist and aspires to a unity among the Turkic people in the region.

The teachers play a central and sophisticated role in achieving this goal. Although religion is avoided consciously in the curriculum and teaching, Gülen's *hizmet*—revitalization of faith in the modern, secular civil society—is not abandoned. Restoration of faith is prescriptively hoped for and implicitly ingrained through socialization and discipline. The schools have a distinct philosophy of education: the reconciliation of moral education and rationality (Durkheim 1961, 11), as well as of faith and science. This reconciliation is inherited from the Nur movement and Said Nursi's writings (Yavuz 2000a, 15). Accordingly, morality is considered rational because "it sets in motion only the ideas and sentiments deriving from reason" (Durkheim 1961, 5). The project reflects Gülen's school of thought, which aims to reconcile through secular teaching the presumably dichotomous approaches to faith and reason as well as to modernity and tradition (Gülen 1996b, 1997g, 1997h). In this sense, although the followers do not present religion as their primary goal in Almaty, it is an undeclared and fluid cultural component of education and cultivation in general.[12] The KATEV teachers can be compared to the elite of the early Turkish republic (especially the Terakki Perver Party), who regarded religion as a necessary means to strengthen the social and moral foundation of society (Mardin 1983b, 142, 1991b, 31). For them, it was the cure against rootlessness and degeneration. Similar to the secular founding fathers, the teachers in Almaty stated:

> These kids need discipline. What an unlucky destiny that they were born into a complete immoral disorder! It is only normal that they are so loose, disengaged, and therefore [have] nihilist tendencies. They suffered for so many years under the antireligious Soviet rule, which cut people off from their spirituality, faith, and morality. We know that it will take time, but they will gradually acquire the sensibility for order and discipline and communal feelings along with a sound scientific background. . . . We have the time, the energy, the commitment, but more important the determination. . . . Interestingly, we already started to see the change in their attitudes. Their parents report their surprise by the rapid effects of our education and thank us.[13]

In Almaty, the followers of the community in *hizmet*—the coordinating staff in KATEV, the teachers, and the experts in education—not only make educa-

---

12. On the republican conception of religion as civic and secondary to social cohesion, see Mardin 1983b, 142.

13. Quoted from an interview, June 1999, Almaty. I heard positive comments from the parents with regard to the change in their children's attitudes and how they became more responsible and acquired more self-control and discipline after they entered the Turkish schools.

tional policy but also implement the curriculum (Lipski 1980). This double responsibility endows the Gülen movement with considerable power over the arrangements of education in an international setting. KATEV and the teachers are both implementers and initiators of this particular kind of education.[14]

The civilization project is, indeed, the extension of Gülen's *hizmet* to the international sphere. On the one hand, the teachers believe that a strong moral education along with a scientific curriculum will help Kazak society develop into a moral, civilized, and progressive society. On the other hand, they also believe that progress and prosperity require the revitalization of faith in society. Their ultimate goal is to save and recover lost souls by cultivating faith through moral education, although they barely declare this goal in the international domain.

In addition to the altruistic teachers, responsive parents are needed to collaborate in this ambitious educational project. Similar to the extension of education to extracurricular activities in the dormitories, discipline and socialization are carried over to the home environment. The educators and teachers visit students' homes and ask for the parents' cooperation. They monitor students in their family life and follow their progress by psychological tests in school. They make sure that the home environment does not contradict the education and discipline in the schools. Moreover, they interfere with order in the private sphere if they find it not conducive to the moral education they implement. They rely heavily on psychological counseling. They also attempt to persuade noncooperating parents to collaborate by convincing them that it is for the good of their children. The educational project is all-encompassing, extending to all spheres of the students' lives. The liberal concerns of freedom of experimentation and space to develop one's own path and identity are not concerns within the project.

Not surprisingly, the local people and the parents' initial responses to the schools were negative. Kazaks were initially suspicious about the aims of the schools. Some of them thought that the Turks were simply "replacing the Soviet hegemony" and taking advantage of the power vacuum to dominate Kazaks through their missionary agendas.[15] They even rejected the naming of the schools "Turk-Kazak." After these reactions and a period of discomfort, "Turk-Kazak" was adopted as part of the official name. Moreover, the initial backlash

14. Lipski uses the phrase "street-level bureaucrats," wherein he designates the implementers of the policies as policymakers. Thus, on top of participation in educational policymaking, the Gülen followers also have some space to remake and interpret curriculum while they implement it.

15. These issues came out in my interviews with the principal of the boys' high school in Almaty and with the head of KATEV in May 1999.

and suspicion were replaced with trust and cooperation from the parents and from the Kazak government.

The teachers are the crucial part of the project. They came to Kazakhstan to serve a specific goal and mission. Most have lived under harsh conditions for uncertain time periods.[16] Among the teachers, self-sacrifice and self-denial[17] are the main characteristics of the *hizmet* abroad. Altruism in the name of God is transferred to self-sacrifice for the nation in the international sphere of the community. The legendary teachers who died for this goal in some Asian countries are recalled with pride and gratitude. As Hedetoft argues,

> the most valued form of nationalism (which is interpreted as a manifestation of a national identity—not vice versa) is that which is based on the courageous acceptance of sacrifice, death being its highest form, war its most hitting context and heroism its official designation. The ultimate litmus test of national identity resides in one's readiness for sacrifice. . . . For it is here that the ideal pertaining to the unity of state and nation is realized in the most radical manner possible. . . . It is only in those—or parallel—situations that the difference between the interest of the nations is clarified beyond any doubt, and where hostile images of the Other are not just allowed but, indeed, demanded. (1995, 25)

Instead of contradicting each other, loyalty to the community and loyalty to the nation reinforce each other in the case of *hizmet* in the international domain. It is not surprising, then, to find extreme forms of self-sacrifice among the followers who serve outside of Turkey: the teachers are not just altruistic believers of the Gülen community, but also loyal citizens of the Turkish republic. However, they openly present their *hizmet* as a service to the nation but do not publicly announce their deeper motivation—self-sacrifice for God—in Kazakhstan. The duality of the teachers' self-sacrifice is reduced conveniently to a single cause of nationhood and thereby celebrated as a matter of diplomacy and international affairs. The progressive daily newspaper *Yeni Yüzyıl* reported: "Four thousand teachers work like diplomats in Gülen's schools abroad."[18] *Zaman,* the community's daily newspaper, also appreciates the teachers as international ser-

---

16. The principal of the boys' high school in Almaty reported how during the days of initiating the projects in Central Asia, he had to endure extreme cold because there was no heat in his building and how he had to go without being paid for several months during his first appointment in the northern territories of the former Soviet Union. From an interview in May 1999.

17. Hedetoft (1995, 20) depicts self-denial for the collective good as a prominent characteristic of nationalism.

18. *Yeni Yüzyıl,* 26 Jan. 1998.

vants of the Turkish state whom the community provides.[19] The Gülen community is proud to replace the state's functions at the international level, which is thought of as a higher platform of the world order.

Combining faith with reason and communal duty with loyalty to the nation, the teachers contribute to the making of educated, civilized, and moral future generations, which eventually will be united by their Turkic identity. They also feel that they shelter a subaltern Turkic people who were suppressed and oppressed many years under the Soviet rule. They claim to help the students in revitalizing (or perhaps creating) commitment to their own origins, such as in learning and appreciating the Kazak language. From this perspective, the exposure of Gülen's project to the region seems purely cultural and apolitical. The teachers claim that the project is immune to politics, a claim in line with the community's self-presentations in Turkey.

The community's followers envision and plan a future in which Turkish culture and language will be prevalent in many parts of the globe, especially in Central Asia. They also imply that Turkish Islam is a recognized and living aspect of the region, despite the fact that the repressive Soviets attempted to bury it. The community's most pronounced objective sounds merely cultural—namely, to bring the Turkic cultures closer to each other. The cultural engineering claims a multicultural identity politics and recognition of differences.

However, it is important to note the paradox with regard to the claims for diversity. On the one hand, the educational project aspires for cultural unity and homogenization in the region. On the other hand, the nationalist project creates the platform for wide-ranging nationalist agendas and attracts and gathers different faces of Turkish nationalism. It should not be surprising, then, that KATEV, the internationalist patriot, accommodates and nurtures many different degrees and kinds of nationalisms under its roof. It is important to explore the nature of these various kinds of nationalisms. Do the different faces of nationalism qualify for civil society?

One of the teachers stated, "The aim is not to Turkify Central Asia, but to bridge the Turkic cultures. It is about familiarity and proximity."[20] However, when I probed this multicultural discourse further, he added:

> We do not simply teach the Turkish language, but also the Turkish culture and make students familiar and comfortable with it. When they are asked about their

19. *Zaman,* 27 Mar. 1998.
20. Author interview, May 1999, Almaty.

national affiliation, they say they are Kazak. But they really lack the cultural sensitivity and "blood consciousness." These human characteristics were eroded in the Soviet times. However, we work on this loss of affiliation. In the future, they will define themselves as Turks, the Kazak Turks. It only takes a decent education for them to realize their roots and how much we have in common. Is not education all about self-awareness and self-realization?

The officers in KATEV introduced me to one of the leading benefactors of the schools, who was a self-designated ultranationalist restaurant owner. He explained that Gülen's vision and public talks were his inspiration to relocate to Almaty. He was moved and incited by the encouragement of this leader—his pathfinder—to go and seek Turkic roots in Central Asia. However, he was also born into an *ülkücü* family (people who are committed to the ultranationalist goal)[21] and thus was raised according to its utopian philosophy. Yet his vision and aspirations have found expression only through his participation in Gülen's undertakings in Central Asia. He was fully satisfied by the opportunity to contribute to the cause of the Turkish schools.

> My kin came from Middle Asia, and I am so proud to be back to where I belong. This was my goal since my childhood. . . . All these lands are sacred Turkish lands. They were stolen from us by the Russians. As you see, we are getting our land back with a huge Muslim population in it. . . . However, these things take time. They will come to terms with their true self gradually. It would take at least fifty years if we try to Türkleştirmek [Turkify] them through nationalist education, through everyday life socialization and dissemination of our traditions. But if a smart political leader appeared on the stage, [one] who would cooperate and agree to consolidate Kazaks under the Turkish rule, we would save time. . . . The cultural way is a long time. The political way is just practical and a short cut, and it only takes a powerful and clever president. . . . However, we all know that it is very unlikely that the political solution would come from the heaven. . . . Thus, Hocaefendi's [Gülen's] vision is precious and the most promising project to our *ülkü*.

On the one hand, the pan-Turanist overtone of the Gülen community's exposure to Central Asia is far from implicit, and the educational projects, as well

---

21. *Ülkü* is a specific political term that refers to the nationalist utopian aim of the ultranationalist Nationalist People's Party in Turkey, wherein all Turkic-speaking peoples will be unified in one nation.

as the variety of nationalist identities that the community attracts, suggest homogenizing tendencies. On the other hand, in accord with the community's domestic patterns of mobilization, Gülen manages to attract and accommodate a diverse collectivity around a new sensibility for the nation. However, the diversity-friendly sites of the community, which try to catch as much support as possible, should not be confused with Gülen's inner logic and agendas. The lives of devout followers are structured by strict rules that impose moral and cultural uniformity. Similar to the dorms, the lighthouses, and summer camps in Turkey, the schools and dorms in Almaty are operated in accordance with strict discipline. Emphasizing the need for time for gradual reform and fluid cultural changes, the teachers I talked to highlighted that schooling is the best and direct way to shape fresh minds. How, then, does this inner logic fit with the definitions of civil society? Does not civil society exclude or contradict some forms of nationalism? The complex relationship between nationalism and civil society has to be examined further.

Pan-Turanist agendas over Central Asia have a long history. Ottoman sultan Abdülhamid II used Islam as a strategy during his rule (1876–1909) to expand influence into Central Asia and as a weapon against imperialism (Mardin 2000a, 16–17). Furthermore, Gülen's agenda in Central Asia shares a good deal with the "Türk Tarih Tezi" (the thesis of Turkish history), which claimed that the Turks contributed to civilization in Central Asia much before the founding of the Ottoman Empire. This thesis was created in the 1930s as part of the nation-building process and became a cornerstone of official ideology. The original aim was to create feelings of belonging, national identity, and pride in being Turkish. Until the late period of the Ottoman Empire, the term *Turk* was used synonymously for "nomad" or "rural." The main effectiveness of "Türk Tarih Tezi" ideology has been to make being a Turk a source of pride. Turkish nationalism has been the most successful and the only complete ideology of Kemalism (Mardin 2000b, 142). Considering its contemporary ultranationalist utopian ideals, it is rather ironic that pan-Turanism claims to be "civilizing" Central Asia after the fall of the Soviet rule.

International Undertakings: In the Service of the "State of the Nation"

It is important to note that the Gülen community initiates an international approach to education that involves educational policymaking in Turkey and in the host countries. In other words, the states recognize the Gülen community as an international actor and cooperate with it in formulating curricula. Because each curriculum reflects the educational policies of both Turkey and the host country, it should not contradict the national interest of any nation-state. Stressing the principle of the universality of science and knowledge, the Gülen movement becomes a creator and implementer of an international approach to education. However, this internationalism ironically is triggered by its strong national loyalties.

"Why should there be only American and German schools all over the world and not Turkish?" several followers in KATEV asked critically.[22] Many nonreligious (as well as religious) businessmen benefactors of the schools reported that their national feeling was satisfied and pampered by watching Kazak students singing the Turkish national anthem and speaking proper Turkish fluently. Admitting that they burst into tears while they watched those students, the followers expressed their emotions and national sentiments: "Who would not feel proud seeing the Turkish flag in the schools abroad?"[23] The emerging sensibility is not simply globalization or transnationalization of Islam. What was so touching for them was to observe the representation of the national culture and *milli emanet*s[24] in the international sphere. The process of nationalizing Islam and Islamic identities coincides with aspirations for the internationalization of these identities.[25]

Moreover, Gülen's aspirations for Central Asia have to be differentiated from a desire for globalist expansion. His international undertakings in the Turkic world anticipate regionalization. The community's followers clearly express that they are in the service of the Turkish state, that their work is the ultimate expression of their devotion to the nation. "An international network in Central Asia would strengthen *our* Turkic nation-states," said one of KATEV's distinguished educators, Hüsamettin Bey. He was especially admired for his sheltering, supporting, and connecting the "real ethnic diaspora Turks" in the different countries of Central Asia.[26] His ultranationalist affiliation fueled his efficacy and capacities at the international level. On the basis of his Turanist, ultranationalist feelings, he was performing as a whole-hearted, engaged, and passionate internationalist who has won awards as a distinct international educator in Kaza-

22. From the author's field notes.

23. For further analysis of various kinds of nationalism, see Nairn 1997.

24. National symbols of objects left to their trust.

25. Indeed, in the interviews, the informants generalized this collaboration to apply to all Central Asian countries, rather than just to Kazakhstan.

26. One of my informants was a very old man who defined himself as "a real Turk," explaining that he belonged to a displaced group in the diaspora, one that had been repressed and discriminated against under Soviet rule; he spoke Turkish with a heavy accent (different from the local Kazak language).

khstan. Moreover, he proudly expressed his closeness to the president of the Kazak state and personal connection to several high-ranking politicians. Hüsamettin Bey is a good example of how the community directs different nationalist goals to new ties between Turkey and host countries.

Rather than confirming suspicions that Turks may be trying to replace Soviet hegemony, the Gülen schools smoothly try to establish a "dialogue between civilizations." This humanist goal was the higher platform on which Gülen initially convinced the Kazaks to cooperate with the formation of schools based on the principles of international peace, mutual recognition, and belief in the universality of science and knowledge. He presented these objectives as higher goals, which were to transcend local concerns and ethnic differences. In this sense, the international arena was a higher platform (Nairn 1997, 28) over which the state's interest was extended and was co-constructed with the good of both the Gülen community and the host country in mind.

Moreover, the followers have pride in representing the nation at a "higher" level—that is, at the international level. The Gülen community is distinct from other Islamist movements and communities in Turkey in its particular conformist, pro-state attitude, which developed hand in hand and in relation with their internationalist aspirations and undertakings. Gülen often highlights this attitude in his books: "Turkey is the candidate to be a super power on the basis of its past and present situation. Many Muslim countries, including the ones in Central Asia, do trust and seem to have hopes and expectations from Turkey. We do not want to lose this [international] credibility" (1997g, 282–83).

However, the question still remains: What kinds of nationalism(s) and internationalism(s) does Gülen nourish? Nairn brilliantly distinguishes different sorts of nationalisms and their counterparts—namely, internationalisms. Instead of an abstract approach to internationalism, he suggests a deeper understanding of it. Accordingly, nationalism needs to be explicated and analyzed critically in order to understand "its alter ego, internationalism" (Nairn 1997, 46) This explains why Gülen's seemingly contradictory claims for nationalism and internationalism are actually complementary tenets of the same promulgation. These claims may be regarded as twin concepts of the same cultural and political agenda.

KATEV attracts and accommodates various faces of nationalisms and their related internationalisms. The Turkish community in and around KATEV displays a diversity of nationalist identities (secular, nonreligious, and Islamist businessmen; liberal intellectuals; education specialists; fascist activists; and so on). Depending on the kind of nationalism they adhere to, their internationalist aspirations differ. However, they all associate with the nationalist cause mobilized and coordinated by KATEV. Hence, KATEV effectuates both a nationalist and an internationalist front. Its mobilization capacity is high in turning different kinds and degrees of nationalist feelings to common goals—that is, in achieving an ethnic politics through the implementation of educational projects.

KATEV manages to attract a variety of local ethnic identities in addition to Turks. Although the Gülen community operates on the basis of unquestioned and discernible borders of Turkish nationhood, it displays a readiness to welcome the Kazak people by inviting and encouraging them to cooperate at different levels of the educational projects and business outlets.[27] This practical incorporation of the Kazaks into the Turkish community is realized by an explicit and outspoken pan-Turanism, but also by an implicit and often unspoken pan-Islamism. The (imagined or real) associations range from the less-pronounced dispositions (such as race, blood) to explicitly emphasized and celebrated qualities (such as culture, linguistics). Moreover, a political discourse accompanies the ethnocultural aspects of their nationalism and internationalism. There is a consensus that international alliances between the Kazak and Turkish states and a prospective regional front are in the interest of both societies. However, the political agendas also display multiple facets, which range from peaceful cooperation between Turkic countries to the extremist *ülkü,* the latter occasionally amounting to the utopian ideal of consolidating all Turkic peoples under the same state, the imagined pan-Turkic nation.

We are witnessing an Islamic community mobilizing a variety of national affiliations to achieve a common goal. This community manages the moral, cultural, and implicitly political approximation of Turkic countries and the regionalization of the Turkic world. To the extent that it employs civil means and civilizational goals (such as dialogue between civilizations, international peace, and progress of science), the Gülen community legitimizes itself as a civil society organization. This legitimation is extremely important in the face of the yearnings for civil society in Kazakhstan.

Paradoxically, the Kazak state tolerates and cooperates with Gülen although it discourages local religious organizations and associations through strict policies. Any religious organization with less than one hundred members is illegal in Kazakhstan, which makes the formation of a religious organization extremely difficult (Ruffin and Waugh 1999, 13). Post-Soviet Central Asian countries suffered not only many years of suppression of Islam, but also the destruction of civic initiative. After many years of isolation, the region seems to have the pri-

---

27. The best graduates of Gülen's schools are offered jobs in KATEV or other Turkish companies with relatively better salaries than those from local jobs.

mary goal of establishing "real ties . . . to the outside world" (Ruffin and Waugh 1999, 4). Kazak society calls for the international community to be involved in its first experimentation with the rule of law, citizenship, and the development of civil society (Zhovtis 1999). The Gülen community is participating in this experiment, claiming to help the host country achieve successful results.

On the basis of extensive ethnographic evidence, this chapter described and analyzed the complex relationship between Islam, nationalism, and civil society.

As this evidence illustrates, political processes do not take place in a vacuum. Rather, they are intermingled with cultural practices and transformations. The strong association of Islam with the nation, its culture, and its state facilitates a formal recognition of the Gülen community as a civil society organization. The community's primary loyalty to the nation strengthens its organizational capacities to cooperate not only with the Turkish state but also with the Kazak state. It operates as a legitimate international actor in the host states where it opens schools.

These findings shed light on the theories of civil society. It is neither merely the diversity that Islam claims to produce in society nor a presumably inherent communal homogeneity or solidarity that qualifies the Gülen movement as a civil society organization. I argued that the Gülen community's distinction from other Islamic groups can be explained by its particular devotion to the nation.

Moreover, the romanticization of Islamic civic culture (reciprocal, egalitarian, and communalist) in comparison with the universalistic, impersonal contractual relations of the "Western-originated" civil society is problematic. It is evident that modernity manifests itself in the Gülen community as alternative combinations of tradition and creativity and as adoptions of Western science, commerce, and business. Perhaps the warmth of the moral community is comforting and tempting in the face of continuous adaptation to others' norms. Not withstanding this fact, however, empirical evidence reveals that the Gülen community is distinct in its adaptability to the West and in its grasp of geopolitical changes in the world order. Combining tradition with modernity and bridging faith with secular regimes, it displays both formal and informal types of organization.

Bringing presumably abstract and universalistic concepts such as the nation-state, nationhood, civil society, and Islam down to the level of everyday life, extensive ethnographic evidence speaks to larger concerns. Such evidence helps to problematize the focus of the debates on modern Islam—that is, the compatibility or incompatibility of civil society and Islam. A new Islamic sensibility of nation and ethnicity is transforming the Gülen community's interaction with the "state of the nation" as well as with the international world order. This interaction has important implications for the community's capacities as a civil society organization.[28] It is largely a post-Soviet phenomenon. The potential influence of Turkish Islam—of Gülen's organizations in particular—on the development of civil society in the Turkic world still needs further exploration. The relationship between ethnicity, Islam, and civil society is becoming an increasingly important issue in the Central Asian context and for the new states of the region. Moreover, the emergent similarities between Islamic and secular Turkish nationalism invite further thinking about the pan-Turanist agendas in Central Asia.

The Gülen movement qualifies as an international bridge between the West and Islamic and Turkic ways of lives, especially by its emphasis on English instruction, universality of science, progress, and secular education. On the basis of these civilizational accomplishments, its claim for developing civil society can be regarded with less suspicion. In contrast to the predicted clash between civilizations (Huntington 1996; Lewis 1993), Gülen's volunteers create dialogue between civilizations, not only between the West and Islam, but especially among various Turkic cultures. This evidence also challenges pessimistic theories about the incompatibility of Islam with nationalism, with secular nation-states, and with civil society and the West. The Gülen community is not only nationalist but also secularization-friendly.

As discussed in detail, Gülen's undertakings reconcile the positive and negative faces of civil society by attracting a wide-ranging form of nationalisms. National loyalties sheltered and fostered by the Gülen movement do not entail guaranteed paths to civil and democratic consequences or to uncivil and antidemocratic consequences. The intended long-term outcomes of these educational projects may be surpassed by the unintended consequences of Gülen's appeal for wide-ranging nationalist agendas, including state-framed ones. Further research is needed to explore how the Gülen community will reconcile several types of nationalisms and internationalisms with modern versions of Turkish Islam.

---

28. Interestingly, although a substantial literature highlights the importance of the penetrations between the state and civil society (see Hall 1995 or Mann 1993), little has been written on this issue in contemporary Muslim countries.

11

Ijtihad and *Tajdid* by Conduct

The Gülen Movement

IHSAN YILMAZ

LAW IS A SOCIOCULTURAL CONSTRUCT and local knowledge. Because law and sociocultural phenomena are interlinked and there is no absolute autonomy, any change in law or culture inevitably will influence the other. Because culture must be conceived as law in Muslim understanding and life, any discussion of change, transformation, or renewal inevitably will be intermingled with the discussions surrounding *ijtihad*. Thus, any new discourse is directly or indirectly a result of a new *ijtihad,* and it does not have to be in the field of law only, as strictly defined and understood by legal modernity.

In Muslim jurisprudence, an internal diversity of legitimate opinions is a sociolegal reality. The existence of different types of Muslim legal pluralism poses both challenges and opportunities regarding neo-*ijtihad* and *tajdid* (renewal) of Islam in the decades to come. In this regard, the movement that has evolved around the ideas of the charismatic figure of Fethullah Gülen provides an example of a renewal with a potential for influencing the Muslim world.

Muslim advocates of renewal have been arguing for a return to the use of *ijtihad* to facilitate reinterpretation of the Islamic heritage to face the challenges of modernity. Yet the question is no longer whether the gate of *ijtihad* is open (Hallaq 1984, 1986), but which *ijtihad*s are necessary and can be followed. Today, many individuals and institutions claim a right to exercise *ijtihad,* and they indeed exercise it. If a state makes *ijtihad,* it can end in civil disobedience, as it has in the case of Pakistan (Yılmaz 2001a, 2001c, forthcoming b). If *ijtihad* is civil, then some people will adopt it freely, and some not. However, at this point, the problem of postmodern fragmentation arises. To prevent this fragmentation and at the same time to implement new changes and *ijtihad*s without confronting civil disobedience, to renew religious thought and practice, and to transform society, leaders of faith-based and faith-inspired movements have a role to play (see in detail Yılmaz forthcoming a).

In this context, I suggest that Gülen has reinterpreted Islamic understanding in tune with contemporary times and has developed and put into practice a new Muslim discourse with respect to some traditionally sensitive issues. His discourse and practice seem to be in tune with the zeitgeist. I suggest in this chapter that Gülen's case consists of renewed Muslim discourses and practices on religion, pluralism, jurisprudence, secularism, democracy, politics, and international relations.[1] The Gülen movement, appealing to an increasing number of Muslims and non-Muslims all over the world, is a successful example of neo-*ijtihad* and *tajdid,* with its origins in Turkey, where the encounter between modernity and traditional Islam has been experienced most deeply.

I argue mainly that the transformative influences of Gülen's discourse can be observed initially and primarily in the movement he has inspired. At a secondary level, this transformation affects the surrounding wider society. In this regard, I briefly highlight Gülen's ideas on *ijtihad,* neo-*ijtihad,* diversity, pluralism, secularism, democracy, politics, international relations, and dialog, and elaborate on what Gülen achieves in practice with respect to these issues.

Internal Muslim Legal Pluralism, Islamic Law, Fiqh, and Ijtihad

In a plural society, the issue of legal pluralism (aside from political, cultural, religious, or structural pluralism) arises where normative heterogeneity exists.[2] Legal pluralism can be found within both the most sophisticated and the less developed polity; it is a global phenomenon. The theory of legal pluralism tries to define legal pluralism not in terms of the state, but in terms of authority and in-

1. Owing to lack of space, I do not discuss the issues of science and education that other contributors to this volume discuss in detail.

2. Even though the formal legal institutions enjoy a kind of monopoly in terms of the legitimate use of power, there are some other forms of effective coercion or effective inducement. The individual belongs to various interposed fields between the individual and the body politic. These social fields have their own rules and the means of coercing or inducing compliance. Literature on legal pluralism suggests that in all communities a number of modes of normative orderings coexist with the official state law. Local law, custom, and ethnic minority laws and customs can be cited as major factors that both influence and impede the effectiveness of law in modern societies. These factors are the sources of multiple interpretations, incoherence, legal authorities, local interests, and local concerns. Other than being a source of justification for popular resistance, they also may affect the degree of respect for the official lawmaker.

stitutions. This theory envisages competing, contesting, and sometimes contradicting orders outside official law and their mutually constitutive relations to official law.

Muslim law is a repertoire of precedents, cases, and general principles, along with a body of well-developed hermeneutical techniques (Al-Azmeh 1996, 12). There is a kind of plurality of Muslim laws and customs. This plurality stems mainly from three different cases: first, the four main law schools (*madhhab*); second, written law (high Islam), which does not completely coincide with people's practices (custom); and third, some differences between the state's Islam and folk or local Islam. From a legal pluralist point of view, Muslim law is not only the law stated in the Muslim law books, but also what Muslim people apply in everyday life. In traditional Islam, the legal system is diffuse, lacking coherence in codes and enforcement, and entailing a multiplicity of authorities and sources of law. Thus, different changes have come into existence in a variety of contexts, which has caused a plurality of Muslim laws that vary depending on local context. It even has been asserted that the different perceptions of Islam throughout the world in various local contexts have led to different "Islams."

Islam demands full allegiance from a person once he or she has chosen to embrace it. Law is an essential and central part of a Muslim's religion. Thus, many Muslims in both Muslim and non-Muslim polities relate themselves to the Islamic law rather than to the legislation of particular countries. Islamic law is a source of legal pluralism in our age. Furthermore, the legal pluralism inherent within Islam maintains a legally plural society even within a Muslim environment. Law in Muslim understanding is a system of meanings and a cultural code for interpreting the world. It "represents an order which governs all spheres of life, in which . . . even the rules of protocol and etiquette are of a legal nature" (Hoffman 1993, 126). Scholars such as Lawrence Rosen (1984, 1989) and Clifford Geertz (1968, 1973, 1983) thus conceive Muslim law as culture.

Because Muslim legal pluralism is inevitable, even in non-Muslim spheres (Yılmaz 2000b, 2001b) and regardless of any official nonrecognition, and because nonrecognition does not make Muslim law disappear, discussions regarding *ijtihad* and *tajdid* are still relevant wherever Muslims live.

Muslim concern about knowing God's will in order to implement it produced classical Islamic law. Islamic law is a territory of considerable textual complexity, for there is no simple set of rules that constitute it, but rather a body of texts—including the Qur'an, hadith, and legal texts of various genres—that supplied the authoritative base for Islamic legal thought and practice (Tucker 1999, 2).

Fiqh is the product of human understanding that sought to interpret and apply the Islamic law in space-time (Esposito 1980, 240). When faced with new situations or problems, scholars looked for a similar situation described in the Qur'an and sunna. The key is the discovery of the effective cause or reason behind a shariah rule. If questions arose about the meaning of a Qur'anic text or tradition, or if revelation and early Muslim practice were silent, jurists applied their own reasoning (*ijtihad*) to interpret the law (Esposito 1998, 83; see also in detail Nyazee 1995, 47–50, and Hallaq 1996).

Ijtihad is not a source of law. It is an activity, an effort, and a process to discover the law from the texts (Qur'an and sunna) and to apply it to the set of facts awaiting decision. There is no *ijtihad* within an explicit rule in the texts.

The Qur'an and sunna are the two most important and primary authorities and sources. The other instruments referred to as sources are consensus (*ijma,* the unanimous agreement of the jurists of a particular age on a specific issue) and analogical reasoning (*qiyas),* which is defined as establishing the relevance of a ruling in one case because of a similarity in the attribute (*illa',* reason or cause) upon which the ruling was based. Although the Qur'an contains prescriptions about matters that would rank as legal in the narrow sense of the term, these injunctions comprise only eighty out of six thousand or so verses. Other verses are mainly about the belief, essentials of the faith, historical lessons, general directives as to what Muslims' aims and aspirations should be—in other words, the "ought" of the religious ethic of Islam. Qur'anic values were interpreted, applied, explained, lived, and concretized by the sunna of the Prophet, which are the second material source of law.

Although jurists generally agreed on the four sources of Islamic law—namely, the Qur'an, the sunna, *qiyas,* and *ijma*—they differed widely in their interpretations of the texts, in the value they attached to *qiyas,* and in their definition of *ijma.* The definition of *ijma* as given by the Shafi'i School includes the agreement of the entire Muslim community (*umma).* Arriving at such an agreement was difficult, considering that the other schools of law opposed the Shafi'i view, and al-Ghazzali worked out a modus vivendi confining unanimity of the community to the fundamentals, leaving matters of detail to the agreement of the scholars (Muslehuddin 1975, 65).

There are also several controversial kinds of legal reasoning and procedures on which there is not a total agreement among jurists as to their validity: public benefit (*istislah* or *maslaha),*[3] necessity (*darura),* custom (*urf),* presumption of con-

---

3. *Maslaha* is based on the belief that God's purpose in Islamic law is the promotion of human welfare (public interest). It is accepted as a source of law, provided that the case is suitable and relevant to either a universal legal principle or to specific textual evidence. Although not textually

tinuity (*istishab*),[4] and juristic preference (*istihsan*).[5] Traditional Muslim jurisprudence employs these legal instruments where the primary sources are silent.

Ijtihad is a very important aspect of Islam with regard to its dynamism and universality.[6] Within practical life, thanks to *ijtihad*, Islam dynamically develops itself in accordance with changing conditions in different contexts.

Muslim jurists and Islamic legal culture not only experienced legal change but also were aware of change as a distinct feature of the law. Muslim jurists were acutely aware of both the occurrence of and the need for change in the law, and they articulated this awareness through such maxims as "the *fatwa* changes with changing times" or through the explicit notion that the law is subject to modification according to the changing of the times or to the changing conditions of society.

Certain *ijtihad*s were accepted over time by more and more *fiqh* scholars and endured the test of time, but others disappeared. Consensus (*ijma*) contributed to the creation of a relatively fixed body of laws or legal schools, *madhhab*s. Legal developments in the formative period of *fiqh* took place via the *madhhab* traditions, whereby jurists of different pedigrees operated within the broad interpretive frameworks of *madhhab* founders. The *madhhab* tradition "also developed a formidable and sophisticated intellectual and legal edifice. The coherence and continuity of this legal tradition was mainly secured by a systematic methodology that favored adherence to the interpretive framework of the founders of the law schools" (Moosa 1999, 164).

The term *madhhab* acquired different meanings throughout history. Its earliest use was merely to signify the opinion(s) of the jurist. It later acquired a more technical meaning to refer to the totality of the *corpus juris* belonging to a leading *mujtahid*, whether or not he was a founder of a school. It also meant the doctrine adopted by a founder and by his followers and sympathizers. Then it was used to

---

specified, public interests can be served by determining what is in a person's or community's best interest in a case and by rendering a judgment that will promote that interest. In classical Muslim jurisprudence, this concept "is not simply utilitarian; it did not develop as free-wheeling practice, but rather as a discipline of law with definite limits within which it was to function. The case involved must be one that concerns social transactions (*muamalat*), rather than religious observances (*ibadat*), and the determination of public interest must be in harmony with the spirit of the *Shariah*" (Esposito 2001b, 9).

4. *Istishab* is a principle of equity that refers to the presumption in the law that conditions known to exist in the past continue to exist or remain valid until proven otherwise.

5. Where strict analogical reasoning leads to an unnecessarily harsh result, *istihsan* is exercised to achieve equity.

6. Author's interview with Fethullah Gülen, 27 Mar. 2000, New York.

mean a corporate entity in the sense of an integral school to which individual jurists considered themselves to belong (Hallaq 2001, 155). Although many *madhhab*s developed, four withstood the test of time in the Sunni jurisprudential realm: Hanafi, Maliki, Shafi'i, and Hanbali.

The interaction between *ijtihad* and *ijma* was dynamic: the community either accepted or rejected a scholar's fresh *ijtihad*. At work was a free-market mechanism, as it were. In the civil realm, the *mujtahid*s supplied a new "product" (*ijtihad*), and if the "consumers" liked it, then this new product would become permanent in the market (see, in more detail, Yılmaz forthcoming a).

Neo-ijtihad

For some time, until the eighteenth and nineteenth centuries, *fiqh* functioned effectively. Although we should not freeze it into a utopian past, it has been observed that certain events coinciding with the emergence of modernity disrupted its continuity. The most notable of these events was the advent of the West (modernity) and the displacement of the traditional Muslim educational systems. Modernity also dramatically changed the cumulative social, cultural, and economic systems of Muslim peoples. These changes affected all spheres of life, including laws (Moosa 1999, 164). The adoption of new bureaucratic processes in line with legal modernity transformed conceptions of time, space, property, work, identity, marriage, body, and the state (Moosa 1999, 166). Coupled with Muslim jurists and lawyers' (*fuqaha*) inability to renew the *fiqh* in accordance with the changing realities of Muslims' sociocultural lives, the juggernaut of modernity limited the role of Muslim law. In some countries, it gradually was removed from public life and then totally abolished, as in Turkey in 1926. In many, it is limited only to family law issues. Even on these matters, *fiqh* has to obey legal modernity. The modern nation-state decides centrally for everybody which opinion is to be followed; it codifies that opinion and makes it obligatory, rendering other opinions invalid.

Especially after the decline of Muslim power and the advance of the West and its hegemony, Muslim advocates of renewal (*tajdid*)[7] and reformers have argued for a return to the right to exercise *ijtihad* to facilitate reinterpretation and renew the Islamic heritage. Most of these late-nineteenth- and early-twentieth-century responses to the impact of the West on Muslim societies resulted in substantial at-

---

7. Muslims are not happy with the term *reform* because it has connotations of Christianity and its reform, which was a radical departure from the past.

tempts to reinterpret Islam to meet the changing circumstances of Muslim life. Ebrahim Moosa gives us a succinct picture of what has been happening:

> In recent years there has been an ongoing debate among scholars as to whether *ijtihad* had ceased in the Sunni legal tradition and, if so, for what reasons and by whose authority. The main reason provided for its discontinuity was that jurists capable of doing comprehensive *ijtihad* were no longer to be found. However, *ijtihad* of a lesser kind was still theoretically and practically possible. Modern Muslim reformers have spiritedly argued for the reintroduction of *ijtihad* into the fiber of Muslim intellectual life. Some traditionalist quarters, especially religious scholars in the Indo-Pakistani subcontinent, Turkey, and the Muslim republics of Central Asia still believe that a regime of *taqlid* is a necessary and a worthwhile methodology not to be abandoned. Other traditionalists in Egypt, Saudi Arabia, and elsewhere in the Middle East will either approve of *ijtihad* with some caution or allow it without restraint. Needless to say, the issue remains the subject of great controversy. (1999, 164)

Several leading modernist Muslim scholars have sought to demonstrate a clearer understanding of the complex origins and development of Islamic law in order to provide grounds for ongoing reinterpretation and renewal to meet the needs of changing Muslim societies. The purpose of reinterpretation is not to formulate new answers, but to rediscover forgotten guidelines from the past.[8] These pragmatic efforts have resulted in the emergence of a utilitarian approach to traditional jurisprudence, wherein certain legal concepts and instruments are taken selectively and arbitrarily from the traditional *fiqh* and then given a new function and value. Ceaseless invocation of the legal instruments of *darura* and *maslaha* is an example of this pragmatic attitude. These two instruments are very prominent in the present Muslim jurisprudential discourse but had a limited

8. The three key authors in making a generic reform movement in Islam—al-Afghani, Abduh, and Rida—were active in restating motifs of the Enlightenment, romanticism, and positivism. They all believed that the restoration of Islamic vitality required the reconstruction of the sources of Islamic law. Al-Afghani was the leading figure. Following Abduh, Rida relied on the Maliki principle of the public interest or general welfare, *maslaha*. In classical Islamic jurisprudence, this principle was only a subsidiary legal principle used in deducing new laws by analogy from the Qur'an and sunna. Rida also relied on Hanbali law and Ibn Taymiyya. Like Ibn Taymiyya, he argued that laws regarding social affairs are not immune from change. Abduh, Rida, and their Salafiyyah movement espoused the view that those injunctions of Qur'an and sunna that governed social relations (*muamalat*) were revealed for the promotion of human welfare. They espoused the view that where social needs were not covered by specific Islamic law texts, reason might be used to interpret the law in light of the public interest (Esposito 1980, 242).

place in traditional *fiqh*. This new approach can be characterized as making constant reference to the primary sources, avoiding the inherited juridical legacy with a claim to the right to interpret the sources (Moosa 1999, 167).

At this point, the approach of Bediüzzaman Said Nursi (1873–1960) is very original and reflects "the middle way"; in his opinion, "the door to *ijtihad* is open, but there are [several] obstacles that block up the way to it" (1997, 154). In sum, the obstacles he names are as follows: the increase in innovations in the Muslim world that put the essentials of religion in danger; the environmental factor in educating *mujtahids*; forced *ijtihad* rather than naturally developing *ijtihad;* distance from the age of bliss; the domination of Western civilization and atheistic philosophy over Muslims and increased difficulties in making a livelihood; consideration of current questions of *fiqh* from the point of view of wisdom and benefit rather than from that of reason (*illa'*) so that everyone's attention is the life of this world rather than on the life of the hereafter; and misunderstanding of the principle of *darura* (Nursi 1997, 154–62). In his view, because of these conditions, many Muslims are inclined to take advantage of *darura,* which is possibly against the spirit of Islamic law (see also Baktir 1998; Sanu 1998).

The reaction to the Westernizing of Islam and Muslim society led to the formation of modern Islamic societies or organizations, such as the Muslim Brotherhood and the Jama'at-i Islami, that combine religious ideology and activism (Esposito 1986, 125–26). Although premodern revivalist movements were motivated internally for the most part, Islamic modernism was a response both to continued internal weaknesses and to the external political and religiocultural threat of colonialism (Esposito 1986, 125–26). Like Muslim revivalists and modernists, Jama'at-i Islami and the Muslim Brotherhood rejected *taqlid* (imitation) and upheld the right of *ijtihad*. Although they advocated change through *ijtihad,* they tended to accept past practice and to undertake change only in those areas not already covered by Islamic law (Esposito 1986, 156).

Micromujtahids and Postmodern Fragmentation
of the Sociolegal Sphere

In these *darura* times (*asr al-darura),* some young Muslims have developed adaptive strategies to cope with the challenges of modern life. They navigate at the *madhhab* level across unofficial Muslim law. The legal pluralism inherent in Islamic jurisprudence helps them to find answers to the dilemmas of everyday life. They select eclectically and pragmatically a convenient answer from one of the mainstream—that is, Sunni—*madhhab*s. By employing this kind of modern individual *takhayyur* (preference, selection),[9] a Muslim "becomes his/her own mufti" (Murad 1999), or a micro*mujtahid,* making sometimes swift decisions in the face of a minor but instant problem (Yılmaz forthcoming a).

As a result, one can observe many Muslims surfing on the inter-*madhhab*-net.[10] A Hanafi follows the Shafi'i *madhhab* and combines the noon prayer with the afternoon one or the evening prayer with the night one (for such a permission, see Türk Dışticaret Vakfı 1999, 43). Hanafi law normally does not permit this change. Surfing in the area of ablution is also possible.[11] Regarding alcohol, although there is a consensus that drinking is prohibited, some Hanafi scholars permit external usage (Beöer 1991, 183–87). Thus, surfers from other *madhhab*s usually benefit from this process. Abu Hanifa and Shaybani are of the view that in *dar al-harb* (non-Muslim lands) the charging of interest is permissible between a Muslim and a non-Muslim. Others oppose this opinion, so if an individual wants to accept interest, he follows the former view (see Beşer 1991, 197).

Although some of these micro*mujtahid*s confine their rulings to the boundaries of the four *madhhab*s, many others claim that they can deduce their own interpretations directly from the Qur'an and sunna. It is even suggested that "in the absence of sanctioned information from recognized institutions, Muslims are increasingly taking religion into their own hands" (Mandaville 1999). Thus, one frequently hears young Muslims say that they can now find all the necessary information on the Qur'an and on hadith on CD-ROMs—information that even *madhhab* founders could not access (see, for example, Islahi 1999).

It is obvious that eventually this approach will lead to millions of *madhhab*s (Beşer 1991, 9), and there will be a postmodern fragmentation. In traditional Islamic jurisprudence, consensus served as a brake on the vast array of individual

9. *Takhayyur* originally referred to the right of an individual Muslim to select and follow the teaching of a *madhhab* other than his or her own with regard to a particular issue. Later, justification for reform was based on any opinion of any jurist regardless of *madhhab*. The doctrine of one school or jurist is combined occasionally with another (*talfiq*). *Takhayyur* in its institutionalized form, first seen in the *Majalla,* has become the most notable basis for reforms in the field of family law. This right of individual Muslims has been adopted in Muslim countries in draft legislation to justify the selection of one legal doctrine from among divergent opinions of the four Sunni *madhhab*s. This usage of *takhayyur* in fact departed from traditional understanding, in which *takhayyur* was the individual Muslim's right in a specific case and not a government's right in legislating change for all Muslims.

10. As elaborated in Yılmaz forthcoming b, the inter-*madhhab*-net is composed of and maintained by the following materials: (*a*) intra-*madhhab* texts; (*b*) inter*madhhab* texts; (*c*) new inter*madhhab fatwa* books; (*d*) newspaper inter*madhhab fatwa* columns; (*e*) radio and television programs; and (*f*) inter*madhhab fatwa*s in cyberspace.

11. For examples, see http://sunnah.org/msaec/articles/*madhhab*_issues.htm.

interpretations of legal scholars and contributed to the creation of a relatively fixed body of laws (Esposito 1998, 83). In *asr al-darura,* there is a danger of post-modern fragmentation as individuals claim to be and act as *mujtahid*s.

To prevent this fragmentation, a new activity is required that will respect the tradition, but also will satisfy the demands of Muslims in the postmodern age. The case of micro*mujtahid*s shows that the question is no longer whether the gate of *ijtihad* is open or not, but which *ijtihad*s are necessary and which ones are to be followed. Many people and institutions claim a right to exercise *ijtihad* and indeed do practice *ijtihad.* Whether or not these claims are legitimate in the people's eyes is another question. The problems of doctrinal authority, legitimacy, and postmodern fragmentation still will need to be dealt with.

Intellectual Leaders, Neo-ijtihad, and Tajdid

Because culture is conceived as law in Muslim understanding and life, any discussion of change, transformation, or renewal inevitably intermingles with discussions surrounding *ijtihad.* Thus, any new discourse is directly or indirectly a result of a new *ijtihad,* which does not have to be in the field of law only, as strictly defined and understood by legal modernity. That is why, especially after the decline of Muslim power and the advance of the West and its hegemony, Muslim advocates of renewal and reformers have argued for a return to the right to exercise *ijtihad* [12] to facilitate reinterpretation and to renew the Islamic heritage (Eickelman 1998, 89; Esposito 1980, 240, 1998, 83; Hassan 1997, 120; Karaman 1996, 536).

Modernists, revivalists, and Muslim activists stress the dynamism, flexibility, and adaptability that characterized the early development of Islam. They argue for internal renewal through *ijtihad* and selective adaptation (Islamization) of Western ideas and technology. Several Muslim scholars have sought to demonstrate a clearer understanding of the origins and development of Islamic law that will provide the grounds for ongoing reinterpretation and renewal to meet the needs of changing Muslim societies.

Esposito argues that even though earlier reformists and advocates of the

---

12. Menski provides a concise account of the issue of the purported closing of the gates of *ijtihad* and skillfully explains that "the impression given was that there would be no more legal development in Islamic law. Western observers loved this, because it seemed to indicate that Muslims had restricted themselves to medieval states of knowledge and development. The modernists rejoiced: Islam was not able to handle the modern world, it would not be part of a global future. All of that has been challenged recently, not only by clever research arguments but by a plethora of new developments in Islamic law itself" (2000, 283).

new *ijtihad* "attracted a circle of followers, these reformers were not succeeded by comparable charismatic figures, nor did they create effective organizations to continue and implement their ideas" (1998, 145). It is for this reason that the role of intellectual leaders, especially faith-based and faith-inspired movement leaders, gains importance.

The Sunan-i Abu Davud hadith that says "At the beginning of every century God will send to this community someone who will *tajdid* [renew, revive, restore] religion" is generally accepted as authentic (Algar 2001, 292). According to this hadith, every century Allah will send an individual to renew the understanding and practice of religion by the *umma* (Algar 2001, 297). This person with the mission of *tajdid* is called *mujaddid* (renewer). As Algar puts it, "There is broad agreement that the function of the *mujaddid* is the restoration both of correct religious knowledge and of practice, and act as its corollary the refutation and eradication of error" (2001, 295). The essence of *tajdid* is in the traditional understanding that in "the revival of sunna and the eradication of *bid'a,* it is not part of the *mujaddid*'s responsibility to bring about comprehensive change on the political plane" (Algar 2001, 295). In Bediüzzaman Said Nursi's view, *mujaddids* "fulfill their duties by employing new methods of explanation, new means of persuasion that are consonant with the age, and new forms of detailed instruction" (n.d., 670, trans. and qtd. by Algar 2001, 304). In every century, there is at least one *mujaddid,* with the possible existence of a number of them. There is also "the possibility of legitimate plurality of opinion concerning the identity of the *mujaddid*" (Algar 2001, 296). Al-Suyuti (849–911, the *mujtahid* imam and renewer of the tenth Islamic century) claims that the key element in defining a *mujaddid* is "palpable and broad influence attested by one's contemporaries" (qtd. in Algar 2001, 310).

Muslim scholarly interest in the hadith has focused almost exclusively on personalities—that is, on the identity of the *mujaddids* (Algar 2001, 242; Turner 1998, 1). Seyyid Reza Nasr's analysis of the role of individual leader-intellectuals in contemporary developments in Islamic thought suggests the reason for this focus:

> It is they who advanced the formative ideas, spoke to the concerns of various social groups, shaped public debates by selecting the ideas that would be included in them and those that would not, and related individual and social experiences to lasting questions and concerns about freedom, justice, good, evil, and salvation. It is they who initiated the process of interpretive reading of the Islamic faith with the aim of leading the struggle with Western thought, and helped give

it a role in rapidly changing Muslim social life. In short, they articulated the foundational ideas that are associated with contemporary Islamic thought, which uses social impulses to make a new discourse possible. (1998, 20–21)

Because of the overconcentration on personalities, the concept of the nature and necessity of *tajdid* rarely, if ever, has been discussed (Turner 1998, 1). In Colin Turner's view, the true meaning of *tajdid* is that whenever necessity dictates, God inspires a person or persons who, through their lives and works, present the realities of belief and Islam to the people as they were meant to be presented. The *mujaddid* thus re-reveals the Qur'an to the people of his own time just as it was intended to be revealed, and indeed as it was revealed by the Prophet some fourteen hundred years ago. And he does so in a way that is accessible to the level of thinking of people in his own time (Turner 1998, 2). As noted, Muslim advocates of *tajdid* have argued for a return to the right to exercise *ijtihad* to facilitate reinterpretation and to renew the Islamic heritage. Yet, as noted earlier, the question now is no longer whether the gate of *ijtihad* is to be opened, but which *ijtihad*s are necessary and which ones are to be followed.

With the exception of Abu Yusuf, none of the great imams was an official of the state apparatus. On the contrary, they refused all kinds of requests, orders, and oppression to make them official servants of the state. These *mujtahid*s were totally independent, and nobody was required to follow them. People went to several *mujtahid*s to ask questions. In a sense, there was a "free-market economy" in which people could consume a number of "competing" *fatwa*s and *ijtihad*s (Yılmaz forthcoming a). The interpretations that endured the test of time became the rule and practice.

In the postmodern age, people are more inclined to be independent, to judge for themselves, and to select from different views. Thus, it seems that, from a sociological point of view, in the future a number of *fatwa*s and *ijtihad*s will "compete" in the "market," and people will choose from them. Already we see many people and institutions claiming a right to exercise *ijtihad*. Whether these claims are legitimate in the people's eyes has to be tested. As noted earlier, state-generated *ijtihad* might end up in civil disobedience, and civil *ijtihad* may create postmodern fragmentation as a result of micro*mujtahid*s and the activities of postmodern Muslim surfers on the inter-*madhhab*-net (Yılmaz forthcoming a). In addition, in the light of Esposito's aforementioned remarks, it is more essential to implement new discourses and *ijtihad*s with effective organizations, followers, and sympathizers, rather than to produce them (Esposito 1998, 145).

Leaders of civil, faith-based, and faith-inspired movements with effective organizations have a significant role to play in preventing postmodern fragmentation and at the same time in implementing new changes and *ijtihad*s without creating civil disobedience (Yılmaz forthcoming a). They can exercise or advocate *ijtihad;* most important, they have the means to implement their ideas in the civil realm, even though in most cases and for different reasons they do not label or flag this practice as *ijtihad* or *tajdid*. Because people follow a movement leader on their own, and nobody, including the state and its laws, forces them to follow a particular leader, the leader's *ijtihad* activity is in the domain of civil *ijtihad*.[13] People may follow that *ijtihad* or not. However, in most cases they probably will follow it. Before they start following a certain movement leader, they more or less judge the leader with different criteria—such as piety, appearance, honesty, knowledge, sincerity, and so on—depending on the individual. Whether these criteria are relevant, scientific, or correct is not important for the simple reason that for the individual's conviction and conscience, they are enough to legitimize a leader and his discourse and practice. After people conclude that a certain movement leader is credible, then they will put their trust in that leader and will start following him in all sorts of ways; the leader's *ijtihad*s and his attitude toward new *ijtihad*s are no exception.

A movement leader has three functions. First, the leader is a *mujtahid* himself and makes *ijtihad*. Second, he follows certain individuals' and institutions' *ijtihad*s. Then, in the eyes of the leader's sympathizers, these *ijtihad*s also become legitimate, and they will follow them, too. Third, the leader can set up an *ijtihad* committee of sympathizers or others. Then, this committee's *ijtihad*s will be followed first by the leader, then by the sympathizers. Thus, postmodern fragmentation of Muslim sociolegal sphere can be avoided while Muslim plurality and diversity are maintained. The case of Fethullah Gülen is illustrative in this regard.

Gülen's Discourse and Its Influence on the Public Spheres

Gülen's discourse has had major influences on Turkey and its region. The transformative influences of his discourse can be observed first in his movement. At a second level, they affect the surrounding wider society in *la longe durée*. Although it is obvious that his discourse has influenced his sympathizers directly

---

13. In the Turkish case, this civil *ijtihad* is also definitely unofficial because the Turkish republic decided to abandon Islamic law in 1926 and made it illegal to make any reference to Islam in sociolegal affairs. Yet many Muslim Turks have persisted despite the Kemalists' Jacobinist aspirations to make Islam a private matter, and they in effect have reconstructed unofficial Turkish Muslim laws (see Yılmaz 2001a, 2002b).

and this influence has propelled the emergence of his movement, it is difficult to formulate a direct correlation between his discourse and Turkish society at large. My observations, as I briefly outline later, suggest that Gülen's discourse not only has been transforming Turkish society, but also will have deeper influences on a more global level in the future. Yet the evidence is neither empirical nor compelling because it is almost impossible to find direct correlations in social phenomena under so many complex interrelated and intermingled influences. The point is that there has been a change in Turkish society on certain issues, and this change has been in the direction of what Gülen has been advocating for the past three decades.

Changing Times and Ijtihad

Gülen's perception of Islam is not based on an abstract model that excludes reinterpretation and thus other interpretations, but it is open to experiences—to the cultural accumulation of this world. Gülen believes that there is a need for *ijtihad* in our age. He says that he respects the scholars of the past but also believes that *ijtihad* is a necessity because to freeze *ijtihad* means to imprison Islam in a given time and space (Yılmaz 2000b). He argues that Islam is a dynamic, universal religion that is beyond time and space, but that also renews itself in real-life situations and changes from one context to another; he believes that *ijtihad* is a major tool for this renewal.[14]

> Taking the Qur'an and sunna as our main sources and respecting the great people of the past, in the consciousness that we are all children of time, we must question the past and present. I am looking for laborers of thought and researchers to establish the necessary balance between the constant and changing aspects of Islam and, considering such juridical rules as abrogation, particularization, generalization, and restriction, who can present Islam to the modern understanding. During Islam's first 5 centuries . . . when the freedom of thought was very broad, many researchers and scholars were involved in such an undertaking. (Ünal and Williams 2000, 53)

He also states that

14. Having said this, Gülen states clearly that "Belief in God, the hereafter, the prophets, the holy books, angels, and divine destiny [has] little to do with changing times. Likewise, worship and morality's universal and unchanging standards have little to do with time and worldly life" (2001a, 133).

The issues brought forth by time and changing circumstances are referred to as secondary methods (*furuat*) of jurisprudence. For example, when sea trade was not so complex, Islam, Christianity, and Judaism had no specific rules for it. Such matters are to be referred to *ijtihad* in the light of basic principles of Islamic belief, morality, and lifestyle. Time and conditions are important means to interpret the *Qur'an*. The *Qur'an* is like a rose that develops a new petal every passing day and continues to blossom. In order to discover its depth and obtain its jewels in its deeper layers, a new interpretation should be made at least every 25 years. (Ünal and Williams 2000, 52)

Yet he also underlines that discussing *ijtihad* is sometimes a luxury because many more serious problems challenge Muslims, and everybody might claim to be a *mujtahid* under today's circumstances. Thus, he places a strong emphasis on raising and educating individuals to have the qualifications of a *mujtahid*.

Gülen emphasizes that in the name of *maslaha* and *darura,* people are inclined to follow the easiest option at all times (1995a, 285–86); if everything is permitted under the name *darura,* then the essence of religion will not remain. He argues that if earlier generations had given permission to everything and relaxed the requirements, then today nothing of the religion would remain (Yılmaz forthcoming a).

It is asserted that in the age of specialization, the possibility of any individual possessing all the qualifications of a *mujtahid* is doubtful; thus, a collective group of *mujtahid*s have become specialists in the required fields (Esposito 1980, 243). In this regard, Gülen also in principle strongly advocates *ijtihad* committees (1995a, 288). He is of the opinion that it is no longer possible for individuals to be *mujtahid-i mutlaq* (absolute *mujtahid*s); *ijtihad* committees can perform this task instead. He believes it is quite possible that in future people from all sorts of disciplines might come together in research centers and constitute *ijtihad* committees that will consult on particular issues. They should also use all technological advances of the age (Yılmaz forthcoming a).

In his view, even today's scholars might come together to try to answer some contemporary questions put to them. In the future, Gülen says, if more suitable *mujtahid*s emerge, they may come up with their own *ijtihad*s and better solutions to the problems Muslims face. For *ijtihad* committees, theology faculties might be suitable bases, or the Directorate of Religious Affairs might set up such a committee or turn its already existing *fatwa* committee into an *ijtihad* committee. The state will espouse one of these *ijtihad*s and enact it; then Muslims will follow this official law (Yılmaz forthcoming a). In Gülen's view, states should establish these committees as a service to society. Yet if a state fails to do so, Muslims should employ civil *ijtihad.* In this regard, he encourages his sympathizers to work on issues such as genetic engineering, organ transplantation, music, art, secularism, modern law, and so on, and to formulate possible Muslim responses to these issues in this age (Yılmaz forthcoming a).

Religious and Legal Pluralism of Turkish Islam and Secularism

Gülen sees diversity and pluralism as natural facts. He wants those differences to be admitted and professed explicitly. He believes that the only method to spread faith to the civilized world is through persuasion. *Tolerance* is the magic word, and practice of it is important (see Ünal and Williams 2000, 256–58, for a detailed discussion of this idea).

He is of the firm opinion that Turks have interpreted and applied Islam in a certain way so that it could be called Turkish Islam (see Ünal and Williams 2000, 54–58). He states that

> Turkish Islam is composed of the main, unchanging principles of Islam found in the *Qur'an* and *Sunna,* as well as in the forms that its aspects open to interpretation assumed during Turkish history, together with Sufism. . . . This is why Turkish Islam always has been broader, deeper, more tolerant and inclusive, and based on love. . . . The Hanafi understanding and Turkish interpretation dominates [*sic*] more than three-fourths of the Islamic world. This understanding is very dear to me. If you like you can call this Turkish Islam. Just as I see no serious canonical obstacle to this, I don't think it should upset anyone. . . . The Turkish nation interpreted Islam in the areas open to interpretation . . . [I]t attained a very broad spectrum and became the religion of great states. For this reason, I think the Turkish Muslimness is appropriate. Another aspect of this is that in addition to profound devotion to the *Qur'an* and *Sunna,* the Turks always have been open to Sufism, Islam's spiritual aspect. (Ünal and Williams 2000, 43, 52, 56)

In making reference to the Turkish Islam of the Seljuks and Ottomans and their practice of religious pluralism, he underlines that "the Muslim world has a good record of dealing with the Jews: there has been almost no discrimination, and there has been no Holocaust, denial of basic human rights, or genocide. On the contrary, Jews have always been welcomed in times of trouble, as when the Ottoman State embraced them after their expulsion from Andalusia" (Ünal and Williams 2000, 243).

He emphasizes that a legally pluralist system existed at these times as well. He is also tolerant of and advocates internal Muslim legal and cultural pluralism. In this context, for instance, he states that "Alawis [*sic*] definitely enrich Turkish culture" (Ünal and Williams 2000, 67) and encourages Alevis to transition to a written culture from an oral culture in order to preserve their identities (Ünal and Williams 2000, 67–70). He stresses that "Alawi [*sic*] meeting or prayer houses should be supported. In our history, a synagogue, a church, and a mosque stood side by side in many places" (Ünal and Williams 2000, 67).

In Gülen's philosophy, secularism is not understood as a non-Muslim way of life. The separation between sacred and profane and the projection of secularism onto social life are acceptable. The rejection of the sacred is not acceptable. Gülen argues that within the boundaries of the Western type of secularism, Islam and the state can be compatible. He emphasizes that such an understanding of secularism existed for the Seljuks and Ottomans: they employed *ijtihad* in worldly matters and enacted laws and decrees to respond to challenges in their times.

Politics

Gülen argues that democracy, in spite of its many shortcomings, is now the only viable political system and that people should strive to modernize and consolidate democratic institutions in order to build a society where individual rights and freedoms are respected and protected, where equal opportunity for all is more than a dream. Humankind, he feels, has not yet designed a better governing system than democracy (Yılmaz forthcoming a).

In his understanding, democracy in its current shape is not an ideal that has been reached, but rather a method and a process "that is being continually developed and revised" (Gülen 2001a, 134):

> Just as [democracy] has gone through many different stages, it will continue to go through other stages in the future to improve itself. Along the way, it will be shaped into a more humane and just system, one based on righteousness and reality. If human beings are considered as a whole, without disregarding the spiritual dimension of their existence and their spiritual needs, and without forgetting that human life is not limited to this mortal life and that all people have a great craving for eternity, democracy could reach its peak of perfection and bring even more happiness to humanity. Islamic principles of equality, tolerance, and justice can help it do just that. (Ünal and Williams 2000, 137)

He does not see a contradiction between "Islamic administration" and democracy (Ünal and Williams 2000, 137):

As Islam holds individuals and societies responsible for their own fate, people must be responsible for governing themselves. The *Qur'an* addresses society with such phrases as: "O people!" and "O believers!" The duties entrusted to modern democratic systems are those that Islam refers to society and classifies, in order of importance, as "absolutely necessary, relatively necessary, and commendable to carry out." People cooperate with one another in sharing these duties and establishing the essential foundations necessary to perform them. The government is composed of all of these foundations. Thus, Islam recommends a government based on a social contract. People elect the administrators, and establish a council to debate common issues. Also, the society as a whole participates in auditing the administration. (Gülen 2001a, 135, 136)

Islam, for Gülen, is not a political project to be implemented. It is a repository of discourse and practices for the evolution of a just and ethical society. He strongly states that "Islam does not propose a certain unchangeable form of government or attempt to shape it. Instead, Islam establishes fundamental principles that orient a government's general character, leaving it to the people to choose the type and form of government according to time and circumstances" (2001a, 134). Because he is critical of the "instrumentalization" of religion in politics, he constantly, if implicitly, criticizes the discourses, rhetorics, practices, and policies of the "political Islam" of Turkey.

Thus, although encouraging everybody to participate in elections and to vote, Gülen never points to any specific party or candidate. He merely gives the guidelines for judging candidates—such as honesty, advocacy of democratic principles, suitability for the job, and so on. In any party, one can find such candidates. At the end of the day, if every voter follows these guidelines, all the elected will be in tune with Gülen's ideals, regardless of party affiliation. Most important, because Gülen is not categorically affiliated with any of the parties, they will always be hopeful and will try to earn his sympathy. Moreover, his supraparty discourse easily attracts people from all walks of life.

Regarding an Islamic state, it is obvious that he is in favor of a bottom-up approach, and his desire is to transform individuals, a desire that cannot be fulfilled by force or from the top (Altınoğlu 1999, 102).

As noted earlier, he advocates a Turkish Islam or an Anatolian Sufism (as an alternative to Saudi or Iranian versions of Islam) that puts an emphasis on tolerance and Turkish modernity, demonstrating that this Islam is not in contradiction with the modern world. His discourse represents a kind of "moderate Islam," even though he strongly rejects such a definition because in his view Islam is already moderate.

In a written response to questions from the *New York Times,* Gülen clarified that "he was not seeking to establish an Islamic regime but did support efforts to ensure that the government treated ethnic and ideological differences as a cultural mosaic, not a reason for discrimination" (Frantz 2000). Gülen's discourse utilizes Mustafa Kemal as a commonly appreciated Turkish hero and polishes aspects of Kemalism that are in tune with his own ideal of a "golden generation."

Gülen addresses people from all walks of life and, as mentioned previously, does not affiliate himself with any political party, although mainstream conservative parties always have been close to him and his movement. Former prime minister Mesut Yılmaz (brief periods in 1991, 1996, and 1997–98), the leader of the Motherland Party, and former prime minister Tansu Çiller (1993–95), the leader of the True Path Party, paid several visits to Gülen and publicly praised him and his movement. Late president Turgut Özal (1989–93) and former president Süleyman Demirel (1993–2000) supported the Gülen schools by sending letters to their colleagues in other countries, by visiting the schools, by attending their opening ceremonies, and so on. They always publicly supported the movement. Muhsin Yazıcıoglu, the leader of the Great Unity Party, is fully supportive of the movement, too.

The National Outlook Movement has been the notable representative of "political Islam" in Turkey. Until 1998, the movement was under the influence of Middle Eastern political Islam to a certain extent, and its ideology was based on the binary opposition of West versus East.[15] Yet, later, some members of the movement (*yenilikçiler,* or "renewalists") established the Justice and Development Party and declared that the failure of political Islamists was that they confused the conditions of Turkey with Middle Eastern experiences and that they were under the influence of the Middle Eastern political Islamists rather than of local Muslim intellectuals. These young renewers—who formed the Turkish government after 3 November 2002, when they received an election landslide of 34 percent of the votes and almost two-thirds of the parliamentary seats—are much more liberal than their elders. Their discourse is more sophisticated, and they have learned to avoid confrontational rhetoric, opting instead for a message of democracy and human rights. The emergence of the Justice and Development Party has shown that Muslim politics in Turkey is evolving from an instrumentalist usage of Islam to a new understanding of practicing Muslims who

---

15. This being said, it must be underlined that the political Islam of this movement is specific to Turkey and might be regarded as "moderate" when compared with other representations of political Islam in the Muslim world. See Şahin Alpay, *Milliyet,* 19 Sept. 2000.

have to deal with daily politics.[16] This evolution is obviously what Gülen has been advocating over the past three decades.

There also has been a change on the left side of the political spectrum. Democratic Leftist prime minister Bülent Ecevit (1999–2002) was supportive of Gülen and his activities. On several occasions, he praised these activities. In a speech he gave at the World Economic Forum in Davos, Switzerland, in 2000, he emphasized the importance of Gülen schools all over the world and how these schools contribute to the Turkish culture.[17] When receiving representatives of the Journalists and Writers Foundation, a Gülen organization, at his office, he reiterated that he supports these schools because he believes that they are spreading the Turkish culture to an extent not achieved by the six-hundred-year-old Ottoman state.[18]

The atmosphere of tolerance and mutual understanding has influenced the founding party of the republic as well, the People's Republican Party. This party has undergone a transformation recently. After losing heavily at the 1998 elections, Deniz Baykal quit as the leader of the party; some time later he returned to politics, saying that he and his discourse had changed, and subsequently was re-elected as leader of the party. Now he defends tolerance of Anatolians; he pays respect to the Ottomans and to the religious scholars of the past; and he employs warm language regarding the issues of religion.[19] He argues that "he wants to come to power in this world while desiring to go to heaven in the hereafter."[20] He says he admires Jalalu'ddin Rumi, Yunus Emre, Hacı Bektaş, and Yesevi and finds their ideas progressive and revolutionary.[21] In an interview by liberal *Hürriyet* columnist Cüneyt Ülsever on Samanyolu TV (part of the Gülen media network) on 24 April 2001, Baykal called his new politics "Anatolian leftism." It is obvious that most of these ideas are what Gülen has been arguing for more than thirty years. Baykal, when asked if he had made similar statements previously, replied that "[the ideology of] social democracy has come to this point very recently."[22] Indeed, this transformation process began some ten years ago at the

16. I discuss this changing discourse of the National Outlook Movement in detail elsewhere (Yılmaz 2000a, 6–7).

17. *Zaman,* 23 Feb. 2000.

18. Ibid.

19. *Aksiyon,* 7 Apr. 2001.

20. *Zaman,* 7 Feb. 2001.

21. *Aksiyon,* 7 Apr. 2001.

22. Ibid. Some party members found this change so radical that they quickly left the party, encouraged and led by Ismet Inönü's son Erdal Inönü.

grassroots level. The ordinary people already had left their ideological camps of the pre-1980s and have been tolerant of each other; this transformation is what has forced Baykal to change as a receptive leader.[23]

Most scholars agree that "Gülen continues a long Sufi tradition of seeking to address the spiritual needs of [the] people, to educate the masses, and to provide some stability in times of turmoil. Like many previous Sufi figures (including the towering thirteenth-century figure, Jalalu'ddin Rumi), he is suspected of seeking political power. However, any change from this apolitical stance will harm his movement first" (Altınoğlu 1999, 102). Even though Gülen consistently reiterates that he has no political claims, that he is against the instrumentalist use of religion in politics, that his emphasis is on individuals, and so on, the militarist elite who see themselves as the staunch guardians of the regime regard him and his movement as potential threats to the state. Those fears seemed confirmed two years ago when television stations broadcast excerpts from videocassettes in which he apparently urged his sympathizers to infiltrate the government "patiently and secretly" (Frantz 2000). He also made some statements vaguely critical of the Turkish establishment. Gülen said his words were taken out of context, and some were altered; he said he was counseling patience to sympathizers faced with corrupt civil servants and administrators intolerant of workers who were practicing Muslims (Frantz 2000). "Statements and words were picked with tweezers and montaged to serve the purposes of whoever was behind this [television program]" (qtd. in Frantz 2000). The militarist elite remains suspicious and claims that Gülen seeks to gain political power over state institutions, including the army. That Gülen employs such vague language on certain issues is understandable given that the authoritarian state does not tolerate any rivals in the social sphere, one of the major reasons for Turkish civil society's immaturity and weakness.

The militarist elite's and the state's suspicious attitude is not confined to Gülen.[24] As liberal leftist intellectuals Etyen Mahcupyan and Murat Belge of the

23. When I was administering a questionnaire in 1993 for an undergraduate course on Turkish local politics taught by Professor Artun Ünsal at Bosphorus University, a former mayor of Kagithane Borough exclaimed, "My party is the best party, CHP [the Republican People's Party], and my *hoca* is the best *hoca*, Fethullah Hoca!"

24. In this regard, Turkey's leading sociologist Nilüfer Göle writes that "The shared aversion of the intelligentsia and the army to the autonomization of civil society in politics—whether expressed through Islamism, Kurdish identity, leftist ideology or liberalism—shaped Kemalism, the ideology underpinning the Turkish mode of Westernization. Throughout Republican political history, these four phobias—whose relative importance varied with the conjuncture—constituted the ideological rationale for political authoritarianism" (1996a, 20).

Daily Radikal wrote many times, civil society is something to be afraid of in Turkey, as it is in any other underdeveloped authoritarian country. In the social realm, the state does not tolerate any rival in the name of authority, unity, national security, or laicism. For instance, soon after the 18 August 1999 earthquake, many civil society institutions, from all walks of life, were very quick to respond to the crisis and arrived at the badly affected areas with all kinds of help. The state and the army were harshly criticized because they were slow to react. Even in the media, these criticisms were aired, which is very unusual in Turkey. Those wanting to help financially channeled their money to these civil society institutions, saying that the corrupt politicians and bureaucrats would not give the funds to the needy. Fearing that the respect for and authority of the state would be harmed, Turkish rulers halted and then prohibited all the private activities. The financial accounts of some of these civil institutions, such as the highly respected nonideological Search and Rescue Team, were confiscated; the state got rid of its rivals. In response, however, all the civil society institutions, from ultra-laicists to Islamists, got together and condemned the state in advertisements in national dailies, a first in Turkey's history.

To sum up, given that Gülen has achieved relative autonomy from state power, that he has been able to mobilize a large segment of society, and that he is of an Islamic background with which the laicist state's policies have felt unease, he always will be depicted as a potential threat.[25]

Jihad for Tolerance, Dialogue, and Cooperation among Civilizations

As noted previously, Gülen sees diversity and pluralism as natural facts; he wants those differences to be admitted and to be professed explicitly. He argues that "The Prophet says that all people are as equal as the teeth of a comb. Islam does not discriminate based on race, color, age, nationality, or physical traits. The Prophet declared 'You are all from Adam, and Adam is from earth. O servants of God, be brothers (and sisters)' " (Gülen 2001a, 134).

Gülen is an adamant supporter and promoter of interfaith dialogue (see Ünal and Williams 2000, 193–304). He underscores that

> Islam recognizes all religions previous to it. It accepts all the prophets and books sent to different epochs of history. Not only does it accept them, but also regards belief in them as an essential principle of being Muslim. By doing so, it acknowledges the basic unity of all religions. A Muslim is at the same time a true

---

25. See further "Islamic Evangelists" 2000.

follower of Abraham, Moses, David, Jesus, and of all other Hebrew prophets. This belief explains why both Christians and Jews enjoyed their religious rights under the rule of Islamic governments throughout history. (2001a, 137)

He argues that there is no rule requiring that the style used in the Qur'an to express some Jews and Christians' obstinacy and enmity toward "truth" also should be used for every Jew or Christian in every era: "the verses condemning and rebuking the Jews and Christians are either about some Jews and Christians who lived in the time of the Prophet Muhammad or their own Prophets" (Ünal and Williams 2000, 260).

He believes that "The Islamic social system seeks to form a virtuous society and thereby gain God's approval. It recognizes right, not force, as the foundation of social life. Hostility is unacceptable. Relationships must be based on belief, love, mutual respect, assistance, and understanding instead of conflict and realization of personal interest" (Gülen 2001a, 137).

In his view, a believer must communicate with any kind of thought and system; "such a person is like a compass with one foot well-established in the center of belief and Islam and the other foot with people of many nations" (Ünal and Williams 2000, 206). To this end, Gülen pioneered the establishment of the Journalists and Writers Foundation in 1994, whose activities promote dialogue and tolerance among all strata of society.[26] Gülen is the honorary president of the foundation. According to its president, Harun Tokak, the foundation took as its principle the performance of activities that develop and consolidate love, tolerance, and dialogue, first among journalists and writers, and then throughout Turkish society and even humankind.[27]

The foundation organized a large Ramadan dinner (*iftar*) in a grand hotel in February 1995.[28] In terms of diversity of the participants, it was the first of its kind. More than one thousand guests attended, including the elite of several social groups. The foundation organized another major event in the same year: the

26. A number of people and groups constantly criticize Gülen's dialogue discourse and activities. See, for example, Mehmet Şevket Eygi's articles in *Milli Gazete* (2000a and 2000b). See also the Kemalist-leftist daily *Cumhuriyet* (specifically 3 Dec. 2000); see Necip Hablemitoglu in the nationalist monthly *Yeni Hayat* (in particular no. 52); Maoist Dogu Perinçek's Workers' Party weekly *Aydınlık;* and Sheikh Haydar Baş's daily *Yeni Mesaj* (for examples, see the 6 May, 7 June, 8 June, 17 June, 29 June, and 23 Sept. 2000 issues).

27. Author's interview with Harun Tokak, 1 Sept. 2000, Istanbul.

28. Ünal and Williams (2000, 208–40, 262–304) provide a detailed account of such organizations, Gülen's speeches, and the presence of some eminent members of the Turkish elite at these events, plus their repercussions.

Awards of Tolerance '95. In 1996, it organized an international conference called "Dialogue of Civilizations." The aim of the conference was to replace the "clash of civilizations" thesis with a dialogue approach. Orthodox Patriarch Bartholomeos; the Istanbul representative of the Vatican, Monsignor Georgi Marovitsch; a leader of the Catholic community; a representative of the Turkish Protestant Presbyterian community; and the consul general of Greece also attended the conference. The president of the foundation emphasizes that they are against the idea of a future determined by conflict among civilizations.[29]

In 1997, the foundation organized an international intercivilization congress, emphasizing the themes of tolerance and intercultural cooperation. In 1998, Gülen met the pope in the Vatican and then the chief rabbi of Jerusalem. Cemal Uşşak, secretary general of the foundation, points out that "there were reactions from radicals and fanatics, but the majority of people, who support moderation, congratulated him."[30] In April 2000, the Intercultural Dialogue Platform of the foundation organized an international symposium in Sanli Urfa and Istanbul, entitled "Abraham: A Symbol of Hope and a Bond of Unity in Dialogue for Jews, Christians, and Muslims" (Journalists and Writers Foundation 2000b).

The foundation also has a busy publishing program. Some of the books it has published include: *Islam and Laicism; Science and Technology in the Ottoman Society; From the Clash of Civilizations to Dialogue; Living Together According to Eastern-Western Sources; Religion, State, and Society;* and *Tolerance in the Ottoman Society.*

The movement tries to bring in all scholars and intellectuals, regardless of their ethnic, ideological, religious, and cultural backgrounds. The Journalists and Writers Foundation also works as a think-tank. The Abant Conference is a result of the attempt at finding solutions to Turkey's problems by bringing together scholars and intellectuals of all stripes. This platform is the first of its kind in Turkish history where intellectuals could agree to disagree on sensitive issues such as laicism, secularism, religion, and state relations. The foundation organizes Abant conventions annually, and every convention ends with a declaration. In 1998, the theme was "Islam and secularism"; in 1999, "religion and state relations"; and in 2000, "the democratic state within the framework of rule of law."

The 1998 Abant Declaration (Gündem 1998) attempts to redefine the meaning of laicism in accordance with the way it is practiced in Anglo-Saxon cultures. Moreover, it reinterprets Islamic theology to respond to modern challenges. It underscores that revelation and reason do not conflict; that individuals should use their reason to organize their social life; that the state should be neutral on

---

29. *Zaman,* 2 Nov. 1996.

30. Author's interview with Cemal Uşşak, 3 Sept. 2000, Istanbul.

beliefs and faiths prevalent in the society; that governance of the state cannot be based on the dominance of one religious tradition; and that secularism should expand individual freedoms and rights and should not exclude any person from the public sphere.

Gülen's discourse and practice have obtained the support of a number of well-known liberal intellectuals, such as the journalists Mehmet Altan, Ali Bayramoğlu, Mehmet Barlas, Etyen Mahcupyan, Mehmet Ali Birand, Gülay Göktürk, Taha Akyol, Cüneyt Ülsever, and Cengiz Çandar, who argue that the solution to Turkey's problems depends on consensus.

Moreover, scholars formerly deemed "radical Islamists" now fully support Gülen's thought and practice. Such influential Muslim scholars as Ali Bulaç and Fehmi Koru, who also are known to the Western academic audience, have modified their discourses in line with Gülen's and have expressed ideas that are different from their earlier thoughts. For instance, Bulaç now fully supports the view that Islam does not a have a specific form of government. He affirms that "if the meaning of political Islam is to establish a theocratic state, it is finished," pointing out that although Islam was once a cause for conflict and polarization, it should now be a base for conciliation.[31] He was formerly against Turkey's entrance to the European Union, but now he advocates accession. Although he once perceived "the Copenhagen criteria" to be a "Christian club," he now sees those criteria as *amr bil ma'ruf* (ordering the good).[32] Very recently he wrote about immigrating to non-Muslim lands and referred to this immigration as *"hijra."*[33] Ahmet Selim, another respected Muslim scholar and intellectual, once wrote, "until Gülen came up with his dialog discourse we were not aware that there were so many verses in the Qur'an encouraging interreligious dialog and cooperation."[34]

Despite the Directorate of Religious Affairs' mission to create a tailor-made national modern Islam by suppressing transnational links, its role has been changing for two years.[35] This change is most observable in the issues of interreligious dialogue, the European Union, and the Turkic world. Put differently, the directorate's main task has been to control and domesticate Islam in accordance with the needs of the secular nation-state (Yavuz 2000b), in the process creating

31. *Zaman,* 4 June 2000.
32. Ibid.
33. *Zaman,* 19 Apr. 2001.
34. *Zaman,* 5 June 1999.
35. Elsewhere (Yılmaz 2000a), I have shown in detail the direct correlation between Gülen's dialog activities and the directorate's recently changing attitude.

a secular, modern "Turkish Islam" cut off from all international and transnational ties, specific and limited to the nation-state's official borders. Interfaith dialog was not on the Turkish power elite's agenda, and thus it was not on the directorate's agenda either.

The Kemalist establishment now has begun to "encourage" the directorate to play a transnational role in order to counterbalance the activities of the Gülen movement. Interreligious dialogue has taken a place only recently on the state's agenda because laicist circles criticized the directorate for remaining inactive even while an unofficial leader with no authority—that is, Gülen—was promoting interreligious dialogue and paying a visit to the pope. Underlying the psychology of this criticism, however, was the laicist elite's fear that religion would spiral out of control.[36] After a while, the directorate started including elements of interreligious dialogue. Although the directorate's discourse did not necessarily include anything against these themes, it did not mention them either. These themes were irrelevant for the state-sponsored "Turkish religion." Only recently has the directorate established a unit for interreligious dialogue.

Now the directorate authorities voice their desire to reinterpret Islam in the face of the challenges of modernity, new developments of the age, Muslims living in non-Muslim western territories, interreligious dialogue, and peaceful coexistence; they emphasize that the directorate's future activities will address such issues.[37] The director, Mehmet Nuri Yılmaz, also paid a visit to the Vatican and on 16 June 2000 had a private meeting with the pope.[38] This event attracted impressive media attention in Turkey, with headlines such as "First Ever in History!" Columnists emphasized that it was a good idea to enter into dialogue with other religions, an idea that never concerned the Kemalist elite until Gülen took the lead and threatened the fictive public monopoly of the state on religious matters.

As mentioned previously, Gülen also has been encouraging his sympathizers to write works on modern-day issues such as genetic engineering, organ transplantation, music, art, modern theology, *tafsir* (Qur'anic exegesis), the Muslim-Christian dialog, and Islam's possible opinions on these subjects in this age

36. For such a comment, see Yenibahar 2000.

37. I had a long discussion with Yusuf Kalkan on these issues and the role of the directorate in the future. He sincerely stated that their intention is not to export any ideology, but to play their part in shaping the future face of Islam in Europe and in the world, with an emphasis on tolerance and dialogue (interview, 16 Aug. 2000, Ankara).

38. Detailed information can be found in the Turkish dailies of the time of visit, or see in detail "Tarihi" 2000. On the front cover, the journal features a picture of Mehmet Nuri Yılmaz, the director, shaking hands with the pope. See also *Diyanet Avrupa* 15 (15 June–15 July 2000).

(Yılmaz 2000b). Now, many of his sympathizers publish papers and books and write Ph.D. theses on these issues, and the movement's publishing houses—such as Nil, Kaynak, Töv, Fountain, Light, Truestar—have been supporting and publishing these works. These publishing companies publish new *fatwa* books, too. The movement has been disseminating these ideas for the past decade in its theology journal *Yeni Ümit*. A new intelligentsia formed along the lines of Gülen's discourse also has been evolving.

Living in Non-Muslim Lands (Dar al-harb) and Cooperation with the West

In modern times, one of the areas that motivates *ijtihad* is the situation of Muslims in non-Muslim polities. The juristic discourse with regard to such issues as whether Muslims may reside in a non-Muslim polity and under what circumstances, the relationships of these Muslims to *dar al-Islam,* and the ethical and legal duties that these Muslims owe both to Muslim law and to their host non-Muslim polity (*dar al-harb*) have been debated since the eighth century. This discourse on the issue has not been dogmatic. Other than the mutually exclusive concepts of *dar al-harb* and *dar al-Islam,* the persistent existence of Muslim minorities voluntarily residing outside *dar al-Islam* has challenged this dichotomous view. Islamic jurisprudence has developed several mechanisms and concepts to facilitate compromise: duress (*ikrah*), necessity (*darura*), and public welfare (*maslaha*). As a result, the concepts *dar al-ahd* (country of treaty, covenant), *dar al-aman* (country of security), *dar as-sulh* (country of peace), and *dar al-darura* (country of necessity) have come into operation, in which it is held that Muslims can live according to their religion in non-Muslim lands perhaps with difficulty but peacefully (Fadl 1994; Masud 1989).

Gülen's frequently used term *dar al-hizmet* (country of service) is a new concept in this regard, reflecting his vision (Pearl and Menski 1998, 64). If one's intention is to serve Islam by presenting a good example, then one can stay wherever one desires, says Abdullah Aymaz, former editor in chief of the daily *Zaman* and Gülen's close friend and colleague for more than thirty years. Gülen stresses that wherever a Muslim is, even outside a Muslim polity, he or she has to obey the *lex loci,* to respect others' rights and to be just, and has to disregard discussions of *dar al-harb* and *dar al-Islam*. In Gülen's understanding, *umma* is more of a transnational sociocultural entity, not a politicolegal one. He hopes that this sociocultural entity will be instrumental in bringing general universal peace.[39]

39. Author's interview with Abdullah Aymaz, 3 Sept. 2000, Istanbul.

He formulates a project of cooperation between Islam and the West to reach this desired, almost utopian, universal peace:

> The West cannot wipe out Islam or its territory, and Muslim armies can no longer march on the West. Moreover, as this world is becoming even more global, both sides feel the need for a give-and-take relationship. The West has scientific, technological, economic, and military supremacy. However, Islam possesses more important and vital factors: Islam, as represented by the Holy Book and the *Sunna* of the Prophet, has retained the freshness of its beliefs, spiritual essence, good works, and morality as it has unfolded over the last fourteen centuries. In addition, it has the potential to blow spirit and life into Muslims who have been numbed for centuries, as well as into many other peoples drowned in the swamp of materialism. (Ünal and Williams 2000, 247)

He further states, "I don't see any harm in joining the West and Western thought on points where it's necessary and where there's no danger. . . . I don't see any harm in taking things the West developed" (Ünal and Williams 2000, 191). Gülen has been quick to respond to the challenges and opportunities of globalization, and his efforts at dialog should be evaluated in this context as well. He has been supportive of Turkey's accession to the European Union (Ünal and Williams 2000, 189). He says, "If both Europe and Turkey could come to a mutually acceptable agreement, the future could be promising. But this demands intelligent people with one eye on the larger world and one eye on their own world" (Ünal and Williams 2000, 58).

He has also encouraged Turkish people to migrate to these countries in order to be honorary representatives and ambassadors of Turkey. In Gülen's discourse, realism has a substantial place. He frequently states that the United States is currently the leader in the international arena (Ünal and Williams 2000, 192), and as an alternative in the leadership stakes, it is better than nondemocratic countries such as China.

The Gülen movement's global vision has been shaped along the lines of Gülen's thought. It is the only Turkish civil society entity that has established institutions in so many different countries. With Gülen's global vision in mind, *Zaman* is published in sixteen countries, sometimes in a bilingual format. It is also the first Turkish daily to be published on the Internet, and very recently its English version was launched. Also with this global vision in mind, Samanyolu TV broadcasts to Europe, Central Asia, and Caucasus. Gülen's books in English, Turkic languages, Russian, Albanian, and other languages are sold in several countries.

Interfaith dialogue all over the world is on the movement's agenda. In the countries where sympathizers reside, they utilize the concept of *dar al-hizmet* and either establish interfaith organizations, associations, and societies or are in close contact with people of faith. Thus, for instance, Turkish businessmen in Korea take the Buddhist priests to Turkey to visit historical places where believers of different faiths lived peacefully. In Thailand, the administrators of Fatih College regularly visit Buddhist authorities and priests and report to them the progress of the Thai pupils in the Gülen schools. In Russia, Romania, Georgia, South Africa, Senegal, and so on, the praxis is the same. They all believe that interfaith and intercultural dialogue is necessary to reach a general universal peace and that the first step in establishing dialogue is to forget past tensions, ignore polemical arguments, and give precedence to common values. The teachers, administrators, and businessmen who immigrated to these countries for *hijra* (emigration) reiterate that their intention is "to prepare mankind for the birth of the century of tolerance and understanding that will lead to the cooperation of civilizations, and to strengthen bonds among all the peoples of the world; what people have in common, not only within a nation, but across national-political boundaries in the world as a whole, is far greater than what divides and separates them."[40]

The movement's schools are virtually the only Turkish presence in many countries, a fact acknowledged by the Turkish intelligentsia. Özdem Sanberk, director of the Economic and Social Studies Foundation and former Turkish ambassador to London, summarizes the liberal democratic Turkish intellectual approach to the schools: "Strategically speaking, the schools are something that should be supported by the state because you have a Turkish presence in these countries" (qtd. in Frantz 2000).[41] It must be noted that until the movement established these schools, the state, think-tanks, research centers, and academics in Turkey made no mention of such an international project, even in theory.[42]

In the Gülen schools, Muslims, Christians, Jews, Buddhists, Shamans, and others study together in peace, affirms Cemal Uşşak, who adds, "in the larger Muslim world, this tolerance poses a potential challenge to Islamism, for its ideas may find receptive audiences among those with access to the outside world."[43]

40. These quotations are also based on my observations and interviews with these people in Japan, Korea, Taiwan, Thailand, and Pakistan between 25 Jan. and 7 Mar. 1998; in Kazakhstan and Kyrgyzstan, 16–23 May 1998; and in Indonesia and Malaysia, 19–26 Dec. 2001.

41. See further "Islamic Evangelists" 2000.

42. Scholars have noted the movement's potential importance in strengthening Turkey's position in the international arena. See, for example, Çandar and Fuller 2001.

43. Author's interview with Cemal Uşşak, 3 Sept. 2000, Istanbul.

Gülen now is described as an opinion leader in Turkey.[44] Newspapers sometimes refer to him as the unofficial civil religious leader of Turkey.[45] His discourse does not reside only at a rhetorical level; in praxis, he encourages all his sympathizers to realize his ideals. As elaborated earlier, after espousing Gülen as a prominent intellectual and religious leader, many people may adapt themselves to his discourse and follow his *ijtihad*s, even though he does not label his precepts as *ijtihad*s.

It is evident that a new Muslim politics, new international relations, a renewed juristic discourse, and a renewed Muslim educational practice have been developing slowly but steadily, paving the way for a modern and harmonious society through an evolving bottom-up approach. It goes without saying that more empirical research definitely is needed to substantiate the arguments I put forward here.

Some elements, if not all, of Gülen's discourse may not be unique. A number of Muslim thinkers, intellectuals, and *mujtahid*s developed new ideas and understandings in the face of the challenges of the modern juggernaut, without making concessions to the Islam of the past, the so-called Golden Age. Yet what makes Gülen's case unique is that he successfully has persuaded and mobilized many people—numbering up to a few million—to establish institutions and to put into practice his discourse and realize his ideals.

Preliminary observations indicate that Gülen not only is renewing Muslim discourses and practices, but also transforming the public sphere, without claiming or boasting that he is doing so. In this regard, the movement is evolving into a school of thought based on Gülen's discourse and with the potential to influence the whole Muslim world. This transformation process is definitely a *tajdid* in the Turkish public sphere. The reality of internal Muslim legal pluralism requires that different *ijtihad*s take place in different parts of the Muslim world at the same time, shaped by local conditions. Thus, it is quite possible that other *tajdid*s exist in places other than Turkey. Yet with the increasing importance and weight of the Turkic world in global sociopolitics, Gülen's *tajdid* will be more influential. The impact of this renewal will be felt even in the distant corners of the global village as his sympathizers in more than fifty countries spread the "renewed word" by conduct.

---

44. Enis Berberoglu, *Hurriyet,* 10 Aug. 2000.
45. Avni Özgürel, *Radikal,* 2 Mar. 2001.

12

Fethullah Gülen

Transcending Modernity in the New Islamic Discourse

JOHN O. VOLL

FETHULLAH GÜLEN is one of the major figures in defining the contemporary global Islamic experience. Although he is not as widely known as some Muslim leaders whose actions attract the attention of the mass news media, his work helps to redefine the nature of Islamic discourse in the contemporary world. He does not stand isolated from the mainstreams of Islamic experience but can be described as a significant fruit of the tree of Islamic spirituality, whose roots are in the Qur'an and prophetic revelation.[1] However, although it is important to note the fruit and the tree, it is also important to look at the context of this image.

The imagery of the tree is useful, but in such imagery the assumed and often unnoticed context and framing of such images shape the understanding of the significance of that image. When one looks at a picture, one seldom actually sees the frame, but the framing context of a picture shapes what we see in the picture itself.[2] If we think of the image of "the tree and fruit" of Fethullah Gülen, it becomes important to be conscious of the frame within which we place that image. A picture of a tree on a foggy day or in a very dark frame can be dismal, whereas a picture of the same tree in a light frame on a sunny day presents a very differ-

1. This is the description Zeki Sarıtoprak gave in the oral presentation "Fethullah Gülen: A Sufi in His Own Way" at the conference "Islamic Modernities: Fethullah Gülen and Contemporary Islam" at Georgetown University on 26 April 2001. Although Sarıtoprak did not carry these specific words into the written version of the paper, chapter 8 in this volume, the basic theme of Gülen's being the product of the long continuity of Islamic spirituality is the core of that chapter.

2. A discussion of the importance of the influence of the framing on how we see the images in a picture can be found in the more general discussion of the art of Rene Magritte in Michel Foucault's *This Is Not A Pipe* (1982).

ent mood. Similarly, the image of the great tree of Islamic spiritual experience and the fruits of Fethullah Gülen can appear very different if the frame for the narrative picture is the frame of modernity or the frame of the world of spiritual experience after modernity. The chapters in this volume illustrate this complexity, sometimes interpreting Gülen in his "modern" context and sometimes in the "transcending modernity" context.

One possible frame for viewing Gülen's movement at the beginning of the twenty-first century is to identify the new Islamic discourses that now are beginning to transcend the discourses of modernity. To consider the issues of "transcending modernity," it is necessary to break out of the now-sterile debates about the nature of the label *postmodern*. If *modern* is used in accord with the older definition as "pertaining to the present and recent times" (*Oxford Universal Dictionary* 1964, 1268), then there can never be a "postmodern," and the content of the meaning of modernity changes constantly. In the older meaning, *modern* simply referred to the major *current* ideas and institutions, regardless of the content.

In recent decades, *modern* has come to have a more defined set of meanings. People began to identify it with a particular perspective and content, and one could speak of "the agenda of modernity" as it began to be defined in western Europe in the seventeenth and eighteenth centuries.[3] When Crane Brinton wrote an influential study called *The Shaping of the Modern Mind* (1953) in the middle of the twentieth century, he was defining a distinctive worldview and perspective, with a particular content. By the 1960s, this "modern" worldview, described by one analyst as "mechanistic, positivist Cartesian 'Science'" (Drucker 1965, 14), was seen as being superceded or transcended by new perspectives, worldviews, and institutions. In this context, it was possible for the well-known management consultant, economist, and societal analyst Peter Drucker to argue in the mid-1960s that at "some unmarked point during the last twenty years we imperceptibly moved out of the Modern Age" and to speak of the "postmodern world" before the term *postmodern* had become a controversial battle cry in the field of literary criticism (1965, xi). By the end of the century, a prominent scholar in the philosophy of science, Stephen Toulman, could argue: "If an historical era is ending, it is the era of Modernity itself. . . . What looked in the 19th century like an irresistible river has disappeared in the sand. . . . The very project of Modernity thus seems to have lost momentum" (1990, 3).

The frame within which contemporary events can be viewed is no longer necessarily the frame of modernity; the context is *not* modern, at least from some perspectives. When various movements and thinkers within the Muslim

---

3. See, for example, the broad analysis in Toulman 1990.

world are discussed, the analysis frequently places the subject within the framework of modernity. Thus, it is possible to state, in examining the development of the ideology of the Muslim Brotherhood in the Arab world, that Hasan al-Banna "embraced modernity, reworking modern political concepts . . . so that they became an integral part of his Islamic political discourse. In contrast, [Sayyid] Qutb rejected modernity as an expression of the negation of God's sovereignty, refusing to adopt the political idiom of the modern nation-state in the service of a rediscovery of Islamic authenticity" (Taji-Farouki 1996, 46). Such an analysis views Qutb and al-Banna in the context of their relationships with modernity in the age of continuing modernity. In the "postmodern" contexts noted by Drucker and Toulman, it also might be possible to see Qutb as not just being "antimodern" but also being "postmodern" in some significant ways. This possible different perspective can be useful in examining the ideas and place of many major intellectuals and activists in the Muslim world and beyond. It is especially helpful in trying to determine Fethullah Gülen's place in the contemporary world. His portrait can be framed by the analysis of the intellectual constructs of modernity; it also can and should be framed in the intellectual world of "beyond modernity."

The New Context

The new global context has many features that reflect new dynamics of interactions of peoples and of emerging societal structures and perspectives. Two important dimensions of this context involve the continuation and intensification of the processes of globalization and the redefinition of the role of religion in society as it becomes clear that the predictions of secularization theory were wrong.

Globalization was an important part of the broader experience of modernity. Many aspects of "modern" society involved significant global connections. "The industrial revolution was an international event from the first. It resulted from changes that had been occurring in global economic relations, and then it redefined those relations. . . . [I]ndustrialization was a global phenomenon" (Stearns 1998, 1). However, local responses to globalization opposed the forms that the new societal world was taking. In the processes of industrialization, this local opposition to the more cosmopolitan industrial forces could be seen even in the region of the origins of the Industrial Revolution in England. Artisans in the cotton trades saw their way of life "begin to give way to an intruding industrial society and its new technologies and systems . . . [and to] new configurations of countryside and city, beyond their ken or control" (Sale 1995, 3). They began a direct action campaign in 1811–12 to destroy new factory machines. Their particular movement became identified by the name of their mythic leader, Ned Ludd, and "Luddite" became the label for activist opposition to the new industrial order.

In the *modern* world, there was polarity between the various processes of modern globalization, including industrialization, and local elements, such as the Luddites, who opposed this modernization and defended essentially premodern, local institutions and social orders. This opposition between global and local was visible in many ways, including the global expansion of European imperial regimes at the expense of local political systems. One could speak of the conflict between global and local as a significant dimension of the world experience of globalization and view global and local as two different options representing contrasting modes of societal organization and worldviews.

During the second half of the twentieth century, an intensification of the processes of globalization led to significant dissolution of the dividing lines between global and local, between cosmopolitan and parochial. As the meaning of modernity itself was being transformed, the worldwide dynamics of human life reached a new level of intensive interaction. Some of these developments are portrayed in the titles (and in the analyses) of two best-selling books in the United States on the global realities of the 1990s: *Jihad vs. McWorld* by Benjamin Barber (1995) and *The Lexus and the Olive Tree* by Thomas Friedman (2000). However, the visible tensions of the late twentieth century described in these and other discussions were no longer conflicts between premodern and modern modes of human life. No longer are the followers of Ned Ludd fighting against the machines of a new industrial way of life. Barber notes that in the relationships between jihad and McWorld, "McWorld cannot . . . do without Jihad: it needs cultural parochialism to feed its endless appetites. Yet neither can Jihad do without McWorld: for where would culture be without the commercial producers who market it and the information and communication systems that make it known? . . . Jihad stands not so much in stark opposition as in subtle counterpoint to McWorld" (1995, 155, 157). In the contexts of human experience "after modernity," the global and the local become joined together in defining the emerging forms of cultural and societal life.

In the world of the late twentieth century and the beginning of the twenty-first, "the processes of globalization and localization are inextricably bound together" (Featherstone 1996, 47), and it is possible to speak of the emerging "global/local synergy" (Wilson and Dissanayake 1996, 2). This conflictual synthesis has been given the label *glocalization* by some analysts and scholars (see, for example, Friedman 2000 and Robertson 1995). The term began as a description of business practices in which one organized "one's business on a global scale while taking account of local considerations and conditions" (Tulloch 1991, 134) and now has come to include the broader and more complex interactions of global and local dynamics in the contemporary world. We need now to understand the world not in the modern terms of *local* "traditional" society in opposition to modern *global* society, but rather in terms of both global and local within the dynamics of the *glocalization* of the world.

Desecularization, along with glocalization, is also a major dynamic in the frame and context surrounding the image of the tree and fruit of Fethullah Gülen. This process is also a long-term historical development that represents a significant transcending of the agendas and modes of modernity. The desecularization of contemporary society is not the vision or program of some fundamentalist or televangelist. The concept is part of the changing understanding of modern and postmodern society. In the modern understanding of the processes of modernization, it was believed that as societies modernized, the public role of religion would be reduced. This secularization theory was based on a key idea that "Modernization necessarily leads to a decline of religion, both in society and in the minds of individuals." But in his reassessment, Peter Berger, one of the major scholars in the development of the theory, claims that "it is precisely this key idea that has turned out to be wrong" (1999, 2–3).

Rodney Stark describes the situation in rather dramatic terms: "For nearly three centuries, social scientists and assorted Western intellectuals have been promising the end of religion. . . . Modernization . . . [was viewed as] the causal engine driving the gods into retirement" (1999, 249, 251). At the conclusion of his analysis, Stark recommends: "Let us declare an end to the social scientific faith in the theory of secularization, recognizing that it was the product of wishful thinking. . . . After nearly three centuries of utterly failed prophecies and misrepresentations of both past and present, it seems time to carry the secularization doctrine to the graveyard of failed theories" (1999, 269–70). Although there is still considerable debate about whether or not secularization theory has failed, those who affirm the continuing importance of secularization do so by extending the concept in the context of recognizing that "culture generally must have a sacred component if it is to compel allegiance" (Demerath 2001, 226). This characterization is substantially different from the expectations of a "religionless" society that many earlier articulators of modernization theory described.

In this framing context, it is possible to see a transformation of the old battle between "the secular" and "the religious" in modern society. In the established perspectives of modernity, secularization was a part of the set of a priori postulates that defined the meaning and nature of "being modern." As the desecularization of society becomes more obvious, however, more and more people recognize that the proposition that secularization is an inherent part of modernity is, in fact, a belief and represents an important doctrine in a modern ideology that can be called secular*ism*. Secularism is increasingly recognized as one of a number of competing visions of modern society rather than an axiomatic part of modernity. When secularism is viewed as a competing world vision and not as an inherent part of modernity, it is possible to ask a common question in a new form: Is secularist modernity a viable option? This question provides an appropriate parallel to the old question frequently asked from the secularist perspective: Is there such a thing as a viable Christian modernity or a viable Jewish modernity or a viable Islamic modernity?

Humanity is now entering an era where the discussions must go beyond the debates in the context of modernity where religious and secular are seen as opposites. The desecularization of the world does not simplistically refute the ideas of secularization theory; it transcends those ideas. Just as global and local are becoming increasingly interdependent in the processes of glocalization, the religious and secular dimensions of contemporary society are coming together in ways that defy the logic of the old conflict between religion and secularism within modernity. In the Muslim world, as in other major faith traditions, articulation of this new relationship takes many different forms that clearly go beyond the main lines of the old assumed polarity between religious and secular. Abdullahi An-Na'im notes the clash between the visions of "fundamentalist" advocates of "political Islam" and the proponents of European-style secularism in Muslim countries and concludes that whenever "Islamic societies exercise their right to self-determination by choosing their own system of government, the outcome is unlikely to favor European conceptions of secularism" (1999, 120–21). That outcome, however, will not involve a simple victory for old-style fundamentalism, but a new synthesis that is clearly Islamic and involves, as "an Islamic imperative," the "strict observance of the principle of pluralism and the protection of human rights" (An-Na'im 1999, 120).

The new framing is not a simple rejection of or an end of secularization. It is a new synthesis of elements of the older modern secularism and religion. This combination, like glocalization, includes many different approaches and visions that may share a sense that to be secular and religious in some way involves "not two coins but two faces of the same coin"; it affirms, as one Turkish intellectual notes, "that Islam includes the secular and the religious. That Islam is *deen wa dunya* (religion and the world)" (Yaşar Nuri Öztürk, as cited in Badran 2001). If we have a world of increasing integration of secular and religious, in a way parallel to the process of glocalization, it might be possible to speak of the growing *relicularization* or *seculigiosity* of the contemporary, postmodern world that goes beyond the simple polarity of fundamentalism and secularism in the modern context.

The old polarities of the recent past are being transcended and transformed. This is not simply a process of creating an artificial and syncretistic middle ground between the secular and the religious or the global and the local. Instead, the glocalized, desecularized world is a world now moving rapidly beyond modernity. These processes are creating a significant frame that is useful to recognize around the picture of Fethullah Gülen in the arenas of religion, faith, and life at the beginning of the twenty-first century.

Fethullah Gülen and the Turkish Experience

The transformations of the Ottoman Empire and modern Turkey are an important part of the modern experience and the historical developments going beyond that experience. The early reformers in the Ottoman Empire of the nineteenth century were modernizers who accepted the vision of modernity that was being defined at that time. Although policies were not stated explicitly in terms of secularization theory as it was articulated in the twentieth century, nineteenth-century reformers worked to reduce the importance and power of "traditional" religious institutions and attitudes in society. The reform program of Sultan Mahmud II (c. 1808–39), for example, is frequently discussed within this framework. One of the standard studies of Ottoman reform notes that the "most significant aspect of the innovations initiated by Mahmud II was the emergence of an Ottoman state . . . based on secular principles of sovereignty as contrasted with the medieval concept of an Islamic empire. The real beginning of modernization and secularization was in this change" (Berkes 1998, 90).

The reformers viewed modernization and secularization as being inherently related, and secularization was an important component of major reform programs in the Ottoman Empire, reaching a culmination in the reforms of Mustafa Kemal Atatürk in the new Turkish republic during the 1920s and 1930s. The Turkish experience was an important case study in one of the significant presentations of modernization theory as it developed in the 1950s. In his influential study *The Passing of Traditional Society* (1958), Daniel Lerner examined the transformation of Turkish peasant life. In the model he constructed, he viewed what was called "traditional" society as his starting point. The process of modernization involved the transformation of "traditionals" into "moderns," with those people who were still in the process identified as "transitionals" (1958, chaps. 4 and 5). In his description of Turkish transitionals, Lerner says that they "are secularizing, acquiring a common concern with problems identified as socio-economic rather than religious. They are becoming activist: problems are to be dealt with by policy rather than by prayer" (1958, 165).

This vision within the frame of modernization theory maintains a set of polarities: modern versus traditional, secular versus religious, activism versus fatalist acceptance. Although these polarities may have been a significant part of the realties of the 1950s, at the beginning of the twenty-first century they are not as important in trying to understand the basic dynamics of continuing transformations of human experience. Again, it may be important to assume that we are now beyond the contexts and issues of modernity and in a new era. In the era of desecularization, policy and prayer may be combinable rather than opposing options.

Fethullah Gülen presents a significant example of the emerging mode of faith articulation that is becoming important at the beginning of the twenty-first century. He is neither "fundamentalist" nor "secularist" (in the old understandings of those identifications framed in the idiom of modernity), and his positions provide a vision that transcends the modern in a context of "glocalization" and "relicularization." The new world is one of both interfaith competition and interfaith dialogue. Many within the faith communities still see the interactions of these elements as relations between belief and unbelief, as can be seen in the shrill debates between Muslim and Christian fundamentalists or in the rigidly old-fashioned positions of militants in the Taliban or bin Laden organizations. However, these now-anachronistic efforts are conceptually tied to the types of competitions of the previous "modern" era, rather than to contemporary global realities. The technologies of the old-style combatants may be contemporary, but their conceptualizations are embedded in the polarities of an older world.

Fethullah Gülen presents faith and tradition in ways that provide effective transitions to the new era. The combination of the ideas as expressed in his book *Questions This Modern Age Puts to Islam* (1998j), and his views on dialogue presented in *Fethullah Gülen: The Advocate of Dialogue* (Ünal and Williams 2000), present an important introduction to some of the basic themes of this perspective. Fethullah Gülen engages in a new mode of competitive discourse in which there are competing faith-based ways of life, but the competition takes place within the "glocal" context of pluralistic experience rather than within an assumed homogeneity of truth. The starting point is the continuing affirmation of the power and necessity of religion. Gülen argues: "Regardless of changes, advancements in science and technology, and new ways of thinking, the feeling of attachment to a religion always has been the primary factor in forming humanity's scientific and intellectual life, developing human virtues, and establishing new civilizations. With its charm and power, religion is still and will be the most influential element and power in people's lives" (Ünal and Williams 2000, 43).

The chapters in this volume provide substantial information and analysis of Gülen's vision of religion in contemporary society and of his place in the modern and contemporary history of Islam. In the introduction, Hakan Yavuz and John Esposito examine the longstanding traditions of secularism in Turkey and how they provide a context for Gülen's thought and movement, discussing how the return of religious activism provides an important example of religious glocalization through what they term the attempt to *vernacularize modernity*. Similarly, Ahmet Kuru's conclusion (chapter 6) that Gülen's thought represents a "middle way between tradition and modernity" also suggests the possibility that Gülen also represents a middle way between modernity and postmodernity. The chapters on education show how this mediation is put into pragmatic programs of learning and practice. Gülen's neo-*ijtihad* in the postmodern era provides the content for this new middle way. Ihsan Yılmaz (chapter 11) provides analysis of the broad spectrum of Gülen's thought in this complex context.

Muslims at the beginning of the twenty-first century are engaged in many vast projects of reframing the basic narratives of their identity and faith. Some remain tied to conservative visions that were defined centuries ago and are therefore considered to be normative because of their age and because of reverence for longstanding tradition. However, these religiocultural conservatives, like the old Luddites in England, have long since lost the real battle for influence in shaping the nature of Muslim societies and discourses. The old battles between tradition and modernity are over. The real battles now are among those who represent different visions of the future in a globalized (glocalized) and desecularized world. Some of the struggles are between those who continue to see the more long-standing visions of modern, secular society as crucial and those who advocate a postmodernity either of multicultural pluralism or of militant normative fundamentalisms that divide the world into believers and unbelievers or into coalitions of the virtuous opposed to axes of evil.

The nature of the basic divisions in this new world is very different from what it was even just a century ago. It may be that the great global divisions were between "civilizations" in the premodern and modern world order. In that context, one might understand the great lines of conflict as "clashes of civilizations."[4] However, by the end of the twentieth century, it was clear that the great

---

4. This phrase was made an important part of policy discourse in the 1990s by the scholarship of Samuel Huntington, beginning with his article "The Clash of Civilizations?" (1993).

conflicts were not among discrete, separate "civilizations." They were between different visions of globalized futures, viewed in terms of more traditional modern secularism, in terms of globalized rigid fundamentalisms, or in terms of multicultural, pluralist, interconnected societies. Such conflicts have been aptly called the "clash of globalizations" (see Hoffman 2002).

In the clashing visions of globalizations, Fethullah Gülen is a force in the development of the Islamic discourse of globalized multicultural pluralism. As the impact of the educational activities of those influenced by him attests, his vision bridges modern and postmodern, global and local, and has a significant influence in the contemporary debates that shape the visions of the future of Muslims and non-Muslims alike.

Appendix

References

Index

Appendix

Abant Declarations

First Abant Final Declaration on "Islam and Secularism" (July 1998)

Today, Turkey appears to be passing through a deep crisis tied to the axes of religions and secularism. As a group of Turkish intellectuals, we came together at Abant and concluded that agreement regarding the following points would be beneficial:

1. According to Islam, the basic goal of revelation is to guide man as to how to attain goodness, beauty, and happiness in this world and the afterlife. Revelation addresses the intelligence and requires comprehension and interpretation from it. Although in the history of Islamic thought there are some conceptions that belittle the importance of the mind, there is no conflict between revelation and intelligence in the dominant line of thought. The responsibility for comprehending and interpreting revelation falls on every believing person to the degree of his strength and knowledge. Every believer must use his intelligence. No individual or class can claim divine authority on the matter of understanding and interpreting revelation.

2. In the first periods of Islam the relation between revelation and life was much more concrete, and importance was given to functional intelligence. In fact, in spite of the clear expression of some Qur'anic verses, and taking into considerations the main objectives and necessities of religion, different interpretations of rules were able to be made and implemented. In this framework, today's Muslims have the authority to bring solutions to the daily problems of the Islamic world.

3. Recently one of the concepts that cause confusion in the Islamic world is the concept of "sovereignty." When looked at from the perspective of the Qur'an, without doubt God is the absolute sovereign of the world with His knowledge, will, mercy, justice, and power. All creatures are under this universal sovereignty. For believers, God is the teacher and guide to moral and social values. However, this concept of sovereignty should not be confused with the concept of sovereignty in the principle, "Sovereignty belongs to the nation without limitations or conditions." The expression "sovereignty is the nation's" means that it is not the natural or divine right of any individual, class, or group; politically it means taking "national will" as basic and not recognizing any power superior to it.

4. In the metaphysically or political sense, *state* means a human institution that does not possess sanctity. The state exists to fulfill natural human interests and needs, and it finds its purpose and function in these interests and needs. Life, security, justice, and freedom are the most basic and natural of these interests and needs. The state should keep the same distance from every kind of ideology, belief, and philosophical view. The state can not have a totalitarian, authoritative, and forceful official ideology. All state officials responsible for carrying out the above mentioned main state duties must act with the consciousness that the duties are under the command of the nation and without causing abuse of their authority. We do not see values and requests such as democracy, human rights, and living in freedom and peace as elements of a particular ideology. The state removes all obstacles from religions, beliefs, and religious interpretations; it guarantees everyone freedom of religion, freedom of conscience, and the freedom to fulfil the requisites of religious beliefs.

5. We think that other than the universal and basic values and the principles of Islam's democratic state based on law, the organization of details of political regimes should be left to the society.

6. Within a legal framework, the state should be unbiased regarding religious beliefs and philosophical views. It should protect the citizens' rights to believe or not believe and remove obstacles to the implementation of beliefs. Secularism is essentially an attitude of the state, and a secular state cannot define religion or pursue a religious policy. Secularism should not be used as a restricting principle in the definition and enumeration of basic rights and freedoms.

7. Interference in the lifestyle of citizens and sensitive points in this issue lie at the source of a number of current difficulties in Turkey. Secularism is not in opposition to religion, and it should not be understood as interference in people's lifestyles. Secularism should not broaden the field of individual freedom. It especially should not lead to discrimination against women and should not deprive them of rights in public.

8. To overcome Turkey's difficulties, democracy based on freedom must take root, and obstacles preventing nongovernmental organizations from growing stronger must removed. Citizens should forego the habit of expecting everything from the government, and the state should refrain from seeing the citizen as in need of guardianship.

9. People should use their rights to live according to their religious or philosophical beliefs and views, as long as there is no clear public law to the contrary that takes its legality from the principle of legal supremacy. No one should be punished, removed from their public duty, or deprived of education and other public services because of it [that belief]. The principle of secularism should be constitutionally defined to the effect that no concession of religious or philosophical views should be made in the unbiased implementation of the principle of absolute equality of human rights and the principles of justice. As a second step, the body of laws should be reviewed, and the citizens' anxiety, which has reached serious proportions, should be alleviated.

10. We who have gathered at this Abant meeting believe: having different views and inclinations and preferring different lifestyles are not obstacles to people in making

sound decisions that take the country's welfare into consideration. However big our problems might be, they can be solved with the initiative of the people. We believe the conclusions that we have arrived at after three days of discussions on religion-state relations will help answer Turkey's common aspirations and expectations.

Third Abant Platform Final Declaration on "Islam and Democracy" (July 2000)

As a group of academics and intellectuals, we came together at Abant on 21–23 July 2000. We discussed solutions to the problems of infringements of human rights, the southeastern question, torture, unsolved murder cases, and the freedom to live according to one's beliefs, etc., which occupy an important place in the national agenda. We decided to submit these [solutions] to public attention, taking the attachment to the principle of constructing a democratic state ruled by law as our starting point and in conformity with the following principles.

1. A democratic state ruled by law accepts the will of society, within the framework of the principle of the supremacy of law and basic rights and freedoms, and derives its legitimacy from these universal values.

2. A democratic state ruled by law stands at an equal distance from all systems of belief and thought and from ways of life depending on them that do not encompass violence.

3. A democratic state ruled by law depends on the idea of a social contract. This guarantees the basic rights and freedoms of all the elements within a differentiated society, the latter being a natural phenomenon.

4. Islam is no obstacle to the existence of a democratic state ruled by law.

5. In the solution of all the economic, political, administrative, social, and cultural questions that our country faces, the establishment of a democratic state ruled by law, in its fullest sense, should be a basic aim. From this standpoint, even though some serious faults and deficiencies remain, the gains that Turkey has made so far in the process of democratization should not be ignored. In fact, following the Ottoman constitutional projects, which were aimed at restricting arbitrary state power by means of a constitution, our republic has become progressively more democratic.

6. The establishment of a democratic state ruled by law constitutes a prior condition to allow different sections of society with different views of the world or cultural characteristics to live together in a peaceful manner, and to allow the realization of a common citizenship to develop. Within this framework, it is essential that no individual or group should be alienated from politics or public life.

7. Although the steps to be taken in this direction are important because Turkey must remain faithful to its international undertakings regarding human rights and democratization, essentially this is a problem relating to the existence, harmony, and order of Turkish society itself.

8. Our country urgently needs a new and civilian constitution. Within this frame-

work, we support civil initiatives and the idea that citizens should compose their own constitutional proposals. It is essential that the civil and democratic constitutional initiative be completed by the improvement of basic laws, chiefly those relating to our legislation regarding political parties, elections, and the Penal Code.

9. The safeguarding of civil and political freedoms is an indispensable condition for the establishment of a democratic state ruled by law. In this context, it should be a basic principle that all schools of thought should be freely expressed and organized, on condition that they do not use violence or openly advocate its use.

10. No state institution should ignore the principle of the supremacy of law in any of its executive acts by appealing to the notion of "reasons of state." In democracies, the state has no legitimate existence outside or above the law.

11. A democratic state ruled by law cannot be reconciled with the idea of the absolute sovereignty of the will of the majority. Even pluralist democratic systems have no right to abolish basic freedoms or the guarantees provided by a state ruled by law.

12. Protecting and developing democracy does not mean maintaining official institutions unchanged, but [rather] protecting democratic administration and institutions and reconstructing them. The way to overcome our problems in the public domain is not to postpone democracy, but to enlarge the sphere of democratic politics.

13. In a democratic state ruled by law, there can be no abandonment of the principle of the independence and neutrality of the judiciary. It should be a basic principle that those who are responsible for implementing the law should not act in accordance with political or ideological considerations.

14. Possession by the state of a large part of the economic wealth of the country creates opportunities for arbitrary interventions by governments. This can constitute a threat to these basic freedoms, besides being one of the causes of political deterioration. For the health of democracy, it is extremely important that the concept should be established among citizens of the moral obligation to pay taxes, and that public authorities should be transparent in their expenditures and be held accountable for them. In this connection, an important goal to be achieved is that the state should remove defects in the distribution of income in accordance with social justice.

15. An administrative reform is necessary that will construct a participatory administration—making local communities partners in the system at the level of province, district, town, and village—in place of the present centralized, clumsy, and bureaucratic administration, and within the concept of a unitary state.

16. One of the factors that damages democracy is that the media, which are an important element in a democratic system, use their power as an instrument to advance their economic and business interests, which have nothing to do with their democratic functions, and publish or broadcast items infringing the principles of press morality and neutrality.

17. Monopolization of ownership of the media, their [the media's] entry into shady relationships with the state, and their tendency to influence the judicial process cannot be reconciled with the concept of a democratic state ruled by law.

18. In a democratic state ruled by law, the authority to take political decisions belongs to the democratically elected representatives of the people. The civil service and the military have the sole job of putting into effect policies defined by democratic methods.

Fourth Abant Declaration on "Pluralism" (July 2001)

Pluralism conveys the recognition of differences in ideas, belief, identity, and interests and of the lack of obstruction to the representation of these differences in a democratic regime. However, the current conditions in Turkey are not on a level that allows for the establishment and continuity of pluralism. For this reason, the "Fourth Abant Platform" felt the necessity of taking up the subject of pluralism and its natural result, the question of social reconciliation.

1. Pluralism can be realized only in a democratic and secular regime that takes the supremacy of the law as its basis and that is based on human rights. Civil and political freedoms, headed by the freedoms of belief, thought and expression, education and organization, are the prerequisites of pluralism. Just as in this sense there can be no pluralism without freedom; neither can permanent social harmony and agreement be established.

2. Democratic pluralism eliminates polarization and enables political and national unity to gain strength and continuity. Social harmony that takes pluralism into consideration should be expressed in a new constitution based on social reconciliation. This issue is tied to understanding being reached among different segments of society that come together as equals and conform to the principle of "unity in plurality."

3. The main goal of pluralism based on the recognition of differences is social harmony. What is meant by this harmony is not changing those who are different, but rather establishing of peaceful coexistence together with these differences.

4. Just as pluralism, which aims at reconciliation, and different identities living together can enrich every identity and culture, they also allow for interaction and change. It is important in this process to strengthen the society's common values and to produce new ones.

5. Social reconciliation is a moral issue at the same time. In this respect, the necessary reconciliation cannot be reached without accepting the other to be as "worthy of respect" as we are.

6. Political pluralism does not contradict the law of "majority rule." However, while implementing the choices of the majority, observing the rights of those who remain outside the majority comprises one of the basic and irrevocable principles of a democratic regime.

7. The society's material well-being plays an important role in the application of pluralism. On the other hand, a democratic pluralistic way of life makes a large contribution to economic development. The distribution of economic well-being among citizens not only consolidates the foundation blocks, but serves to increase belief and trust in democracy as well.

8. The pluralism of each society is nourished by its own historical and social experiences. Our society's historical and sociocultural heritage and experience comprise an important resource for pluralism.

9. Efforts to create a homogeneous society in the name of modernization are unacceptable; politics cannot be a vehicle for social transition in the direction of homogeneity. One of Turkey's basic problems is the conflict between government administration and the demands of the people. The government must stop seeing the society as a construction site and forego "social engineering." It must recognize the differences in society and take their demands into consideration. Turkey needs an understanding that allows the government to remain at an equal distance from all citizens and social segments and to represent all differences in the public sphere.

10. In order for the door to political pluralism to open, there is an immediate need for changes in democracy, in accordance with universal laws, to be made in the Constitution, political parties, and election laws. In this respect, it is important that parties that do not include any kind of violence in their ideas or activities should not be prohibited from politics. In addition, arrangements must be made to provide for more transparency in the financing of politics and public spending and for the strengthening of local administration.

11. In order to put into action these decisions related to pluralism and social reconciliation, education should be reorganized with the help of civil organizations along the lines of Turkey's sociocultural realities.

In summary, while speaking of "pluralism" in all our recommendations, our not naming various social groups was owing to our concern that giving a name would lead to a political posture. Our wish is for a Turkey in which every kind of name and political posture can express itself. Pluralism and social reconciliation necessitate that every individual can benefit from all basic rights and freedoms without prejudice based on gender, race, language, or religion, and especially based on inequality between the sexes.

References

Abu-Zahra, Nadia. 2000. "Islamic History, Islamic Identity, and the Reform of Islamic Law: The Thought of Husayn Ahmad Amin." In *Islam and Modernity: Muslim Intellectuals Respond,* edited by John Cooper, Ronald L. Nettler, and Mohamed Mahmoud, 82–104. London and New York: I. B. Tauris.

Açıkel, Fethi. 1996. "Kutsal Mazlumluğun Psikopatolojisi." *Toplum ve Bilim* 70: 153–98.

"Ahir Zaman'da Islam Batı' dan Dogacak." 2002. *Zaman,* 19 Aug.

Ahmed, Sara. 2000. *Strange Encounter: Embodied Others in Post-coloniality.* London: Routledge.

Akman, Nuriye. 1995. Interview with Fethullah Gülen. *Sabah,* 25–30 Jan.

Akpınar, Turgut. 1993. *Türk Tarihinde İslamiyet.* Istanbul: İletişim Yayınları.

Akşin, Şina. 1994. *Şeriatçı Bir Ayaklanma: 31 Mart Olayı.* Istanbul: Imge.

Akşit, Bahattin. 1991. "Islamic Education in Turkey: Medrese Reform in Late Ottoman Times and Imam-Hatip Schools in the Republic." In *Islam in Modern Turkey: Religion, Politics, and Literature in a Secular State,* edited by Richard Tapper, 145–70. London: I. B. Tauris.

Aktay, Yasin. 1993. "Political and Intellectual Disputes on the Academisation of Religious Knowledge." Master's thesis, Middle East Technical Univ., Ankara.

———. 1997. "Body, Text, Identity: Islamist Discourse of Authenticity in Modern Turkey." Ph.D. diss., Middle East Technical Univ., Ankara.

———. 1999. *Türk Dininin Sosyolojik İmkanı.* Istanbul: İletişim Yayınları.

Akyüz, Yahya. 1999. *Türk Eğitim Tarihi (Başlangıçtan 1999'a).* Istanbul: Alfa.

Albayrak, Sadık. 1987. *31 Mart Vak'ası Gerici bir Hareket Mi?* Istanbul: Bilim-Araştırma.

Algar, Hamid. 1990. "A Brief History of the Naqshbandî Order." In *Naqsibandis,* edited by Marc Gaborieau and Alexandre Thierry Zarkane, 3–44. Istanbul: L'institut francais d'Anatoliennes d'Istanbul.

———. 2001. "The Centennial Renewer: Bediuzzaman Said Nursi and the Tradition of *Tajdid.*" *Journal of Islamic Studies* (Oxford) 12, no. 3: 291–311.

Alkan, Ahmet Turan. 1996. "Entellektüel ile Arifin Kesişme Noktası." In *Fethullah Gülen Hocaefendi ile Ufuk Turu,* edited by Eyüp Can, 203–4. Istanbul: Milliyet Yayınları.

Altınoğlu, Ebru. 1999. *Fethullah Gülen's Perception of State and Society.* Istanbul: Bosphorus Univ.

Anderson, Benedict. 1998. *Imagined Communities: Reflections on the Origin and Spread of Nationalism.* London: Verso.

An-Na'im, Abdullahi A. 1999. "Political Islam in National Politics and International Relations." In *The Desecularization of the World,* edited by Peter L. Berger, 103–21. Washington, D.C.: Ethics and Public Policy Center.

Aras, Bülent. 1998. "Turkish Islam's Moderate Face." *Middle East Quarterly* 5, no. 3: 23–31.

Aristotle. 1996. *Nicomachean Ethics.* In *Classics of Moral and Political Theory,* edited by Michael L. Morgan, 247–71. Indianapolis, Ind.: Hackett.

Armağan, Mustafa, and Ali Ünal, eds. 1999. *Medya Aynasında Fethullah Gülen: Koza'dan Kelebeğe.* Istanbul: Gazeteciler ve Yazarlar Vakfı Yayınları.

———, eds. 2001. *Aydınların Kaleminden Fethullah Gülen: Diyaloğa Adanmış Hayat.* Istanbul: Gazeteciler ve Yazarlar Vakfı Yayınları.

Asad, Talal. 1993. *Genealogies of Religion: Discipline and Reasons of Power in Christianity and Islam.* Baltimore: Johns Hopkins Univ. Press.

Aydın, Selim. 1996. *Bilgi Çağında İnsan.* İzmir: T.Ö.V.

al-Azmeh, Aziz. 1996. *Islams and Modernities.* 2d ed. London and New York: Verso.

Badran, Margot. 2001. "The Religious Face of Secularism." *Al-Ahram Weekly On-line,* no. 519 (1–7 Feb.). Available at: www.ahram.org.eg/weekly/2001/519/intrvw.htm.

Baktir, Mustafa. 1998. "Bediuzzaman's Views on *Ijtihad.*" Available at: http://www.nesil.com.tr.

Balcı, Bayram. 2000. "Les écoles privées de Fethullah Gülen en Asiecentrale Missionnaires de l'Islam ou hussards de la turcité?" Ph.D. diss., IEP Université Pierre Mendès France, Grenoble.

———. 2002. "Orta Asya'da Fethullah Gülen'in Neo-Nurcu Okulları: Yerleşmeleri, Işleyişleri ve Eğitim Yoluyla Aktardıkları Mesajın Doğası." *Toplum ve Bilim* 93 (summer): 251–83.

Barber, Benjamin R. 1995. *Jihad vs. McWorld: How Globalism and Tribalism Are Reshaping the World.* New York: Ballantine.

Barlas, Mehmet. 2000. *Hocaefendi Sendromu.* Istanbul: Birey.

Baydar, Mustafa. 1955. *31 Mart Vak'ası.* Istanbul: Milli Tesanüt Birliği.

Beck, Ulrich. 1994. "Reinvention of Politics: Towards a Theory of Reflexive Modernization." In *Reflexive Modernization: Politics, Tradition, and Aesthetics in the Modern Social Order,* edited by U. Beck, A. Giddens, and S. Lash, 1–55. Stanford, Calif.: Stanford Univ. Press.

Berger, Peter L. 1973. *The Social Reality of Religion.* London: Allen Lane.

———. 1999. "The Desecularization of the World: A Global Overview." In *The Desecularization of the World,* edited by Peter L. Berger, 1–18. Washington, D.C.: Ethics and Public Policy Center.

Berkes, Niyazi. 1984. *Teokrasi ve Laiklik.* Istanbul: Adam.

———. 1998. *The Development of Secularism in Turkey.* New York: Routledge.

Bermann, Marshal. 1988. *All That Is Solid Melts into Air: The Experience of Modernity.* New York: Penguin.

Beşer, Faruk. 1991. *Fetvalar.* İzmir: Nil.

Binder, Leonard. 1988. *Islamic Liberalism: A Critique of Development Ideologies.* Chicago: Univ. of Chicago Press.

Birand, M. Ali. 1997. "Fethullah Gülen'in Gelişmelere Bakışı." *Sabah,* 1 Nov.

Brinton, Crane. 1953. *Ideas and Men.* New York: New American Library.

Bulut, Faik. 1998. *Kim Bu Fethullah Gülen? Dünü-Bugünü-Hedefi.* Istanbul: Ozan.

Çakır, Ruşen. 1999. "Fethullah'ı Kullanıp Attılar." *Milliyet,* 26 June.

Calhoun, Craig. 1992. *Habermas and the Public Sphere.* Cambridge, Mass.: MIT Press.

———. 1994. "Nationalism and Civil Society: Democracy, Diversity, and Self-determination." In *Social Theory and the Politics of Identity,* edited by Craig Calhoun, 304–35. Oxford: Blackwell.

Çalışkan, Kerem. 1998. "Fethullah Hoca ve Laiklik." *Yeni Yüzyıl,* 21 July.

Çalışlar, Oral. 1995. "Interview with Fethullah Gülen." *Cumhuriyet,* 20 Aug.

———. 1997. *Fethullah Gülen'den Cemalettin Kaplan'a (İslamiyet Üzerine Söyleşiler).* Istanbul: Pencere.

Can, Eyüp. 1996. *Fethullah Gülen ile Ufuk Turu.* 13th ed. Istanbul: A.D.

Canan, İbrahim. 1996. "Bediüzzaman Said Nursi'de Sahabe Telakkisi." In *Uluslarası Bediüzzaman Sempozyumu,* 416–51. Istanbul: Yeni Asya.

Çandar, Cengiz. 1993–94. "Değişim Sürecinde İslâm." *İslâmî Araştırmalar* (Kış): 3–9.

Çandar, Cengiz, and Taha Akyol. 1998. "Interview with Fethullah Gülen." Available at: http://www.m-fgulen.org/hayat/article.php?id=1847. Retrieved 2 Feb. 2003.

Çandar, Cengiz, and Graham E. Fuller. 2001. "Grand Geopolitics for a New Turkey." *Mediterranean Quarterly* 12, no. 1. (winter): 22–38.

Casanova, Jose. 1994. *Public Religions in the Modern World.* Chicago: Univ. of Chicago Press.

"Catholics Act in Defense of Gülen." 2001. *Turkish Daily News,* 31 May.

Cells, Michael A. 1996. *Early Islamic Mysticism.* New York: Paulist Press.

Çınar, Menderes, and Ayşe Kadıoğlu. 1999. "An Islamic Critique of Modernity in Turkey: Politics of Difference Backwards." *Orient* 40, no. 1: 53–69.

Collins, Randall. 1982. *Sociological Insights: An Introduction to Non-obvious Sociology.* New York: Oxford Univ. Press.

Connolly, William. 1999. *Why I Am Not a Secularist.* Minneapolis: Univ. of Minnesota Press.

Cooper, John. 1998. "The Limits of the Sacred: The Epistemology of 'Abd al-Karim Soroush." In *Islam and Modernity,* edited by John Cooper, Ronald L. Nettler, and Mohamed Mahmoud, 38–56. London: I. B. Taurus.

Cucchiari, Salvatore. 1988. " 'Adapted for Heaven': Conversion and Culture in Western Sicily." *American Ethnologist* 15: 417–41.

Danişmend, İsmail Hami. 1961. *31 Mart Vak'ası.* Istanbul: Kitabevi.

Değer, M. Emin. 2000. *Bir Cumhuriyet Düşmanının Portresi ya da Fethullah Gülen Hocae-fendi'nin Derin Misyonu.* Istanbul: Cumhuriyet.

Demerath, Nicholas J. 1995. "Rational Paradigms, A-rational Religion, and the Debate over Secularization." *Journal for the Scientific Study of Religion* 34: 105–12.

————. 2001. "Secularization Extended: From Religious 'Myth' to Cultural Common-place." In *The Blackwell Companion to Sociology of Religion,* edited by Richard K. Fenn, 211–28. Oxford: Blackwell.

Demir, C. Engin, Ayşe Balcı, and F. Akkok. 2000. "The Role of Turkish Schools in the Educational System and Social Transformation of Central Asian Countries: The Case of Turkmenistan and Kyrgyzstan." *Central Asian Survey* 19, no. 1: 141–55.

Derrida, Jacques. 1974. *On Grammatology.* Translated by G. C. Spivak. Baltimore: Johns Hopkins Univ. Press.

————. 1978. *Writing and Différance.* Translated by Alan Bass. Chicago: Univ. of Chicago Press.

"Diyalog İçin Cesur Adım." 1996. *Aksiyon* (13–19 Apr.): 4–7.

Drucker, Peter F. 1965. *Landmarks of Tomorrow: A Report on the New "Post-Modern" World.* New York: Harper and Row.

Durkheim, E. 1961. *Moral Education.* London: Free Press.

Dursun, Turan. 1996. *Müslümanlık ve Nurculuk.* Istanbul: Kaynak Yayınları.

————. 1998. *Dua.* Istanbul: Kaynak Yayınları.

Eickelman, Dale F. 1998. "Inside the Islamic Reformation." *Wilson Quarterly* 22, no. 1: 80–89.

————. 2000. "The Coming Transformation in the Muslim World." *Current History* 99, no. 633 (Jan.): 16–20.

Eisenstadt, S. N. 1999. *Fundamentalism, Sectarianism, and Revolution: The Jacobin Dimension of Modernity.* New York: Cambridge Univ. Press.

Eliade, Mircea. 1985. *A History of Religious Ideas.* Vol. 3. Translated from the French by Alf Hiltebeitel and Diane Apostolos-Cappadona. Chicago: Univ. of Chicago Press.

Erdoğan, Lâtif. 1997. *Fethullah Hocaefendi "Küçük Dünyam."* 40th ed. Istanbul: A.D.

Erdoğan, Mustafa. 1999. "Islam in Turkish Politics: Turkey's Quest for Democracy Without Islam." *Critique* 15: 25–49.

Ersoy, Ahmed. 1993. *Eğitimde Depremli Yıllar.* İzmir: Feza.

Ersoy, Mehmed Akif. 1989. *Safahat.* Ankara: Kültür Bakanlığı Yayınları.

Esposito, John L. 1980. "Perspectives on Islamic Law Reform: The Case of Pakistan." *Journal of International Law and Politics* 13, no. 2: 217–45.

————. 1986. "Islam, Ideology, and Politics in Pakistan." In *The State, Religion, and Ethnic Politics,* edited by Myron Weiner and Ali Banuazizi, 333–69. Syracuse, N.Y.: Syracuse Univ. Press.

————. 1998. *Islam: The Straight Path.* 3rd ed. Oxford: Oxford Univ. Press.

————. 2001a. "Islam and Secularism in the Twenty-First Century." In *Islam and Secular-*

ism in the Middle East, edited by John Esposito and Azzam Tamimi, 1–12. New York: New York Univ. Press.

———. 2001b. *Women in Muslim Family Law.* Syracuse, N.Y.: Syracuse Univ. Press.

Esposito, John L., and James Piscatori. 1991. "Democratization and Islam." *Middle East Journal* 45, no. 3: 427–44.

Esposito, John L., and John Voll. 1996. *Islam and Democracy.* New York: Oxford Univ. Press.

Eygi, Mehmet Şevket. 2000a. "Turkic World." *Milli Gazete,* 5 May.

———. 2000b. "Secret Agreement with Papacy." *Milli Gazete,* 26 May.

Fadl, K. A. E. 1994. "Islamic Law and Muslim Minorities: The Juristic Discourse on Muslim Minorities from the 2nd/8th to the 11th/17th Centuries." *Islamic Law and Society* 1, no. 2: 141–87.

Featherstone, Mike. 1996. "Localism, Globalism, and Cultural Identity." In *Global/Local: Cultural Production and the Transnational Imaginary,* edited by Rob Wilson and Wimal Dissanayake, 46–77. Durham, N.C.: Duke Univ. Press.

"Fethullah Gülen Met with Pope John Paul II." 1998. *Turkish Times,* 1 Mar.

"Fethullah'ın Hocaları Türban Attı." 1998. *Yeni Yüzyıl,* 16 Sept.

Finke, Roger. 1990. "Religious Deregulation: Origins and Consequences." *Journal of Church and State* 32: 609–26.

Fischoff, Ephraim. 1963. *The Sociology of Religion.* Boston: Beacon.

Foucault, Michel. 1982. *This Is Not a Pipe.* Translated by James Harkness. Berkeley and Los Angeles: Univ. of California Press.

Frantz, Douglas. 2000. "Turkey Assails a Revered Islamic Moderate." *New York Times,* 25 Aug.

Friedman, Thomas L. 2000. *The Lexus and the Olive Tree.* Expanded ed. New York: Random House.

Gaborieau, Marc, and Alexandre Thierry Zarkane, eds. 1990. *Naqsibandis.* Istanbul: L'institut francais d'Anatoliennes d'Istanbul.

Gadamer, Hans-Georg. 1991. *Truth and Method.* Translated by Joel Weinsheimer and Donald G. Marshall. 2d rev. ed. New York: Crossroad.

Geertz, Clifford. 1968. *Islam Observed.* New Haven, Conn.: Yale Univ. Press.

———. 1973. *Interpretation of Cultures.* New York: Basic.

———. 1983. *Local Knowledge: Further Essays in Interpretive Anthropology.* New York: Basic.

Gellner, Ernest. 1981. *Muslim Society.* Cambridge: Cambridge Univ. Press.

———. 1994a. *The Conditions of Liberty: Civil Society and Its Rivals.* London: Hamish Hamilton.

———. 1994b. "Kemalism." In *Encounters with Nationalism,* 81–91. Oxford: Blackwell.

———. 1994c. *Nations and Nationalism.* Ithaca, N.Y.: Cornell Univ. Press.

al-Ghazzali, Abu Hamid Muhammad. 1991. *The Alchemy of Happiness.* Translated by Elton L. Daniel. New York: M. E. Sharpe.

Giddens, Anthony. 1990. *The Consequences of Modernity.* Stanford, Calif.: Stanford Univ. Press.

————. 1999. *Capitalism and Modern Social Theory: An Analysis of the Writings of Marx, Durkheim, and Max Weber.* Cambridge: Cambridge Univ. Press.

Godzo, Azra. 1998. *Bediüzzaman Said Nursi: Svjetlost u Poslanicama o Svjetlosti.* Sarajevo: Mega.

Göktürk, Gülay. 1999. "Devletin İnayetiyle." *Sabah,* 25 June.

Göle, Nilüfer. 1996a. "Authoritarian Secularism and Islamist Politics: The Case of Turkey." In *Civil Society in the Middle East,* vol. 2, edited by Augustus Richard Norton, 19–39. Leiden: E. J. Brill.

————. 1996b. *The Forbidden Modern: Civilization and Veiling.* Ann Arbor: Univ. of Michigan Press.

————. 1996c. "Muhafazakarlığın Manalandırdığı Modernlik." In *Fethullah Gülen Hocaefendi ile Ufuk Turu,* 13th ed., edited by Eyüp Can, 205–6. Istanbul: A.D.

————. 2000a. *Islam ve Modernlik üzerine Melez Desenler.* Istanbul: Metis Yayınları.

————. 2000b. "Snapshots of Islamic Modernities." *Daedalus* 129, no. 1: 91–117.

Gülen, M. Fethullah [as M. Abdülfettah Şahin]. 1992. *Ilim ve Bilim: Ilim ve Bilim Kavramlarının Tahlili.* İzmir: T.Ö.V.

————. 1993. *Questions This Modern Age Puts to Islam.* London: Truestar.

————. 1995a. *Fasıldan Fasıla.* Vol. 1. 7th ed. İzmir: Nil.

————. 1995b. *Fasıldan Fasıla.* Vol. 2. 2d ed. İzmir: Nil.

————. 1995c. *Kur'an ve Sünnet Perspektifinde Kader.* İzmir: Işık Yayınları.

————. 1995d. *Prophet Muhammad: The Infinite Light.* London: Truestar.

————. 1996a. *Criteria or the Lights of the Way.* Vol. 1. London: Truestar.

————. 1996b. *İnancın Gölgesinde.* Vols. 1 and 2. İzmir: Nil Yayınları.

————. 1996c. *Prophet Muhammad as Commander.* London: Truestar.

————. 1996d. *Towards the Lost Paradise.* London: Truestar.

————. 1997a. *Asrın Getirdiği Tereddütler.* Vol. 2. 11th ed. İzmir: T.Ö.V.

————. 1997b. *Asrın Getirdiği Tereddütler.* Vol. 3. 8th ed. İzmir: T.Ö.V.

————. 1997c. *Buhranlar Anaforunda İnsan (Çağ ve Nesil 2).* 11th ed. İzmir: T.Ö.V.

————. 1997d. *Fasıldan Fasıla.* Vol. 3. 3rd ed. İzmir: Nil.

————. 1997e. *Kalbin Zümrüt Tepeleri.* İzmir: Nil.

————. 1997f. "Orta Asya Eğitim Hizmetleri." *Yeni Türkiye* 15: 685–95.

————. 1997g. *Prizma.* Vol. 1. Istanbul: Zaman.

————. 1997h. *Prizma.* Vol. 2. Istanbul: Zaman.

————. 1997i. *Understanding and Belief: The Essentials of Islamic Faith.* İzmir: Kaynak.

————. 1997j. *Yeşeren Düşünceler (Çağ ve Nesil 6).* 2d ed. İzmir: T.Ö.V.

————. 1997k. *Yitirilmiş Cennete Doğru (Çağ ve Nesil 3).* 10th ed. İzmir: T.Ö.V.

————. 1997l. *Zamanın Altın Dilimi (Çağ ve Nesil 4).* 10th ed. İzmir: T.Ö.V.

————. 1998a. *Asrın Getirdiği Tereddütler.* Vol. 1. İzmir: Nil.

————. 1998b. *Asrın Getirdiği Tereddütler.* Vol. 4. 10th ed. İzmir: Nil.

————. 1998c. *Çağ ve Nesil.* Vol. 1. 15th ed. İzmir: Nil.

————. 1998d. *Hoşgörü ve Diyalog İklimi.* Istanbul: Merkür Yayıncılık.

————. 1998e. *Irşad Ekseni.* İzmir: Zaman.

————. 1998f. *Ölçü veya Yoldaki Işıklar.* Vol. 1. 12th ed. İzmir: Nil.

————. 1998g. *Ölçü veya Yoldaki Işıklar.* Vol. 4. 8th ed. İzmir: T.Ö.V.

————. 1998h. *Prophet Muhammad as Commander.* İzmir: Kaynak.

————. 1998i. *Prophet Muhammad: The Infinite Light.* 2 vols. İzmir: Kaynak.

————. 1998j. *Questions This Modern Age Puts to Islam.* Translation of vol. 1 of *Asrın Getirdiği Tereddütler.* İzmir: Kaynak.

————. 1998k. *Ruhumuzun Heykelini Dikerken.* İzmir: Nil.

————. 1998l. "Takdim." In *Yeni bir Bakış Açısıyla Ilim ve Din,* vol. 1, edited by Irfan Yılmaz, Hakkı İhsanöğlu, Selim Aydın, Fuat Bozer, Hevzat Bayhan, and İhsan İnal, 1–6. Istanbul: Feza Gazetecilik.

————. 1999a. "The Necessity of Interfaith Dialogue: A Muslim Approach." Speech given at the Parliament of the World's Religions, Capetown, 1–8 Dec.

————. 1999b. *Prizma.* Vol. 3. 6th ed. İzmir: Nil.

————. 1999c. *Key Concepts in the Practice of Sufism.* Translated by Ali Ünal. Fairfax, Va.: The Fountain.

————. 2000a. "At the Threshold of a New Millennium." *The Fountain* 3, no. 29. (Jan.-March): 5–9.

————. 2000b. *Kur'an'dan İdrake Yansıyanlar.* Vol. 2. Istanbul: Zaman Gazetesi.

————. 2000c. *Prophet Muhammad: Aspects of His Life.* Translated by Ali Ünal. Fairfax, Va.: The Fountain.

————. 2000d. *Questions and Answers about Faith.* Fairfax, Va.: The Fountain.

————. 2001a. "A Comparative Approach to Islam and Democracy." *SAIS Review* 21, no. 2: 133–38.

————. 2001b. *Fasıldan Fasıla.* Vol. 4. Istanbul: Nil Yayınları.

————. 2003. "Hoşgöraü ve Medya." Available at: http://www.m-fgulen.org/eser/article.php?id-442. Accessed 18 July 2003.

————. n.d.a. *Altın Nesil.* Izmir: N.p.

————. n.d.b. *Key Concepts in the Practice of Sufism.* İzmir: Kaynak.

Gülerce, Hüseyin. 2002. "Türkiye'nin Üç Koordinatı." *Zaman,* 14 Feb.

Gündem, Mehmet. 1998. *Abant Toplantıları 1: Islam ve Laiklik.* Istanbul: Gazeteciler ve Yazarlar Vakfı.

Güngor, Erol. 1981. *Islam'ın Bugünkü Meseleleri.* Istanbul: Ötüken Yayınları.

Habermas, Jürgen. 1979. *Communication and the Evolution of Society.* Boston: Beacon.

————. 1984. *The Theory of Communicative Action.* Vol. 1. Translated by Thomas McCarthy. London: Heinemann.

————. 1997a. "Further Reflections on the Public Sphere." In *Habermas and the Public Sphere,* edited by Craig Calhoun, 421–61. Cambridge, Mass: MIT Press.

————. 1997b. "Modernity: An Unfinished Project." In *Habermas and the Project of Modernity: Critical Essays on the Discourse of Modernity,* edited by Maurizio Passerin d'Entreves and Seyla Benhabib, 38–55. Cambridge, Mass.: MIT Press.

————. 2001. "The Public Sphere: An Encyclopedia Article." In *Media and Cultural Studies: Keyworks,* edited by Meenakshi Gigi Durham and Douglas M. Kellner, 102–7. Oxford: Blackwell.

Haddad, Yvonne Yazbeck. 1999. *"Ghurba* as Paradigm for Muslim Life: A *Risale-i Nur* Worldview." *The Muslim World* 89, nos. 3–4: 297–313.

Hakim, Halkawt. 1990. "Mawlana Khalid et Les Pouvo in Naqshibandi." In *Naqsibandis,* edited by Marc Gaborieau and Alexandre Thierry Zarkane, 360–70. Istanbul: L'institut francais d'Anatoliennes d'Istanbul.

Hall, John A. 1995. *Civil Society: Theory, History, and Comparison.* London: Polity.

————. 1998a. "Genealogies of Civility." In *Democratic Civility: The History and Cross-cultural Possibility of a Modern Political Ideal,* edited by R. W. Hefner, 53–77. New Brunswick, N.J.: Transaction.

————. 1998b. "The Nature of Civil Society." *Society* (May-June): 32–41.

————. 1998c. *The State of the Nation.* Cambridge: Cambridge Univ. Press.

Hallaq, Wael. 1984. "Was the Gate of *Ijtihad* Closed?" *International Journal of Middle East Studies* 16, no. 1: 3–41.

————. 1986. "On the Origins of the Controversy about the Existence of *Mujtahids* and the Gate of *Ijtihad.*" *Studia Islamica* 63: 129–41.

————. 1996. "Ifta' and *Ijtihad* in Sunni Legal Theory: A Developmental Account." In *Islamic Legal Interpretation: Muftis and Their Fatwas,* edited by Muhammad Khalid Masud, Brinkley Messick, and David Powers, 33–43. Cambridge, Mass.: Harvard Univ. Press.

————. 2001. *Authority, Continuity, and Change in Islamic Law.* New York: Cambridge Univ. Press, 2001.

Hasnaoui, Ahmed. 1977. "Certain Notions of Time in Arab-Muslim Philosophy." In *Time and Philosophies,* edited by Paul Ricoeur, 49–79. Paris: UNESCO.

Hassan, Hussain Hamid. 1997. *An Introduction to the Study of the Islamic Law.* Islamabad: International Islamic Univ.

Hayatı, Mesleği, Tercüme-i Hali. 1976. Istanbul: Sözler.

Hedetoft, Ulf. 1995. *Signs of Nations: Studies in the Political Semiotic of Self and Other in Contemporary European Nationalism.* Aldershot, England: Dartmouth.

Hefner, Robert W. 1998. "Multiple Modernities: Christianity, Islam, and Hinduism in a Globalizing Age." *Annual Review of Anthropology* 27: 83–104.

————. 2000. *Civil Islam: Muslims and Democratization in Indonesia.* Princeton, N.J.: Princeton Univ. Press.

Heft, James L. 1999. *A Catholic Modernity? Charles Taylor's Marianist Award Lecture.* New York: Oxford Univ. Press.

Helliwell, John F., and Robert D. Putnam. 1999. *Education and Social Capital.* National Bureau of Economic Research (NBER) Working Paper no. 7121. Cambridge, Mass.: NBER.

Heper, Metin. 1997. "Islam and Democracy in Turkey: Toward a Reconciliation?" *Middle East Journal* 51, no. 1 (winter): 32–45.

Hermann, Rainer. 1996. "Fethullah Gülen—eine muslimische Alternative zur Refah Partei?" *Orient* 37, no. 4: 619–46.

Hirschkind, Charles. 2001. "Civic Virtue and Religious Reason: An Islamic Counterpublic." *Cultural Anthropology* 16, no. 1: 3–34.

Hobsbawm, E. J. 1996. "Language, Culture, and National Identity." *Social Research* 63, no. 4: 1065–80.

"Hocaefendi'den Güncel Yorumlar." 1997. *Zaman,* 16 Apr.

Hoffman, Murad. 1993. *Islam: The Alternative.* Reading, England: Garnet.

Hoffmann, Stanley. 2002. "The Clash of Globalizations." *Foreign Affairs* 81, no. 4. (July-Aug.): 104–15.

Huntington, Samuel. 1993. "The Clash of Civilizations?" *Foreign Affairs* 72, no. 3 (summer): 22–49.

———. 1996. *The Clash of Civilizations: Remaking of the World Order.* New York: Simon and Schuster.

Ibn Taymiyya. 1985. *Siyasetu's Shar'iyyah.* Translated into Turkish by Vecdi Akyüz. Istanbul: Dergah.

Ilıcak, Nazlı. 1998. "Fethullah Gülen'in Gönül Penceresinden." *Akşam,* 13 Mar.

Inglehart, Ronald. 1997. *Modernization and Postmodernization: Cultural, Economic, and Political Change in Forty-three Countries.* Princeton, N.J.: Princeton Univ. Press.

Inkeles, Alex, and David Horton Smith. 1976. *Becoming Modern: Individual Change in Six Developing Countries.* Cambridge, Mass.: Harvard Univ. Press.

İnsel, Ahmet. 1997. "Yeni Muhafazakarlık ve Fethullah Gülen." *Yeni Şafak,* 26 Apr.

"Interview with Fethullah Gülen." 1998. *Aksiyon* (6 June). Available at: http://www.m-fgulen.org/hayat/article.

Islahi, Abdul Azim. 1999. "Prerequisites for *Ijtihad:* A Reappraisal." Available at: http://islamic-finance.net/research/ijtihad-islahi.html.

"Islamic Evangelists." 2000. *The Economist* 356, no. 8178 (7 Aug.): 52.

Izzetbegoviç, Ali. n.d. *Doğu ve Batı Arasında İslam.* Translated by Salih Şaban. Istanbul: Nehir Yayınları.

Jäschke, Gotthard. 1972. *Yeni Türkiye'de İslâmcılık.* Ankara: Bilgi Yayınevi.

Jepperson, Ronald, Alexander Wendt, and Peter J. Katzenstein. 1996. "Norms, Identity, and Culture in National Security." In *The Culture of National Security, Norms, and Identity in World Politics,* edited by Peter J. Katzenstein, 33–75. New York: Columbia Univ. Press.

Journalists and Writers Foundation (Gazeteciler ve Yazarlar Vakfı). 1999. *Medya Aynasında Fethullah Gülen.* Istanbul: Gazeteciler ve Yazarlar Vakfı.

———. 2000a. *Abant Platformu 2: Din Devlet ve Toplum.* Istanbul: Gazeteciler ve Yazarlar Vakfı.

———. 2000b. *Journalists and Writers Foundation.* Istanbul: Gazeteciler ve Yazarlar Vakfı.

———. 2001. *Abant Platformu 4: Çogulculuk ve Toplumsal Uzlaşma.* Istanbul: Gazeteciler ve Yazarlar Vakfı.

Kara, İsmail. 1997. "Ha Türk Müslümanlığı, ha Türk-Islam Sentezi." *Milliyet,* 7 Sept.

Karabaşoğlu, Metin. 1996. "Bilime Nasıl Bakmalı." *Köprü* 53: 3–14.

Karakoç, Sezai. 1968. *Kıyamet Aşısı.* Istanbul: Diriliş Yayınları.

Karal, Enver Ziya. 1981. "The Principles of Kemalism." In *Atatürk, Founder of a Modern State,* edited by Ali Kazancıgil and Ergun Özbudun, 11–36. London: Hurst.

Karaman, Hayrettin. 1996. *İslamın Işığında Günümüzün Meseleleri.* Istanbul: Yeni Şafak.

Kasaba, Reşat. 1998. "Cohabitation? Islamist and Secular Groups in Modern Turkey." In *Democratic Civility: The History and Cross-Cultural Possibility of a Modern Political Ideal,* edited by Robert W. Hefner, 265–82. New Brunswick, N.J.: Transaction.

Kepel, Gilles. 1991. *La revanche de Dieu: Chrétiens, juifs et musulmans à la reconquête du monde.* Paris: Editions du Seuil.

Kepenek, Yakup. 1998. "Abant Bildirgesi." *Cumhuriyet,* 27 July.

Khan, Mujeeb R. 1995. "Bosnia-Herzegovina and the Crisis of the Post-Cold War International System." *East European Politics and Societies* 9, no. 3 (fall): 459–98.

Kırkıncı, Mehmet. 1993. *İrşad Sahasında Bediüzzaman.* Istanbul: Zafer.

———. 1994. *Bediüzzaman'ı Nasıl Tanıdım.* Istanbul: Zafer.

Kısakürek, Necip Fazıl. 1988. *Çile.* Istanbul: Büyük Doğu Neşriyat.

———. n.d. *Son Devrin Din Mazlumları.* Istanbul: Büyük Doğu Neşriyat.

Köker, Levent. 1990. *Modernleşme, Kemalizm ve Demokrasi.* Istanbul: İletişim Yayınları.

Kömeçoğlu, Uğur. 1997. "A Sociologically Interpretative Approach to the Fethullah Gülen Community Movement." Master's thesis, Boğaziçi Univ.

———. 2000. "Kutsal ile Kamusal, Fethullah Gülen Cemaat Hareketi." In *İslamın Yeni Kamusal Yüzleri,* edited by Nilüfer Göle, 148–94. Istanbul: Metis.

Kozanoğlu, Can. 1997. *Internet, Dolunay, Cemaat.* Istanbul: İletişim Yayınları.

Laçiner, Ömer. 1995. "Postmodern bir Dini Hareket: Fethullah Hoca Cemaati." *Birikim* 76: 3–11.

Laclau, Ernesto, ed. 1995. *The Making of Political Identity.* London: Verso.

Lapidus, Ira. 1988. *A History of Islamic Societies.* New York: Cambridge Univ. Press.

———. 1996. "State and Religion in Islamic Societies," *Past and Present* 151 (May): 3–27.

Lerner, Daniel. 1958. *The Passing of Traditional Society.* New York: Free Press.

Lewis, Bernard. 1969. *The Emergence of Modern Turkey.* Oxford: Oxford Univ. Press.

———. 1993. "Islam and Liberal Democracy." *Atlantic Monthly* (Feb.): 89–94.

———. 1994. *Islam and the West.* Oxford: Oxford Univ. Press.

———. 1997. "The West and the Middle East." *Foreign Affairs* 76, no. 1: 114–30.

Lichbach, Mark Irving. 1997. "Social Theory and Comparative Politics." In *Comparative Politics: Rationality, Culture, and Structure,* edited by Mark Irving Lichbach and Alan Zuckerman, 239–76. Cambridge: Cambridge Univ. Press.

Lindholm, Charles. 1996. *Islamic Middle East: An Historical Anthropology.* London: Blackwell.

Lings, Martin. 1993. *A Sufi Saint of the Twentieth Century.* Cambridge: Islamic Text Society.

Lipski, M. 1980. *Street-Level Bureaucracy.* New York: Russell Sage Foundation.

Lubeck, Paul. 2001. *Antinomies of Islamic Movements under Globalization.* Center for Global, International, and Regional Studies (CGIRS) Working Paper. Santa Cruz, Calif.: CGIRS.

Lyotard, Jean-François. 1997. *The Postmodern Condition: A Report on Knowledge.* Minneapolis: Univ. of Minnesota Press.

Majeed, Javed. 1998. "Nature, Hyperbole, and the Colonial State: Some Muslim Appropriations of European Modernity in Late-Nineteenth-Century Urdu Literature." In *Islam and Modernity: Muslim Intellectuals Respond,* edited by John Cooper, Ronald L. Nettler, and Mohamed Mahmoud, 10–37. London: I. B. Tauris.

Malmisanij. 1991. *Said Nursi ve Kürt Sorunu.* Istanbul: Doz.

Mandaville, Peter. 1999. "Digital Islam: Changing Boundaries of Religious Knowledge?" Available at: http://isim.leidenuniv.nl/newsletter/2/isim/1.html.

Mann, M. 1993. *Sources of Social Power.* Vol. 2. Cambridge: Cambridge Univ. Press.

Mardin, Şerif. 1981. "Atatürk ve Pozitif Düşünce." In *Atatürk ve Cumhuriyet Dönemi Türkiyesi,* 57–67. Istanbul: Türkiye Ticaret Odaları, Sanayi Odaları ve Ticaret Borsaları Birliği Yayınları.

———. 1983a. *Jön Türklerin Siyasi Fikirleri.* Istanbul: İletişim Yayınları.

———. 1983b. "Religion and Politics in Modern Turkey." In *Islam in the Political Process,* edited by James Piscatori, 138–59. Cambridge: Cambridge Univ. Press.

———. 1989. *Religion and Social Change in Modern Turkey: The Case of Bediuzzaman Said Nursi.* New York: State Univ. of New York Press.

———. 1991a. "The Just and the Unjust." *Daedalus* 120, no. 3: 113–30.

———. 1991b. *Türkiye'de Din ve Laiklik Makaleler.* Vol. 2. Istanbul: İletişim Yayınları.

———. 1994. "Culture, Change, and the Intellectual: A Study of the Effects of Secularisation in Modern Turkey: Necip Fazıl and the Nakşibendi." In *Cultural Transitions in the Middle East,* edited by Şerif Mardin, 190–213. Leiden: E. J. Brill.

———. 2000a. *Türkiye'de Din ve Siyaset.* Istanbul: İletişim Yayınları.

———. 2000b. *Türkiye'de Din ve Siyaset Makaleler.* Vol. 3. Istanbul: İletişim Yayınları.

Masud, Muhammad Khalid. 1989. "Being Muslim in a Non-Muslim Polity: Three Alternate Models." *Journal of the Institute of Muslim Minority Affairs* 10, no. 1: 118–28.

"Medeniyetler Diyaloğu." 1996. *Zaman,* 2 Nov.

Meeker, Michael E. 1991. "The New Muslim Intellectuals in the Republic of Turkey." In *Islam in Modern Turkey,* edited by Richard Tapper, 205–10. London: I. B. Tauris.

Menski, Werner F. 2000. *Comparative Law in a Global Context: The Legal Systems of Asia and Africa.* London: Platinium.

Mermer, Ali. 1997. "The Ways to Knowledge of God in the *Risale-i Nur.*" In *The Third International Symposium on Bediuzzaman Said Nursi,* edited by the Nesil Foundation, 54–66. Istanbul: Nesil Foundation.

Mert, Nuray. 1994. *Laiklik Tartışmasına Kavramsal bir Bakış: Cumhuriyet Kurulurken Laik Düşünce.* Istanbul: Bağlam.

Milli Eğitim Bakanlığı. 1997. *Yurt Dışında Açılan Özel Öğretim Kurumları Temsilcileri: İkinci Toplantı.* Ankara: Milli Eğitim Bakanlığı.

Moosa, Ebrahim. 1999. "Language of Change in Islamic Law: Redefining Death in Modernity." *Journal of Islamic Studies* 38, no. 3: 12–34.

Murad, Abdal-Hakim. 1999. "The Problem of Anti-madhhabism." Available at: http://sunnah.org/fiqh/antimadhhabism.htm.

Mürsel, Safa. 1995. *Bediüzzaman Said Nursi ve Devlet Felsefesi.* Istanbul: Yeni Asya Yayınları.

Muslehuddin, Mohammad. 1975. *Islamic Jurisprudence and the Rule of Necessity and Need.* Islamabad: Islamic Research Institute.

Nairn, T. 1997. *Faces of Nationalism.* London: Verso.

Nasr, Seyyed Hosein. 1980. "Reflections on Islam and Modern Life." *Al-Serat* 6, no. 1. Available at: http://www.al islam.org/al-serat/reflect-nasr.htm.

———. 1991. *Sufi Essays.* Albany: State Univ. of New York Press.

Nasr, Seyyid Vali Reza. 1998. "Qur'anic Commentary and Social Change: Modern South Asian *Tafsir* and *Risale-i Nur* in Comparative Perspective." Paper presented at the Fourth International Symposium on Bediuzzaman Said Nursi, Istanbul, 22 Sept.

Nietzsche, Friedrich. 1968. *Will to Power.* Translated by W. Kaufman and R. J. Hollingdale. New York: Random House.

———. 1995. *Anti-Christ.* Translated into Turkish from the German by Oruç Auroba. Istanbul: Hil.

Nursi, Said. 1987. *Tarihçe-i Hayatı.* Istanbul: Tenvir.

———. 1992. *The Words.* Translated by Şükran Vahide. Istanbul: Sözler.

———. 1993. *Emirdağ Lahikası.* Istanbul: Yeni Asya Yayınları.

———. 1994. *Risale-i Nur Külliyatı.* Istanbul: Yeni Asya Yayınları.

———. 1996a. *Risale-i Nur Külliyatı.* Vol. 1. Istanbul: Nesil.

———. 1996b. *Risale-i Nur Külliyatı.* Vol. 2. Istanbul: Nesil.

———. 1997. *The Words.* Vol. 2. Izmir: Kaynak.

———. n.d. *Şualar.* Istanbul: Sözler.

Nyazee, Imran Ahsan Khan. 1995. *Theories of Islamic Law.* Islamabad: International Institute of Islamic Thought.

Ocak, Ahmet Yasar. 2000a. *Türkler, Türkiye ve Islam.* Istanbul: İletişim Yayınları.

———. 2000b. *Türk Sufiliğine Bakışlar.* Istanbul: İletişim Yayınları.

Olson, Robert W. 1989. *The Emergence of Kurdish Nationalism and the Sheikh Said Rebellion, 1880–1925.* Austin: Univ. of Texas Press.

The Oxford Universal Dictionary on Universal Principles. 1964. 3rd ed., rev. Oxford: Clarendon.

Öz, Esat. 1992. *Tek Parti Yönetimi Siyasal Katılım.* Ankara: Gündoğan Yayınları.

Özdalga, Elisabeth. 1997. "Modern bir Haçlının Kusurları, W. Montgomery Watt ve Islâm'ı Entelektualizmle Fethetmenin Zorlukları." *Tezkire* 11–12: 24–38.

———. 1998a. *Modern Türkiye' de Örtünme Sorunu Resmi Laiklik ve Popüler Islam.* Istanbul: Sarmal.

————. 1998b. *The Veiling Issue, Official Secularism, and Popular Islam in Modern Turkey.* Surrey: Curzon.

————. 2000. "Worldly Asceticism in Islamic Casting: Fethullah Gülen's Inspired Piety and Activism." *Critique* 17 (fall): 83–104.

Özdemir, Hikmet. 1993. *1960'lar Türkiyesinde Sol Kemalizm Yön Hareketi.* Istanbul: İz.

Özdenören, Rasim. 1979. *Gül Yetiştiren Adam.* Istanbul: Akabe Yayınları.

Özsoy, Osman. 1997. "Interview with Gülen." *Haber Kritik,* STV, 29 Mar.

————. 1998. *Fethullah Gülen Hocaefendi ile Canlı Yayında Gündem.* Istanbul: Alfa.

Papastergiadis, N. 1993. *Modernity as Exile: The Stranger in John Berger's Writing.* Manchester: Manchester Univ. Press.

Parla, Taha. 1992. *Kemalist Tek Parti İdeolojisi ve CHP'nin Altı Oku.* Istanbul: İletişim Yayınları.

Pattaro, Germano. 1976. "The Christian Conception of Time." In *Cultures and Time,* edited by Paul Ricoeur, 169–95. Paris: UNESCO.

Pearl, David, and Werner F. Menski. 1998. *Muslim Family Law.* 3rd ed. London: Sweet and Maxwell.

Piscatori, James. 1983. *Islam in the Political Process.* New York: Cambridge Univ. Press.

————. 1986. *Islam in a World of Nation-States.* New York: Cambridge Univ. Press.

Politella, J. 1963. "Sufism as a Bridge Between Eastern and Western Religious Thought." *Muslim World* 53: 50–58.

Putnam, Robert. 1993. *Making Democracy Work: Civic Traditions in Modern Italy.* Princeton, N.J.: Princeton Univ. Press.

Rahman, Fazlur. 1982. *Islam and Modernity: The Transformation of an Intellectual Tradition.* Chicago: Univ. of Chicago Press.

Reichmuth, Stefan. 1995. "Christian and Muslim Communities and Their Influence on Education in Nigeria." In *Pluralism and Education: Current World Trends in Policy, Law, and Administration,* edited by Peter M. Roeder, Ingo Richter, and Hans-Peter Füssel, 279–92. Berkeley and Los Angeles: Univ. of California Press.

Rıfat, Mevlanzade. 1996. *31 Mart-Bir İhtilalin İçyüzü.* Istanbul: Pınar.

Robertson, Roland. 1995. "Glocalization: Time-Space and Homogeneity-Heterogeneity." In *Global Modernities,* edited by Mike Featherstone, Scott Lash, and Roland Robertson, 25–44. London: Sage.

Rodrigues, Melanie Portilla. 1997. *Social Capital in Developing Societies: Reconsidering the Links Between Civil Agency, Economy, and the State in the Development Process.* Working Paper Series no. 248 (May). The Hague: Institute of Social Studies.

Rosen, Lawrence. 1984. *Bargaining for Reality: The Construction of Social Relations in a Muslim Community.* Chicago: Univ. of Chicago Press.

————. 1989. *The Anthropology of Justice: Law as Culture in Islamic Society.* Cambridge: Cambridge Univ. Press.

Rosenthal, Erwin I. J. 1962. *Political Thought in Mediaeval Islam.* Cambridge: Cambridge Univ. Press.

Ruffin, M. H., and D. Waugh, eds. 1999. *Civil Society in Central Asia*. Seattle: Univ. of Washington Press.

Rumi, Jalalu'ddin. 1990. *The Mathnawi, Book V*. Translated by Reynold A. Nicholson. Cambridge: E. J. W. Gibb Memorial Trust.

Sachedina, Abdulaziz. 2001. *The Islamic Roots of Democratic Pluralism*. New York: Oxford Univ. Press.

Sadri, Mahmoud, and Ahmad Sadri, eds. 2000. *Reason, Freedom, and Democracy in Iran: Essential Writings of Abdolkarim Soroush*. New York: Oxford Univ. Press.

Şahiner, Necmeddin. 1979. *Bilinmeyen Taraflaryla Bediüzzaman Said Nursi*. Istanbul: Yeni Asya Yayınları.

———. 1996. *Belgelerle Bediüzzaman'ın Kabir Olayı*. Istanbul: Timaş.

Sale, Kirkpatrick. 1995. *Rebels Against the Future: The Luddites and Their War on the Industrial Revolution, Lessons for the Computer Age*. Reading, Mass.: Addison-Wesley.

Salt, Jeremy. 1999. "Turkey's Military 'Democracy.' " *Current History* (Feb.): 72–78.

Sanu, Qutb Mustafa. 1998. "A Critical Analysis of Bediuzzaman's Treatise on *Ijtihad*." Available at: http://www.nesil.com.tr.

Sayyid, S. 2000. "Beyond Westphalia: Nations and Diasporas—the Case of the Muslim Umma." In *Un/settled Multiculturalisms: Diasporas, Entanglements, Transruptions*, edited by Barnor Hesse, 33–50. London: Zed.

Şen, Mustafa. 2001. "Turkish Enterprises in Central Asia: The Case of Kazakhstan and Kyrgyzstan." Ph.D. diss., Middle East Technical Univ., Ankara.

Sevindi, Nevval. 1997. *Fethullah Gülen ile New York Sohbeti*. Istanbul: Sabah.

Shah, Idries. 1968. *The Way of the Sufi*. Ankara: Penguin.

Singh, Sir Jogendra. 1939. *The Invocations of Sheikh Abdallah Ansari*. London: Wisdom of the East Series.

Smith, Anthony D. 1986. *The Ethnic Origins of Nations*. Oxford: Blackwell.

———. 1999. "Ethnic Election and National Destiny: Some Religious Origins of Nationalist Ideals, Nations, and Nationalism." *Nations and Nationalism* 5, no. 3: 331–55.

Soydan, Mehmet Ali. 1999. *Devlet, Medya ve Siyaset Üçgeninde Fethullah Gülen Olayı*. Istanbul: Birey Yayıncılık.

Stark, Rodney. 1994. "A Supply-Side Reinterpretation of the 'Secularization' of Europe." *Journal for the Scientific Study of Religion* 33: 230–52.

———. 1999. "Secularization, R.I.P." *Sociology of Religion* 60, no. 3 (fall): 249–73.

Stark, Rodney, and Roger Finke. 2000. *Acts of Faith: Explaining the Human Side of Religion*. Berkeley and Los Angeles: Univ. of California Press.

Stearns, Peter N. 1998. *The Industrial Revolution in World History*. 2d ed. Boulder, Colo.: Westview.

Stirling, Paul. 1958. "Religious Change in Republican Turkey." *Middle East Journal* 12: 395–408.

Taji-Farouki, Suha. 1996. "Islamic State Theories and Contemporary Realities." In *Islamic Fundamentalism*, edited by Abdel Salam Sidahmed and Anoushiravan Ehteshami, 35–50. Boulder, Colo.: Westview.

"Tarihi Görüşme: Yilmaz Papa'yı Ziyaret Etti." 2000. *Diyanet Aylık Dergi* 115 (July): 6–17.

Taşgetiren, Ahmet. 1998. "Abant'ın Çözemediği Sorun." *Yeni Şafak,* 27 July.

Taylor, Charles. 1985. *Philosophy and the Human Science.* New York: Cambridge Univ. Press.

———. 1989a. "Cross Purposes: The Liberal Communitarian Debate." In *Liberalism and Moral Life,* edited by N. Rosenblum, 159–83. Cambridge, Mass.: Harvard Univ. Press.

———. 1989b. *Sources of the Self: The Making of the Modern Identity.* Cambridge, Mass.: Harvard Univ. Press.

———. 1992. *Multi-culturalism and the Politics of Recognition.* Princeton, N.J.: Princeton Univ. Press.

———. 1998. "Modes of Secularism." In *Secularism and Its Critic,* edited by Rajeev Bhargava, 31–53. Delhi: Oxford Univ. Press.

———. 1999. "Nationalism and Modernity." In *Theorizing Nationalism,* edited by Ronald Beiner, 219–45. Albany: State Univ. of New York.

Tibi, Bassam. 1995. "Culture and Knowledge: The Politics of Islamization of Knowledge as a Postmodern Project? The Fundamentalist Claim to De-Westernization." *Theory, Culture, and Society* 12: 1–24.

Timur, Taner. 1971. *Türk Devrimi ve Sonrası, 1919–1946.* Ankara: Doğan Yayınları.

Tocqueville, Alexis de. 1955. *The Old Regime and the French Revolution.* Translated by Stuart Gilbert. Garden City, N.Y: Doubleday.

Toprak, Binnaz. 1981. *Islam and Political Development in Turkey.* Leiden: E. J. Brill.

———. 1987. "The Religious Right." In *Turkey in Transition,* edited by Irvin C. Schick, 218–36. Oxford: Oxford Univ. Press.

———. 1993. "Islamist Intellectuals: Revolt Against Industry and Technology." In *Turkey and the West: Changing Political and Cultural Identities,* edited by Metin Heper, Ayse Öncü, and Heinz Kramer, 237–57. London: I. B. Tauris.

Toulman, Stephen. 1990. *Cosmopolis: The Hidden Agenda of Modernity.* New York: Free Press.

Touraine, Alain. 1992. *Critique de la modenité.* Paris: Fayard.

Tschannen, Olivier. 1991. "The Secularization Paradigm: A Systematization." *Journal for the Scientific Study of Religion* 30: 395–415.

Tucker, Judith E. 1999. "Revisiting Reform: Women and the Ottoman Law of Family Rights, 1917." Available at: http://sfswww.georgetown.edu/sfs/prgrams/ccas/asj/tucker.htm.2.

Tulloch, Sara. 1991. *The Oxford Dictionary of New Words.* Oxford: Oxford Univ. Press.

Tunaya, Tarik Zafer. 1964. *Devrim Hareketleri İçinde Atatürk ve Atatürkçülük.* Istanbul: Baha.

———. 1991. *Islâmcılık Akımı.* Istanbul: Simavi.

Tuncay, Mete. 1981. *Türkiye Cumhuriyetin'de Tek Parti Yönetimi (1923–1931).* Ankara: Yurt.

Turam, Berna. 2000. "Between Islam and the State: The Politics of Engagement." Ph.D. diss., McGill Univ., Montreal.

Türk Dıyanet Vakfı (TDV). 1999. *Günümüz Meselelerine Fetvalar*. Ankara: TDV.

"Turkish Court Voids Warrant for Islamic Leader." 2000. *New York Times,* 29 Aug.

"Turkish Press Scanner: Gülen Is Like Khomeini." 2000. *Turkish Daily News,* 8 Sept.

Turner, Colin. 1998. "Renewal in Islam and Bediuzzaman." Paper presented at the Fourth International Symposium on Bediuzzaman Said Nursi, Istanbul, 20–22 Sept.

Ünal, Ali. 1998. "Başörtüsü Meselesi." *Zaman,* 30 Sept.

———. 2002. *M Fethullah Gülen: Bir Portre Denemesi*. Istanbul: Nil.

Ünal, Ali, and Alphonse Williams, eds. 2000. *The Advocate of Dialogue: Fethullah Gülen*. Fairfax, Va: The Fountain.

Ünal, İsmail. 2001. *Fethullah Gülen'le Amerika'da bir Ay*. Istanbul: Işık Yayınları.

Vergin, Nur. 1998. "Türkiye Müslümanlığı ve Sözde Türk Islami," *Yeni Yüzyıl,* 6 Sept.

Voll, John. 1982. *Islam, Continuity, and Change in the Modern World*. Boulder, Colo.: Westview.

———. 1999. "Renewal and Reformation in the Mid-Twentieth Century: Bediuzzaman Said Nursi and Religion in the 1950s." *The Muslim World* 89, nos. 3–4: 245–59.

Waltz, Kenneth N. 1979. *Theory of International Politics*. Reading, Mass: Addison-Wesley.

Walzer, M. 1983. *Spheres of Justice: A Defense of Pluralism and Equality*. New York: Basic.

Webb, Emily Lynne. n.d. *Fethullah Gülen: Is There More to Him Than Meets the Eye?* Paterson, N.J.: Zinnur.

Weber, Max. 1976. *Protestant Ethic and the Spirit of Capitalism*. Translated by Talcott Parsons. New York: Scribner.

———. 1980. *Wirtschaft und Gesellschaft*. 5th ed. Tübingen: Mohr.

———. 1991. *Die Protestantische Ethik*. Vol. 1. Edited by Johannes Winckelman. Gütersloh, Germany: Siebenstern.

Weldes, Jutta. 1999. *Cultures on Insecurity States, Communities, and the Production of Danger*. Minneapolis: Univ. of Minnesota Press.

Wendt, Alexander. 1999. *Social Theory of International Politics*. New York: Cambridge Univ. Press.

White, Jenny. 1996. "Civic Culture and Islam in Urban Turkey." In *Civil Society: Challenging Western Models,* edited by C. Hann and E. Dunn, 143–55. London: Routledge.

Wight, Martin, Gabriel Wight, and Brian Porter, eds. 1991. *International Theory: The Three Traditions*. Leicester: Leicester Univ. Press.

Wilson, Bryan. 1982. *Religion in Sociological Perspective*. Oxford: Oxford Univ. Press.

Wilson, Rob, and Wimal Dissanayake. 1996. "Introduction: Tracking the Global/Local." In *Global/Local: Cultural Production and the Transnational Imaginary,* edited by Rob Wilson and Wimal Dissanayake, 1–18. Durham, N.C.: Duke Univ. Press.

Yack, B. 1999. "The Myth of the Civic Nation." In *Theorizing Nationalism,* edited by R. Beiner, 103–18. New York: State Univ. of New York Press.

———. 2000. "Popular Sovereignty, Nationalism, and the Liberal Democratic State." Paper presented in the workshop "What Can States Do Now?" McGill Univ., Montreal.

Yavuz, M. Hakan. 1993. "Nationalism and Islam: Yusuf Akçura, Üç Tarz-i Siyaset." *Oxford Journal of Islamic Studies* 4, no. 2: 175–207.

———. 1995a. "Efsanevi Islam-Folk Islam: Alexander Benningsen." *Nehir* (May): 58–60.

———. 1995b. "Orta Asya'daki Kimlik Oluşumu: Yeni Kolonizatör Dervişler-Nurcular." *Türkiye Günlüğü* 33 (Apr.-Mar.): 160–65.

———. 1995c. "The Patterns of Political Islamic Identity: Dynamics of National and Transnational Loyalties and Identities." *Central Asian Survey* 14, no. 3: 341–72.

———. 1995d. "Türkistan'da Halkın Manevi Dünyası: Efsanevi Islam." *Dergah* 62 (Apr.): 12–13.

———. 1996a. "Nurculuk Millileşiyor." *Milliyet,* 18 Sept.

———. 1996b. "Yayına Dayalı Islami Söylem ve Modernlik: Nur Hareketi." In *Uluslarası Bediüzzaman Sempozyumu III,* 641–66. Istanbul: Yeni Asya.

———. 1997a. "Nasıl bir Türkiye." *Milliyet,* 11 Aug.

———. 1997b. "Print-Based Islamic Discourse and Modernity: The Nur Movement." In *The Third International Symposium on Bediuzzaman Said Nursi,* edited by the Nesil Foundation, 324–50. Istanbul: Nesil Foundation.

———. 1998. "Efsanevi Islam: Atalar Dini ve Modern Bağlantılar." In *Türk Dünyasının Dini Meseleleri,* 11–24. Ankara: Türkiye Diyanet Vakfı Yayınları.

———. 1999a. "The Assassination of Collective Memory: The Case of Turkey." *The Muslim World* 99, nos. 3–4: 193–207.

———. 1999b. "Societal Search for a New Social Contract in Turkey: Fethullah Gülen, the Virtue Party, and the Kurds." *SAIS Review* 29, no. 1 (winter): 114–43.

———. 1999c. "Towards an Islamic Liberalism? The Nurcu Movement and Fethullah Gülen." *Middle East Journal* 53, no. 4 (fall): 584–605.

———. 2000a. "Being Modern in the Nurcu Way." *ISIM Newsletter* (Leiden Univ.) 6 (Oct.) (entire issue).

———. 2000b. "Cleansing Islam from the Public Sphere." *Journal of International Affairs* 54, no. 1: 20–42.

———. 2000c. "Turkish Identity Politics and Central Asia." In *Islam and Central Asia: An Enduring Legacy or an Evolving Threat?* edited by Roald Sagdeev and Susan Eisenhower, 193–211. Washington, D.C.: Center for Political and Strategic Studies.

———. 2001. "Five Stages of the Construction of Kurdish Nationalism in Turkey." *Nationalism and Ethnic Politics* 7, no. 3. (fall): 1–24.

———. 2003. *Islamic Political Identity in Turkey.* Oxford: Oxford Univ. Press.

Yenibahar, Asim. 2000. "Diyanet Baskani Neden Papayi Ziyaret Etti?" *Akit,* 20 June.

Yılmaz, Ihsan. 2000a. "Changing Institutional Turkish-Muslim Discourses on Modernity, West, and Dialogue." Paper presented at the Congress of the International Association of Middle East Studies, Freie Universität, Berlin, 5–7 Oct.

———. 2000b. "Muslim Law in Britain: Reflections on the Socio-legal Sphere and Differential Legal Treatment." *Journal of Muslim Minority Affairs* 20, no. 2: 353–60.

————. 2001a. "Is Having a Personal Law System a Solution? Towards a Supra-modern Law." *Journal for Islamic Studies* 20: 99–124.

————. 2001b. "Legal Pluralism in Turkey: Persistence of Muslim Laws." *International Journal of Turkish Studies* 7, nos. 1–2 (spring): 110–24.

————. 2001c. "Law as Chameleon: The Question of Incorporation of Muslim Personal Law into the English Law." *Journal of Muslim Minority Affairs* 21, no. 2: 297–308.

————. 2002. "Secular Law and the Emergence of Unofficial Islamic Law in Turkey." *Middle East Journal* 56, no. 1 (winter): 113–31.

————. Forthcoming a. "Inter-*madhhab* Surfing, Neo-*ijtihad,* and Faith-Based Movement Leaders." In *The Islamic School of Law: Evolution, Devolution, and Progress,* edited by Frank Vogel, Peri Bearman, and Ruud Peters. Cambridge, Mass.: Harvard Univ. Press.

————. Forthcoming b. "Limits of Law: Reform in Muslim Family Law and Civil Disobedience in Pakistan." *Die Welt des Islams* 44.

————. Forthcoming c. "Muslim Legal Pluralism in *Asr al Darura,* Surfers on the Inter-*madhhab*-net and Neo-*ijtihat.* In *The Islamic School of Law: Evolution, Devolution, and Progress,* edited by Frank Vogel, Peri Bearman, and Ruud Peters. Cambridge, Mass.: Harvard Univ. Press.

Yılmaz, İrfan, Hakkı İhsanoğlu, Selim Aydın, Fuat Bozer, Hevzat Bayhan, and İhsan Inal, eds. 1998. *Yeni bir Bakış Açısıyla Ilim ve Din.* Vols. 1 and 2. Istanbul: Feza Gazetecilik.

Yu, Bingyi, and Zhaolu Lu. 2000. "Confucianism and Modernity: Insights from an Interview with Tu Wei-ming." *China Review International* 7, no. 2: 377–87.

Zhovtis, E. A. 1999. "Freedom of Association and the Question of Its Realization in Kazakhstan." In *Civil Society in Central Asia,* edited by M. H. Ruffin and D. Waugh, 57–70. Seattle: Univ. of Washington Press.

Zizek, Slavoc. 1989. *The Sublime Object of Ideology.* London: Verso.

Index